RETIRING ABROAD

A SURVIVAL HANDBOOK
by
David Hampshire

SURVIVAL BOOKS · LONDON · ENGLAND

First published 2002

Survival Books Limited, 1st Floor, 60 St James's Street
London SW1A 1ZN, United Kingdom
☎ +44 (0)20-7493 4244, ▤ +44 (0)20-7491 0605
✉ info@survivalbooks.net
💻 www.survivalbooks.net

British Library Cataloguing in Publication Data.
A CIP record for this book is available from the British Library.
ISBN 1 901130 56 8

Printed and bound in Finland by WS Bookwell Ltd

ACKNOWLEDGEMENTS

My sincere thanks to all those who contributed to the successful publication of this book, in particular Joanna Styles who researched and wrote the country profiles, Joe and Kerry Laredo (proof-reading and desktop publishing), Graeme & Louise Chesters and the many other people who helped who I have failed to mention. Finally a special thank you to Jim Watson for the superb cover and cartoons.

What Readers and Reviewers

When you buy a model plane for your child, a video recorder, or some new computer gizmo, you get with it a leaflet or booklet pleading 'Read Me First', or bearing large friendly letters or bold type saying 'IMPORTANT – follow the instructions carefully'. This book should be similarly supplied to all those entering France with anything more durable than a 5-day return ticket. It is worth reading even if you are just visiting briefly, or if you have lived here for years and feel totally knowledgeable and secure. But if you need to find out how France works then it is indispensable. Native French people probably have a less thorough understanding of how their country functions. – Where it is most essential, the book is most up to the minute.

Living France

We would like to congratulate you on this work: it is really super! We hand it out to our expatriates and they read it with great interest and pleasure.

ICI (Switzerland) AG

Rarely has a 'survival guide' contained such useful advice. This book dispels doubts for first-time travellers, yet is also useful for seasoned globetrotters – In a word, if you're planning to move to the USA or go there for a long-term stay, then buy this book both for general reading and as a ready-reference.

American Citizens Abroad

It is everything you a!ways wanted to ask but didn't for fear of the contemptuous put down – The best English-language guide – Its pages are stuffed with practical information on everyday subjects and are designed to complement the traditional guidebook.

Swiss News

A complete revelation to me – I found it both enlightening and interesting, not to mention amusing.

Carole Clark

Let's say it at once. David Hampshire's *Living and Working in France* is the best handbook ever produced for visitors and foreign residents in this country; indeed, my discussion with locals showed that it has much to teach even those born and bred in l'Hexagone. – It is Hampshire's meticulous detail which lifts his work way beyond the range of other books with similar titles. Often you think of a supplementary question and search for the answer in vain. With Hampshire this is rarely the case. – He writes with great clarity (and gives French equivalents of all key terms), a touch of humour and a ready eye for the odd (and often illuminating) fact. – This book is absolutely indispensable.

The Riviera Reporter

Have Said About Survival Books

What a great work, wealth of useful information, well-balanced wording and accuracy in details. My compliments!

Thomas Müller

This handbook has all the practical information one needs to set up home in the UK – The sheer volume of information is almost daunting – Highly recommended for anyone moving to the UK.

American Citizens Abroad

A very good book which has answered so many questions and even some I hadn't thought of – I would certainly recommend it.

Brian Fairman

A mine of information – I may have avoided some embarrassments and frights if I had read it prior to my first Swiss encounters – Deserves an honoured place on any newcomer's bookshelf.

English Teachers Association, Switzerland

Covers just about all the things you want to know on the subject – In answer to the desert island question about the one how-to book on France, this book would be it – Almost 500 pages of solid accurate reading – This book is about enjoyment as much as survival.

The Recorder

it's so funny – I love it and definitely need a copy of my own – Thanks very much for having written such a humorous and helpful book.

Heidi Guiliani

A must for all foreigners coming to Switzerland.

Antoinette O'Donoghue

A comprehensive guide to all things French, written in a highly readable and amusing style, for anyone planning to live, work or retire in France.

The Times

A concise, thorough account of the DOs and DON'Ts for a foreigner in Switzerland – Crammed with useful information and lightened with humorous quips which make the facts more readable.
American Citizens Abroad

Covers every conceivable question that may be asked concerning everyday life – I know of no other book that could take the place of this one.

France in Print

Hats off to *Living and Working in Switzerland*!

Ronnie Almeida

CONTENTS

APPENDICES   319

INDEX   335

SUGGESTIONS PAGE   344

ORDER FORMS   345

NOTES   349

IMPORTANT NOTE

All countries have their idiosyncrasies and most encompass a variety of ethnic groups, languages, religions and customs, not to mention continuously changing rules, regulations (particularly regarding business, visas, and work and residence permits), laws and costs. Note also that a change of government or regime can have far-reaching effects on many important aspects of life in many countries. **I cannot recommend too strongly that you check with an official and reliable source (not always the same) before making any major decisions or taking an irreversible course of action. However, don't believe everything you're told or read – even, dare I say it, herein!**

Useful addresses and references to other sources of information have been included in all chapters and in **Appendices A B and C** to help you obtain further information and verify details with official sources. Important points have been emphasised, in **bold** print, some of which it would be expensive, or even dangerous, to disregard. **Ignore them at your peril or cost!** Unless specifically stated, the reference to any company, organisation or product in this book doesn't constitute an endorsement or recommendation. Any reference to any place or person (living or dead) is purely coincidental.

AUTHOR'S NOTES

- Times are shown using am (latin: ante meridiem) for before noon and pm (post meridiem) for after noon (see also **Time Difference** on page 143).

- Costs and prices (shown in US$, GB£ or local currency) should be taken as estimates only, although they were mostly correct at the time of publication.

- His/he/him also means her/she/her (please forgive me ladies). This is done to make life easier for both the reader and (in particular) the author, and isn't intended to be sexist.

- All spelling is (or should be) English and not American.

- Warnings and important points are shown in **bold** type.

- The following symbols are used in this book: ☎ (telephone), ▤ (fax), 💻 (Internet) and ✉ (e-mail).

- Lists of **Useful Addresses**, **Further Reading** and **Useful Websites** are contained in **Appendices A, B and C** respectively.

- For those unfamiliar with the Metric system of weights and measures, imperial conversion tables are included in **Appendix D**.

INTRODUCTION

Whether you're already retired and living abroad or just thinking about it – this is **THE BOOK** for you. It was written especially with you in mind and is worth its weight in sunshine. *Retiring Abroad* is designed to meet the needs of anyone with the time and money to spend a few months a year ('seasonal retirement') or live permanently abroad, including retirees, the 'idle' rich, lottery winners, long-stay tourists, holiday homeowners and anyone else who yearns for a change of scenery. However long your intended stay abroad, you'll find the information contained in this book invaluable.

Basic information isn't difficult to find about most countries and a multitude of books is published on retirement. However, reliable and up-to-date information in English specifically intended for retirees planning to live abroad isn't so easy to find, least of all in one volume. Our aim in publishing this book was to help fill this void and provide the comprehensive practical information necessary for a relatively trouble-free life. You may have travelled abroad on holiday, but living in a foreign country for an extended period or permanently is a different matter altogether – adjusting to a different environment, culture and language, and making a home abroad can be a traumatic and stressful experience.

You need to adapt to new customs and traditions and discover the local way of doing things, for example, finding a home, acquiring cash and obtaining affordable health insurance. For most foreigners, overcoming the everyday obstacles of life abroad has previously been a case of pot luck. But no more! With a copy of *Retiring Abroad* to hand you'll have a wealth of information at your fingertips. Information derived from a variety of sources, both official and unofficial, not least the hard won personal experiences of the author and his researchers, family, friends, colleagues and acquaintances. *Retiring Abroad* is a comprehensive handbook on a wide range of everyday subjects and represents the most up-to-date source of general information available to anyone planning to retire abroad. It isn't, however, simply a monologue of dry facts and figures, but a practical and entertaining look at the life in a foreign country.

Adapting to living in a new country is a continuous process, and although this book will help reduce your 'novice phase' and minimise the frustrations, it doesn't contain all the answers (most of us don't even know the right questions to ask!). What it will do is help you make informed decisions and calculated judgements, instead of uneducated guesses and costly mistakes. **Most importantly, it will help save you time, trouble and money, and repay your investment many times over.**

Although you may find some of the information a bit daunting, don't be discouraged. Most problems occur only once and fade into insignificance after a short time (as you face the next half a dozen!). The majority of people who retire abroad would agree that, all things considered, they love it – and wild horses couldn't drag them away. Living abroad, even for a short period each year, is a wonderful way to enrich and revitalise your life, and may even help you live longer. I trust this book will help you avoid the pitfalls of life abroad and smooth your way to a happy and rewarding future in your new home.

Good luck!   **David Hampshire**
                                                             May 2002

1.

WHY RETIRE ABROAD?

R etiring abroad, whether permanently or for just part of the year (so-called 'seasonal retirement'), is an increasingly popular choice, particularly among retirees from countries with 'poor' (cold, wet, etc.) climates, high taxes or soaring property prices. For many people, the dream of spending their golden years in the sun has become an affordable option, although retiring abroad (even for part of the year) isn't without its pitfalls and shouldn't be attempted without careful consideration and planning. Before deciding where, when or indeed, whether to retire abroad, it's important to do your homework thoroughly and investigate the myriad implications and possibilities. Recognising and preparing for potential difficulties in advance is much easier than dealing with disappointment, or even a crisis, later.

However, if you do decide to take the plunge, you will be in good company. Tens of millions of people have successfully retired abroad, including some 2 million Americans (around 400,000 in Mexico alone), over a million Britons, plus many thousands of Canadians and northern Europeans (notably Dutch, Germans and Scandinavians). Hundreds of thousands of British pensioners live in France, Italy and Spain, and countries such as Canada, Germany, Ireland, New Zealand and Portugal also have significant numbers of British retirees. Over 4 million Canadians, colloquially known as 'snowbirds', regularly spend the winter months in Arizona, Florida, the Caribbean or Latin America, returning to Canada for the warmer summer months.

As when making all major life decisions, it isn't wise to be in too much of a hurry. Many people make expensive (even catastrophic) errors when retiring abroad, often because they don't do sufficient research or take into account the circumstances of their partners and family members. It isn't unusual for people to uproot themselves and after some time wish they had chosen a different region or country – or even that they had stayed at home! (A significant number of people who retire abroad return home within a relatively short period.)

WHY DO YOU WANT TO RETIRE ABROAD?

The first question to ask yourself is exactly why you want to retire abroad. Do you wish to live abroad permanently or spend only part of the year abroad? For example, many retirees spend the winter abroad in a warmer country, returning to their home country for the summer. If you're planning to retire abroad for health reasons, the climate will be an important consideration. Do you primarily wish to live somewhere with a lower cost of living? Do you want to make frequent return trips to your home country, to visit your family and friends? What do your family and friends think of your plans to live abroad? The fewer family ties you have, the wider your choice of countries and possibly the more difficult it will be to make a decision. Can you afford to retire abroad? What of the future? Is your income secure and protected against inflation?

You will need to take into account the availability and cost of accommodation, communications, travelling times (and cost), security, health facilities, leisure and sports opportunities, culture shock, the cost of living and local taxes, among other things. Many retirees wishing to retire abroad are North Americans or northern Europeans, who can often buy a home abroad for much less than the value of their family home. The difference between the money raised on the sale of your family home and the cost of a home abroad can be invested to supplement your pension, allowing you to live comfortably in retirement, particularly when a lower cost of living is taken into consideration. However, if you plan to buy a second home abroad, you will need to maintain two homes, although the running costs can usually be offset by letting your home(s) when you're absent.

ADVANTAGES & DISADVANTAGES

Before planning to live abroad permanently, you must take into account many considerations. There are both advantages and disadvantages to retiring abroad, although for most people the benefits outweigh the drawbacks.

Advantages

Climate: For most people, the main advantage of retiring abroad is a more moderate climate, which may include southern Europe, the southern states of the USA (e.g. Arizona, California and Florida), Central and South America, the Caribbean and the southern hemisphere in general (e.g. Australia, New Zealand and South Africa). For most people, one of the principal benefits is improved health as a result of living in a warmer climate and a more relaxing environment (provided you don't expect things to be done the same way as at 'home'!). Your general sense of well-being will be greatly enhanced when you live in a warm and sunny climate. Those who suffer from arthritis, colds, influenza and other illnesses exacerbated by cold and damp generally live longer and enjoy a better quality of life in a warm climate, while those who are prone to stress benefit from the relaxed lifestyle in most hot countries. However, if you're planning to retire abroad for health reasons, you should ask your doctor for his advice regarding suitable countries and locations (see also **Health** on page 72).

Living in a warmer climate often results in an increased life expectancy for retirees. A better climate also provides ample opportunities to enjoy outdoor activities, such as gardening, golf, tennis or walking, during your increased leisure time. On the financial side, you'll save a considerable sum on heating bills, although you shouldn't automatically assume that because your retirement destination is hot in the summer it will also be warm in winter. For example, in many Mediterranean resorts it can be surprisingly cool in winter, when you will need some form of heating. On the other hand, countries that experience warm winters often have very hot and humid summers, when costly air-conditioning is essential. It's wise to visit the country of your choice at different times of the year before making your decision, to find out exactly how cold and hot it *really* is in the winter and summer. Make sure you aren't caught unawares by a country that turns out to be unbearably hot or cold at times, or which frequently suffers from natural disasters such as torrential rain, flooding or hurricanes (see also **Climate** on page 120).

Lower Taxation: Some countries provide generous, tax-free concessions for retirees, while others have considerably lower tax bills than North America and northern European countries. Many popular retirement countries have low direct and indirect taxation, including property taxes, and no wealth or inheritance taxes. Note, however, that citizens and residents of some countries (e.g. the USA and South Africa) are subject to tax on their world-wide income, irrespective of its source, and residents of certain countries must declare their foreign assets (e.g. property) to the tax authorities in their country of origin.

Tax planning is a complex subject and all aspects should be carefully considered after consultation with an expert (see also **Finance** on page 90). However, you should bear in mind that, in general, retirees who consider *only* the financial benefits of retiring abroad are more likely to be dissatisfied than those whose main motivation is the lifestyle and other reasons!

Lower Cost of Living: Many countries surveyed in this book (see **Chapter 8**) have a relatively low cost of living, often considerably lower than North America or northern Europe (although countries from these regions are also included!). This is particularly true as far as property is concerned and many goods also aren't subject to such high levels of duty or tax. The cost of fresh food and locally-produced wine or beer is generally reasonable in popular retirement countries, where dining out is also an affordable option.

Higher Standard of Living: If your retirement destination has favourable tax rates or concessions and a low cost of living, the chances are that your standard of living will rise proportionately. When this is added to the benefits of a warmer year-round climate, your quality of life will also improve significantly.

Lower Property Prices: Property prices in North America and northern Europe (and in most of the world's capital cities) have risen considerably in recent years, and many people find themselves caught in a spiralling property market, unable to buy a home that represents good value. In contrast, many popular retirement countries offer affordable homes and in some countries real bargains can be found. You may be surprised to discover that for the price of a small apartment in London or New York, you can buy a detached home with a swimming pool in many countries! (See **Buying a Home** on page 48.)

Increased Leisure and Sports Options: The availability of a wide range of leisure and sports activities at an affordable cost is an added attraction of many popular retirement destinations. Most have excellent leisure facilities, such as golf and tennis clubs, with affordable membership prices. If you retire to a country with a mild climate, you will also have more time and opportunities to practise your chosen sport or activity, which will rarely be interrupted by rain!

Disadvantages

As with all major life decisions, there are also disadvantages to retiring abroad and you should consider these and their implications carefully before making a decision. However, it's worth noting that the majority are avoidable or easily surmountable, provided you choose your destination carefully and do your homework before retiring abroad.

Communication Problems: For many, the main disadvantage of retiring abroad is the separation from family and loved ones, particularly from grandchildren who have a habit of growing up fast. This barrier can be reduced by keeping in touch regularly by phone (many countries now offer inexpensive international calls), by e-mail (most countries provide widespread Internet access) or by choosing a country within easy travelling distance of your home country.

Culture Shock and Language Problems: Many retirees underestimate the cultural isolation that you can feel living abroad, particularly if you're planning to move to a country with a different language where you will have few compatriots. Many people find that coping with retirement and the lack of structure to life without a daily work regime is made doubly stressful by the sense of isolation (and possible frustration) created by a new culture and language. Are you prepared to be in a minority and to be treated as a foreigner? Are you open to different ways of doing things? Do you make friends easily? Can you cope with a slower pace of life and a high level of bureaucracy?

It's also generally accepted that the older you are, the more difficult it is to learn a new language. A new culture and language don't, however, have to make your life more frustrating and can do much to enrich it, although it's important to be aware of the potential difficulties. Culture shock (see page 126) can be significantly reduced if you retire to a country with an established expatriate community, as there is in most popular retirement destinations.

Boredom and Isolation: Although most people look forward to retirement, many find the reality of not working difficult and the prospect of full-time leisure daunting. The question of 'what are you going to do all day?' can be difficult to answer – even more so abroad, where there may not be the same facilities and familiar leisure activities that you have in your home country. You may miss your social life back home and find it difficult to be accepted into (or to accept) your new expatriate or 'native' community. It's wise to visit your prospective retirement destination a number of times at different times of the year and to rent a property (see page 44) before buying a home and making a long-term commitment.

Financial Problems: Without careful planning, retirement abroad can involve financial problems, such as those caused by exchange rate fluctuations, poor investments and possible loss of pension indexation. Tax and cost of living benefits may also turn out to be lower than originally thought.

Bureaucracy and Underdevelopment: Many countries (particularly those in southern Europe and Latin America) are notorious for their bureaucracy and red tape, which, if you aren't prepared for it, can be frustrating and daunting. Less-developed countries may look 'exotic' in tourist brochures, but many have poor or non-existent services.

Immigration Laws: Some countries have strict immigration laws regarding the status of foreigners and how long you can remain there at a time. You may find that you cannot stay longer than six months or that a retirement visa isn't indefinite, which can heighten your insecurity. Some countries impose high permit and visa fees or require that you meet certain, usually financial, criteria (see **Permits and Visas** on page 26).

Health Concerns: In some countries there are dangers of disease and infection, and local medical facilities may be poor or not be up to the standard you're used to. Private health insurance (see page 82) may also be necessary and is prohibitively expensive in some countries (see **Health** on page 72).

Old Age & Infirmity: Before planning to live abroad, you should consider how you would cope if your mobility was restricted. Many countries have inadequate facilities and support for those with disabilities, and social services may provide little or no help for the elderly and infirm. Another consideration is the provision of retirement homes or sheltered accommodation (see page 49), which are either non-existent or in their infancy in many countries; even when available, places may be in short supply.

Other Considerations

The following points should also be taken into account when considering whether or where to retire abroad:

- One of the main considerations in choosing a retirement location should be the 'pleasantness' of the location. You should be aware that an area can change considerably over a period; for example a village may be quiet and undeveloped when you buy a property and retire there, but it could rapidly become a major tourist spot. This is particularly true of unspoilt and 'undiscovered' Mediterranean resorts and little-known parts of Central America and the Caribbean. Before committing yourself to a location, make sure that you're aware of the government's and local authorities' plans for it.

- Be cautious about choosing your favourite holiday destination as your place of retirement. Holiday memories tend to be recalled through rose-tinted spectacles, but the reality of daily life can be very different, and your perspective and requirements as a resident are quite different from those of a tourist. Before buying a home, you should visit an area at different times of the year and rent a property for an extended period (up to six months) before taking the plunge (see page 44).

- Investigate local public transport thoroughly. This is particularly important if you're elderly, as you may not always be able (or wish) to drive. There's little point in choosing an isolated spot or somewhere with a limited public transport system, when in a few years' time you may have to rely on local bus and train services for your transportation. You should also consider the terrain of your chosen home, as a location with lots of hills or steps can become an insurmountable problem if you have mobility problems or become disabled.

● Do as much research as possible on your prospective retirement destination, preferably by visiting a country or area several times before making a decision. If you're planning to retire abroad with a partner, you should do the research together, so that both of you are aware of the benefits and drawbacks.

● **Most importantly – <u>and it bears repeating</u> – if you aren't <u>absolutely certain</u> where you want to retire, rent for an extended period before buying a home and burning your bridges!**

2.

CHOOSING THE COUNTRY

After having decided to retire or live part of the year abroad, the next thing you need to do is choose the country. Anyone planning to retire abroad usually has a host of countries to choose from and therefore it's important to do extensive research in order to make the right decision. Unless you already own a home abroad or have family ties in a particular country, you could be faced with a wealth of choices. There is, of course, no perfect country for everybody, although most people manage to find their particular ideal country – sometimes after a few false starts.

When choosing the country, there are numerous considerations to be made. Can you speak the language or are you willing to learn? What is the cost of living? Do you wish to buy a home (which isn't permitted by foreigners or is prohibitively expensive in some countries) and could you sell at a realistic price should the need arise? Do you plan to let your home abroad to supplement your income (this isn't permitted in some countries or there are high taxes)? Do you need or wish to be 'close' (measured in driving or flying time) to your home country or another country? How important is the climate?

You may already have some preferences, possibly influenced by where you have spent a number of enjoyable holidays or countries where you have family and friends. If you're planning to start a new life, you should choose a country that suits your personality and taste, as this will be a key factor in your future enjoyment. Before deciding on a country it's advisable to do as much research as possible and to read books especially written for those planning to live or buy a home abroad (such as those published by Survival Books! – see page 345). It will also help to read magazines such as *Resident Abroad* and visit expatriate websites such as 💻 www.escapeartist.com, www.internationalliving.com, www.livingabroad.com, www.transitionsabroad.com and www.ftexpat.com (see **Appendix C** for a list). **Bear in mind that the cost of investing in a few books or magazines (and other research) is tiny compared to the expense of making a big mistake!**

This chapter will help you decide on the country and includes important considerations such as permits, communications, getting there and getting around, particularly motoring.

DO YOU NEED A PERMIT OR VISA?

If you wish to retire or spend long periods each year abroad (e.g. in a holiday home), you must ensure that this will be possible before making any plans and that you will be able to afford to live abroad. Note that if you don't qualify to live permanently in a country by birthright or as a national of a country with which it has a residence agreement, it may be impossible to obtain a residence permit. For example, Americans may find it difficult to retire in a European country and the USA doesn't permit most foreigners without a green card to retire in America, irrespective of their income or whether they own a home there. Unless you're a citizen of Canada or the USA, you won't be permitted to live in North America for longer than three months a year without an appropriate permit or visa.

In most countries it's necessary for retirees to have a minimum income to qualify for a residence permit, and in some countries they must also own a property (although a long-term lease on a property may be sufficient). For example, although a national of a European Union (EU) country can live in any other EU country, there's no automatic right to a residence permit and retirees must meet minimum income levels.

In some countries the rules and regulations governing permits and visas change frequently, so it's important to obtain up-to-date information from an embassy or consulate in your home country. **Permit infringements are taken seriously by the authorities in all countries and there are penalties for breaches of regulations, including fines and even deportation for flagrant abuses.**

KEEPING IN TOUCH

The availability, quality and cost of local services such as post and telephone (including mobile phones, fax and the Internet/e-mail) may be important considerations when planning to retire abroad, particularly if you wish to keep in close touch with family and friends. The range of services and the reliability and speed of postal deliveries varies considerably with the country. In some countries airmail letters can take weeks to be delivered, even to neighbouring countries, and thousands of items of mail go astray each year. Nowadays it's possible to set up what's called a 'portable office' whereby your postal, telephone, fax and e-mail addresses are 'transparent' and can be taken with you wherever you live. To set up world-wide phone and fax numbers, see 🖳 www.jfax.com. See also **Mail** and **E-mail** below.

Telephone: Most western countries provide an excellent telephone service and a phone can be installed in days, while in others there may be a long wait to have a telephone line installed and the service is antiquated and prone to breakdowns. The cost of international telephone calls varies considerably with the country and can be *very* expensive. However, there are a number of ways to reduce the cost, including obtaining an international calling card, e.g. from an American telephone company, or using a callback or resale company (see below). Note that if you will be absent from a home abroad for long periods, you should pay your telephone bill (and all other regular bills) by direct debit from a local bank or post office account. If you fail to pay a bill on time your service could be terminated and it could take weeks to have it reconnected.

Home Country Direct: You can obtain an international calling credit card from telephone companies in most countries, which allows you to make calls (at local rates) from as many as 120 countries and charge them to your telephone bill in your home country. Many European countries subscribe to a Home Country Direct service, which enables you to call a special number giving you direct and free access to an operator in the country you're calling. The operator will connect you to the number required and will also accept credit card and reverse charge calls. However, you should be wary of making international reverse charge calls to some countries using this scheme, as you will pay at least double the cost of using a local payphone. For a list of countries served by the Home Country Direct service, consult your telephone directory or call the local operator.

International Calling Cards: You can obtain an international calling card from telephone companies in many countries, which allows you to make calls from abroad and charge them to your telephone bill in your home country. American long-distance telephone companies (e.g. AT&T, MCI and Sprint) compete vigorously for overseas customers and offer calling cards allowing customers to bill international calls to a credit card. The benefits of international calling cards are that they are fee-free and calls can be made to/from most countries and usually from any telephone (including hotel telephones), and via an English-speaking operator in America (foreign-language operators are also available). Some companies offer conference call facilities, which allow you to talk to a number of people in different countries simultaneously. Other features may include a 'world office' facility allowing you to retrieve voice and fax messages at any time, from anywhere in the world. Note that if you do a lot of travelling, it's wise to carry a number of calling cards, as the cheapest card often depends on the countries you're calling from and to.

Callback or Resale Companies: Callback and resale telephone companies buy international line time at a cheap rate from major telephone companies, thus enabling them to offer inexpensive international calls. Callback companies were so-called because you called a special number, usually in the UK or the USA, and after letting the phone ring you simply hung up. The telephone company automatically called you back and provided you with a line as if you were calling from the UK or the USA. In this way you could bypass expensive local telephone companies. Nowadays this has been replaced in most countries by a system whereby you simply dial a code before making a call, which connects you to the resale company's services. Using these companies may entail dialling more digits, although this can be reduced by buying a phone with a memory facility. Calls must usually be paid for with a credit card, possibly in advance, or by direct debit each month from a bank account or credit card.

Mobile Phones: Many countries provide a mobile phone service in the major population centres or countrywide. A mobile phone is particularly useful in countries where there's a long wait for the installation of a fixed phone line. Note, however, that in some countries mobile phones are expensive to buy and operate, and have high connection fees, standing charges and call rates. **International tariffs can vary by hundreds of per cent according to your network provider and your contract.** Digital mobile phones that subscribe to the Global System for Mobile (GSM) communications system can be used to make and receive calls in over 160 countries (called international roaming). For information about individual countries, see the Internet (⌨ www.gsmworld.com/gsminfo/gsminfo.htm) or contact the GSM Association, 6–8 Old Bond Street, London, UK (☎ 020-7518 0530, ✉ info@ gsmworld.com).

Before using a GSM phone abroad, you should contact your service provider to verify that your tariff allows this facility. You must also ensure that your phone will operate in the country you're planning to visit, e.g. in North America you normally need a tri-band phone that operates across three frequencies. Note that when you take a GSM phone abroad, all calls made to your phone will go via the country where the phone is registered and you must pay for the call from that country to the country where you're located. You can, however, divert all incoming calls to voicemail when abroad. Calls made from abroad are routed automatically via a local GSM service provider.

Internet 'Telephone' Services: The success of the Internet is built on the ability to gather information from computers around the world by connecting to a nearby service provider for the cost of a local telephone call. If you have correspondents or friends who are connected to the Internet, you can make international 'calls' for the price of a local telephone call (which is free in some countries) to an Internet provider. Once on the Internet there are no other charges, no matter how much distance is covered or time is spent online. Internet users can buy inexpensive software that effectively turns their personal computer into a voice-based telephone (both parties must have compatible computer software). You also need a sound card, speakers, a microphone and a modem, and access to a local Internet provider. While the quality of communication isn't as good as using a telephone (it's similar to a CB radio) and you need to arrange call times in advance (e.g. via e-mail), making international 'calls' costs virtually nothing. The Internet can also be used to send and receive e-mail (see below).

Post: Postal services are notoriously slow and unreliable in many countries, and post often takes weeks to arrive or may even be lost entirely. One way around this is to have you post sent to a PO box or accommodation address in your home country, from where it can be sent on to you (to anywhere in the world) at regular intervals by registered post or courier. You can send important items by courier or give them to returning friends and family to post (in some countries returning expatriates co-operate to provide an international postal delivery service). Using fax and e-mail (see below) for most communications will also considerably reduce the amount of post you need to send.

Fax Services: Fax machines are available in all countries, although the cost varies considerably. It may be possible to take a fax machine abroad, but you must check that it's compatible or that it can be modified at a reasonable cost. Most fax machines made for use in a European country will operate in most other European countries, although getting a fax machine repaired abroad may be difficult unless the same model is sold locally. Public fax services are provided by main post offices in many countries, although they may only send faxes, not receive them. Faxes can also be sent and received via major hotels, libraries and office service providers in most countries.

E-mail: One of the easiest ways to keep in touch with family and friends abroad is by e-mail. This provides almost instantaneous communication and allows you to circumvent the local postal service. It isn't even necessary to have your own computer and Internet service provider, as in most countries there are cyber-cafes, libraries, hotels, bookshops and office service providers, where you can pick up your e-mail for a small fee (or maybe even for free). You can obtain a free, portable e-mail address (or a number) from a number of websites, including 🖥 www.mailexcite.com, www.hotmail.com, www.mail.lycos.com, www.shanjemail.com and www.yahoo. com. Then by simply by connecting to the Internet you can pick up your e-mail from anywhere in the world.

Office Services: In major towns and tourist areas in many countries there are offices (such as Mail Boxes Etc. – 🖥 www.mbe.com) which offer a wide range of business and communications services. These may include telephone, fax (transmission and receipt), mailbox service, mail-hold, mail forwarding, call-in service and 24-hour access, stamps, envelopes, postcards, packing supplies, air shipping/receiving, postal metering, money orders and transfers, telegrams, voicemail, e-mail, Internet, telex, copy service, telephone message service and various other business services.

GETTING THERE

Although it isn't so important if you're moving to a neighbouring country within a reasonable driving or flying distance of your family and friends, one of the major considerations when retiring abroad is often transport links with your home country. How long will it take to get there, e.g. by air, taking into account journeys to and from airports? Is it possible to drive? One of the main advantages of being able to drive is that you can take much more luggage with you and the cost for a family may be significantly lower than flying. Could you travel by bus, train or ferry? What does it cost? How frequent are buses, flights, trains or ferries at the time(s) of year when you plan to travel. Is it feasible to travel home for a long weekend, given the cost and travelling time involved?

Note that scheduled airline fares are prohibitively expensive to some countries, while charter flight companies can be unreliable and over-booking is often a problem in the high season. If you intend to make frequent trips back home, it obviously makes sense to choose a country that involves a relatively short journey that isn't too expensive. If a long journey is involved, you should bear in mind that it takes most people a day or two to fully recover, particularly when a long flight (and possibly jet-lag) is involved. **Note also that local airlines in some countries have a poor safety record and should be avoided if at all possible.**

Regular travellers, e.g. with ferry companies and airlines, can often take advantage of travel clubs, season tickets, discount schemes for shareholders and special deals for frequent fliers. For example, those travelling between the UK and the continent by ferry can make savings by joining a 'Property Owners Club', such as those operated by Brittany Ferries for homeowners in France and Spain, while P&O shareholders owning a minimum of 600 P&O 5.5pc concessionary stock receive discounts of up to 50 per cent on most routes. Note that if flying is your only alternative, you should bear in mind that if you need to take a flight at short notice it can be prohibitively expensive, as you may be unable to get an inexpensive charter or apex fare. Also bear in mind that in some countries, ferry services are severely curtailed outside the main holiday season and services are often cancelled altogether in bad weather.

Shop around for the lowest fares available. For some destinations it may be cheaper to fly via another country than to take a direct scheduled flight, assuming that this is possible. British readers should compare the fares listed in newspapers such as *The Sunday Times*, *Observer* and London's *Time Out* entertainment magazine. In the USA the best newspapers include the Sunday editions of the *New York Times*, the *Los Angeles Times* and the *Chicago Tribune*.

Useful publications for frequent fliers include the Official Airline Guides (OAG) Worldwide *Pocket Flight Guide*, *The Complete Sky Traveler* by David Beaty (Methuen), and *The Round the World Air Guide* by Katie Wood and George McDonald (Fontana). Regular air travellers may also be interested in subscribing to *Frequent Flyer* (💻 www.frequentflier.com) or *WebFlyer* (💻 www.webflyer.com).

Allow plenty of time to get to and from airports, ports and railway stations, particularly when travelling during peak hours, when traffic congestion can be horrendous.

GETTING AROUND BY PUBLIC TRANSPORT

For many people, an important aspect of retiring abroad is being able to get around easily, safely and relatively cheaply by public transport. This is particularly important if you're elderly and can longer (or no longer wish to) drive. Public transport services in most countries vary considerably from excellent to terrible, or are even non-existent, depending on where you live. In some countries, there's no rail service and only an infrequent and unreliable local bus service. Public transport tends to be excellent to adequate in major cities, where there may be an integrated system encompassing buses, trains, trams and possibly an underground railway or ferry system. However, most people who live in rural areas find it necessary to have their own car. Taxis are common and plentiful in most countries, although they can be prohibitively expensive or dangerous in others. In some countries there are inexpensive shared taxis or mini-buses, which pick up and drop off passengers at any point along their route.

If you don't drive or aren't planning to own a car abroad, you'll usually need to live in a city or large town where there's adequate public transport and should investigate the frequency and cost of local public transport such as buses, trains, ferries and taxis. Note that if you don't have a car, you may need to use taxis to carry your shopping home or have it delivered.

Bear in mind that in some countries, public transport can be unsafe, e.g. old 'equipment', a lack of safety equipment and procedures (life-belts, life-rafts, seat-belts, etc.), overloading, and drivers and operators who are poorly trained or otherwise unfit to operate public transport. In some countries foreigners are warned not to use public transport except for official taxis. Information about public transport is obtainable from tourist offices and any good guide book.

MOTORING

If you're wedded to your car (or at least to having your own transport), you probably wouldn't consider living anywhere you cannot get around independently. Having your own transport will also allow you a much wider choice of where you can live. However, it isn't always necessary to own a car, and many people use taxis for local trips and rent a car for longer journeys.

Bear in mind that driving is a nerve-wracking and even dangerous experience in many countries, and most people are more accident-prone when driving abroad. Driving in cities is often totally chaotic at the best of times, particularly when traffic drives on a different side of the road from that in your home country. A car can be a liability in towns if you don't have private parking and you will save a lot of money if you can manage without one (which is why many people on a limited budget live in towns). A private garage or parking space can be prohibitively expensive in major cities and towns.

If you're planning to become a resident, you may be able to import a new or second-hand car, duty and tax-free. Check the regulations in any country you must pass through to reach your destination (you may need a *Carnet de Passage* for travel outside Western Europe). When buying a car for use abroad, you will find that in many countries it pays to buy a model that runs on diesel fuel, which is much cheaper than regular fuel (or petrol), and has air-conditioning, which is a blessing in a hot country. Note that if you're planning to import a car (new or second-hand) into most countries, it must have local type-approval and meet certain technical standards. You usually also need to have owned and operated a vehicle abroad for six months to qualify for tax-free importation. This isn't a problem when taking a car from one European Union (EU) country to another or from Canada to the USA, but can be a problem when exporting a vehicle from the US or Japan to Europe or vice versa, when it may need expensive modifications.

EU nationals who are moving to another EU country can use a vehicle registered in their home country abroad without paying local taxes. However, the period of use is determined by the time that a non-resident is permitted to remain in another EU country without becoming a resident, which is a maximum of six months (182 days) in a calendar year. Note that you must be resident in some countries in order to own and operate a car on local registration plates.

Car Rental

The major multinational rental companies, such as Alamo, Avis, Budget, Hertz and Thrifty, have offices in many countries, particularly at major airports and in major cities. There are also cheaper local rental companies. Car rental companies are listed in yellow pages and local companies are listed by town. You may be approached at airports by representatives of local rental companies, who may not be reputable (check their credentials). It's best to reserve a rental car before arriving abroad, particularly during peak periods. When booking, remember to specify an automatic model if you aren't used to a manual (stick-shift) gearbox, as most rental cars in most countries are manual. Fly-drive deals are available from most airlines and travel agents.

Car rental rates vary considerably and are usually much higher in Europe than North America, although they vary with the location and season. Many companies have lower rates for weekend rentals, e.g. from 4pm on Fridays to noon on Mondays, and for rentals of 14 days or longer. The rates charged by major international companies vary little, although you may get a better deal by booking in advance. One of the advantages of hiring with a national company is that you can rent a car in one town and drop it off in another, although you should check the cost of this service. Although cheaper, small local companies require you to return a car to the office you hired it from or to the local airport. **Note also that some of the cheaper rental companies cut corners on maintenance and repairs, and cars can sometimes be unsafe to drive.**

When comparing rates, check that they are inclusive of insurance and taxes, that the insurance cover is adequate and that there are no hidden costs, e.g. collision damage waiver (CDW), theft cover, personal accident insurance (PAI), airport tax, additional drivers and local taxes (e.g. sales, goods and services or value added tax). Some companies don't offer unlimited kilometres/miles, which usually works out more expensive unless you plan to cover a relatively short distance. If required, check that you're permitted to take a car out of the country where you rent it, as you may need extra insurance.

Where applicable, you should ensure that you have sufficient power for mountain driving, e.g. at least a 1.6 litre engine for two people and their luggage. If you're going to be doing a lot of driving in summer, air-conditioning is a must (which again requires a larger engine). Always check the contract and car, e.g. for body damage and to ensure that everything works, before setting out.

To rent a car in most countries you must be aged at least 21, which is increased to 25 for certain categories of cars. Note that some companies also have an upper age limit, e.g. 70. Drivers must produce a valid licence (a copy isn't acceptable) and photographic identity and some drivers require an international driving permit. If more than one person will be driving a vehicle, all the drivers' names must be entered on the rental agreement. If a credit card isn't used, there's usually a high cash deposit and possibly the whole rental period must be paid for in advance. **When paying by credit card, carefully check your bill and statement, as unauthorised charges aren't unknown.** It may be possible to sign a credit card authorisation slip and then pay by cash when you return a car. However, if you do this, you must make sure that you obtain (and destroy) the credit card payment slip.

Renting a car is prohibitively expensive in some countries, particularly during the high season or for long periods. One way to reduce the cost is to rent a car through the American office of an international car rental company such as Alamo, Avis, Budget or Hertz and pay by credit card. This is a legitimate practice and can save considerably on local rates. The US telephone numbers of international rental companies can be obtained from international directory enquiries or via the Internet.

Driving Licence

Ensuring that you're licensed to drive in some countries can be simple or infuriatingly complicated. This depends, not on your nationality, but on the country, or in some cases the state within a country (such as the USA), that issued your licence. All licences issued by European Union member states are recognised in all other EU countries and in most other European countries. However, if you're a non-EU citizen planning to live in an EU country, obtaining a local driving licence can be a frustrating experience (this also applies to many Americans). In some countries you can drive with a foreign licence (possibly with a translation) for a limited period, although many countries require foreigners to have an international driving permit (IDP). Usually residents have a limited period (e.g. six months or a year) in which to exchange a foreign licence for a local one, after which it becomes invalid and you must take a driving test.

If your current licence isn't recognised in the country where you're planning to live, it may be possible to obtain a licence from a country whose licences are recognised, although you must do this before taking up residence abroad. Recognition of your licence will depend on whether your home country (or the country or state that issued your licence) has a reciprocal agreement with the country where you're planning to live. If it doesn't, you may need to do some or all of the following:

● take a first-aid course;

● take a number of lessons with a local driving school;

● pass written and practical driving tests;

● undergo a medical and eye examination;

● provide a copy and official translation of your driving licence;

● supply a number of photographs;

● obtain a residence permit;

● complete various forms;

● produce your passport;

● pay a hefty fee.

If your driving licence isn't recognised in a country where you're planning to live, make sure that you start the process for obtaining a local licence as soon as possible after your arrival, as it can take some months. If you don't obtain a local licence by the deadline, you may be prohibited from driving or may need to take a driving test, even if one wasn't originally required.

Note that if you wish to drive a car with a manual gearbox (stick shift) and passed your test in a car with an automatic gearbox, you will need to take a driving test. Your existing licence may be stamped and returned to you, retained until you leave the country, or returned to the country of issue. If you will need it to drive in your home or another country, be sure to obtain a copy before going abroad.

Car Insurance

When driving abroad, ensure that you have valid car insurance. This is a complicated subject and the types of insurance, what's included and the cost vary considerably from country to country. In some countries such as the USA, it isn't mandatory to have liability insurance in all states and, even when it is, the minimum liability limits are usually woefully inadequate (special motor insurance that provides added protection is available from some travel agents). Never take it for granted that your motor insurance is sufficient for you and your passengers, but check in advance and obtain it in writing – this is particularly important when renting a car. When driving abroad, you should also consider breakdown insurance (see below).

Motorists insured in an EU country, the Czech Republic, Hungary, Liechtenstein, Norway, Slovakia and Switzerland are automatically covered for basic third party liability in all the above countries. **However, always check, as some insurance companies may restrict the countries where you're covered.** In Europe, an international insurance certificate (green card) is compulsory when driving in certain countries and it's mandatory to buy car insurance at the border to enter some countries. A green card is available at no extra cost when you're insured in most Western European countries, which extends your normal insurance (e.g. fully comprehensive) to other countries covered by the green card agreement – but check which countries are covered.

Breakdown Insurance: When driving abroad, it's important to have breakdown insurance (which may include holiday and travel insurance), including repatriation for your family and your car in the event of an accident or breakdown. If you're a member of a motoring organisation, you may be covered when travelling abroad by a reciprocal agreement with national breakdown services, although cover is usually fairly basic. When motoring in some countries, it's also wise to take out special legal protection insurance such as bail bond insurance, without which the authorities may lock you up and throw away the key if you're involved in an accident. In some European countries breakdown insurance is provided by car insurance companies. More comprehensive policies are available from motoring organisations in many countries. Many companies providing European breakdown insurance operate multilingual, 24-hour, emergency centres where assistance is available for motoring, medical, legal and travel problems.

Car Security

Most countries have a problem with car theft and thefts from cars, particularly in major cities and resort areas. In many countries, foreign-registered vehicles, especially camper vans and mobile homes, are targeted by thieves. If you drive anything other than a worthless wreck you should have theft insurance that includes your car stereo and personal belongings (although this may be prohibitively expensive). If you drive a new or valuable car it's wise to have it fitted with an alarm, an engine immobiliser (the best system) or other anti-theft device, and to also use a visible deterrent such as a steering or gear stick lock. It's particularly important to protect your car if you own a model that's desirable to professional car thieves, e.g. most new sports and executive models, which are often stolen by crooks to order.

The best security system (available in many western countries) for a valuable car is a tracking device that's triggered by concealed motion detectors. The vehicle's movements are tracked by radio or satellite and the police are automatically notified and recover over 90 per cent of vehicles. Some systems can immobilise a vehicle while it's on the move (which may not be such a good idea!). The main drawback is that tracking systems are expensive, although many insurance companies offer a discount on comprehensive insurance when you have a tracking system fitted.

Few cars are fitted with deadlocks and most can be broken into in seconds by a competent thief. A good security system won't usually prevent someone from breaking into your car or even stop it from being stolen, but it will make it more difficult and may persuade a thief to look for an easier target. Radios, cassette and CD players attract thieves like bees to a honey pot in many countries. If you buy an expensive stereo system, buy one with a removable unit or with a removable control panel that you can pop into a bag or pocket. Never forget to remove it (and your mobile phone), even when parking for a few minutes.

Thieves often smash windows (in some countries BMW stands for 'break my window') to steal stereo systems and other articles from cars, even articles of little value such as sunglasses or cigarettes. When leaving your car unattended, store any valuables, including clothes, in the glove box or boot (trunk). Note, however, that storing valuables in the boot isn't always safe, particularly if the boot can be opened from inside the car. If a car is empty, a thief may be tempted to force open the boot with a crowbar. It's never sensible to leave your original car papers in your car (which may help a thief dispose of it). When parking overnight or when it's dark, it's best to park in a secure overnight car park or garage, or at least in a well-lit area.

Car-jacking (or highway piracy) is an increasing problem in some countries, where gangs deliberately bump or ram cars to get drivers to stop, or block the road, usually late at night when there's little traffic about. Crooks may also pose as plainclothes policemen and try to get you to stop by flashing a 'badge'. In the worst cases, thieves take not only the car and its contents, but even the victims' clothes they are wearing. Travelling at night in some countries is hazardous and should be avoided.

If your car is stolen or anything is stolen from it, report it to the police in the area where it was stolen. You can usually report it by telephone but must go to the station to complete a report. Don't, however, expect the police to find it or even take any interest in your loss. Report a theft to your insurance company as soon as possible.

Driving Abroad

You may be unfamiliar with the road rules and regulations in the country where you're planning to live, which may differ considerably from those in your home country. The following tips are designed to help you survive driving abroad:

- If you're taking a car with you, don't forget your car registration and insurance papers, test and tax certificates (if applicable). If you intend to drive to the country where you're planning to take up residence, ensure that you have sufficient local currency (for petrol, road tolls, food, traffic fines, etc.) for all the countries you will pass through.

- You're probably aware that not all countries drive on the same side of the road – in some countries drivers use both sides (when not driving in the middle!). It saves confusion if you drive on the same side as the majority. If you aren't used to driving on the left or right, take it easy until you're accustomed to it. Be particularly alert when leaving lay-bys, T-junctions, one-way streets, petrol stations and car parks, as it's easy to lapse into driving on the wrong side. It's helpful to display a reminder (e.g. 'Think Left!' or 'Think Right!') on your car's dashboard.

- Note that the procedure following an accident isn't the same in all countries, although many (e.g. European) countries use a standard accident report form provided by insurance companies. As a general rule, you should call the police to the scene for anything other than a minor accident.

- Drivers of foreign-registered cars must have the appropriate nationality plate or sticker affixed to the rear of their car when motoring abroad. In many countries you can be fined on the spot for not displaying it, although it isn't often enforced judging by the number of cars without them. Cars must show the correct nationality plate only and not an assortment.

- Ensure that your car complies with local laws and that you have the necessary equipment, e.g. spare tyre, bulbs and fuses, warning triangle (in some countries such as Spain you need two), first-aid kit, fire extinguisher, petrol can (note that carrying a can of petrol or petrol in plastic cans is forbidden in some countries) and headlight beam deflectors. Check the latest regulations with a motoring organisation in your home country.

- Make sure that you have sufficient spares, particularly if you're driving a rare or exotic car (i.e. any car that isn't sold locally). A good map will come in handy, particularly when you're lost. Make sure that the type of petrol you require is freely available locally and in all the countries you intend to visit or pass through. If you need leaded or lead replacement petrol (LRP) and it isn't available locally, you may need to have your car's engine modified. Make sure that you know the local name for the type of fuel you require, which can be confusing, e.g. *gasolio* in Italy is diesel (and not gasoline), while *gasolina* in Spain is petrol (gasoline) and *pétrole* in France is paraffin!

- Seat belts must be worn at all times in European countries, North America and in many other countries. In some countries dipped headlights (low beam) must be used at all times.

- If you're planning a long journey, a mechanical check-up for your car is recommended, particularly if it hasn't been serviced for a while.

- The legal blood alcohol level when driving varies depending on the country and is 80mg per 100ml of blood in some Western European countries, although it's zero in many Eastern European countries. Alcohol is estimated to be a major factor in at least a third of all road accidents and in countries with a 'drink-drive culture' it's much higher. Note that the strength of alcoholic beverages (and the size of drinks) varies considerably from country to country. The best policy is not to drink alcohol at all when you're driving.

- In continental Europe, where all traffic drives on the right, most main roads are designated priority roads indicated by a sign, the most common of which is a yellow diamond on a white background (the end of priority is shown by the same sign with a black diagonal line through it). On secondary roads without priority signs and in built-up areas, you must give way to all vehicles coming from your RIGHT. **Failure to observe this rule is the cause of many accidents.** If you're ever in doubt about who has priority, give way to trams, buses and all traffic coming from your RIGHT (particularly large trucks!). Emergency (ambulance, fire, police) and public utility (electricity, gas, telephone, water) vehicles attending an emergency have priority on all roads in most countries. Note that at roundabouts (traffic circles) vehicles on the roundabout normally have priority and not those entering it, usually indicated by a give way sign.

● Never carry anything across an international border unless you're absolutely sure what it contains, as it could contain drugs or other illegal substances. The same applies to any passengers (and their baggage) that you pick up on your journey. Note that it's illegal to transport produce, plants, alcohol and under-age children (apart from your own) across international or state borders in some countries.

When driving anywhere, **NEVER** assume that you know what another motorist is going to do next. Just because a motorist is indicating left doesn't mean he's actually going to turn left – in some countries he's just as likely to be turning right, stopping or about to reverse – and in many countries motorists make turns without any indication at all! Don't be misled by any semblance of road discipline and clearly marked lanes. Try to be courteous, if only in self-defence, but don't expect others to reciprocate.

The most dangerous countries in which to drive vary according to the newspapers and magazines you read and whose statistics they use. What is indisputable is that you can minimise your chance of having an accident by careful and 'defensive' driving. Take extra care in winter, when ice and snow can make driving particularly hazardous. Driving in many countries is chaotic and nerve-racking at the best of times. If you're in doubt about your ability to cope with the stress or the risks involved, you would be wiser to use public transport.

3.

ACCOMMODATION

In most countries, finding accommodation to rent or buy isn't difficult, provided your requirements aren't too unusual. There are, however, a few exceptions. For example, rented accommodation in major cities is usually in high demand and short supply, and rents can be *very* high. Accommodation usually accounts for around 25 per cent of the average family's budget, but can be up to 50 per cent in major cities. Property prices and rents vary considerably according to the region and city and have increased steadily in most major cities in recent years. In cities and large towns, apartments are much more common than detached houses, which are rare and prohibitively expensive.

People in most countries aren't very mobile and move house much less frequently than the Americans and British, which is reflected in the fairly stable property market. It generally isn't worth buying a home abroad unless you plan to stay in the country for the medium to long term, say a minimum of five years and preferably 10 to 15. People in most countries don't buy domestic property as an investment, but as a home for life, and you shouldn't expect to make a quick profit when buying property abroad.

TEMPORARY ACCOMMODATION

On arrival abroad, it may be necessary to stay in temporary accommodation for a few weeks or months, e.g. before moving into permanent accommodation or while waiting for your furniture to arrive. Many hotels and bed and breakfast establishments cater for long-term guests and offer reduced weekly or monthly rates. In many areas, particularly in major cities, serviced and holiday apartments are available. These are fully self-contained, furnished apartments with their own bathrooms and kitchens, which are cheaper and more convenient than a hotel, particularly for families. Serviced apartments are usually rented on a weekly basis. Self-catering holiday accommodation is available in most countries, although it's prohibitively expensive during the main holiday season (e.g. June to August in Europe).

RENTED ACCOMMODATION

It's prudent when looking for a permanent home abroad to rent for a period until you know exactly what you want, how much you wish to pay and where you want to live. This is particularly important for retirees who don't know a country well, when renting allows you to become familiar with an area, its weather, amenities and the local people' to meet other foreigners who have made their homes abroad and share their experiences' and not least, to discover the cost of living at first hand. Renting is also a good option for those wishing to spend only a few months a year abroad or for 'seasonal retirees' intending to spend the winter abroad, particularly in resort areas in Florida and Spain.

Many western countries have a strong rental market and it's possible to rent every kind of property, from a tiny studio apartment to a huge rambling castle. Rental properties are mostly privately owned, but include investment properties owned by companies and public housing owned by local councils. If you're looking for a home for less than a year, you're better off looking for a furnished apartment or house. Rental properties in most countries are let unfurnished, particularly for lets longer than a year, and long-term furnished properties are difficult to find. Bear in mind that in some countries, unfurnished means a property that is completely empty, except perhaps for the bathroom porcelain and possibly a kitchen sink. There will be no kitchen cupboards, appliances, light fitting, curtains or carpets, although you may be able to buy these from a departing tenant. Semi-furnished apartments usually have kitchen cupboards and bathroom fixtures, and possibly a few pieces of furniture, while furnished properties tend to be fully equipped, including crockery, bedding and possibly towels (similar to renting a self-catering apartment).

Furnished Rentals: Many countries have an abundance of self-catering accommodation and a wide choice. You can choose from cottages, apartments, villas, bungalows, mobile homes, chalets, and even castles and palaces, if your budget runs to them. Most property is available for short holiday lets only, particularly during the peak summer season. However, some owners let their homes long-term, particularly outside the peak summer period. Note that when the rental period includes the peak letting months of July and August, the rent may be prohibitive. If you rent for a short period from an agent, you should try to negotiate a lower commission than the usual one month's rent, e.g. 10 per cent of the total rent payable. You can make agreements by fax when renting from abroad.

Standards vary considerably, from dilapidated ill-equipped cottages to luxury villas with every modern convenience. A typical holiday rental is a small cottage or self-contained apartment with one or two bedrooms (sleeping two to four and usually including a sofa bed in the living-room), a large living-room/kitchen with an open fire or stove, and a toilet and bathroom. Always check whether a property is fully equipped (which should mean whatever you want it to mean!) and whether it has central heating if you're planning to rent in winter.

For short-term lets, the cost is calculated on a weekly basis (Saturday to Saturday) and depends on the standard, location, number of beds and the facilities provided. For holiday rentals, the year is generally split into three rental periods: low (e.g. October to April), mid (e.g. May and September) and peak (e.g. July and August). Rents vary considerably with the country, the region, the time of year, and, not least, the size and quality of the property. As a rough guide, a rural property in Europe sleeping two costs from around GB£150 (US$240) per week in the low season to GB£250 (US$350) per week in the peak season. A property sleeping four costs from GB£150 (US$225) per a week in the low season to GB£400 (US$550) in the high season. At the other end of the scale, you can easily pay GB£2,000 to £4,000 (US$3,000 to $5,500) or more per week in summer for a large farmhouse or villa with a swimming pool.

If you're looking for a rental property for say three to six months, it's best not to rent unseen, but to rent a holiday apartment for a week or two to allow you time to look around for a long-term rental or a property to buy. Note that rental laws and protection for tenants doesn't usually extend to holiday lettings, furnished lettings or sub-lettings. For holiday letting, parties are free to agree such terms as they see fit concerning the period, rent, deposit and the number of occupants permitted, and there's no legal obligation for the landlord to provide a written agreement. However, you shouldn't rent a furnished property long-term without a written contract, which is important if you wish to have a deposit returned.

Hotels: Hotel rates vary with the time of year, the location and the individual establishment, although you may be able to haggle over rates outside the high season and for long stays. A single room in most western countries (excluding major cities) costs from around GB£20 (US$30) and a double room from around GB£30 (US$45) per night. You should expect to pay at least double these rates in a major city, where inexpensive hotels are often used as permanent accommodation. Hotels aren't usually a cost-effective solution for anyone planning to stay in a country long term, although in some countries they are the only alternative and may have special low rates for long-term residents. Bed and breakfast accommodation is also available in many countries, although it isn't always budget accommodation, when you need to choose a hostel or pension, which may have self-catering apartments or studios.

Finding a Rental Property

Your success in finding a suitable rental property depends on many factors, not least the kind of rental you're seeking (a one-bedroom apartment is easier to find than a four-bedroom detached house), how much you want to pay and the area where you wish to live. There are a number of ways of finding a property to rent, including the following:

- If you have friends, relatives or acquaintances in the area, ask them to help spread the word. In many countries, the best properties are often found by word of mouth, particularly in major cities, where it's almost impossible to find somewhere with a reasonable rent unless you have connections.

- Rental properties are advertised in local newspapers and magazines, including expatriate publications, and can also be found through property publications in many countries. Many estate agents offer short-term rentals, and builders and developers may also rent properties to potential buyers. Short-term rentals can be found through local and state tourist offices abroad, travel agents, the Internet and many overseas newspapers.

● Check the small ads. in local newspapers and magazines (see below).

● Look for properties with a 'to rent' sign in the window.

● Visit accommodation and letting agents (listed in the yellow pages). Most cities and large towns also have estate agents (or realtors) who act as letting agents for homeowners. It's often better to deal with an agent than directly with owners, particularly regarding contracts and legal matters.

● Look for advertisements in shop windows and on bulletin boards in shopping centres, supermarkets, universities and colleges, and company offices.

● Check newsletters published by companies, colleges, churches, clubs and expatriate organisations, and their notice boards.

You must usually be quick off the mark to find accommodation through small ads in local newspapers Buy newspapers as soon as they're published and start phoning straight away. You can also view rental advertisements on the Internet, where all major newspapers have websites. Other sources include expatriate publications published in major cities and small ad newspapers. Some estate agents also provide apartment listings in their own magazines. You must be available to inspect properties immediately or at any time. Even if you start phoning at the crack of dawn, you're likely to find a queue when you arrive to view a property in a major city.

The best days for advertisements are usually Fridays and Saturdays. Advertisers may be private owners, property managers or letting agencies (particularly in major cities). You can insert a 'rental wanted' advertisement in many newspapers and on notice boards, but don't count on success using this method. Finding a property to rent in major cities in many countries is similar to the situation in London and New York, where the best properties are usually found through personal contacts (word of mouth). The worst time to look is during September and October when people return from their summer holidays and students are looking for accommodation.

Rents: Note that rents are very high in some countries, particularly in major cities where rental property is in high demand and short supply. Rents may also be astronomical in relation to the local cost and standard of living. In many countries you must pay a year's rent in advance or for the whole period of your contract and landlords may demand a non-returnable deposit (called 'key' money), usually equal to a few months' rent, simply for the 'privilege' of being able to rent a property.

BUYING A HOME

Buying a home in most countries is usually a good long-term investment and for permanent residents is usually preferable to renting. For those planning to retire abroad indefinitely, buying is usually the better option, particularly as buying a home is often no more expensive (or even cheaper) than renting in the long term, and could yield a handsome profit. Provided you avoid the most expensive areas (i.e. major cities), property can be relatively inexpensive in many countries compared with the UK or USA, although the fees associated with a purchase usually add between 5 and 15 per cent to the cost. Note, however, that in some countries foreigners aren't permitted to buy property.

Property ownership is high in some countries, e.g. as high as 80 per cent, although people in most countries don't generally buy property as an investment and you shouldn't expect to make a quick profit when buying property abroad. In most countries, property values increase at an average of around 5 per cent a year or in line with inflation, meaning that you must own a house for a few years simply to recover the fees associated with buying. Property prices rise faster than average in some fashionable areas, although this is generally reflected in higher purchase prices. The stable property market in most countries acts as a discouragement to speculators wishing to make a quick profit, as does capital gains tax.

It isn't wise to be in too much of a hurry when buying a home. Have a good look around in your preferred area(s) and make sure that you have a clear picture of the relative prices and the kinds of property available. There's a huge variety of properties for sale in most countries ranging from derelict farmhouses and village houses requiring complete restoration to modern luxury apartments and villas with all modern conveniences. Some people set themselves impossible deadlines in which to buy a property (e.g. a few days or a week) and often end up bitterly regretting their impulsive decision.

It's a wise or lucky person who gets his choice absolutely right first time, which is why most experts recommend that you rent before buying unless you're absolutely certain what you want, how much you wish to pay and where you want to live. To reduce the chances of making an expensive error when buying in an unfamiliar country or region, it's often prudent to rent for 6 to 12 months. This allows you to become familiar with the region and the weather, and gives you plenty of time to look around for a permanent home at your leisure. There's no shortage of properties for sale in most countries and whatever kind of property you're looking for, you'll have an abundance to choose from. Wait until you find your 'dream' home and then think about it for another week or two before signing a contract.

To get an idea of property prices, check the prices of properties advertised in English-language property magazines and local newspapers, magazines and property journals (see **Appendix A**). In some countries, property price indexes for various regions are published by local property magazines, although these should be taken only as a rough guide. Before deciding on the price, make sure you know exactly what's included, as it isn't unusual for people to strip a house or apartment bare when selling and even remove the kitchen sink, toilets, light fittings and even the light switches! If applicable, have fixtures and fittings listed in the contract.

For anyone planning to buy a home abroad, our sister publication, *Buying a Home Abroad* by your author, David Hampshire, is essential reading (see the rear of the book to order a copy). A comprehensive list of other books is contained in **Appendix B**.

RETIREMENT HOMES

Over the last decade, the demand for purpose-built retirement homes and developments has grown rapidly, and there's a huge demand in Australia, Canada, New Zealand, the UK and the USA, where retirement homes usually sell quickly. Retirement developments are rarer in other countries, although they are becoming more popular in southern European countries such as Spain and Portugal as developers become aware of the market potential.

Retirement developments have a variety of names depending on the country: in the UK they are generally known as 'sheltered housing', in Australia and New Zealand the term 'retirement village' is popular, while in Canada and the USA a retirement development may be called an 'adult community' or a 'Continuing Care Retirement Community' (CCRC). Developments may be a combination of apartments, townhouses and detached houses. In most countries it's necessary to buy a property, although it may also be possible to rent, lease or buy a 'lifetime occupancy'.

The advantages of retirement housing are many, not least that help is on hand 24 hours a day, either from a live-in warden or caretaker, or via an alarm system linked to a control centre. A nurse and maintenance man are usually on call and there may also be visiting doctors and dentists. Many developments or villages provide 24-hour, seven days a week emergency care and some also have their own nursing homes. Within a retirement development or village you will also find a ready-made community, where company is always available and a wide range of activities is organised. Note, however, that some people make the mistake of moving into a purpose-built retirement home before they really need to, and find that the maintenance and service costs are prohibitively high or discover that the community lifestyle of a retirement village isn't for them. Sheltered housing developments may be tailored for active retirees (e.g. aged 50+) or elderly people (aged 70+) with limited mobility, and you should check exactly who a development is intended for.

Facilities vary considerably, although retirement developments and villages generally offer a wide variety of amenities and services. Before buying a retirement home, you should visit a number of villages and talk to residents, as they vary enormously in the quality and variety of housing, amenities and cost. Retirement villages offer a luxurious lifestyle, a supportive environment, safety and security, and some are more like country estates or luxury hotels, with corresponding prices.

Homes usually have central heating, air-conditioning (where necessary), fully-fitted kitchens and cable or satellite TV. A wide range of communal facilities and services may be provided, including medical and dental clinics (possibly with a resident doctor and dentist), nursing facilities, lounges, laundry, housekeeping, spa complex (with sauna and Jacuzzi), restaurant and bar, meal delivery, landscaped gardens, handyman, mini-supermarket, post and banking facilities, library service, guest apartments, free local transport, 24-hour security with closed-circuit television (CCTV), intercom, personal emergency alarm system and a 24-hour multi-lingual reception. Sports and leisure services may include a golf course, swimming pools (e.g. heated outdoor and/or indoor pools), tennis courts, lawn bowling, croquet, billiards/pool room, gymnasium, video room, library and a social club.

As with all property purchases, it's important to spend some time visiting different developments and obtain expert advice. In many developments you're required to sign a binding contract before you can purchase a property. Make sure that you fully understand it and its implications before signing, particularly if you're buying in a foreign country with different property laws from those at home. Note that in some countries retirement developments and their standards aren't legally regulated, and buyers may be unprotected by the law.

Retirement developments or villages vary considerably in size and facilities. In some countries, e.g. the UK, they tend to be small developments based around a community building used for social and other purposes, and located within easy access of local shops and amenities. In others, such as the USA, retirement villages may include up to 2,000 homes with their own sports (e.g. golf courses, tennis courts, etc.), shopping, restaurant and other facilities. Villages may be situated in or close to towns or be in rural areas, although most have access to public transport. Retirement villages are usually run by private companies, although in some countries there are a number of state-run developments, and in some cases the private company may be a co-operative or be owned by a religious or ethnic organisation.

In order to ensure that a development or village runs smoothly, there are regulations or statutes which state how it's managed and what the occupants may and may not do. Statute contents can vary considerably, although they are usually agreed between the occupants, the developer and the management. When you visit a retirement development you should ask to see a copy of the statutes, which should be written in clear and easily understandable language. Note particularly any restrictions and consider how they may affect your lifestyle and intentions. For example, most retirement developments have strict regulations regarding the age and status of the occupants and some may not accept anyone under 55 or family units larger than a couple. Some also restrict visits by children or prohibit them from staying overnight. Before committing yourself to a particular development, ensure that you understand the regulations and their implications.

Retirement homes take many different forms, which may all be provided within the same development or village. These generally include the following:

Independent Living Units: These are independent properties in their own right and may be apartments, townhouses or detached houses. They are usually fitted with call systems and may include facilities for the disabled such as ramps or stair lifts. Owners have access to community or village facilities.

Assisted Living Units: These are usually small apartments with limited catering facilities, where residents generally have access to communal dining and recreational areas. Properties include call systems and facilities for the disabled and are generally for retirees who want to remain independent but require help with some daily activities.

Nursing Homes: These are usually chosen by those who need help with most daily activities or require constant nursing care.

Choosing a Retirement Home

The choice of retirement homes, developments and villages can be daunting. The following checklist is designed to help you make your decision:

- The development or village:
  - Is the development or village located in attractive surroundings? Is it well-maintained? Is it noisy? Is it close to local amenities and public transport?
  - What facilities does the development or village offer and are they well maintained? What facilities are planned for the future?
  - How secure is the development or village?
  - What future construction is planned for the development or village? Will you have any say in this?
  - Is the development or village well managed?
  - What are the rules and regulations regarding visitors, children, pets, social activities and the use or alteration of a property?

- The property:
  - Does the property get plenty of sun and is it sheltered from the wind?
  - Does it include facilities for the elderly such as grab rails, easily accessible units and cupboards, and call buttons in every room?
  - Is it secure?
- The fees:
  - What are the monthly and other fees?
  - What exactly is included in the monthly service charge? Does it increase every year and, if so, by how much?
  - Are there additional fees? If so, who decides what they are, the amount payable and how they will be apportioned?
  - Will you have to pay any fees if you decide to leave?
  - Do residents have to pay fees for units that aren't occupied?
- The future:
  - If your requirements change in the future, can you exchange your home for another one within the development? If so, what are the charges?
  - Who controls the sale of your home? Are any fees to be paid to the management?
  - If you can sell your home privately, is the developer entitled to a percentage of the sale price?

Retirement homes or sheltered housing are generally an excellent option for older retirees, and the fact that they are in short supply in most countries underlines their popularity. However, although some countries such as the UK and the USA have introduced legislation protecting buyers' rights, in many countries the purchase of a retirement home in a purpose-built development or village remains a legal grey area. Before committing yourself to the purchase of a home within a retirement development in a foreign country, it's important to obtain expert legal advice and not to sign a contract unless you fully understand its contents. For information about retirement homes in individual countries see **Country Directories** in Chapter 8. Further information is available from the following organisations:

Australia: The Council on the Aging (⌨ www.cota.org.au) can provide detailed information about retirement home options in each state. There are also state Retirement Village Residents Associations.

Canada: The Canadian Association of Retired Persons (⌨ www.50plus.com) provides information about retirement communities in Canada and Florida.

New Zealand: The Retirement Villages Association (⌨ www.retirement villages.org.nz) maintains a country-wide directory of retirement villages.

United Kingdom: The Elderly Accommodation Counsel (EAC), 3rd Floor, 89 Albert Embankment, London SE1 7TP (☎ 020-7820 1343, ⌨ www. housingcare.org) maintains a nation-wide database with comprehensive information about sheltered accommodation in the UK. For further information obtain a copy of *A Buyer's Guide to Retirement Housing* (Age Concern Books, ⌨ www.ageconcern.org.uk).

USA: The Continuing Care Accreditation Commission (⌨ www.ccac online.org) is America's only accrediting body for retirement communities and can provide lists of accredited sheltered accommodation and other information.

AVOIDING PROBLEMS

The problems associated with buying property abroad have been highlighted in the last few decades or so, during which the property market in some countries has gone from boom to bust and back again. From a legal point of view, some countries are much safer than others, although buyers have a high degree of protection under the law in most countries. However, you should take the usual precautions regarding contracts, deposits and obtaining proper title. Many people have had their fingers burnt by rushing into property deals without proper care and consideration. It's all too easy to fall in love with the beauty and allure of a home and sign a contract without giving it sufficient thought. If you're uncertain, don't allow yourself to be rushed into making a hasty decision, e.g. through fears of an imminent price rise or because someone else is interested in a property. Although many people dream of buying a retirement home abroad, it's vital to do your homework thoroughly and avoid the 'dream sellers' (often fellow countrymen) who will happily prey on your ignorance and tell you anything in order to sell you a home.

The vast majority of people who buy homes abroad don't obtain independent legal advice and most of those who experience problems take no precautions whatsoever. Of those who do take legal advice, many do so only after having paid a deposit and signed a contract or, more commonly, after they have run into problems. The most important point to bear in mind when buying property abroad is to obtain expert legal advice from someone who's familiar with local law, and you should never pay any money or sign anything without first taking legal advice. You'll find the relatively small cost (in comparison with the cost of a home) of obtaining legal advice to be excellent value, if only for the peace of mind it affords. Trying to cut corners to on legal costs is foolhardy in the extreme when a large sum is at stake.

There are professionals who speak English and other languages in many countries, and many expatriate professionals (e.g. architects, builders and surveyors) also practise abroad. However, don't assume that because you're dealing with a fellow countryman he'll offer you a better deal or do a better job than a local person (the reverse may be true). It's wise to check the credentials of professionals you employ, whatever their nationality. Note that it's never wise to rely solely on advice proffered by those with a financial interest in selling you a property, such as a builder or estate agent, although their advice may be excellent and totally unbiased.

Declared Value: Don't be tempted by the 'quaint' custom of tax evasion, where the 'official' sale price declared to the authorities is reduced by an 'under the table' cash payment. In many countries, it's possible when buying a property direct from the vendor that he will suggest this, particularly if he's selling a second home and must pay capital gains tax on the profit. Obviously if the vendor can show a smaller profit, he pays less tax. **You should steer well clear of this practice, which is of course strictly illegal (although widespread).** If you under-declare the price, the authorities can re-value the property and demand that you pay the shortfall in tax plus interest and fines. If you're selling a property, you should bear in mind that if the buyer refuses to make the illicit payment after the contract has been signed, there's nothing (legally) you can do about it!

Among the most common problems experienced by buyers abroad are: buying in the wrong area (**rent first!**); buying a home that's difficult or even impossible to sell; buying too large a property and grossly underestimating restoration and modernisation costs; not having a survey done on an old property; not taking legal advice; not including the necessary conditional clauses in the contract; buying a property for business, e.g. to convert to self-catering accommodation, and being too optimistic about the income; being overcharged by vendors and agents (a common practice when selling to foreigners in some countries); taking on too large a mortgage; and property management companies going bust or doing a moonlight flit with owners' rental receipts.

Other problems include: buying a property without a legal title (a particular problem in Eastern Europe); buying a property that has been built or extended without planning permission; buying a property that is subject to embargoes; buying a property that is part of the assets of a company sold illegally by a bankrupt builder or company; undischarged mortgages from the previous owner; builders absconding with the buyer's money before completing a property; claims by relatives after a property has been purchased; properties sold to more than one buyer; and people selling properties they don't own. Always take care when a property is offered at a seemingly bargain price by a builder, developer or other businessman, and run a thorough credit check on the vendor and his business.

One law that property buyers should be aware of is the law of subrogation, whereby property debts, including mortgages, local taxes, utility bills and community charges, remain with a property and are inherited by the buyer in many countries. This is an open invitation to dishonest sellers to 'cut and run'. It is, of course, possible to check whether there are any outstanding debts on a property, and you must ensure that your legal advisor does this after you sign a contract and again a few days before completion.

It's preferable to have your finance in place before you start looking for a property abroad and, if you need a mortgage, to obtain a mortgage guarantee certificate from a bank that guarantees you a mortgage at a certain rate, which is usually subject to a valuation. Note, however, that in many countries a buyer can withdraw from a contract and have his deposit returned if he's unable to obtain a mortgage. You'll need to pay a deposit when signing a contract and must pay all fees and taxes on completion.

Summary: It's important to deal only with qualified and licensed agents, and to engage a local lawyer before signing anything or paying a deposit. A surveyor may also be necessary, particularly if you're buying an old property or a property with a large plot. Your lawyer will carry out the necessary searches regarding such matters as ownership, debts and rights of way. Enquiries must be made to ensure that the vendor has a registered title and that there are no debts against a property. It's also important to check that a property has the relevant building licences, conforms to local planning laws and that any changes (alterations, additions or renovations) have been approved by the appropriate authority. If a property is owned by several members of a family, which is common in some countries, all owners must give their consent before it can be sold. It's also important to ensure that a rural property has a reliable water supply and sewage system.

Finally, if there's any chance that you will need to sell (and recoup your investment) in the foreseeable future, it's wise to buy a home that will be sellable. A property with broad appeal in a popular area will usually fit the bill, although it will need to be *very* special to sell quickly in some areas. A modest, reasonably priced property is usually likely to be much more sellable than a large expensive home, particularly one requiring restoration or modernisation.

CHOOSING THE LOCATION

The most important consideration when buying a home is usually its location – or as the old adage goes, the *three* most important points are location, location and location! A property in a reasonable condition in a popular area is likely to be a better investment than an exceptional property in a less attractive location. There's no point in buying a dream property in a terrible location. The wrong decision regarding location is one of the main causes of disenchantment among foreigners when buying homes abroad.

Where you buy a property will depend on a range of factors, including your personal preferences, whether it will be a permanent or holiday home, whether you plan to let it, and, not least, your financial resources. When seeking a permanent home, don't be too influenced by where you have spent an enjoyable holiday or two. A town or area that was acceptable for a few weeks' holiday may be far from suitable for a retirement home, particularly regarding the proximity to shops, medical facilities and other amenities.

If you have little idea about where you wish to buy, read as much as you can about the countries and regions on your shortlist and spend some time looking around your areas of interest. Note that the climate, lifestyle and cost of living can vary considerably with the country and the region and even within a particular region. Before looking at properties, it's important to have a good idea of the type of property you're looking for and the price you wish to pay, and to draw up a shortlist of the areas or towns of interest. If you don't do this, you're likely to be overwhelmed by the number of properties to be viewed. Estate agents usually expect serious buyers to know where they want to buy within a 30 to 40km (20 to 25mi) radius and some even expect clients to narrow it down to specific towns and villages.

The 'best' area in which to live depends on a range of considerations, including the proximity to a town, shops (e.g. a supermarket), public transport, sports facilities, beach, etc. Don't, however, believe the travelling times and distances stated in adverts and estate agents' brochures. According to some agents' magical mystery maps every home is close to a city or large town, public transport and other amenities. When looking for a home, bear in mind the travelling time and costs to shops and local amenities such as restaurants and bars! If you buy a remote country property, the distance to local amenities and services could become a problem, particularly as you get older and less mobile. If you live in a remote rural area you will need to be much more self-sufficient than if you live in a town and will need to use a car for everything, which will add significantly to the cost of living. **The cost of motoring is high in some countries and may be an important consideration when buying a home.**

If possible, you should visit an area a number of times over a period of a few weeks, both on weekdays and at weekends, in order to get a feel for the neighbourhood (walk, don't just drive around!). A property seen on a balmy summer's day after a delicious lunch and a few glasses of wine may not be nearly so attractive on a subsequent visit on a dull day without the warm inner glow. If possible, you should also visit an area at different times of the year, e.g. in both summer and winter, as somewhere that's wonderful in summer can be forbidding and inhospitable in winter. On the other hand, if you're planning to buy a winter holiday home, you should also view it in summer, as snow can hide a multitude of sins! In any case, you should view a property a number of times before making up your mind to buy it. If you're unfamiliar with a country or area, most experts recommend that you rent for a period before deciding to buy (see **Rented Accommodation** on page 44). This is particularly important if you're planning to buy a retirement home in an unfamiliar area.

Obtain a large-scale map of the area where you're looking, which may even show individual buildings, thereby allowing you to mark off the places that you've seen. You could do this using a grading system to denote your impressions. If you use an estate agent, he'll usually drive you around and you can then return later to those that you like most at your leisure – provided you've marked them on your map!

There are many points to consider regarding the location of a home and can roughly be divided into the immediate surroundings, neighbourhood, and the general area or region. Take into account the present and future needs of all members of your family, including the following (see also **Advantages & Disadvantages** on page 17):

● For most people the **climate** is one of the most important factors when buying a retirement home. Bear in mind both the winter and summer climate, the position of the sun, the average daily sunshine, plus the rainfall and wind conditions.

● You may also wish to check whether the area is noted for fog, which can make driving dangerous. The orientation or aspect of a building is vital; if you want morning or afternoon sun (or both) you must ensure that balconies, terraces and gardens are facing the right direction.

● Check whether an area is particularly susceptible to **natural disasters** such as floods (which are common in some countries), storms (hurricanes, tornadoes, etc.), forest fires, landslides or earthquakes. If a property is located near a coast or waterway, it may be expensive to insure against floods, which are a constant threat in some countries. In areas with little rainfall, there are often severe water restrictions and high water bills. See also **Climate** on page 120.

● **Noise** can be a problem in many cities and resort areas. Although you cannot choose your neighbours, you can at least ensure that a property isn't located next to a busy road, railway line, airport, industrial plant, commercial area, discotheque, night club, bar or restaurant (where revelries may continue into the early hours). Look out for objectionable properties that may be too close to the one you're considering and check whether nearby vacant land has been 'zoned' for commercial activities or tower blocks. In community developments (e.g. apartment blocks) many properties are second homes and are let short term, which means you may have to tolerate boisterous holidaymakers as neighbours throughout the year (or at least during the summer months).

- Bear in mind that if you live in a popular tourist area you'll be inundated with **tourists** in summer. They won't only jam the roads and pack the public transport, but may also occupy your favourite table at your local café or restaurant. A 'front-line' property on a beach or in a marina development may sound attractive and be ideal for short stays, but it isn't always the best choice for permanent residence. Many beaches are hopelessly crowded in the summer, streets may be smelly from restaurants and fast food outlets, parking impossible, services stretched to breaking point, and the incessant noise may drive you crazy. Some people prefer to move inland or to higher ground, where it's less humid, more peaceful and you can enjoy panoramic views. However, getting to and from hillside properties can be hazardous and the often poorly maintained roads (usually narrow and without crash barriers) in many countries are for confident drivers only. Many country roads are also only suited for four-wheel-drive vehicles.

- Do you wish to live in an area with many of your fellow countrymen and other expatriates or as far away from them as possible? If you wish to integrate with the local **community**, avoid foreign 'ghettos' and choose an area or development with mainly local inhabitants. However, unless you speak the local language fluently or intend to learn, you should think twice before buying a property in a village. The locals in some villages resent 'outsiders' buying up prime properties, particularly holiday homeowners, although those who take the time and trouble to integrate into the local community are usually warmly welcomed. If you're buying a permanent home, it's important to check your prospective neighbours, particularly when buying an apartment. For example, are they noisy, sociable or absent for long periods? Do you think you will get on with them? **Good neighbours are invaluable, particularly when buying a second home.**

- Do you wish to be in a **town** or do you prefer the **country**? Inland or on the coast? How about living on an island? Bear in mind that if you buy a property in the country, you'll probably have to tolerate poor public transport (or none at all), long travelling distances to a town of any size, solitude and remoteness. You won't be able to pop along to the local bakery, drop into the local bar for a glass of your favourite tipple with the locals or have a choice of restaurants on your doorstep. In a town or large village, the market will be just around the corner, the doctor and chemist close at hand, and if you need help or have any problems, your neighbours will be close by.

  In the country you will be closer to nature, will have more freedom (e.g. to make as much noise as you wish) and possibly complete privacy, e.g. to sunbathe or swim *au naturel*. Living in a remote area in the country will suit nature lovers looking for solitude who don't want to involve themselves in the 'hustle and bustle' of town life (not that there's much of this in most rural towns). If you're after peace and quiet, make sure that there isn't a busy road or railway line nearby or a church within 'DONGING!' distance. Note, however, that many people who buy a remote country home find that the peace of the countryside palls after a time and they yearn for the more exciting city or coastal nightlife. If you've never lived in the country, it's wise to rent before buying. Note also that, while it's cheaper to buy in a remote or unpopular location, it's often much more difficult to sell.

- If you're planning to buy a large country property with an extensive **garden** or plot, bear in mind the high cost and amount of work involved in its upkeep. If it's to be a second home, who will look after the house and garden when you're away? Do you want to spend your holidays mowing the lawn and cutting back the undergrowth? Do you want a home with a lot of outbuildings? What are you going to do with them? Can you afford to convert them into extra rooms or guest or self-catering accommodation?

- What local **health and social services** are provided? How far is the nearest hospital with an emergency department?

- What **shopping facilities** are provided in the local neighbourhood? How far is it to the nearest sizeable town with good shopping facilities, e.g. a supermarket? How would you get there if your car was out of action? Note that many rural villages have few shops or facilities, and aren't necessarily a good choice for a retirement home.

- What is the range and quality of local **leisure, sports, community and cultural facilities**? What is the proximity to sports facilities such as a beach, golf course, ski resort or waterway? Bear in mind that properties in or close to ski and coastal resorts are usually considerably more expensive, although they also have the best letting potential. If you're interested in a winter holiday home, which area should you choose? While properties in ski resorts are relatively expensive, they tend to appreciate faster than properties in many other areas and generally maintain their value in bad times.

- Is the proximity to **public transport**, e.g. an international airport, port or railway station, or access to a motorway important? Don't, however, believe all you're told about the distance or travelling times to the nearest motorway, airport, railway station, port, beach or town, but check yourself. Being on a local bus route is also advantageous.

- If you're planning to buy in a town or city, is there adequate private or free on-street **parking** for your family and visitors? Is it safe to park in the street? In some areas it's important to have secure off-street parking if you value your car. Parking is a problem in many towns and most cities, where private garages or parking spaces are rare and can be expensive (although you may be able to rent a garage). Bear in mind that an apartment or townhouse in a town or community development may be some distance from the nearest road or car park. How do you feel about carrying heavy shopping hundreds of metres to your home and possibly up several flights of stairs? Traffic congestion is also a problem in many towns and tourist resorts, particularly during the high season.

● What is the local **crime** rate? In some areas, the incidence of burglary is high. Due to the higher than average crime rate (see page 121), home insurance is higher in major cities and resort areas. Check the crime rate in the local area, e.g. burglaries, stolen cars and crimes of violence. Is crime increasing or decreasing? Bear in mind that professional crooks like isolated houses, particularly those full of expensive furniture and other belongings that they can strip bare at their leisure. You're much less likely to be a victim of theft if you live in a village, where crime is usually virtually unknown – strangers stand out like sore thumbs in villages, where their every move is monitored by the local populace.

● Do houses **sell** well in the area? Generally, you should avoid neighbourhoods where desirable properties routinely remain on the market for three months or longer (unless the property market is in a severe slump and nothing is selling).

MOVING HOUSE

Many experts recommend that you take as little as possible with you when retiring abroad and that you sell or give away your furniture and household apparatus. However, this isn't always practical and in any case depends on your home country and your destination. If you're travelling by air, you should take as much as possible with you and ensure that you fully utilise your baggage allowance (or every nook and cranny if you're travelling by car) and pack all the essential items that you will need on arrival. The rest can be sent by air freight (for example small household items) or sea container (furniture and other bulky items). After considering the shipping costs, you may decide that it's cheaper (and easier) to ship only personal effects and buy new furniture and apparatus locally.

After finding a home abroad it usually takes just a few weeks to have your belongings shipped within continental Europe or North America. From anywhere else it varies considerably, e.g. around four weeks between Europe and the east coast of America, six weeks between Europe and the US west coast or the Far East, and around eight to ten weeks between Europe and Australasia. Customs clearance is no longer necessary when shipping your household effects from one European Union (EU) country to another. However, when shipping your effects between other countries you should enquire about customs formalities in advance. When moving to some countries you must present to your local consulate an inventory (usually in the local language) of the items that you're importing, and it must be officially stamped. **In any case, it's wise to have an inventory to hand or give one to your shipper.** If you fail to follow the correct procedure, you can encounter problems and delays and may be charged duty or fined. The relevant forms to be completed may depend on whether your home abroad will be your principal residence or a second home. Removal companies usually take care of the paperwork and ensure that the correct documents are provided and properly completed (see **Customs** on page 148).

It's wise to use a major shipping company with a good reputation. For international moves it's best to use a company that's a member of the International Federation of Furniture Removers (FIDI) or the Overseas Moving Network International (OMNI), with experience in the country you're moving to. Members of FIDI and OMNI usually subscribe to an advance payment scheme providing a guarantee: if a member company fails to fulfil its commitments to a client, the removal is completed at the agreed cost by another company or your money is refunded. Some removal companies have subsidiaries or affiliates abroad, which may be more convenient if you encounter problems or need to make a claim.

You should obtain at least three written quotations before choosing a company, as costs vary considerably. Companies should send a representative to provide a detailed quotation. Most companies will pack your belongings and provide packing cases and special containers, although this is naturally more expensive than packing them yourself. Ask a company how they pack fragile and valuable items, and whether the cost of packing cases, materials and insurance (see below) are included in a quotation. If you're doing your own packing, most shipping companies will provide packing crates and boxes. Shipments are charged by volume, e.g. the square metre in Europe and the square foot in North America. You should expect to pay from GB£2,000 to £4,000 (US$3,000 to $5,500) to move the contents of a three to four-bedroom house within Western Europe, e.g. from London to southern Spain. If you're flexible about the delivery date, shipping companies will quote a lower fee based on a 'part load', where the cost is shared with other deliveries. This can result in savings of 50 per cent or more compared with an individual delivery. Whether you have an individual or shared delivery, obtain the maximum transit period in writing, or you may have to wait months for delivery!

Be sure to fully insure your belongings during removal with a well established insurance company. Don't insure with a shipping company that carries its own insurance, as they may fight every penny of a claim. Insurance premiums are usually 1 to 2 per cent of the declared value of your goods, depending on the type of cover chosen. It's prudent to make a photographic or video record of valuables for insurance purposes. Most insurance policies cover for 'all risks' on a replacement value basis. Note that china, glass and other breakables can usually only be included in an all-risks policy when they're packed by the shipping company. Insurance usually covers total loss or loss of a particular crate only, rather than individual items (unless they were packed by the shipping company). If there are any breakages or damaged items, they should be noted and listed before you sign the delivery bill (although it's obviously impractical to check everything on delivery). If you need to make a claim, be sure to read the small print, as some companies require clients to make a claim within a few days, although seven is usual. Send a claim by registered post. Some insurance companies apply an 'excess' of around 1 per cent of the total shipment value when assessing claims.

If you're unable to ship your belongings directly abroad, most shipping companies will put them into storage and some allow a limited free storage period prior to shipment, e.g. 14 days. **If you need to put your household effects into storage, it's imperative to have them fully insured, as warehouses have been known to burn down!** Make a complete list of everything to be moved and give a copy to the shipping company. Don't include anything illegal (e.g. guns, bombs, drugs or pornographic videos) with your belongings, as customs checks can be rigorous and penalties severe. Provide the shipping company with detailed instructions how to find your home from the nearest motorway or main road and a telephone number where you can be contacted.

If you're moving household goods within North America or Europe, you can rent a self-drive van or truck. Note, however, that you will usually need to return it to the country where it was hired. If you plan to transport your belongings personally, check the customs requirements in the countries that you will pass through. Most people find it isn't worthwhile doing their own move unless it's a simple job, e.g. a few items of furniture and personal effects only. It's no fun heaving beds and wardrobes up stairs and squeezing them into impossible spaces. If you're taking pets (see page 129) with you, you may need to ask your vet to tranquillise them, as many pets are frightened (even more than people) by the chaos and stress of moving house.

Bear in mind when moving home that everything that can go wrong often does, so you should allow plenty of time and try not to arrange your move from your old home on the same day as the new owner is moving in. That's just asking for fate to intervene! **Last but not least, if your new home has poor or impossible access for a large truck you should inform the shipping company (the ground must also be firm enough to support a heavy vehicle).** Note also that if furniture needs to be taken in through an upstairs window, you may need to pay extra. See also **Customs** on page 148 and the **Checklists** on page 153.

MOVING IN

One of the most important tasks to perform after moving into a new home is to make an inventory of the fixtures and fittings and, if applicable, the furniture and furnishings. When you have purchased a property, you should check that the previous owner hasn't absconded with any fixtures and fittings that were included in the price or anything that you specifically paid for, e.g. carpets, light fittings, curtains, furniture, kitchen cupboards and appliances, garden ornaments, plants or doors.

When moving into a long-term rental property, it's necessary to complete an inventory of its contents and a report on its condition. This includes the condition of fixtures and fittings, the state of furniture and furnishings, the cleanliness and state of the decoration, and anything that's damaged, missing or in need of repair. An inventory should be provided by your landlord or agent and may include every single item in a furnished property, down to the number of teaspoons. The inventory check should be carried out in your presence. If an inventory isn't provided, you should insist on one being prepared and annexed to the lease. If you find a serious fault after signing the inventory, send a registered letter to your landlord and ask for it to be attached to the inventory.

An inventory should be drawn up both when moving in and when vacating a rented property. If the two don't correspond, you must make good any damages or deficiencies or the landlord can do so and deduct the cost from your deposit. Although most landlords are honest, some will do almost anything to avoid repaying a deposit. Note the reading on your utility meters (e.g. electricity, gas and water) and check that you aren't overcharged on your first bill. The meters should be read by utility companies before you move in, although you may need to organise it yourself.

It's wise to obtain written instructions from the previous owner concerning the operation of appliances, heating and air-conditioning systems, maintenance of grounds, gardens and lawns, care of special surfaces such as wooden, marble or tiled floors, and the names of reliable local maintenance men who know a property and its quirks. Check with your local town hall regarding local regulations about such things as rubbish collection, recycling and parking.

HOME SECURITY

When moving into a new home it's often wise to replace the locks (or lock barrels) as soon as possible, as you have no idea how many keys are in circulation for the existing locks. This is true even for new homes, as builders often give keys to sub-contractors. In any case, it's wise to change the external locks or lock barrels regularly, e.g. annually, particularly if you let a home. If they aren't already fitted, it's best to install high security (double cylinder or dead bolt) locks. Modern properties may be fitted with high security locks that are individually numbered. Extra keys for these locks cannot be cut at an ordinary hardware store and you will need to obtain details from the previous owner or your landlord. In remote areas it's common for owners to fit two or three locks on external doors, alarm systems, grilles on doors and windows, window locks, security shutters and a safe for valuables. The advantage of grilles is that they allow you to leave windows open without inviting criminals in (unless they are very slim). Many modern developments have security gates and caretakers.

In areas with a high risk of theft (e.g. most major cities and coastal resorts), your insurance company may insist on extra security measures, such as two locks on external doors, internal locking shutters, security bars on windows below a certain height from the ground, and grilles on patio doors. External doors should be of the armoured variety with a steel rod locking mechanism. An insurance policy may specify that all forms of protection must be employed when a property is unoccupied, and if security precautions aren't adhered to, a claim may be reduced by half. It's usually necessary to keep any insured valuables in a safe, which must be approved by your insurance company.

You may wish to have a security alarm fitted, which is usually the best way to deter thieves and may also reduce your household insurance. It should

cover all external doors and windows and include internal infra-red security beams, and may also include an entry keypad with a code (which can be frequently changed and is useful for clients if you let a home) and 24-hour monitoring (with some systems it's possible to monitor properties remotely from another country via a computer). With a monitored system, when a sensor (e.g. smoke or forced entry) is activated, a signal is sent automatically to a 24-hour monitoring station. The duty monitor will telephone to check whether it's a genuine alarm (a number or password must be given) and if he cannot contact you someone will be sent to investigate.

You can deter thieves by ensuring that your house is well lit and not conspicuously unoccupied. External security 'motion detector' lights (that switch on automatically when someone approaches), random timed switches for internal lights, radios and televisions, dummy security cameras, and tapes that play barking dogs (etc.) triggered by a light or heat detector may all help deter burglars.

You can fit UPVC (toughened clear plastic) security windows and doors, which can survive an attack with a sledge-hammer without damage, and external steel security blinds (which can be electrically operated), although these are expensive. A dog can be useful to deter intruders, although he should be kept inside where he cannot be given poisoned food. Irrespective of whether you actually have a dog, a warning sign with a picture of a fierce dog may act as a deterrent. You should have the front door of an apartment fitted with a spy-hole and chain so that you can check the identity of a visitor before opening the door. **Remember, prevention is better than cure, as stolen goods is rarely recovered.**

Holiday homes are particularly vulnerable to thieves and in some countries they are regularly ransacked. No matter how secure your door and window locks, a thief can usually obtain entry if he's sufficiently determined, often by simply smashing a window or even breaking in through the roof or by knocking a hole in a wall! In isolated areas, thieves can strip a house bare at their leisure and an unmonitored alarm won't be a deterrent if there's no-one around to hear it. If you have a holiday home abroad, it isn't wise to leave anything of great value (monetary or sentimental) there.

If you vacate your home for an extended period, it may be obligatory to notify your caretaker, landlord or insurance company, and to leave a key with the caretaker or landlord in case of emergencies. If you have a robbery, you should report it immediately to your local police station, where you must make a statement. You will receive a copy, which is required by your insurance company if you make a claim.

When closing up a property for an extended period, you should ensure that everything is switched off and that it's secure. Another important aspect of home security is ensuring that you have early warning of a fire, which is easily done by installing smoke detectors. Battery-operated smoke detectors can be purchased for around GB£5 (US$7), and should be tested periodically to ensure that the batteries aren't exhausted. You can also fit an electric-powered gas detector that activates an alarm when a gas leak is detected.

LETTING YOUR HOME

Many people planning to retire abroad choose to let their family home rather than sell it, particularly if they're planning to spend only part of the year abroad. You may also wish to let your home until you're certain that you have made the right decision. Letting ensures that your home is more secure and isn't neglected while you're away. The costs incurred when letting a home are usually tax deductible and there may also be other tax advantages such as reduced capital gains tax and being able to offset mortgage interest against income tax. You can either let your home short-term and use it yourself for holidays or, as most people do when going abroad for a number of years, let it long-term. However, you need to be careful with contracts, as in some countries it can be difficult to evict a long-term tenant if they refuse to vacate your home, which is why some people stick to short-term lets. Short-term lets are more lucrative if your home is situated in a major city or resort, but it will need to stand up to a lot more wear and tear.

You will also need a property management company that specialises in short or long-term letting. Before letting an apartment, you must check that letting is permitted. Short-term lets may be prohibited and you may also need to notify the building's administrator, your mortgage lender and your insurance company if a property is let. You can let a property yourself, although this is generally wise only if you're letting it to a close friend or relative. The alternative is to get a reliable friend or relative to handle the letting or use a professional agent, which is usually the best solution. Note that you (or your agent) should never finalise letting agreements via the Internet and should always interview tenants face to face, and obtain personal, professional and financial references.

If you plan to engage a management company and wish to have a tenant in situ as soon as possible after your departure, you will need to make arrangements two or three months in advance. A management company will charge commission based on a percentage of the gross rental income. This is usually around 10 to 15 per cent for letting and collection, and a further 5 to 10 per cent for management services. Take care when selecting a company and ensure that your income is kept in a separate bonded (escrow) account and paid regularly. It's essential to employ an efficient, reliable and honest company, preferably long-established. Ask for the names of satisfied customers and check with them. The rent is usually set in consultation with the management company and based on existing rents in the area for similar properties. It's usually non-negotiable, although the terms of the lease are generally negotiable. **The contract should be checked by your lawyer or solicitor!**

A management company's services should include: the collection and payment of rent; arranging routine maintenance and essential repairs to the building and garden; notifying insurance companies (where applicable) and obtaining approval for essential repairs; regular inspections; paying taxes (e.g. property tax) and insurance premiums (if not done by the owner); and forwarding mail. Give the management company a telephone, fax number or e-mail address where you can be contacted, so that you can approve major repairs or resolve other matters. If you have your own maintenance people or companies, you should give their names to the management company, plus details of anything that's under warranty and the manufacturer's name and model numbers of major systems and appliances (e.g. heating and cooling systems, cooker, refrigerator and freezer).

The landlord is usually responsible for maintaining the structure, major installations and appliances such as the heating and cooling system, cooker, washing machine, refrigerator and freezer. Tenants are usually responsible for any damage other than normal wear and tear to fixtures and fittings, furniture and decoration, and for maintaining the garden. The landlord or agent should check the condition and state of repair of a property at regular intervals, and also make periodic checks when a property is empty (e.g. between lets) to ensure that it's secure and that everything is in order.

If you let a property, it's best to replace expensive furniture and furnishings and remove valuable belongings. Leave them with friends or relatives or put them into storage, and ensure they are insured for their full value with a reputable insurance company (preferably not with the storage company). When furnishing a property that you plan to let, you should choose hard wearing, dark coloured carpets that won't show stains, and buy durable furniture and furnishings. Simple, inexpensive furniture is best in a modest home, as it will need to stand up to hard wear. You will also need to decide whether you wish to let to families with young children or pets (which may result in damage to expensive contents and decor) or smokers. Many people who are letting a luxury home insist on professional tenants or let only to companies. Note that letting to people with diplomatic immunity can be risky, as they're outside the jurisdiction of the local courts.

Other points to bear in mind are deposits (how much and who will hold them – usually a management company if you have one), and building and contents insurance. You will need a special contents insurance policy if you're letting (or leaving a property empty) and may need to obtain a policy from an insurance company that specialises in letting. Tenants should have third party insurance for damage caused to the building and its contents, and contents insurance for their own belongings. Draw up an inventory of all contents and fixtures and fittings, and append it to the lease (a management company will usually arrange this for you). This must be checked and agreed by the tenants on moving in and when vacating the property.

Note that landlords must adhere to strict regulations in many countries, particularly regarding fire and safety matters, e.g. fire-resistant furniture, approved gas installations, fire and gas alarms and fire-fighting apparatus (e.g. fire extinguishers). It may be necessary to have a home inspected by an official inspector and to display a certificate confirming this in a prominent position in your home.

4.

HEALTH

One of the most important aspects of living abroad (or anywhere for that matter) is maintaining good health. The quality of health care and health care facilities vary considerably from country to country, although most western countries provide good to excellent health care for those who can afford to pay for private treatment. However, there's a stark contrast between public and private health facilities in many countries, even western countries, some of which have severely over-stretched and under-funded public health services. The provision of fully-equipped hospitals is rare in many countries (in some countries there's only one major general hospital in the capital city), and nursing care and post-hospital assistance are well below what most westerners take for granted. Health facilities in remote areas, even in developed countries, are often inadequate, and if you have a serious accident or need emergency hospital treatment in some countries, you will need to be evacuated to the nearest major city or possibly to another country.

Public Health Services: Many countries have a public health service providing free or low cost health care for those who contribute to social security, including their families. Retirees from European Union (EU) countries enjoy free or subsidised public health services in other EU countries. If you don't qualify for health care under a public health service, it's essential to have private health insurance (see page 82) – in fact it may be impossible to obtain a residence permit without it. Private health insurance is often desirable in any case, due to the shortcomings of public health services and long waiting lists in some countries. Visitors should have travel insurance (see page 114) if they aren't covered by a reciprocal health care agreement (see page 85). The World Health Organisation (🖳 www.who.int) publishes regular surveys in which it rates countries according to their health care (in 2000, the top ten included France, Italy, San Marino, Andorra, Malta, Singapore, Spain, Oman, Austria and Japan – which will no doubt surprise many Americans!).

Health Problems Abroad: Common health problems experienced by foreigners abroad may include sunburn and sunstroke, stomach and bowel problems (due to the change of diet and more often, water, but they can also be caused by poor hygiene), and various problems related to excessive alcohol. The dangers of disease and infection are considerably greater in some countries and every precaution should be taken. All food must be thoroughly washed and tap water boiled in some countries.

Bear in mind also that in certain countries there are significant risks of illness or death from diseases such as AIDS, hepatitis, malaria, tetanus, tuberculosis, typhoid and yellow fever, which are widespread in some countries – infectious diseases killed 13 million people in 1999! Health problems are also caused or exacerbated by the high level of air pollution in some countries (particularly in major cities), which affects asthma sufferers and others with respiratory problems. Before travelling to many countries, particularly in Africa, Asia and South America, it's necessary to have a number of vaccinations, which may include some of the following: dengue fever, giardiasis, hepatitis, tetanus, tuberculosis, yellow fever, Japanese encephalitis, malaria, paratyphoid, rabies and typhoid (see 💻 www.tmvc. com.au/info10.html for a world-wide vaccination guide).

The World Health Organisation (💻 www.who.int) provides a wealth of information for travellers and those moving abroad, including health topics, communicable/infectious diseases, disease outbreak news, vaccines, environment and health statistics. Other useful websites include the Medical Advisory Service for Travellers Abroad (💻 www.masta.org), Medicine Planet (💻 www.travelhealth.com), and the British Government's Department of Health (💻 www.doh.gov.uk/ traveladvice/index.htm) which also publishes a free booklet *Health Advice for Travellers*. Where applicable heath warnings are included under **Medical Facilities** in **Country Profiles** (Chapter 8).

Climate: A warm, temperate climate is generally considered best for the health, as in areas such as southern California, the Caribbean, Central America, the Costa Blanca in Spain, New South Wales (Australia) and South Africa. Retirees should avoid countries that experience extremely hot conditions for most of the year. If you aren't used to the hot sun, you should limit your exposure and avoid it altogether during the hottest part of the day, wear protective clothing (including a hat) and use a sun block. Too much sun and too little protection will dry your skin and cause premature ageing, to say nothing of the risk of skin cancer. Care should also be taken to replace the natural oils lost from too many hours in the sun, and the elderly should take particular care not to exert themselves during hot weather.

Nevertheless, a warm climate is therapeutic, particularly for sufferers from rheumatism and arthritis, and those prone to bronchitis, colds and pneumonia. The generally slower pace of life in many hot countries is also beneficial for those prone to stress (it's difficult to remain up-tight while relaxing in the sun), although it takes some people a while to adjust. The climate and lifestyle in any country has a noticeable affect on your mental health, and people who live in hot climates are generally happier and more relaxed than people living in cold, wet climates (such as Northern Europe and North America).

Pre-Departure Check: It's wise to have a complete health check (including eyes, teeth, etc.) before going to live abroad, particularly if you have a record of poor health or are elderly. The only immunisation that's mandatory is yellow fever for parts of Africa and South America, although a number of others are recommended for some countries, as are anti-malaria tablets. If you're already taking regular medication, you should note that brand names for medicines vary from country to country and should ask your doctor for the generic name. If you wish to match medication prescribed abroad, you will need a current prescription with the medication's trade name, the manufacturer's name, the chemical name and the dosage. Most medicines have an equivalent in other countries, although particular brands may be difficult or impossible to obtain.

It's possible to have medication sent from abroad and no import duty or tax is usually payable. If you will be living abroad for a short period, you should take sufficient medicines to cover your stay or until you can find a source locally or have it sent from abroad. Note, however, that it's illegal to import certain medicines into some countries, which may even include such things as Codeine! In an emergency a local doctor will write a prescription which can be filled at a local chemist's or a hospital may refill a prescription from its own pharmacy. It's also wise to take some of your favourite non-prescription medicines (e.g. aspirins, cold and flu remedies, lotions, creams, etc.) with you, as they may be difficult or impossible to obtain abroad or may be much more expensive. If applicable, take a spare pair of spectacles, contact lenses, dentures or a hearing aid, plus a comprehensive first-aid kit (many kits are available off the shelf). If you have any serious medical problems, you should make a note of the relevant details, including the treatment you were given with dates, and any medicines you're taking. You should also note your blood group and any medicines that you're allergic to.

If you have an existing medical problem that cannot easily be seen or recognised, e.g. a heart condition, diabetes, a severe allergy (e.g. penicillin) or epilepsy, or you have a rare blood group, you may wish to join MedicAlert. MedicAlert members wear an internationally recognised identification bracelet or necklace, on the back of which is engraved details of your medical condition, your membership number and a 24-hour emergency phone number. When you're unable to speak for yourself, doctors, police or paramedics can obtain immediate, vital medical information from anywhere in the world by telephoning this number. MedicAlert is a non-profit registered charity and members pay for the cost of the bracelet or necklace plus a small annual fee. For more information contact the MedicAlert Foundation (🖥 www.medic alert.org).

There are many Internet sites where medical advice is available, such as the British sites Healthworks (🖥 www.healthworks.co.uk), Net Doctor (🖥 www.netdoctor.co.uk) and Patient (🖥 www.patient.co.uk) and the American Combined Health Information Database (🖥 http://chid.nih.gov), Healthfinder (🖥 www.health finder.gov) and Medline Plus (🖥 www.medline plus.gov). Bear in mind that published information, although usually approved or written by medical experts, shouldn't be used as a substitute for consulting a doctor and that Internet 'doctors' and medical advice must be used with extreme caution.

Among the many useful health guides are the British Medical Association's *Complete Family Health Guide* (Dorling Kindersley), the *Merck Manual of Medical Information: Home Edition* (Merck), *International Travel and Health 2001* (World Health Organisation), the

Rough Guide to Travel Health by Dr. Nick Jones, *The ABC of Healthy Travel* (British Medical Journal), *Traveller's Health* by Dr. R. Dawood (OUP) and the *First Aid Handbook* (National Safety Council).

Checklist

Health (and health insurance) is an important issue for those retiring abroad, many of whom are ill-prepared for old age and the possibility of health problems. In addition to general healthcare considerations, retirees planning to live abroad should also consider the following points before choosing a destination.

● Health screening is particularly important for those aged over 50 and it's prudent to have annual health check-ups. Are these available locally? In some countries retirees over a certain age (usually 60) receive free health screening and tests, although these may not be available abroad. If health screening is provided by the public health service, what are the waiting lists like? If regular health screening is unavailable, can you afford to return to your home country for regular check-ups? Note that you may need to remain a member of your home country's health service and continue to pay contributions while abroad in order to use the services.

● Eye tests should be carried out regularly, e.g. at least every two years. Are trained opticians available? Are eye tests free or will you have to pay?

● Are English-speaking doctors and other practitioners available locally? Are clinics and hospitals available with English-speaking staff. If not, how will you cope when visiting a doctor or hospital? Do doctors make house calls?

● Should you become disabled or unable to walk well, what sort of facilities and help are available? Are wheelchairs available? Can you easily buy home adaptations such as bath rails or stair lifts, or will you have to purchase these (at higher cost) from abroad?

● Does the country provide good facilities for the disabled, e.g. access to public buildings via ramps, reserved disabled parking spaces, toilets for the disabled, etc.? Provision for handicapped travellers and wheelchair access to buildings and public transport is poor or non-existent in many countries.

● Are alarm call systems with 24-hour assistance available?

● What sort of day and home nursing care is available?

● Are there carers and support groups for the sick?

There's a dearth of welfare and home-nursing services for the elderly in most popular 'retirement' countries, either state or private, and many foreigners who can no longer care for themselves are forced to return to their home countries (where you may no longer be eligible for free or subsidised medical treatment). In most countries there are few state residential nursing homes and no hospices for the terminally ill, although many countries offer sheltered accommodation, assisted living units and nursing homes for those who can afford them.

EMERGENCIES

The action to take in a medical emergency depends on the degree of urgency. Keep a record of the telephone numbers of your doctor, local hospital and clinic, ambulance service, dentist and other emergency services (fire, police) next to your telephone. In many countries, emergency numbers are displayed at the front of telephone directories. If you're unsure who to call, dial the emergency number and you will be put in touch with the relevant service. The appropriate course of action to take may include one of the following:

● In a life-threatening emergency, call a free emergency number and request an ambulance. State clearly where you're calling from and the nature of the emergency, give your name and the number of the telephone you're calling from. Don't hang up until the operator tells you to. In many countries, ambulances are equipped with cardiac equipment and manned by paramedics, and special cardiomobiles may be provided for emergency heart cases. There's also an helicopter ambulance service in many countries, this may be privately operated with membership by subscription.

● If you're physically able, you can go to a hospital emergency or casualty department. All foreigners in some countries have the right to be treated free of charge in an emergency, irrespective of whether they have insurance.

● If you're unable to visit your doctor's surgery, your doctor may visit you at home provided you call him during surgery hours. If he's away, his office will usually give you the name and number of a substitute doctor on call. Local newspapers usually list duty chemists (pharmacies) – in major cities some may be open 24 hours a day.

● If you need urgent medical treatment outside surgery hours and cannot get to your nearest casualty department, there may be a local duty doctor service or emergency telephone helpline.

Provided you call in response to a real emergency, you won't usually be charged for the use of the emergency services. Note that in some countries it's an offence to offer medical assistance in an emergency unless you're a doctor or are qualified in first-aid, and you risk being sued by the injured party. However, it may also be an offence *not* to assist someone in an emergency, e.g. by not calling the emergency services or not offering first-aid when qualified to do so.

DOCTORS

The training, proficiency and availability of doctors varies considerably with the country and the city or region where you live. Those who live in a major city in a western country have a far wider choice of practitioners (many English-speaking) than those living in rural areas in a developing country, where the nearest doctor may be hours away. Even in western countries, the quality and choice of doctors in remote areas is often poor, and you may be faced with a long journey to the nearest doctor's surgery or hospital. It's difficult to find English-speaking doctors in some countries, particularly some developing countries, which is why it's essential to have a working knowledge of the local language, which could save your life in an emergency. Embassies and consulates may keep lists of doctors and specialists in their area who speak English and other foreign languages, and your friends or neighbours may also be able to recommend someone. General practitioners or family doctors are also listed in the yellow pages in most countries.

If you wish to take advantage of a free or subsidised public health service, one of the first things to do after arrival in a country is to register at the nearest office. When registering, you may be required to choose a family doctor with a social security agreement. Local health authorities provide you with a list of doctors with whom you can register and you can choose anyone who's willing to accept you (although there may be a requirement to register with a doctor within a certain distance of your home). Each adult member of a family is usually issued with a membership number and card, which you must take with you when visiting a doctor or other health practitioner. If you want a doctor to visit you at home, you must telephone during surgery hours. House calls made by public health service doctors are usually free during normal working hours.

If you have private health insurance, you can usually see a private doctor, specialist or consultant at any time, although (depending on your level of insurance) you may need to pay for their services. Note that in many countries you're expected to settle the bill (usually in cash, although some doctors accept credit cards) immediately after treatment, even if you have health insurance, and you may need to prove that you can pay before any treatment is given. It's very important to keep all medical receipts in some countries, as these can be offset against your income tax bill.

HOSPITALS & CLINICS

All cities and large towns have at least one clinic or hospital, usually indicated by the international sign of a white 'H' on a blue background. Public (state) hospitals may include community hospitals, district hospitals, general hospitals, teaching hospitals and university hospitals (or a combination of these). Major or general hospitals may be designated teaching hospitals, which combine treatment with medical training and research work, and are staffed and equipped to the highest standards.

Some hospitals and most clinics specialise in particular fields of medicine, such as obstetrics and surgery, rather than being full service hospitals. In addition there may be specialist hospitals for children, the mentally ill and handicapped, the elderly and infirm, and for the treatment of specific complaints or illnesses. There are also dental hospitals in many countries. Public hospitals may have a 24-hour accident, casualty or emergency department that provides treatment for medical emergencies and minor accidents, although this may apply only to major hospitals. In some countries there are also walk-in clinics (possibly 24-hour) where you can be treated on the spot for minor emergencies. Except in emergencies, you're normally admitted or referred to a hospital or clinic for treatment only after consultation with a doctor.

In addition to public hospitals, there are usually private hospitals and clinics in major cities and resort areas in many countries, which may include American, British and international hospitals. There's a wide discrepancy between public and private hospital facilities (e.g. medical equipment, number of staff, private rooms, catering, etc.) in many countries, although in western countries there's generally little variation in the quality of medical treatment (e.g. surgery). The best hospitals are invariably found in the wealthiest suburbs of major cities and large towns, so if you wish to have a first class hospital on your doorstep, you may need to live in an up-market (i.e. expensive) area. Note that the best public hospitals often have long waiting lists.

Your choice of hospital and specialist usually depends on whether you choose a public or private hospital and the treatment required. If you're treated in a public hospital under a state's public health service, you must usually be treated or operated on by the medical specialist on duty. If you request the services of a particular specialist or wish to avoid a long waiting list for an operation, you (or your insurance company) must usually pay the full cost of treatment. If you aren't covered by the public health service, you may be required to pay before you receive treatment, irrespective of whether you have private health insurance. However, international health insurance companies usually have arrangements with certain hospitals and pay bills directly. Costs for private operations vary enormously, according to the reputation of the specialists involved and the fees they command. Sometimes it's cheaper to have an operation abroad, e.g. in a neighbouring country. You should check the local hospital facilities in advance and, if necessary, ensure that your health insurance covers you for medical evacuation.

Basic accommodation in public hospitals normally consists of shared rooms, although single rooms are usually available with an en suite bathroom for a supplement or for private patients. In some countries, patients in public hospitals must bring everything they need with them, including towels, toiletries, pyjamas or night-dresses and dressing gowns, although meals are provided. Note, however, that the food may be inedible and you may need some outside assistance (food parcels) if you're to survive a stay! You may also need to get your family or friends to attend to your needs, as nursing services are sparse or non-existent in public hospitals in some countries. In contrast, in private clinics and hospitals, accommodation is generally on a par with a luxury hotel, with air-conditioned rooms, TV and telephone, gourmet food and an extra bed for a relative if required. Public hospitals usually have restricted visiting hours of around two or three hours a day, while private hospitals and clinics may have no restrictions at all.

DENTISTS

The quality of dental treatment and its cost varies considerably from country to country. For example, in the USA and a few other countries, dental treatment is phenomenally expensive, although it's also recognised to be among the best in the world. Many people are sceptical about the quality of foreign dentists and prefer to have treatment in their home country. In some countries, few dentists speak English, which can be an added problem. However, your country's local embassy or consulate may keep a list of English-speaking dentists in your area, or your friends or neighbours may be able to recommend a local dentist. Dentists are also listed in local telephone directories and the yellow pages, although only names and addresses may be listed and information such as specialities and surgery hours may not be provided.

There are public health dental services in some countries, although the treatment provided is usually basic and may consist only of check-ups and emergency treatment. Note also that private dentists in some countries have a better reputation than those working for a public health service, although many dentists treat both public and private patients. You need to be wary of unnecessary treatment, which is a common practice in some countries, where dentists deliberately perform unnecessary treatment ('drill for profit'!). If you have regular check-ups and usually have little or no treatment, you should be suspicious if a new dentist suggests you need a lot of fillings or extractions.

In this case you should obtain a second opinion before going ahead (note, however, that two dentists rarely agree on exactly the same treatment).

Always try to obtain an accurate (preferably written) quotation before beginning a course of treatment, although few dentists will quote an exact fee for work, and often a 'rough estimate' is only a fraction of the final bill. For extensive work, such as root canal treatment or cosmetic work, bills can be astronomical. As with private doctors, it's usual to pay a dentist (credit cards may be accepted) before a course of treatment begins in many countries or at least immediately after it's completed. If your family requires expensive dental treatment, e.g. crowns, bridges, braces or false teeth, it's worthwhile checking whether treatment is cheaper abroad, e.g. in your home country.

OPTICIANS

As with other medical practitioners abroad, it isn't necessary to register with an optician or optometrist. You simply make an appointment with the practitioner of your choice, although it's wise to ask your friends or neighbours if they can recommend someone. Opticians are listed in the yellow pages. The eye care business is competitive in most countries and prices for spectacles and contact lenses aren't controlled, so it's wise to shop around and compare costs. There are large optical chains in some countries, where spectacles can be made on the spot or within 24 hours, although if you have your prescription you can sometimes buy ready-made reading spectacles from chemists'.

To be treated under a public health service, it may be necessary to have your eyes examined by an eye specialist or oculist, for which you generally need to obtain a referral from your family doctor. An oculist can make a more thorough test of your eyesight than an optician and is able to test for certain diseases that can be diagnosed from eye abnormalities, e.g. diabetes and some types of cancer. If glasses are necessary, he will write a prescription that you can take to an optician or spectacle maker.

It's wise to have your eyes tested before going abroad and to take a spare pair of spectacles and/or contact lenses with you. You should also bring a copy of your prescription in case you need to obtain replacement spectacles or contact lenses urgently.

DYING ABROAD

It's an unfortunate but unavoidable fact of life that no one is immortal. However, if you have made arrangements for your death, it will be considerably easier for those you leave behind. This is particularly important in a foreign country, where there may be different religious or social customs regarding funerals and burials, and inheritance and succession laws may be quite different from those in your home country (see **Wills** on page 106).

Funeral and burial arrangements need to be considered carefully. Burial grounds are extremely limited in some countries, where it may be necessary to be buried in a tomb in a wall or in a communal burial ground, which is recycled after a period and used for new burials. Cremation is possible in many countries, although you may be unable to keep the ashes at home or dispose of them as you wish, e.g. by scattering them at sea or on the pitch of the deceased's favourite football club. The body of a deceased person can usually be shipped to another country for burial. You will need to provide the funeral agent with the documents relating to the death and the identity of the deceased, so that he can obtain the necessary permits. Your local embassy may be able to help arrange this.

If you wish your body to be returned to your home country for burial, you will need to plan for the expense involved and may wish to take out insurance to cover the cost (this may be included in international health insurance). If you wish to be buried or cremated in your new country, you should investigate the cost; it's also worth considering insurance for this, as the simplest funeral arrangements can cost thousands of US$ or £ sterling in many countries. A wide choice of insurance plans are available in many countries, including pre-paid plans, where you pay for all your funeral costs in a lump sum or contribute a monthly amount. Before committing yourself to an insurance plan, make sure that you know exactly what it covers, what the total cost is and the cancellation penalty. You should ensure that the company is long-established and reputable, and that your contributions are invested in a trust fund or other secure vehicle.

In most countries a death must be registered within a certain period (e.g. seven days) at the local births and deaths registry office of the town where it occurred, although an undertaker (see below) will usually do this for you. Registration applies to everyone, irrespective of their nationality and whether they are residents or visitors. In the event of a death, all interested parties must be notified. If a death takes place in a hospital, the attending doctor will complete a death certificate; you should make several copies of this, which will be required by banks and other institutions. If death occurs at home, you should call your family doctor or the local police. If a death occurs in suspicious circumstances, a post mortem (autopsy) must usually be performed.

Finally, you should make sure that your family are fully aware of your wishes and arrangements, which you should put in writing.

HEALTH INSURANCE

One of the most important aspects of living abroad is having adequate health insurance, as the cost of being uninsured or under-insured can be astronomical and could even prove fatal! Note, however, that the cost of private health insurance can be prohibitively expensive in some countries (e.g. the USA) and if you have a poor health record you may be unable to obtain insurance for an affordable premium. Long-stay visitors (e.g. up to six months) should have travel or long-stay health insurance or an international health policy. If your stay abroad will be short, you may be covered by a reciprocal agreement between your home country and the country where you will be living.

The majority of residents in many countries (particularly European countries) are covered for health treatment under a public health service or compulsory private health insurance schemes. In European Union countries this includes foreign retirees over the age of 65 who are covered by the public health scheme in their home countries. Many countries provide emergency treatment for visitors under reciprocal agreements (see page 85), although these don't apply to citizens of some countries, e.g. the USA. Visitors spending short periods abroad should have travel health insurance (see page 114) if they aren't covered by a reciprocal agreement or an international health policy.

If you will be living abroad permanently and don't qualify for medical treatment under a public health service, it's usually imperative that you have private health insurance (unless you have a very large bank balance), which is compulsory in many countries. In countries with a public health service, those who can afford it often take out complementary private health insurance, which provides a wider choice of medical practitioners and hospitals, and frees you from inadequate public health services, waiting lists and other restrictions. Private insurance may also allow you to choose an English-speaking doctor or a hospital where staff speak English or other foreign languages.

A health insurance policy should, if possible, cover you for all essential health care whatever the reason, including accidents (e.g. sports accidents) and injuries, whether they occur at your home or while travelling. Policies offered in different countries vary considerably in the extent of cover, limitations and restrictions, premiums, and the free choice of doctors, specialists and hospitals. **Don't take anything for granted, but check in advance.** Note that insurance companies in some countries can (and will) cancel a policy at the end of the insurance period if you have a serious illness with constant high expenses, and some companies automatically cancel a policy when you reach a certain age, e.g. 65 or 70. You should avoid such a policy like the plague, as to take out a new policy at the age of 65 or older for a reasonable premium is difficult or impossible in some countries.

International Policies: If you do a lot of travelling, it's best to have an international health policy. These generally offer wider cover than local policies, although if local medical facilities are adequate and you rarely travel abroad, they can be a waste of money. Most international health policies include repatriation or evacuation (although it may be optional), which may be an important consideration if you need treatment that's unavailable locally but is available in your home or another country. Repatriation may also include shipment (by air) of the body of someone who dies abroad to their home country for burial (see page 80). Some companies offer different policies for different areas, e.g. Europe, world-wide excluding North America, and world-wide including North America. A policy may offer full cover anywhere within Europe and limited cover in North America and certain other countries, e.g. Japan. Note that an international policy also allows you to choose to have non-urgent medical treatment in another country. Most companies offer different levels of cover, e.g. basic, standard, comprehensive and prestige.

There's always a limit on the total annual medical costs, which should be at least GB£250,000 or around US$350,000 (most go up to GB£1 million/US$1.5 million or higher), and some companies limit costs for specific treatment or costs such as specialists' fees, surgery and hospital accommodation. Some policies also include permanent disability cover, e.g. GB£100,000 or US$150,000, for those in full-time employment. A medical isn't usually required for health policies, although pre-existing health problems are usually excluded for a period, e.g. one or two years. Claims are usually settled in all major currencies and large claims are usually settled directly by insurance companies (although your choice of hospitals may be limited). Always check whether an insurance company will settle large medical bills directly; if you're required to pay bills and claim reimbursement from an insurance company, it can take you several months to receive your money. It isn't always necessary to have bills translated into English or another language, although you should check a company's policy. Most international health insurance companies provide 24-hour emergency telephone assistance.

The cost of international heath insurance varies considerably with your age, the extent of cover, the insurer, and, not least, your home country or the country where you're resident. Note that with most international insurance policies, you must enrol before you reach a certain age, e.g. 60, in order to be guaranteed continuous cover in your old age. Companies may also have restrictions on where you live permanently and your nationality. Premiums can sometimes be paid monthly or quarterly, although some companies insist on payment annually in advance. When comparing policies, carefully check the extent of cover and exactly what's included and excluded from a policy (which may be noted only in the *very* small print), in addition to premiums and excess charges.

In some countries, premium increases are limited by law, although this may apply only to residents in the country where a company is registered and not to overseas policyholders. Although there may be significant differences in premiums, generally you get what you pay for and can tailor your premiums to your requirements. The most important questions to ask are whether the policy provides the cover you need and whether it's good value. If you're in good health and are able to pay for your own outpatient treatment, such as visits to your family doctor and prescriptions, then the best value for money policy is usually one covering only specialist visits and in-hospital treatment.

Among the many companies offering international private medical insurance are BUPA International (🖥 www.bupa-intl.com), Expacare (🖥 www.expacare.net), Goodhealth (🖥 www.goodhealth.co.uk), InterGlobal Insurance Services (🖥 www.interglobalpmi.com), International Private Healthcare (🖥 www.iph.uk.net), Medicare International (🖥 www.medicare. co.uk), Morgan Price International Healthcare (🖥 www.morgan-price.com), PPP Healthcare (🖥 www.ppphealthcare.com) and William Russell (🖥 www. william-russell.co.uk). Alternatively you can contact a specialist insurance broker such as Medibroker (🖥 www.medibroker.com).

Make sure that you're fully covered abroad before you receive a large bill. It's foolhardy for anyone living abroad (or even visiting) not to have comprehensive health insurance. If you're inadequately insured, you could be faced with some **very** high medical bills. When changing employers or moving abroad, you should ensure that you have uninterrupted health insurance and, if you're planning to change your health insurance company, that important benefits aren't lost.

Checklist

When comparing the level of cover provided by different health insurance schemes, the following points should be considered:

● Does the scheme offer a choice of cover and can you choose to pay an excess (deductible) to reduce your premiums.

● Are private, semi-private (e.g. a two-bed room) and general hospital cover available? What are the costs? Is there a limit on the time you can spend in hospital?

● Is optional dental cover provided? What exactly does it include? Can it be extended to include extra treatment? Dental insurance usually contains numerous limitations and doesn't cover cosmetic treatment.

- Are private and semi-private rooms available in local hospitals?
- Are accidents covered, e.g. sports injuries and dental treatment, wherever and however they occur? As a general rule, health insurance includes cover for accidents but may exclude car accidents and accidents incurred when participating in certain 'dangerous' sports, such as skiing and hang-gliding.
- What are the restrictions regarding hospitalisation in a region or country other than the one where you have your permanent home? What level of cover is provided in other countries? What are the limitations?
- Are emergency ambulance or other transportation fees are covered?
- Is there a qualification period for specific benefits or services?
- Are all medicines covered or are there restrictions?
- Are convalescent homes or spa treatments covered when prescribed by a doctor?
- What are the restrictions on complementary medicine, e.g. chiropractic, osteopathy, naturopathy, massage and acupuncture? Are they covered? Must a doctor make a referral?
- Are extra costs likely, and if so, what for?
- Are spectacles or contact lenses covered, and if so, how much can be claimed and how frequently? Some insurance policies allow you to claim for a new pair of spectacles every two or three years.
- Is the provision and repair of artificial limbs and other essential health aids covered?
- Is evacuation and the cost of medical treatment abroad covered in full?
- Will the insurer provide a cash deposit or guarantee payment in advance if a hospital requires it?

Reciprocal Health Agreements

Many people are covered by reciprocal health agreements when living abroad, although this may apply in emergencies only. For example, anyone insured under a public health scheme in a European Union (EU) country is covered for medical treatment in other EU countries, provided certain steps are taken in advance. You must usually obtain a form (E111) from your social security office before leaving home and must be covered by your home country's public health scheme to qualify. Full payment (possibly in cash) must usually be made in advance for treatment received abroad, although you will be reimbursed on your return home. **Note, however, that you can still receive a**

large bill, as your local health authority usually assumes only a percentage of the cost.

This applies to all EU countries except the UK, where everyone receives free health care, including visitors. You're also reimbursed for essential treatment in non-EU countries, although you must obtain detailed receipts. Note that reimbursement is based on the cost of comparable treatment in your home country. In certain countries there are no reciprocal agreements, e.g. Canada, Japan, Switzerland and the USA, and medical treatment can be **very** expensive. You're advised to have private health insurance when visiting or living in these countries. In fact this is recommended wherever you're travelling, as insurance provides more comprehensive medical cover than reciprocal health care agreements (and usually includes other services, such as repatriation). If you do a lot of travelling abroad, it's usually worthwhile having an annual international health insurance policy.

5.

FINANCE & INSURANCE

One of the most important aspects of living abroad (even for brief periods) is finance, which includes everything from transferring and changing money to banking, mortgages and local taxes. If you're planning to invest in a property abroad financed with funds imported from another country, it's important to consider both the present and possible future exchange rates (don't be too optimistic!). **Bear in mind that your income can be exposed to risks beyond your control when you live abroad, particularly regarding inflation and exchange rate fluctuations. It's important to obtain expert financial advice before going to live abroad from an independent and impartial source, i.e. NOT someone who's trying to sell you something!**

In many countries, residents and non-resident foreigners with financial interests there must have a fiscal or tax number, which must be used in all dealings with the tax authorities and in various other financial transactions. Without a fiscal number you may be unable to register the title deed of a property, open a bank account or take out an insurance policy.

If you're a non-resident and own a home abroad, it's wise to employ a local professional, e.g. an accountant or tax adviser, to look after your local financial affairs and declare and pay your taxes. You can also have a representative receive your bank statements, ensure that your bank is paying your standing orders (e.g. for electricity, gas, water and telephone bills), and that you have sufficient funds to pay them. If you let a home abroad through a local company, they may perform the above tasks as part of their service. In some countries it's mandatory for foreign non-resident property owners to appoint a fiscal representative, who automatically receives all communications from the local tax authorities.

If you plan to live abroad, you must ensure that your income is (and will remain) sufficient to live on, bearing in mind currency devaluations and exchange rate fluctuations (if your income isn't paid in the local currency), rises in the cost of living (see page 107), unforeseen expenses such as medical bills, and anything else that may reduce your income, e.g. stock market crashes and recessions! Foreigners, particularly retirees, often under-estimate the cost of living abroad and some are forced to return to their home countries after a few years.

Although many people prefer to pay cash (which cannot be traced by the taxman!) rather than use credit or charge cards (see page 95), it's wise to have at least one credit card when living abroad. Note, however, that not all businesses accept credit cards (businesses in developing countries rarely accept them), and you should check in advance.

Your financial arrangements should be carefully organised in consultation with a financial expert, particularly with regard to inheritance and estate laws. It's also wise to make a will (see page 106) in the country where you're resident or any country where you own property, not least because it makes the inheritance procedure considerably easier and quicker for your heirs. Note, however, that financial advisers are totally unregulated in many countries and there are plenty of predators around just waiting to get their hands on your loot. Always shop around for financial services and never sign a contract unless you know exactly what the costs and implications are. Although bankers, financiers and brokers don't like to make too fine a point of it, they aren't doing business with you because they like you, but simply to get their hands on your pile of chips. It's up to you to make sure that their share is kept to a minimum and that you receive the best possible value for your money.

This chapter includes information about the following: importing and exporting money; banking; credit, debit and charge cards; mortgages; pensions; taxes (income, property, capital gains, wealth, inheritance and gift tax); wills; the cost of living; and insurance.

IMPORTING & EXPORTING MONEY

Exchange controls have been abolished in the last few decades in most countries, particularly western countries. However, many countries require foreigners to declare imports or exports of funds above a certain amount and have restrictions on the amount that can be imported or exported in cash, notes and bearer-cheques in any currency, plus gold coins and bars. Where necessary, it's particularly important to declare large sums, e.g. for the purchase of a home abroad, as it may be impossible to legally export funds from some countries if they weren't declared when imported. These regulations are usually designed to curb criminal activities (e.g. money laundering) and tax evasion and may also apply to travellers simply passing through a country. In some countries, foreigners must declare the origin of funds used for the purchase of a home – **if you don't, they may be confiscated.**

International Money Transfers: Making international money transfers between different countries can be a nightmare and can take anything from a few minutes to many weeks (or months if the money gets 'lost'), depending on the banks and countries involved. A bank to bank transfer can usually be made by a 'normal' postal transfer or via an electronic transfer (such as SWIFT). A normal transfer within Europe is supposed to take three to seven days, but in reality it often takes much longer, whereas a SWIFT telex transfer should be completed in a few hours, with funds being available within 24 hours. The cost of transfers varies considerably – not only the commission and exchange rates, but also transfer charges (such as the telex charge for a SWIFT transfer).

Most international transfers are slow and costly, even between banks and countries with state-of-the-art banking systems. The average time taken for international transfers within Europe is around five days and some transfers take many weeks or even get lost completely. Banks in some countries are notoriously slow and have been accused of deliberately delaying transfers in order to earn interest on money 'stuck in the pipeline'. The cost of transfers also varies considerably. Except for the fastest (and most expensive) methods, transfers between international banks are a joke in the age of electronic banking, when powerful financiers can move funds anywhere in the world almost instantaneously.

Shop around banks and financial institutions for the best deal and don't be afraid to change your bank if the service provided doesn't meet your requirements. Many banks subscribe to an international electronic network to (theoretically) facilitate fast and inexpensive transfers between members. You can also make transfers in Europe via Euro giro from post offices, which takes three days and is available between most European Union countries plus Switzerland. Telegraphic transfers can be made via specialist companies such as Western Union between some 200 countries, which is the quickest (around ten minutes!) and safest method, but also one of the most expensive. American Express (AE) operates a similar service for cardholders, who can send money via the AE Moneygram service between offices in Europe and North America in as little as 15 minutes.

Yet another way to transfer money is via a bank draft, which should be sent by registered post. Note, however, that in the unlikely event that it's lost or stolen, it's impossible to stop payment and you must wait six months before a new draft can be issued. In some countries, bank drafts aren't treated as cash and must be cleared like personal cheques. When transferring small amounts it's better to use a money order. **If you intend sending a large amount of money abroad for a transaction such as buying property, you should ensure that you receive the commercial rate of exchange rather than the tourist rate (shop around for the best rate).**

Personal Cheques: It's often possible to pay a cheque drawn on a bank in your home country into a bank account abroad, e.g. in Europe, although it can take a long time to clear and fees are high. A personal cheque drawn on a European or American bank can take three or four weeks to clear, as it must be cleared with the paying bank. However, some banks allow clients to draw on cheques issued by foreign banks from the day they're paid into a client's account. Note that most American banks don't accept cheques drawn on foreign bank accounts written in a foreign currency.

Debit Cards: Many foreigners living abroad keep the bulk of their money in a foreign account (perhaps in an offshore bank) and draw on it using a debit card when abroad, which is a convenient solution for short trips abroad.

Postcheques: Giro postcheques are issued by European post offices and can be cashed (with a guarantee card) for GB£125 (or the foreign currency equivalent) at post offices in most European countries.

Travellers' Cheques: Travellers' cheques are accepted in most countries, but may be restricted to major currencies (if in doubt, buy them in US$) and may only be cashed by banks in major cities. The commission for cashing travellers' cheques is usually 1 per cent (you need your passport), depending on the issuer and where you cash them. Lost or stolen travellers' cheques can be replaced in most countries (the easiest to replace are American Express), but you must keep a separate record of the cheque numbers.

Footnote: In many countries, there isn't a lot of difference in cost between buying foreign currency or travellers' cheques or using a credit or debit card to obtain cash. However, many people simply take cash when travelling abroad, which is asking for trouble, particularly if you have no way of obtaining more cash, e.g. with a credit or debit card. **One thing to bear in mind when travelling anywhere is not to rely on only one source of funds!**

If you have a computer with Internet access, you can use the universal currency converter (⌨ www.xe.com/ucc) to convert foreign currencies into your home country's currency or the currency in which your income is earned.

BANKS

Although it's possible to live abroad without having a local bank account, by using credit and debit cards and travellers' cheques, this isn't wise and is an expensive option. In any case, residents and homeowners usually need a local bank account to pay their utility and tax bills, which are best paid by direct debit. You can usually have your state pension or social security payments paid directly into a bank account abroad.

If you have a holiday home abroad, you can usually have all documentation (e.g. statements) sent to your permanent home address. Many foreign banks have branches in major cities abroad, although few have extensive networks. Note also that foreign banks abroad usually operate in exactly the same way as domestic banks, so you shouldn't expect, for example, a branch of Barclays or Deutsche Bank in Spain to operate like a branch in the UK or Germany.

Non-residents can open a bank account in most countries by correspondence, although it's best done in person in the country concerned. Ask your friends, neighbours or colleagues for their recommendations and just visit the bank of your choice and introduce yourself. You must provide proof of identity (e.g. a passport or identity card) and of your address abroad and, in some countries, a fiscal or tax number. If you open an account while in your home country, you must obtain an application form from an overseas branch of your chosen bank or from a bank abroad. If you open an account by correspondence, you will also need to provide a reference from your current bank.

Note that banks in most countries make few or no concessions for foreign customers, e.g. the provision of general information and documentation such as statements in foreign languages and staff who speak foreign languages. However, some banks offer a multilingual service and go out of their way to attract foreign customers. In some countries there are restrictions regarding the type of accounts a non-resident foreigner may open, although residents can usually open any type of account.

Note that overdrawing a bank account (bouncing cheques) in many countries is a criminal offence, and offenders can be barred from maintaining a bank account for a period (it will also severely damage your credit rating).

Offshore Banking

If you have a sum of money to invest or wish to protect your inheritance from the tax man, it may be worthwhile investigating the accounts and services (such as pensions and trusts) provided by offshore banking centres in tax havens such as the Caribbean Islands, Channel Islands (Guernsey and Jersey), Gibraltar and the Isle of Man – some 50 locations world-wide are officially classified as tax havens. Offshore banking has had a good deal of media attention in recent years, during which it has also been under investigation by the EU and the OECD. The major attractions are that money can be deposited in a wide range of currencies, customers are usually guaranteed anonymity (although this is changing), there are no double taxation agreements, no withholding tax is payable and interest is paid tax-free. Many offshore banks also provide telephone banking (usually 24 hours a day, seven days a week) and Internet banking.

A large number of American, British and other European banks and financial institutions provide offshore banking facilities in one or more locations. Most institutions offer high-interest, instant-access accounts, deposit accounts for long-term savings and investment portfolios, in which funds can be deposited in most major currencies. It's also possible to invest in a range of bonds, funds, trusts, pensions, equities and other investment vehicles, which are usually intended for long-term investments. Many people living abroad keep a local account for everyday business and maintain an offshore account for international transactions and investment purposes. However, most financial experts advise investors not to rush into the expatriate life and invest their life savings in an offshore financial centre until they know what their long-term plans are.

Most accounts have minimum deposit levels, which usually range from the equivalent of around GB£500 to £10,000 or US$700 to $14,000, with some as high as GB£100,000 or US$140,000. In addition to large minimum balances, accounts may also have strict terms and conditions, such as restrictions on withdrawals or high early withdrawal penalties. You can deposit funds on call (instant access) or for a fixed period, e.g. from 90 days to one year (usually for larger sums). Interest is usually paid monthly or annually; monthly interest payments are slightly lower than annual payments but have the advantage of providing a regular income. There are usually no charges, provided a specified minimum balance is maintained. Many accounts offer a cash or credit card (e.g. Mastercard or Visa) which can be used to obtain cash from automated teller machines (ATMs) throughout the world.

When selecting a financial institution and offshore banking centre, your first priority should be for the safety of your money. In many offshore banking centres, bank deposits are guaranteed under a deposit protection scheme, whereby a maximum sum is guaranteed should the financial institution go to the wall (the Isle of Man, Guernsey and Jersey all have such schemes). Unless you're planning to bank with a major international bank (which is only likely to fold the day after the end of the world!), you should check the credit rating of a financial institution before depositing any money, particularly if it doesn't provide deposit insurance. All banks have a credit rating (the highest is 'AAA') and a bank with a high rating will happily tell you what it is (but get it in writing). You can also check the rating of an international bank or financial organisation with Moodys Investors Service (🖥 www.moodys.com). You should be wary of institutions offering higher than average interest rates; if it looks too good to be true, it probably will be – like the infamous Bank of International Commerce and Credit (BICC) which went bust in 1992!

When choosing an offshore bank, you may also wish to consider its communications network (24-hour telephone banking, fax, e-mail, Internet banking), your personal contact (will you have one?) and the geographical location – if possible it's best to choose a bank in a similar time zone, or you may be calling your advisor in the middle of the night! Useful websites include Investors Offshore (🖥 www. investorsoffshore.com) and Tax News (🖥 www.tax-news.com).

CREDIT, DEBIT & CHARGE CARDS

'Plastic money' in the form of cash, debit, credit and charge cards is widely used in all western countries (less so in developing countries), where banks are busy trying to create a cash-less society. Cash and debit cards are issued by most banks and most can be used world-wide via the American Express, Mastercard and Visa networks. With a cash/debit card (they're usually the same card), cash withdrawals and purchases are automatically debited from a cheque or savings account. All withdrawals or purchases are shown on your monthly statement and you cannot usually run up an overdraft or obtain credit (unless arranged beforehand).

Cards allow holders to withdraw cash, e.g. GB£100 to £500 or US$150 to $700 (or the foreign currency equivalent) per day from ATMs and obtain account balances and mini-statements. Cash can also be obtained from the ATMs of networks other than the one your card belongs to, although there's usually a fee. Most ATMs accept a bewildering number of cards, which may be illustrated on machines, including credit (Eurocard, Mastercard, Visa) and charge (Amex, Diners Club) cards. Note that, although debit cards such as those belonging to the Visa network can be used to obtain cash abroad, they may be treated as credit cards and a charge levied.

Credit and charge cards are usually referred to collectively as credit cards, although not all cards are real credit cards, where the balance can be repaid over a period. Visa and Mastercard are the most widely accepted credit cards in most countries and are issued by most banks. Charge cards such as American Express and Diners Club aren't widely accepted in some countries, particularly by small businesses (who wisely prefer cash). Debit cards may use the American Express, Mastercard or Visa networks, but allow withdrawals or purchases to be made from a personal bank account that's in credit (or has an overdraft facility).

Note that when using a credit card in some countries (e.g. France), you usually need to enter a personal identification number (PIN) into a machine, without which you may be unable to use your credit card. You also need a PIN to withdraw cash abroad from an ATM with a credit card (there's a limit to the amount that can be withdrawn). Note that using a foreign credit card to obtain cash abroad is expensive, as there's a standard charge (e.g. 1.5 per cent), a high interest rate, which is usually charged from the day of the withdrawal, and possibly a poor exchange rate. Never assume that a business (such as a restaurant) accepts a particular credit or charge card but check before running up a bill. Note that small businesses in many countries don't accept credit cards.

Even if you don't like credit cards and shun any form of credit, they do have their uses: e.g. no-deposit car rentals; no pre-paying hotel bills (plus guaranteed bookings); obtaining cash 24-hours a day; telephone, mail-order and Internet payments; more safety and security than cash; and above all, greater convenience. They're particularly useful when travelling abroad. However, in the wrong hands they're a disaster and should be shunned by spendthrifts.

MORTGAGES

Mortgages or home loans for buying a home abroad may be available in your home country, the country where the property is situated, and possibly also from financial institutions in offshore banking centres or other countries. Note, however, that in some countries mortgages are difficult or impossible to obtain from local banks, even for nationals. Therefore you should never pay a deposit on a home and assume that obtaining a mortgage will be a simple matter, but check in advance.

The amount that can be borrowed varies with the country where the property is situated, the country where the loan is to be raised, the lender, and, not least, your financial standing. In the last decade, lenders in many countries have tightened their lending criteria due to the repayment problems experienced by recession-hit borrowers, and some lenders apply strict rules regarding income, employment and the type of property on which they will lend. Foreign lenders, such as banks in offshore financial centres, also have strict rules concerning the nationality and domicile of borrowers, and the percentage they will lend. In theory lenders based in European Union (EU) countries are allowed to make loans anywhere within the EU, but in practice a single market doesn't exist.

In some countries the law doesn't permit banks to offer mortgages or other loans where repayments are more than a third of net income (after deducting existing mortgage or rental payments). Joint incomes and liabilities are included when assessing a couple's borrowing limit (usually a bank will lend to up to three joint borrowers). Most banks require proof of your monthly income and all outgoings, such as mortgage payments, rent and other loans and commitments. Proof of income includes three months' pay slips for employees, confirmation of income from your employer and tax returns. If you're self-employed, you usually require an audited copy of your balance sheets and trading accounts for the past three years, plus your last tax return. However, 'no income qualifier' loans of up to around 60 per cent of a property's value are available in many countries. In many countries it's customary for a property to be held as security for a loan, i.e. the lender takes a first charge on the property, which is recorded at the property registry.

Mortgages are granted on a percentage of a property's valuation, which may be below the actual market value. The maximum mortgage granted in most countries is 70 to 80 per cent of the valuation, although it can be as low as 50 to 60 per cent for non-residents and buyers of second homes. Loans may be repaid over 5 to 30 years, depending on the lender and country, although the usual term in most countries is 10 to 20 years for residents and sometimes less for non-residents. Repayment mortgages are the most common type in most countries, although endowment and pension-linked mortgages may also be offered. Repayments are usually made monthly or quarterly, although bi-weekly payments (which reduce the interest considerably) are also possible in some countries.

Note that you must add expenses and fees totalling from a few per cent to over 20 per cent of the purchase price (depending on the country) to the cost of a property. There are various fees associated with mortgages, e.g. all lenders charge an 'arrangement' fee and, although it's unusual to have a survey in most countries, lenders usually insist on a 'valuation survey' before they grant a loan. **Always shop around for the best interest rate and ask the effective rate, including all commissions and fees.**

Buying Through an Offshore Company: This is (not surprisingly) popular among non-resident property buyers in many countries, as they can legally avoid paying wealth tax, inheritance tax and capital gains tax. Buyers can also avoid transfer tax or stamp duty when buying a property owned by an offshore company, which can be a good selling point. However, it isn't possible in many countries and the owners of properties purchased through offshore companies in some countries (e.g. Spain) must register their ownership with the authorities or face punitive taxes. However, there are still legitimate advantages to buying property through an offshore company in some countries, although you should obtain expert advice from an experienced lawyer before doing so.

Mortgages for Second Homes: If you have equity in an existing home, it may be more cost effective to re-mortgage (or take out a second mortgage) on that property, than to take out a new mortgage for a home abroad. It entails less paperwork and therefore lower fees and a plan can be tailored to meet your requirements. Depending on the equity in your existing property and the cost of a home abroad, this may also enable you to pay cash for a second home. The disadvantage of re-mortgaging or taking out a second mortgage is that you reduce the amount of equity available in your existing property, which is useful if you need to raise cash in an emergency. Note that when a mortgage is taken out on a home abroad, it's usually charged against the property and not the individual borrower, which can be important if you get into repayment difficulties.

Foreign Currency Loans: It's generally recognised that you should take out a mortgage in the currency in which your income is paid or in the currency of the country where a property is situated. However, it's also possible to obtain a foreign currency mortgage in major currencies such as GB£, US$, Japanese Yen, Swiss francs or euros. In the 1980s and 1990s, high interest rates in many countries meant that a foreign currency mortgage was a good deal for many people. **However, most borrowers should be extremely wary of taking out a foreign currency mortgage, as interest rate gains can be wiped out overnight by currency swings and devaluations.**

The advantage of having a mortgage in the currency in which your income is paid is that if the currency is devalued against the currency of the country where you own a property, you will have the consolation that the value of your home abroad will (theoretically) have increased by the same percentage when converted back into your 'income' currency. When choosing between various currencies, you should take into account the costs, fees and interest rates and possible currency fluctuations. Irrespective of how you finance the purchase of a home abroad, you should always obtain professional advice. Note that if you have a foreign currency mortgage, you must usually pay commission charges each time you transfer currency to pay your mortgage or remit money abroad. If you let a home abroad, you may be able to offset the interest on your mortgage against rental income, but pro rata only. If you raise a mortgage abroad or in a foreign currency, you should be aware of any impact this may have on your tax allowances or liabilities.

Payment Problems: If you're unable to meet your mortgage payments, some lenders will renegotiate your mortgage so that payments are made over a longer period, thus allowing you to reduce your payments. Although interest rates have fallen in recent years, many lenders are slow to reduce their interest rates for existing borrowers and some try to prevent existing mortgage holders transferring to another lender offering a lower rate by imposing prohibitive fees. However, some countries have introduced legislation to enable borrowers with fixed rate mortgages to change their mortgage lender or re-negotiate a mortgage with their existing lender at a greatly reduced cost. A mortgage can usually be taken over (assumed) by the new owner when a property is sold, which can be advantageous for a buyer. Note that if you stop paying your mortgage, your lender can embargo your property and could eventually force its sale at auction to recover the loan.

PENSIONS

Before deciding where, or indeed whether, to retire abroad, it's important to ensure that your income will be sufficient to live on (see **Cost of Living** on page 107). You also need to consider how living abroad will affect your state and/or private pensions. In some countries you can continue to contribute to social security (in your home country) when living abroad or when you retire early in order to qualify for a full (or higher) state pension when you reach retirement age. Note that it may be compulsory to contribute to social security in some countries when you're below the state pension age, even when you're retired.

Most countries will pay state pensions or social security payments directly into a bank account abroad. If you receive a British state pension, you should be aware that the amount you receive will be frozen at the current level if you retire in certain countries, including Australia, Canada and New Zealand, and you won't be entitled to annual cost of living increases.

Before making any decisions about pensions, it's important to consult an independent pensions adviser.

TAX

Before planning to retire abroad, it's wise to investigate the taxes that will be payable, particularly income tax, social security and other taxes incurred by residents. If you plan to buy a home abroad, you may also need to take into account property taxes (rates), capital gains tax, wealth tax and inheritance tax. For many people, moving abroad is an opportunity to reduce their overall taxes, particularly when moving from a high to a low-tax country, when the timing of a move can be significant (see **Planning** below). Some countries encourage retirees to take up residence by offering tax incentives.

Income Tax

Income tax is of particular interest (or concern!) to those planning to retire abroad, although most countries also levy income tax on income earned by non-residents, such as the income from letting a home. If you're planning to retire abroad permanently, you may also need to take into account social security contributions, if you're below the official retirement age. Note that the combined burden of income tax, social security and other taxes can make a considerable hole in your income in some countries.

Liability: Under the law of most countries you become a fiscal resident (liable to income tax) if you spend 183 days during a calendar year or your main centre of economic interest, e.g. investments or business, is there. Temporary absences are usually included in the calculation of the period spent abroad, unless residence is shown to have been in another country for 183 days in a calendar year. If your spouse (and dependent minor children) normally resides in a country where you have a home, has a residence permit, and isn't legally separated from you, you may also be considered to be a tax resident in that country (unless you can prove otherwise). Some countries restrict the visits of non-residents, e.g. the UK limits them to 182 days in any tax year or an average of 91 days per year over four consecutive tax years.

Dual Residence: It's possible for some people to have 'dual residence' and be tax resident in two countries simultaneously, in which case your 'tax home' may be resolved under the rules of international treaties. Under such treaties you're considered to be resident in the country where you have a permanent home. If you have a permanent home in both countries, you're deemed to be resident in the country where you have the closest personal and economic ties. If your residence cannot be determined under the above rules, you're deemed to be resident in the country where you have a 'habitual abode'. If you have a habitual abode in both or in neither country, you're deemed to be resident in the country of which you're a citizen. Finally, if you're a citizen of both or neither country, the authorities of the countries concerned will decide your tax residence between them!

Double Taxation Treaties: Residents in most countries are taxed on their world-wide income, subject to certain treaty exceptions. Non-residents are usually taxed only on income arising in a particular country, e.g. non-residents of France pay tax only on income arising in France. Citizens of most countries are exempt from paying taxes in their home country when they spend a minimum period abroad, e.g. a year, although this doesn't apply to US citizens. Many countries have double taxation treaties with other countries, which are designed to ensure that income that has been taxed in one treaty country isn't taxed again in another. The treaty establishes a tax credit or exemption on certain kinds of income, either in the country of residence or the country where the income is earned.

Double taxation treaties vary with the country and, where applicable, have priority over domestic law. In the absence of a double taxation treaty between your home country and the country where you're planning to live or work, check how this will affect you. In many cases, even when there's no double taxation agreement between two countries, you can still usually obtain relief from double taxation. In this case, tax relief is usually provided through direct deduction of any foreign tax paid or through a 'foreign compensation' formula. Note that if your tax liability in one country is less than in another, you may be required to pay the tax authorities the difference in the country where you're resident. If you're in any doubt about your tax liability in your home country or another country where you're living, contact your nearest embassy or consulate for information. The USA is one of the few countries that taxes its non-resident citizens on income earned abroad – Americans can obtain a copy of a brochure, *Tax Guide for Americans Abroad*, from American consulates.

Moving Abroad: Before leaving a country for good, you usually need to pay any tax due for the previous year and the year of departure, and you may also need to apply for a tax clearance. A tax return must usually be filed prior to departure and must include your income and deductions for the current tax year up to the date of departure. The local tax office will calculate the taxes due and provide a written statement. In some countries, a tax clearance certificate is necessary to obtain a 'sailing or departure permit' or an exit visa. A shipping or moving company may also need official authorisation from the tax authorities before they can ship your personal effects abroad.

Tax Havens: If you're looking for a tax haven or a low-tax country, you should investigate countries such as Andorra, Belize, Brunei, the Caribbean islands (e.g. the Bahamas, Bermuda or the Cayman Islands), the Channel Islands, Costa Rica, Cyprus, Ecuador, the Gulf States, Honduras, the Isle of Man, Gibraltar, Liechtenstein, Malta, Mexico, Nicaragua, Monaco, Panama or Switzerland. Note that you need a **very** large bank balance to purchase a property and become a resident in some low-tax countries, e.g. the Caribbean, Channel Islands, Monaco and Switzerland. You should also be aware that owning a home in a particular country won't necessarily qualify you for a residence permit and that to qualify as a resident you must usually spend at least 183 days a year in a country (see above).

Planning: If you're intending to move abroad permanently, you should plan well in advance, as the timing of a move can make a big difference to your tax liabilities, both in your present and your new country of residence. Find out what you must do to become an official non-resident in your current country of residence and how long you will need to be resident in your new home to qualify as a resident for tax purposes. In most countries you automatically become liable for income tax if you spend longer than six months (183 days) there during a calendar year (see above).

If you intend to live abroad permanently, you should notify the tax and social security authorities in your previous country of residence well in advance. You may be entitled to a tax refund if you leave during the tax year, which usually requires the completion of a tax return. The authorities may require evidence that you're leaving the country, e.g. proof of having purchased or rented a home abroad.

Property Taxes

Property taxes (also called real estate taxes or rates) are levied by local authorities in most countries and are payable by all property owners, irrespective of whether they're residents or non-residents, and may also be paid by tenants. In some countries an additional 'residential' or local income tax is also paid by residents. Property taxes pay for local services, which may include rubbish collection, street lighting, sanitary services (e.g. street and beach cleaning), local schools and other community services, local council administration, social assistance, community substructure, cultural and sports amenities, and possibly water rates. Before buying a home, check the tax rate with the local town hall, as rates usually vary from community to community.

Property tax is usually payable irrespective of whether a property is inhabited, provided it's furnished and habitable. It may be split into two amounts, one for the building and another for the land, with the tax on land payable irrespective of whether it's built on or not. Before buying a property you should check that there are no outstanding property taxes for the current or previous years, as in many countries the new owner assumes all unpaid taxes and debts. When you buy a property in any country, ownership must be registered at the local land registry, which is usually done by the lawyer or public notary officiating at the completion of the sale.

Property taxes are normally based on the fiscal or notional letting value of a property, which is usually lower than the actual purchase price or a property's market value. If the fiscal value of your property increases greatly, check that it has been correctly calculated. You can appeal against the valuation of your property if you believe it's too high, particularly if it's higher than that of similar properties in the same area. Note, however, that an appeal must be lodged within a limited period (check with the local town hall). **It's important that the fiscal value of your property is correct, as in some countries a number of taxes are linked to this value, such as**

property letting tax, wealth tax, transfer tax on property sales and inheritance tax.

Wealth Tax

Some countries levy a wealth tax, which is usually applicable only to residents, although it sometimes also applies to non-resident property owners. Your wealth is generally calculated by totalling your assets and deducting your liabilities. When calculating your wealth tax, you should include the value of all property, including real estate, vehicles, boats, aircraft, business ownership, cash (e.g. in bank accounts), life insurance, gold bars, jewellery, stocks, shares and bonds. If you fail to declare your total assets, you can be fined. Assets that are exempt from wealth tax usually include *objets d'art* and antiques (provided their value doesn't exceed certain limits), the vested rights of participants in pension plans and funds, copyrights (as long as they remain part of your net worth), assets forming part of a country's historical heritage, and 'professional assets' in a business. Deductions are usually made for mortgages, business and other debts, and wealth tax paid in another country.

The level at which wealth tax is applicable varies greatly with the country and whether you're a resident or non-resident. For residents in Spain it's payable on assets above €108,182 (although a couple are each entitled to the €108,182 exemption, making a combined exemption of €216,364), while in France no tax is payable on assets below €720,000. Wealth tax may depend on your domicile, e.g. if you're domiciled in France, the value of your estate is based on your world-wide assets, whereas if you're resident in France but not domiciled there, the value of your estate is based only on your assets in France.

Capital Gains Tax

Capital gains tax (CGT) is payable on the profit from sales of certain assets in most countries, which may include property, antiques, art and jewellery, stocks, bonds and shares, household furnishings, vehicles, coin and stamp collections and other 'collectibles', gold, silver and gems, and the sale of a business. International tax treaties usually decree that capital gains on property is taxable in the country where it's situated.

Note that if you move abroad permanently and retain a home in another country, this may affect your position regarding capital gains tax. Had you sold your foreign home before moving abroad, you would usually have been exempt from CGT, as it would have been your principal residence. However, if you establish your principal residence abroad, your property in your home country becomes a second home and thus you may be liable for CGT when it's sold. Capital gains tax can be a complicated subject and you should always obtain legal advice before disposing of property or buying property abroad. **Note that the tax authorities in many countries co-operate to track down those attempting to avoid capital gains tax.**

Most countries provide an exemption if gains don't exceed a certain amount. Certain types of gain are also exempt and may include gains as a result of the death of a taxpayer, gifts to government entities, donations of certain assets in lieu of tax payments, and the exchange of assets for a life annuity for those aged over 65. Capital losses can usually be offset against capital gains, but not against ordinary income, and it's usually possible to carry forward capital losses (or a percentage) in excess of gains and offset them against future gains for a limited period. In most countries, capital gains are treated as ordinary income for residents.

A property capital gain is based on the difference between the purchase price and the sale price. However, in most countries there are exemptions, which usually depend on the number of years a property has been owned. If an asset has been owned for less than a certain period, e.g. two years in France (second homes) and Spain, capital gains are taxed in full. Most countries allow a tax exemption (called indexation relief) on the sale of your principal residence (e.g. the UK and France), although some (such as Spain and the USA) allow an exemption only if you buy another home within a limited period and levy tax on any profits that aren't re-invested. However, residents of France don't pay CGT on a profit made on the sale of their principal home, provided they've occupied it since its purchase, while in Spain residents aged over 65 are exempt from paying CGT. In the USA, if you're a resident aged over 55 you can make a one-time, tax-free profit of US$250,000 (US$500,000 for a couple filing jointly) on the sale of your principal residence before you're liable for CGT. Note that in some countries you're exempt from CGT on a second home if you don't own your main residence, i.e. if you're a tenant or leaseholder, although this may apply only to the first sale of a second home.

In some countries, capital gains made by non-residents are taxed at a flat rate (e.g. 35 per cent in Spain) and there may be no reduction for the length of time you've owned a property. However, in most countries the amount of CGT payable is reduced the longer you've owned a property. In most cases, you cease to be liable for CGT after owning a property for a number of years, e.g. 22 years in France and ten years in Spain. Where applicable, a sum may be withheld by the official handling the sale in lieu of capital gains tax or the buyer must retain a percentage when the seller is a non-resident, e.g. 5 per cent in Spain.

You should keep all bills for the fees associated with buying a property (e.g. lawyer, estate agent and surveyor), plus any bills for renovation, restoration, modernisation and improvement to a second home, as these can usually be offset against CGT and may be index-linked. If you work on a house yourself, you should keep a copy of all bills for materials and tools, as these can also be offset against CGT. Losses on rentals may also be able to be carried forward and offset against a capital gain when a property is sold. Costs relating to a sale can also usually be offset against any gain, as can interest paid on a loan taken out to purchase or restore a property. In some countries you can protect yourself and your survivors from capital gains tax by bequeathing property, rather than giving it away while you're alive.

Inheritance & Gift Tax

Dying doesn't free you (or more correctly, your beneficiaries) entirely from the clutches of the tax man. Many countries impose an inheritance tax (also called estate tax or death duty) and gift tax on the estate of a deceased person. Usually both residents and non-residents are subject to inheritance tax if they own property abroad. The country where you pay inheritance and gift tax is usually decided by your domicile. If you're living permanently abroad at the time of your death, you will be deemed to be domiciled there by the local tax authorities. If you're domiciled abroad, inheritance and gift tax payable there will apply to your world-wide estate (excluding property); otherwise it applies only to assets held abroad, such as a second home. It's important to make your domicile clear so that there's no misunderstanding on your death.

Inheritance Tax: In many countries, inheritance tax is paid by the beneficiaries and not by the deceased's estate. This may mean that if you inherit a home abroad, you may need to sell it to pay tax. The rate of inheritance tax payable usually depends upon the relationship between the donor and the recipient, the amount inherited, and (in some countries) the current wealth of the recipient. Direct descendants and close relatives of the deceased usually receive an allowance before they're liable for inheritance tax. Some countries have strict succession laws (although they don't always apply to foreigners) regarding who you can leave your assets to. To take advantage of lower tax rates, it's usually best to leave property to your spouse, children or parents, rather than to someone who's unrelated.

It's important for both residents and non-residents owning a home abroad to decide in advance how they wish to dispose of it. If possible, this should be done before buying a home abroad, as it can be complicated and expensive to change later. There are many ways to limit or delay the impact of restrictive inheritance laws, including buying property through an offshore company or trust and inserting a clause in a property purchase contract allowing a property to be left in its entirety to a surviving spouse without being shared among the children. A surviving spouse can also be given a life interest in an estate in preference to children or parents, through a 'gift between spouses'. Note that most countries don't recognise the rights to inheritance of a non-married partner, although there are a number of solutions to this problem, e.g. a life insurance policy. Some bequests are exempt from inheritance tax, including certain types of properties and legacies to charities and government bodies.

Gift Tax: Gift tax is calculated in the same way as inheritance tax, depending on the relationship between the donor and the recipient and the size of the gift. There's usually a limit to the amount of money or assets you can give away, e.g. to your children, during your lifetime without paying gift tax, and donations made within a certain number of years of your death may be liable to inheritance tax. A reduction is usually granted depending on the age of the donor (generally the younger the donor, the larger the reduction).

Inheritance law is a complicated subject and professional advice should be sought from an experienced lawyer who's familiar with the inheritance laws of the country where you plan to buy a home and any other countries involved. Your will (see below) is a vital component in keeping inheritance and gift tax to the minimum or delaying its payment.

WILLS

It's an unfortunate fact of life that you're unable to take your hard-earned assets with you when you take your final bow (or to come back and reclaim them in a later life!). All adults should make a will, irrespective of how large or small their assets. The disposal of your estate depends on your country of domicile (see **Income Tax** on page 100). Most countries permit foreigners who aren't domiciled abroad to make a will in any language and under the law of any country, provided it's valid under the law of that country. A will must usually be in writing (but not necessarily in the hand of the testator). Under international rules regarding conflict of law, the law that generally applies is the law of the country where the testator was a citizen at the time of his death.

Note, however, that 'immovable' property, i.e. land and buildings, must usually be disposed of (on death) in accordance with local law. All other property abroad or elsewhere (defined as 'movables') may be disposed of in accordance with the law of your home country or domicile. Therefore, it's important to establish where you're domiciled. One solution for a non-resident wishing to avoid foreign inheritance laws may be to buy a property through a company, in which case the shares of the company are 'movable' assets and are therefore governed by the succession laws of the owner's country of domicile.

In many countries, the law gives the immediate family (i.e. spouse, children and parents) an absolute right to inherit a share of an estate, and therefore it isn't possible to disinherit them as can be done in some other countries (e.g. the UK). Note also that in many countries, marriage doesn't automatically revoke a will, as it does, for example, in the UK.

If you have a large estate abroad, it's wise to consult a lawyer when drawing up a will. It's possible to make separate wills, one relating to property in your home country and another for any foreign property. Experts differ on whether you should have separate wills for property in different countries, written under local law, or have one will in your home country with a codicil (appendix) dealing with any foreign property. However, most lawyers believe that it's better to have a local will in any country where you own immovable property, which will speed up and reduce the cost of probate (the proving of a will). If you have more than one will, you must make sure that they don't contradict each other.

You'll need someone to act as the executor of your estate, which can be particularly costly in relation to modest estates. In some countries, many people appoint their bank manager, lawyer or another professional person to act as executor, although this should be avoided, if possible, as the fees can be astronomical. It's better to make your beneficiaries the executors, who can instruct a lawyer after your death if they require legal assistance. Note that probate can take a long time in some countries.

Keep a copy of your will(s) in a safe place and another copy with your lawyer or the executor of your estate. Don't leave them in a safe deposit box, which in the event of your death may be sealed for a period under local law. You should keep information regarding bank accounts and insurance policies with your will(s), but don't forget to tell someone where they are!

Note that inheritance law is a complicated subject and it's important to obtain professional legal advice when writing or altering your will(s).

COST OF LIVING

No doubt you would like to estimate how far your money will stretch abroad and how much you will have left after paying your bills. The cost of living has risen considerably in most countries in the last decade or so, and some countries that previously enjoyed a relatively low cost of living are no longer quite so attractive, particularly for retirees. On the other hand, foreigners whose income is paid in 'hard' currencies, such as those of most northern European countries and North America, have seen their incomes (when converted to local currency) in many countries rise sharply in recent years. If anything, the difference in the cost of living between 'rich' North American and northern European countries has remained the same or has widened in favour of the richer countries. For example, the cost of living is 25 to 50 per cent lower than in North America and northern Europe in many Caribbean and Central and South American countries.

If you spend only a few months abroad each year, you may not be too concerned about the local cost of living. However, if you plan to live abroad permanently you should ensure that your income is, and will remain, sufficient to live on, bearing in mind currency devaluations (if your income isn't paid in local currency), inflation, and extraordinary expenses such as medical bills or anything else that may drastically reduce your income (such as stock market crashes and recessions). Note that if your pension is paid in a currency that's devalued, this could have a catastrophic effect on your standard of living (as it did on British residents abroad when sterling was effectively devalued by some 20 per cent in 1992 after the UK withdrew from the European Monetary System). Note also that some countries (e.g. the UK) freeze state pensions at the current rate for those going to live permanently in certain countries.

It's difficult to calculate an average cost of living for any country, as it depends very much on your circumstances and lifestyle, and where you live. It's generally cheaper to live in a rural area than in a large city or a popular resort area (and homes are also much cheaper). The actual difference in your food bill will depend on what you eat and where you lived before moving abroad. Food in most southern European and Mediterranean countries, and most Central and South American countries is cheaper than in most northern European countries, although North Americans won't find the difference so great. The equivalent of around GB£150 or US$210 should feed two adults for a month in most popular retirement countries, including inexpensive local beer or wine, but excluding fillet steak, caviar and expensive imported foods.

A couple owning their home (with no mortgage) in many popular 'retirement' countries can 'survive' on a net income of as little as GB£325 or around US$450 per month (some pensioners live on less), and most can live quite comfortably on an income of GB£500 or US$700 a month. However, this covers basic needs only and doesn't include 'luxuries'. In fact, many northern Europeans (particularly Scandinavians) and North Americans find that if they live modestly without overdoing the luxuries, their cost of living abroad can be up to 50 per cent less than in their home countries.

Comparing prices and, where feasible, shopping abroad (possibly by mail or via the Internet – see page 133) for expensive items can yield huge savings. It may also be possible to make savings by buying clothes, general household items, furniture and furnishings, and even your car abroad. Where possible, foreign newspapers and magazines should be purchased abroad on subscription (possibly sharing the cost with friends). If you have a tight budget, you should avoid shopping in fashionable towns or shopping centres and 'tourist' shops, which have proliferated in some countries and may include supermarkets in areas inhabited mainly by foreigners. Ask the locals where to shop for the lowest prices and best value goods.

There are a number of websites providing cost of living comparisons between countries and major cities, including the Economic Research Institute (💻 www. salariesreview.com and www.erieri.com/sources), Runzheimer International (💻 www.runzheimer.com) and Expat Forum (💻 www.expatforum.com).

INSURANCE

An important aspect of living abroad is insurance, including health, travel, home contents and third party liability insurance. It's unnecessary to spend half your income insuring yourself against every eventuality from the common cold to being sued for your last penny, but it's important to insure against any event that could precipitate a major financial disaster, such as a serious accident or your house falling down.

As with anything concerning finance, it's important to shop around when buying insurance. Simply collecting a few brochures from insurance agents or making a few phone calls could save you a lot of money. Note, however, that not all insurance companies are equally reliable or have the same financial stability, and it may be better to insure with a large international insurance company with a good reputation than with a small local company, even if this means paying higher premiums. Major international insurance companies have offices and representatives in many countries.

Read all insurance contracts before signing them. If a policy is written in a language that you don't understand, get someone to check it and don't sign it unless you clearly understand the terms and the cover provided. Some insurance companies will do almost anything to avoid paying out in the event of a claim and will use any available legal loophole. Therefore it pays to deal only with reputable companies – not that this provides a guarantee!

In all matters regarding insurance, you're responsible for ensuring that you and your family are legally insured abroad. Regrettably you cannot insure yourself against being uninsured or sue your insurance agent for giving you bad advice! Bear in mind that if you wish to make a claim on an insurance policy, you may be required to report an incident to the police within 24 hours (this may also be a legal requirement). You should obtain legal advice for anything other than a minor claim, as the law abroad may differ considerably from that in your home country or your previous country of residence and you should **never** assume that it's the same.

See also **Health Insurance** on page 82 and **Car Insurance** on page 36.

Household Insurance

In most countries, insurance for a private dwelling includes third party liability, building and contents insurance, all of which are usually contained in a multi-risk household or homeowner's insurance policy (although in some countries these risks must be insured separately). When buying a home abroad, you're usually responsible for insuring it from the moment you become the owner, e.g. for third party risks. In some countries, many homeowners don't have household insurance, and of those that do, the vast majority have insufficient insurance for their homes and possessions. **This is**

extremely unwise, particularly regarding building insurance, as it isn't unusual for buildings to be severely damaged by floods and storms in some countries.

Third Party Liability: In many countries, property must be insured for third party liability at all times or when building work starts on a new home. The third party liability insurance of the previous owner may automatically transfer to a new owner unless he takes out his own insurance. If you take over the existing insurance, you should ensure that it provides adequate cover and that it isn't too expensive. Third party liability insurance covers you against financial responsibility for injuries to third parties on your property or accidents directly attributed to something connected with your property. Note that if you own a home that's part of a development or community property (see page 49), such as an apartment or a townhouse, you must usually be insured for third party risks in the event that you cause damage to neighbouring properties, e.g. through flood or fire.

Building Insurance: Although it isn't usually compulsory for owners (unless you have a mortgage), it's advisable to take out building insurance which generally covers damage due to fire, lightning, water, explosion, storm, smoke, freezing, snow, theft, riot or civil commotion, vandalism or malicious damage, acts of terrorism, impact (e.g. by aircraft or vehicles), broken glass (constituting part of the building), and natural catastrophes (such as falling trees). Insurance should include glass, external buildings, aerials and satellite dishes, and gardens and garden ornaments. Note that if a claim is made as a result of a defect in the building or design, e.g. the roof is too heavy and collapses, the insurance company won't pay up (yet another reason to have a survey before buying).

The amount for which you should insure your home isn't the current market value, but its replacement value, i.e. the cost of rebuilding a property if it's totally destroyed. This should be increased each year in line with inflation. **Make sure that you insure your property for the true cost of rebuilding.** If you have a mortgage, your lender will usually insist that your home, including most permanent structures on your land, has building insurance. It may be mandatory to take out building insurance with a lender for the whole of the mortgage term, with the premium being paid in a single lump sum.

In some countries (e.g. the USA) many people lose their homes each year due to natural disasters such as earthquakes, fires, floods, hurricanes and tornadoes. In high risk areas, owners must usually pay an extra premium to cover risks such as subsidence (e.g. where homes are built on clay), floods or earthquakes, although the cost may be extremely high (only some 15 per cent of Californians have earthquake insurance, as it's simply too expensive). Read the small print carefully, e.g. some policies don't include water coming in from ground level (e.g. flood water) and provide cover only for water seeping through the roof. **It's prudent to investigate the occurrence of natural disasters in an area where you're planning to buy and the cost of insurance before committing yourself, as the cost can be prohibitive.** Note that in certain countries, claims for damage caused by storms aren't considered by insurance companies unless the situation is declared a natural catastrophe or an 'act of God' by the government.

If you own an apartment or a townhouse that's part of a communal property, building insurance should be included in your service charges, although you should check exactly what is covered. You must, however, still be insured for third party risks in the event that you cause damage to neighbouring properties, e.g. through flood or fire. New buildings should be covered by a builder's warranty, although unless a warranty is guaranteed by an independent national organisation it may not be worth the paper on which it's printed.

Contents Insurance: Your home contents are usually insured for the same risks as a building (see above) and in most countries are insured for their replacement value (new for old), with a reduction for wear and tear for clothes and linen. However, in some countries (e.g. the USA), possessions are insured for their 'actual cash value' (cost minus depreciation). You can, buy 'replacement value' insurance, although policies often include limits and are more expensive. Valuable items are covered for their declared and authenticated value. Most policies include automatic indexation of the insured sum in line with inflation. Contents policies always contain security clauses and if you don't adhere to them a claim won't be considered.

Optional Cover: Contents insurance may include accidental damage to sanitary installations, loss of cash, replacement of locks following damage or loss of keys, alternative accommodation cover, and damage to property belonging to third parties stored in your home, although these may all be optional. Optional items usually also include credit cards (and their fraudulent use), frozen foods, emergency assistance (e.g. plumber, glazier, electrician), redecoration, garaged cars, replacement pipes, loss of rent, and the cost of emergency travel to a home abroad (for holiday homeowners). Many policies include personal third party liability as an option (see **Third Party Liability Insurance** below). A basic policy may exclude items such as musical instruments, jewellery, valuables, sports equipment and bicycles, for which you may need to take out extra cover. A basic policy also *doesn't* usually include accidental damage caused by your family to your own property, e.g. 'accidentally' putting your foot through the TV during a political broadcast!

Valuables: High-value possessions, such as works of art, antiques, furs and jewellery, aren't usually covered (or fully covered) by a standard policy and must be insured separately for their full value. They must usually be itemised, and photographs and documentation such as a professional appraiser's report provided. Some companies even recommend or insist on a video film of belongings. When making a claim, you should produce the original bills if possible (always keep bills for expensive items) and bear in mind that replacing imported items locally may be more expensive than their original cost. All-risks cover is available from some insurance companies, offering a world-wide extension to a household policy and including items such as jewellery and cameras.

Security: Note that in some countries a building must have iron bars on the ground-floor windows and patio doors, window shutters and secure locks. In countries and areas with a high risk of theft (e.g. major cities and most resort areas), an insurance company may insist on extra security measures, e.g. two locks on all external doors (one of a mortise type) and shutters or security gratings on windows. A policy may specify that all forms of protection on doors must be used at night (e.g. after 10pm) and when a property is left empty for more than a few days. It's unwise to leave valuable or irreplaceable items in a holiday home or in a property that's vacant for long periods.

Some companies offer a discount if properties have steel reinforced doors, security locks and alarms (particularly alarms connected to a 24-hour monitoring service). An insurance company may send someone to inspect your property and advise on security measures. Policies usually cover theft only when there are signs of forcible entry and don't cover thefts by a tenant (but may cover thefts by domestic staff).

Inventory: When insuring your possessions, don't buy more insurance than you need. Unless you have valuable possessions, insurance may cost more than replacing your possessions and you may be better off just insuring a few valuable items, rather than everything. To calculate the amount of insurance you need, make a complete list of your possessions containing a description, purchase price and date, and their location in your home. Some insurance companies use a formula based on your building insurance value (i.e. the value of your home), although this is no more than a 'guesstimate'. Keep the list and all receipts in a safe place (such as a safety deposit box), and add new purchases and make adjustments to your insurance cover when necessary.

Under-Insurance: Take care that you don't under-insure your house contents and that you periodically reassess their value and adjust your insurance premium accordingly. Your contents should include everything that isn't part of the fixtures and fittings, and which you could take with you if you were moving house. In many countries, if you under-insure your contents, a claim will be reduced by the percentage by which you're under insured. For example, if you make a claim for GB£1,000 (US$1,400) and you're found to be under-insured by 50 per cent, you will receive only GB£500 (US$700).

Premiums: The cost of household insurance varies considerably with the country, the type of property, its location and the local crime rate. Premiums are usually calculated on the size of the property, either the habitable (constructed) area in square metres (or square feet) or the number of rooms, rather than its value. The sum insured may be unlimited, provided the property doesn't exceed a certain size and is under a certain age, e.g. 200 years, although some companies restrict home insurance to properties with a maximum number of rooms or a maximum value of contents. In general, detached, older and more remote properties cost more to insure than apartments and new properties (particularly when located in towns), due to the higher risk of theft. Premiums are also higher in certain high-risk areas, and some policies impose a small excess (deductible) for each claim.

Holiday Homes: In some countries premiums are higher for holiday homes, due to their high vulnerability, particularly to theft. Premiums are usually based on the number of days a property is inhabited each year and the interval between periods of occupancy. Cover for theft, storm, flood and malicious damage may be suspended when a property is left empty for more than three weeks at a time (or if there's no visible forced entry in the event of theft). It's possible to negotiate cover for periods of absence for a hefty surcharge, although valuable items are usually excluded. If you're absent from your property for long periods, e.g. longer than 30 days at a time, you may also be required to pay an excess on a claim arising from an occurrence that takes place during your absence (and theft may be excluded). Some companies refuse to insure holiday homes in high-risk areas. **You should read all small print in policies.** Note that if you let a home abroad, even for short periods, you may be required to notify your household insurance company.

Claims: If you wish to make a claim, you must usually inform your insurance company in writing (by registered letter) within two to seven days of the incident or 24 hours in the case of theft. Thefts should also be reported to the local police within 24 hours, as the police statement (of which you receive a copy for your insurance company) constitutes `irrefutable' evidence of your claim. Check whether you're covered for damage or thefts that occur when you're away from the property and are therefore unable to inform the insurance company or police immediately.

Settlement of Claims: Bear in mind that if you make a claim you may need to wait months for it to be settled. Generally the larger the claim, the longer you will have to wait for your money, although in an emergency some companies will make an interim payment. If you aren't satisfied with the amount offered, don't accept it and try to negotiate a higher figure. If you still cannot reach agreement on the amount or the time taken to settle a claim, you may be able to take your claim to an ombudsman or an independent industry organisation for arbitration. **Note that some insurance companies will do their utmost to find a loophole which makes you negligent and relieves them of liability.**

Third Party Liability Insurance

It's common practice in many countries to have third party liability insurance. To take an everyday example, if your soap slips out of your hand while you're taking a shower, jumps out of the window and your neighbour slips on it and breaks his neck, he (or his widow) will sue you for around GB£1 million (or US$10 million in the USA). With third party liability insurance you can shower in blissful security. Third party liability insurance covers all members of a family and includes damage done or caused by your children and pets, e.g. if your dog or child bites someone. Where damage is due to severe negligence, benefits may be reduced. In some countries, if your children attend school they're automatically covered by third party liability insurance, in others you may need to take out a special policy. Third party liability insurance also protects you against claims from anyone who injures himself or suffers loss while on your land or in your home. Check whether insurance covers you against accidental damage to your home's fixtures and fittings (which may be covered by your household insurance).

Third party liability insurance is often combined with household insurance (see above). If it isn't included in your household insurance, third party liability insurance is inexpensive and usually costs around GB£10 to £20 (US$15 to $30) a year for each GB£50,000 (US$70,000) of cover, although you may be required to pay the first GB£50 or £100 (US$70 to $140) of a claim.

Travel Insurance

Travel Insurance is recommended for all who don't wish to risk having their journey spoilt by financial problems or to arrive broke. As you probably know, anything can and often does go wrong when travelling, sometimes before you even reach the airport or port (particularly when you *don't* have insurance). Travel insurance is available from many sources, including travel and insurance agents, motoring organisations, transport companies and direct from insurance companies. When you pay for your travel costs with some credit cards, you're provided with free travel accident insurance up to a specified amount. **However, you shouldn't rely on this insurance, as it usually covers death or serious injury only.**

Level of Cover: Before taking out travel insurance, carefully consider the level of cover you require and compare policies. Most policies include cover for loss of deposit or travel cancellation, missed flights, departure delay at both the start and end of a journey (a common occurrence), delayed baggage, personal effects and lost baggage, medical expenses and accidents (including repatriation home if necessary), money, personal liability, legal expenses, and protection against a travel company or operator going bust. You should also insure against missing your flight after an accident or transport breakdown, as some 50 per cent of travel insurance claims are for cancellation. Note that some policies limit the amount you can claim for personal belongings to around GB£200 (US$300) per item, which may be insufficient to cover your Rolex watch or digital camera.

Medical expenses are an important aspect of travel insurance and it isn't wise to rely on reciprocal health arrangements (such as provided by form E111 in European Union countries). You also shouldn't rely on travel insurance provided by charge and credit card companies, house contents policies or private medical insurance, none of which usually provide the necessary cover (although you should take advantage of what they offer). The minimum medical insurance recommended by most experts is around GB£250,000 (US$350,000) in Europe and GB£500,000 to £1 million (US$750,000 to $1.5 million) in North America and some other countries, e.g. Japan.

If applicable, check whether there are any restrictions for those over a certain age, e.g. 65 or 70. Third party liability cover should be GB£500,000 to £1 million (US$750,000 to $1.5 million) in Europe and GB£1 million to £2 million (US$1.5 to $3 million) in North America. **Note that most travel and holiday insurance policies don't provide the minimum level of cover that most people need.** Always check any exclusion clauses in contracts by obtaining a copy of the full policy document, as all relevant information isn't included in insurance leaflets.

Annual Policies: For people who travel abroad frequently or spend long periods abroad, an annual travel policy usually provides the best value. Many insurance companies offer annual travel policies for a premium of around GB£100 to £150 (US$140 to $210) for an individual (the equivalent of around three months' insurance with a standard travel insurance policy), which are excellent value for frequent travellers. The cost of an annual policy may depend on the area covered, e.g. Europe, world-wide excluding North America and world-wide including North America, although it doesn't usually cover travel within your country of residence. There's also a limit on the number of trips a year and the duration of each trip, e.g. 90 or 120 days. An annual policy is usually a good choice for owners of a home abroad who travel there frequently for relatively short periods. **However, check exactly what's covered or omitted, as an annual policy may not provide adequate cover.** A policy recommended by the Medical Advisory Service for Travellers Abroad is the Worldwide Travel Protector policy (☎ UK 0870-120 0112).

Claims: Although travel insurance companies will gladly take your money, they aren't so keen to honour claims and you may have to persevere before they pay up. Fraudulent claims against travel insurance are common, and unless you can produce evidence to support your claim the insurers may think you're trying to cheat them. Always be persistent and make a claim irrespective of any small print, as this may be unreasonable and therefore invalid in law. **All insurance companies require you to report any loss (or any incident for which you intend to make a claim) to the local police or carriers within 24 hours and to obtain a report. Failure to do this usually means that your claim won't be considered.**

6.

FURTHER CONSIDERATIONS

This chapter contains important miscellaneous considerations and information for those planning to retire abroad, including climate, crime, culture shock, pets, religion, safety, shopping abroad, social customs, television and radio, and time difference.

CLIMATE

For most people, the climate is one of the most important factors when deciding where (or whether) to retire abroad, particularly if you have a wide choice of countries. When choosing where to live you should bear in mind both the winter and summer climate, the average daily sunshine, plus the rainfall and wind conditions. You may also wish to check whether an area is noted for fog, which can make for hazardous driving conditions. The best climate in which to live is generally considered to be one without wide extremes of cold and heat, and where the average temperature over the year has the smallest swings between the coldest and hottest days. This includes areas such as southern California, the Caribbean, Central America, the Costa Blanca in Spain, New South Wales (Australia) and South Africa.

It's important to check whether an area is prone to natural disasters such as floods (which are common in some countries), storms (hurricanes, tornadoes, whirlwinds, etc.), forest fires, landslides or earthquakes. Forest fires are a danger in summer in most hot countries, including many US states, southern European countries and Australia, while earthquakes are a constant threat in California, many southern and eastern European countries (e.g. Armenia, the Balkans, Italy, Turkey), the Middle East (e.g. Iran), Japan, Chile, Indonesia and the Philippines, among other countries.

Many countries have experienced severe flooding in recent years, including France, Germany, Italy, the UK and the USA. There was severe flooding in many US states (e.g. California and Texas) in the '90s (record rainfall in 1992 caused the worst flash floods since 1938) and in 1993 the Mississippi and Missouri rivers broke their banks and flooded some 23 million acres. It's said (only half-jokingly) that some US states experience four seasons: fire, flood, drought and earthquakes/hurricanes! Flash floods can be dangerous in some countries, particularly in mountainous areas, and if you live near a coast or waterway it can be expensive to insure against floods. The good news is that your chances of experiencing a cyclone, hurricane, tornado, flood, earthquake or forest fire are rare in most areas. On the other hand, in regions with little rainfall there are often droughts and severe water restrictions (plus high water bills).

In some countries (e.g. the USA) people overreact to extremes of climate, with freezing air conditioning in summer and sweltering heating in winter. Because most buildings are either too hot or too cold, it's often a problem knowing what to wear and people dress in layers that they take off or put on, depending on the indoor or outdoor temperature. Many people use humidifiers to counteract the dry air caused by powerful heating or air conditioning.

Weather forecasts are given in daily newspapers and broadcast on radio and TV stations (there are 24-hour dedicated weather TV stations in North America), and world weather conditions are also available via numerous websites, including:

⌨ www.worldclimate.com;

⌨ www.worldweather.com;

⌨ www.cnn.com/weather;

⌨ http://weather.yahoo.com;

⌨ www.bbc.co.uk/weather.

See also **Health** on page 72.

CRIME

The crime rate (and what constitutes a crime) varies considerably from country to country, so it's important to investigate the level in a particular country, region or city before deciding where to retire. Most western European, Middle Eastern, Asian and Australasian countries are safe places to live and Canada also has relatively little serious crime. The crime rate, however, in the USA varies considerably from state to state and city to city, and can be high. Many Central and South American and African countries can be dangerous places in which to live, and precautions may have to be taken at all times. Major cities have the highest crime rates, some areas of which are best avoided at almost any time of the day or night. Many cities are notorious for 'petty' crime such as handbag snatching, pickpockets and thefts of (and from) vehicles. In contrast, crime in villages and rural areas (away from tourist areas) is virtually unknown in most countries, and windows and doors are often left unlocked.

The most common crime is theft, which embraces a multitude of forms. One of the most common in southern European, Asian and South American countries is the bag snatcher, possibly on a motorbike or moped, which involves grabbing a hand or shoulder bag (or a camera) and riding off with it, sometimes with the owner still attached (occasionally causing serious injuries). It's advisable to carry bags on the inside of the pavement and to wear shoulder bags diagonally across your chest, although it's better not to carry a bag at all (the strap can be cut) and wear a wrist pouch or money belt. You should also be wary of bag-snatchers in airport and other car parks, and never wear valuable jewellery and watches in high-risk areas. Motorcycle thieves may smash car windows at traffic lights to steal articles left on seats, so bags should be stowed on the floor or behind seats.

Tourists and travellers are the targets of many of the world's most enterprising criminals, including highwaymen, who pose as accident or breakdown victims and rob motorists who stop to help them. Car-jacking (or highway robbery) is also a problem in some countries (see **Crime Prevention & Safety** below). Don't leave cash or valuables unattended when swimming or leave your bags, cameras or jackets lying around on chairs in cafés or bars (always keep an eye on your belongings in public places). Beware of gangs of child thieves in cities, pickpockets and over-friendly strangers. Always remain vigilant in tourist haunts, queues and anywhere there are large crowds, and never tempt fate with an exposed wallet or purse or by flashing your money around. One of the most effective ways of protecting your passport, money, travellers' cheques and credit cards is with an old-fashioned money belt.

Foreigners are often victims of housebreaking and burglary (particularly holiday homeowners), which is rife in resort areas in many countries. Always ensure that your home is secure (see page 63) and that your belongings are well insured, and never leave valuables lying around. It's advisable to install a safe if you keep valuables (e.g. jewellery) or cash in your home. In some countries, developments may be patrolled by security guards, although they may have little influence on crime rates and may instil a false sense of security. It's advisable to arrange for someone to periodically check a property when it's left unoccupied.

Fortunately, violent crime is still relatively rare in most countries, although muggings, murders, rapes and armed robbery have increased considerably in the last decade or so in many countries. There are also dangers for women travelling alone and hitch-hiking isn't recommended anywhere. Sexual harassment is also a problem in some countries, where women (particularly blondes) are often the subject of unwanted attention. It's advisable for lone women to use taxis rather than public transport late at night.

Drug addiction is the main impetus for crime in many countries, where the bulk of crime may be drug related. Drug addiction is a huge and growing problem throughout the world and drug addicts (and prostitutes) are a common sight in many towns and cities. It's an offence to possess soft drugs such as hashish in many countries, while in some it's legal for personal use or the law tends to turn a blind eye to its use. On the other hand, the possession and use of hard drugs such as heroin and cocaine is strictly prohibited in most countries and the penalty for trafficking can be death! Many countries are particularly harsh in their treatment of foreign drug dealers, who may be held on remand for years without trial. **When travelling to and from any country in a vehicle you should take particular care, as vehicles are frequently found to contain hidden drugs planted by drug dealers.** You should also be wary of giving strangers lifts and **never** transport anyone across an international border.

Many Asian and Middle Eastern countries have strict laws regarding matters such as the sale and consumption of alcohol, pornography, age of consent, homosexuality, adultery, dress for women and dress in holy places. Often these have religious connotations, particularly in Muslim countries, and it's important to be aware of them. It's easy to unwittingly offend your hosts and in certain cases even to be arrested for what may appear to be an innocuous matter. In some countries 'petty' laws (such as illegal parking and jaywalking) may be widely ignored, while in others they're strictly enforced, so that it's important to know the local 'ropes'.

One of the biggest financial threats to foreigners abroad isn't from the locals, but from your own countrymen and other foreigners. It's common for expatriate 'businessmen' in some countries to run up huge debts, either through dishonesty or incompetence, and cut and run owing their clients and suppliers a fortune. In many resort areas, confidence tricksters, swindlers, cheats and fraudsters lie in wait around every corner and newcomers must constantly be on their guard (particularly when buying a home). Fraud of every conceivable kind is a fine art in many countries and is commonly perpetrated by foreigners on their fellow countrymen. Always be wary of someone who offers to do you a favour or show you the ropes, or anyone claiming to know how to 'beat the system'. **If anything sounds too good to be true, you can bet it almost certainly is.** It's a sad fact of life, but you should generally be more wary of doing business with your fellow countrymen abroad than with local people.

Despite the foregoing catalogue of disasters, in most countries you can usually safely walk almost anywhere at any time of the day or night, and there's absolutely no need for anxiety or paranoia about crime. You should, however, be 'street-wise' and take certain elementary precautions, which include learning the 'ground rules' (which vary from country to country). If you follow the rules your chances of being a victim of crime are usually low – but break the rules and they rise dramatically. These include avoiding high-risk areas, particularly those frequented by drug addicts, prostitutes and pickpockets. When you're in an unfamiliar city, ask a tourist office official, policeman, taxi driver or other local person whether there are any unsafe neighbourhoods – and avoid them! As with most things in life, prevention is better than cure. This is particularly true when it comes to crime prevention, as only a relatively small percentage of crimes are solved and the legal process in many countries is agonisingly slow. It's also important to have adequate insurance for your possessions.

Crime Prevention & Safety

Staying safe in a large city is largely a matter of common sense (plus a little luck), although you need to develop survival skills in some cities. Most areas are safe most of the time, particularly when there are a lot of people about. At night, stick to brightly lit main streets and avoid secluded areas (best of all, take a cab). Walk in the opposite direction to the traffic so no one can curb crawl (drive alongside) you at night and walk on the outside of the pavement (sidewalk), so you're less likely to be mugged from a doorway. Avoid parks at night and keep to a park's main paths or where there are other people during the day.

If you find yourself in a deserted area late at night, remain calm and look as though you know where you're going by walking briskly. If you need to wait for a train or bus at night, do so in a main waiting room, a well lit area, or where there's a guard or policeman. If possible, avoid using subways in the late evening. Most major cities have 'no-go' areas at night and some have areas that are to be avoided at any time. Women should take particular care and should never hitch-hike alone; rape statistics are extremely high in some countries and most go unreported.

It's advisable to carry the bare minimum of cash on you, say GB£10 to GB£30 (ca. US$20 to US$50), referred to as 'mugger's money' in the USA. This is because in the event that you're mugged, it's usually sufficient to satisfy a mugger and prevent him from becoming violent (or searching further). In some countries, parents give their children mugger's money as a matter of course whenever they leave home.

Some experts advise you to carry your cash in at least two separate places and to split cash and credit cards. Don't keep your ID card or passport, driver's licence and other important documents in your wallet or purse where they can be stolen. Never resist a mugger. It's far better to lose your wallet and jewellery than your life! Many muggers are desperate and irrational people under the influence of drugs, and they may turn violent if resisted. Anaesthetic sprays sold in drugstores or ordinary hair or insect sprays are carried by some people to deter assailants (as are pepper sprays and mace, although usually illegal). These are, however, of little use against an armed assailant and may increase the likelihood of violence.

Don't leave cash, cheques, credit cards, passports, jewellery and other 'valuables' lying around or even hidden in your home (the crooks know all the hiding places). Good-quality door and window locks and an alarm will help, but may not deter a determined thief. In many cities, triple door locks, metal bars and steel bars on windows are standard fittings. If you live in a city, you should be wary of anyone hanging around outside your home or apartment block. Have your keys ready and enter your home as quick as possible. Most city dwellers always lock their doors and windows, even when going out for a few minutes only.

Often apartments are fitted with a security system, so that you can speak to visitors before allowing them access to your building. Luxury apartment buildings may have (armed) guards in the lobby with closed-circuit TV and voice identification security systems. In addition, most apartment doors have a peephole and security chain, so you can check a caller's identity before opening the door. Be careful who you allow into your home and check the identity of anyone claiming to be an official inspector or an employee of a utility company. Ask for ID and confirm it with their office before opening the door. Also beware of bogus policemen (they may flash an imitation badge), who may stop you in the street and ask to see your money and passport – and then run off with them!

Store anything of value in a home safe or a bank safety deposit box and ensure that you have adequate insurance. Never make it obvious that no one is at home by leaving tell-tale signs such as a pile of newspapers or mail. Many people leave lights, a radio or a TV on (activated by random timers) when they aren't at home. Ask your neighbours to keep an eye on your home when you're on holiday. Many towns have 'crime watch' areas, where residents keep an eye open for suspicious characters and report them to the local police.

If you're driving, keep to the main highways and avoid high-risk areas. Never drive in cities with your windows or doors open or valuables (such as handbags or wallets) on the seats. Take extra care at night in car parks and when returning to your car, and never sleep in your car. If you have an accident in a dangerous or hostile area (any inner-city area), police often advise you not to stop, but to drive to the nearest police station to report it. In remote areas, accidents are sometimes staged to rob unsuspecting drivers (called 'highway hold-ups') and cars are deliberately bumped to get drivers to stop; again, don't stop but seek out the nearest police station. Thieves may stop in front of you to prevent you driving away; if this happens you should reverse and get away as fast as you can! If you stop at an accident in a remote area or are flagged down, keep the engine running and in gear and your doors locked (ready to make a fast getaway), and only open your window a fraction to speak to someone. Be aware, however, that they're likely to immediately smash the window if they're crooks. Note that in some countries rental cars are targeted by muggers and you should be wary of collecting a rental car from an airport at night.

In many countries, police forces, governments, local communities and security companies all publish information and advice regarding crime prevention, and your local police station may also carry out a free home security check. See also **Car Security** on page 37 and **Home Security** on page 63.

CULTURE SHOCK

'Culture shock' is the term used to describe the psychological and physical state felt by foreigners when they relocate abroad. Culture shock can also be regarded as the period of adjustment to a new country. The symptoms are essentially psychological and are caused by the sense of alienation you feel when you're bombarded on a daily basis with cultural differences in an environment where there are few, if any, familiar references. There are, however, also physical symptoms that may manifest themselves in the form of an increased incidence of minor illnesses (e.g. colds and headaches) or more serious psychosomatic illnesses brought on by depression. Culture shock takes a number of forms, but is typically as follows:

● The first stage is known by expatriates as the 'honeymoon stage' and usually lasts from a few days to a few weeks after arrival. This stage is essentially a positive one, when a newly-arrived expatriate finds everything is an exciting and interesting novelty. This feeling is similar to that of being on holiday.

● The second stage is usually completely opposite to the first and is essentially negative and a period of crisis, as the initial excitement and holiday feeling wears off and the expatriate starts daily life, except of course that this daily life is nothing like any he has previously experienced. This crisis is characterised by a general feeling of disorientation and confusion as well as loneliness. Physical exhaustion brought on by jet lag, extremes of hot or cold, and the strain of having hundreds of settling-in tasks to do is an important physical symptom of this stage.

● The third stage is sometimes known as the 'flight' stage (because of the overwhelming desire to escape) and is usually the one that lasts the longest and is the most difficult to cope with. During this period the expatriate feels depressed and angry, as well as resentful towards the new country and its people. Depression is worsened by the fact that at this stage you can see nothing positive or good about the new country and focus exclusively on the negative aspects of the relocation, refusing to acknowledge any positive points.

It's generally agreed that the period of readjustment lasts around six months, although there are expatriates who adjust earlier and those who never get over the 'flight' stage and are forced to return home. Experts agree that all expatriates suffer from culture shock and there's no escaping the phenomenon, although its negative effects can be reduced and there are certain things you can do about it before you relocate:

● The key to reducing the negative effects of culture shock is a positive attitude towards your retirement country – if you don't look forward to the move, you should question why you're doing it!

● Discover as much as possible about your chosen retirement country before you go, so that your arrival and settling-in period aren't quite as much of a surprise as they might be. There are literally hundreds of publications about all countries as well as numerous websites designed for expatriates (see **Appendix C**). Many websites provide access to expatriates, already living in a country, who can answer questions and provide useful help and advice. There are also 'notice boards' on some websites where you can post a message or question. Before you go, try to find someone in your local area who has visited the country and talk to them about it. Some companies organise briefings for families before departure. **Most importantly, you should visit and get to know the country where you're planning to retire before making the leap. Rent a property before buying a home and don't burn your bridges until you're sure you've made the correct decision!**

● **Learn the language.** As well as a positive attitude, overcoming the language barrier will probably be the most decisive factor in your time abroad. The ability to speak the local language isn't just a practical and useful tool (the one that will allow you to buy what you need, find your way around, etc.), but it's also the key to understanding a country and its culture. If you can speak the local language, even at a low level, your scope for possible friends and acquaintances is immediately widened beyond the usual limited expatriate circle. Obviously not everyone is a linguist and learning a language can take time and requires motivation. However, with sufficient motivation and perseverance virtually anyone can learn enough of another language to participate in the local culture. Certainly the effort pays off and expatriates who manage to overcome the language barrier find their experience abroad decidedly richer and more exciting than those who don't. If you make an effort at communicating with the local people in their own language, the chances are that you'll also find them far more receptive to you and your needs.

● Make a conscious effort to get involved in the new culture. There are often plenty of local clubs where you can practise sport or keep fit, join an arts club, learn to cook local dishes, taste wine, etc. Not only will this fill some of your spare time, giving you less time to miss home, but you'll also meet new people and make friends. If you feel you cannot join a local club, perhaps because the language barrier is too great, then you can always participate in activities for expatriates, of which there are usually many in the most popular retirement destinations.

- Talk to other expatriates. Although they may deny it, they've all been through exactly what you have and faced the same feeling of disorientation. Even if they may not be able to provide you with advice, it helps to know that you aren't alone and that it gets better in the end.

Culture shock is an unavoidable part of retiring abroad, but if you're aware of it and take steps to lessen its effects before you go and while you're abroad, the chances are that the period of adjustment will be shortened and its negative and depressing consequences reduced.

There are a number of books designed to help you understand and overcome culture shock, including *Breaking Through Culture Shock – How to Survive an International Assignment*, Dr. Elizabeth Marx (Nicolas Brealey), which although intended for employees is useful for anyone. Many expatriate websites also offer advice and help, including many of those listed in **Appendix C**.

HOME HELP

If you spend long periods at a home abroad or live abroad permanently, you may wish to employ someone to help around the home such as a cleaner, housekeeper, maid, nanny, cook, gardener, chauffeur, nurse or baby-sitter. This can cost just a few dollars an hour or even a day in some countries, although you should avoid exploitation. If you need or wish to hire a full-time employee, there are, however, a number of important points to take into consideration. These may include work and residence permits, employment contracts, working conditions, minimum wages, holidays and time off, income tax and social security; meals, room and board, dismissal, redundancy payments, and accident and health insurance.

In most countries there are strict regulations concerning the employment of full-time domestic staff, including minimum salaries, time off and paid holidays. Minimum salaries may vary considerably according to the nationality, age and experience of an employee. You may have to apply for a work or residence permit and pay an employee's pension, accident and health insurance (or part). It may also be necessary to deduct tax at source from your employee's income (including lodging and meals, if part of his salary) and complete all the associated official paper work. In many countries, an employer and a domestic employee must have a written contract of employment, and if there's no written contract the law may assume that there's a verbal agreement for a minimum period, e.g. one year. If you break the law regarding the hiring and firing of employees, an employee may have redress to a labour court, which can result in a substantial compensation award.

Most regulations apply to full-time staff only and not to temporary staff employed for less than a specified number of hours per week, e.g. 15 or 20. In many countries you should ensure that employees are covered by social security, as you can be held responsible should they have an accident on your property. Always ask to see an employee's social security card and obtain legal advice if you're unsure of your obligations under the law. Note that if you're found to be employing someone who isn't paying social security (and income tax), you can be heavily fined and may have to pay any unpaid social security payments.

In some countries you should ask for a written quotation from temporary staff stating the work to be done and the cost, as this will then make them legally responsible for their own insurance and social security. Note that, although there are statutory minimum wages in many countries for full-time employees, you may have to pay a higher rate for a temporary employee who's employed by the hour, half-day or day. Enquire among your neighbours and friends to find out the going rate, as if you pay too much you could find yourself unpopular. If you need to hire someone who speaks English or another 'foreign' (non-local) language, you may need to pay a premium.

PETS

If you plan to take a pet abroad, it's important to check the latest regulations. Make sure that you have the correct papers, not only for your country of destination, but for all the countries you will pass through to reach it, e.g. when travelling overland. Particular consideration must be given before exporting a pet from a country with strict quarantine regulations, such as the UK. If you need to return prematurely, even after a few hours or days abroad, your pet may need to go into quarantine, e.g. for six months in the UK (but see **British Pet Owners** on page 131).

Many other countries in addition to the UK operate a quarantine period (e.g. Australia), which may be in the owner's own home, and some (such as the UK and Sweden) have a pet's passport scheme. Most countries require pets to have a health certificate, issued by an approved veterinary surgeon, and vaccination certificates for rabies and possibly other diseases. A rabies vaccination must usually be given not less than 20 days or more than 11 months prior to the date of issue of the health certificate. Pets aged under 12 weeks are usually exempt, but must have a health certificate and a certificate stating that no cases of rabies have occurred for at least six months in the local area. Note that there's no quarantine period (or only a token one) in many countries when pets are exported from countries without rabies.

If you're transporting a pet by ship or ferry, you should notify the shipping company. Some companies insist that pets are left in vehicles (if applicable), while others allow pets to be kept in cabins. If your pet is of nervous disposition or unused to travelling, it's best to tranquillise it on a long sea crossing. Pets can also be transported by air (contact airlines for information) and there are specialist companies in some countries. Animals may be examined at the port of entry by a veterinary officer in the country of destination.

In many countries, pets must be registered and may be issued with a disc to be worn on a collar around their neck, while others require dogs to be tattooed on their body or in an ear as a means of registration. In recent years, some countries have introduced a microchip identification system for dogs (which has replaced tattooing), whereby a microchip is inserted under the skin. Registration can be expensive, particularly if you have more than one dog. Irrespective of whether your dog is tattooed or micro-chipped, it's advisable to have it fitted with a collar and tag with your name and telephone number on it and the magic word 'reward'. Most countries have rules regarding the keeping of dogs, which may require a health card if they're older than three months. In public areas, a dog may need to be kept on a lead (and muzzled if it's dangerous) and wear a health disc on its collar. Dogs are often prohibited from entering places where food is manufactured, stored or sold, and may also be barred from sports and cultural events, and banned from beaches.

If you intend to live abroad permanently, dogs should also be vaccinated against certain other diseases in addition to rabies, which may include hepatitis, distemper and kennel cough. Cats should be immunised against feline gastro-enteritis and typhus. Pets should also be checked frequently for ticks and tapeworm. Note that there are a number of diseases and dangers for pets in some countries that aren't found in North America and Northern Europe. For example, in Spain there are a number of diseases and dangers for pets, some of which aren't found in most other European countries. These include the fatal leishmaniasis (also called Mediterranean or sandfly disease), which can be prevented by using a spray such as Defend Dog, processionary caterpillars, leeches, heartworm, ticks (a tick collar can prevent these), feline leukaemia virus and feline enteritis. Obtain advice about these and other diseases from a veterinary surgeon in your home country or on arrival abroad. Take extra care when walking your dog in country areas, as hunters sometimes put down poisoned food to control natural predators. Don't let your dog far out of your sight or let it roam free, as dogs may be stolen or mistakenly shot by hunters.

Health insurance for pets is available in most countries (vet fees can be astronomical) and it's advisable to have third-party insurance in case your pet bites someone or causes an accident. In areas where there are poisonous snakes, some owners keep anti-venom in their refrigerator (which must be changed annually). Note that in some countries the keeping of dogs may be restricted or banned from long-term rental or holiday accommodation (so check when renting an apartment). Some countries also have strict laws regarding cleaning up after pets in public places (so called 'poop-scoop' laws) and you can be heavily fined for not doing so.

Veterinary surgeons are well trained in most countries, where there are also kennels, catteries and animal hospitals and clinics, which may provide a 24-hour emergency service, and even pet cemeteries. There are also animal welfare organisations in many countries which operate shelters for stray and abused animals, and inexpensive pet hospitals.

British Pet Owners

On 28th March 2000, the UK introduced a pilot 'Pet Travel Scheme (PETS)' which replaced quarantine for qualifying cats and dogs. Under the scheme, pets must be micro-chipped (they have a microchip inserted in their neck), vaccinated against rabies, undergo a blood test and be issued with a 'health certificate' ('passport'). **Note that the PETS certificate isn't issued until six months *after* the above have been carried out!** Pets must also be checked for ticks and tapeworm 24 to 48 hours before embarkation on a plane or ship.

The scheme is restricted to animals imported from rabies-free countries and countries where rabies is under control – initially 24 European countries (the 15 European Union (EU) countries plus Andorra, Gibraltar, Iceland, Liechtenstein, Monaco, Norway, San Marino, Switzerland and the Vatican), but has now been extended to Australia, New Zealand, Cyprus, Malta and a number of other rabies-free islands. It may also be extended to North America, although the current quarantine law will remain in place for pets coming from Eastern Europe, Africa, Asia and South America. The new regulations cost pet owners around GB£200 (for a microchip, rabies vaccination and blood test), plus GB£60 per year for annual booster vaccinations and around GB£20 for a border check. Shop around and compare fees from a number of veterinary surgeons. To qualify, pets must travel by sea via Dover or Portsmouth, by train via the Channel Tunnel or via London Heathrow airport (only certain carriers are licensed to carry animals and they can usually take only one animal per flight). Additional information is available from the Department of the Environment, Food and Rural Affairs (DEFRA, formerly MAFF, ☎ UK 0845-933 5577, ✉ pets.helpline@defra.gsi.gov.uk).

British owners must complete an Application for a Ministry Export Certificate for dogs, cats and other rabies-susceptible animals (form EXA1), available from the DEFRA, Animal Health (International Trade) Division B, Hook Rise South, Tolworth, Surbiton, Surrey KT6 7NF, UK (☎ 020-8330 4411). A health inspection must be performed by a licensed veterinary officer before you're issued with an export health certificate valid for 30 days.

RELIGION

Most countries have a tradition of religious tolerance and citizens and foreigners alike generally have total freedom of religion without hindrance by the state or community. Nevertheless, in some countries certain sects have been declared to be dangerous to the community and have been banned. Note that there have been violent clashes between religious groups, notably in Israel and Palestine between Muslims and Jews (which are ongoing), in Indonesia between Muslims and Christians, and in the Balkans, which have resulted in civil wars and massacres. You should be aware of any religious tensions in a country where you're planning to live and how it will affect your lifestyle.

It's necessary to take care not to offend anyone's religion and to be careful what you wear when visiting religious sites and holy places, where there are often strict rules regarding dress (particularly in Muslim countries). Note also that many Muslim countries ban alcohol (its importation and consumption), the importation of certain literature and videos, and there are severe penalties for blasphemy against the Islamic religion.

SAFETY

It's important to be aware of anything that's happening in a country where you're planning to retire that could affect your personal safety, such as wars, riots, military coups, terrorism, kidnappings and general civil unrest, to name but a few. You also need to be aware of crime and drugs (see page 121), health (see **Chapter 4**), motoring problems (see page 38), and how to deal with local officials and matters such as bribery and corruption, which is a way of life in some countries. If you have any problems concerning safety while abroad, you should contact your local consulate or embassy for advice. If you register with your local embassy (see page 151) they will contact you in times of serious civil unrest or wars and may assist you in returning home (if necessary).

Most governments post warnings on official websites for their nationals, which, in many cases, apply to all travellers and can (of course) be referred to by anyone. These include the US Department of State (🖥 http://travel.state. gov/travel_warnings. html and http://travel.state.gov/warnings_list.html); this website also contains warnings about drugs (🖥http://travel.state.gov/ drug_warning.html) and a list of useful travel publications (🖥 http://travel. state.gov/travel_pubs.html). Other useful websites include the British Foreign and Commonwealth Office (🖥 www.fco.gov.uk/travel), Gov Spot (🖥 www. govspot.com/ask/travel.htm), SaveWealth Travel (🖥 www.save wealth.com/ travel/warnings), and the Australian Department of Foreign Affairs and Trade (🖥 www.dfat.gov.au/consular/advice/advices_mnu.html).

There are also a number of books about safety for travellers, these include *World Wise – Your Passport to Safer Travel*, Suzy Lamplugh (Thomas Cook). Safety information may also be available via your local television Teletext service (e.g. BBC2 Ceefax page 470+ in the UK).

Where applicable, warnings are also included under **Political Stability** or **Crime Rate** in the Country Profiles (**Chapter 8**), although these aren't comprehensive and are intended only as a guide.

SHOPPING ABROAD

Shopping by mail-order, phone, fax or via the Internet is popular among retirees in many countries, particularly those where it's difficult or impossible to buy many western goods (or they're prohibitively expensive). Direct retailing by companies (cutting out the middle man) has become much more widespread in recent years and many companies sell goods and services by mail, often via their own websites.

Many major stores publish catalogues and will send goods anywhere in the world, particularly American and British stores. Many companies provide account facilities or payment can be made by credit card. Buying goods mail-order from the USA can result in huge savings, even after paying postage and local taxes. Companies of interest to avid mail-order shoppers include Catalog Link (🖥 www.cataloglink.com), which has a comprehensive index of catalogues from around the world, and the Buyer's Index (🖥 www.buyersindex.com).

Internet Shopping: Retailers and manufacturers in most countries offer Internet shopping, but the real benefit comes, when shopping abroad, when savings can be made on a wide range of products (you can buy virtually anything via the Internet). On the other hand, when comparing prices, take into account shipping costs, insurance, duty and VAT. Shopping on the Internet is generally secure (secure servers, with addresses beginning https://rather than http://, are almost impossible to crack) and in most cases safer than shopping by phone or mail-order. **It isn't, however, guaranteed and credit card fraud is a growing problem.**

To find companies or products via the Internet, simply use a search engine such as Altavista, Google or Yahoo. Useful websites include:

🖥 www.myprimetime.com;

🖥 www.pricewatch.com;

🖥 www.mytaxi.co.uk (which contains the Internet addresses of 2,500 world-wide retail and information sites);

🖥 www.amazingemporium.co.uk;

🖥 www.abargain.co.uk;

⌨ www.myamericanmarket.com;

⌨ www.shopsmart.com;

⌨ www.buy.com;

⌨ www.iwanttoshop.com;

⌨ www.shopguide.co.uk;

⌨ www.grouptrade.com;

⌨ www.euroffice.co.uk;

⌨ www.virgin.net/shopping/index.html (which has a good directory of British shopping sites).

Many websites offer online auctions, such as:

⌨ www.ebay.com (and ⌨ www.ebay.co.uk);

⌨ www.loot.com;

⌨ www.qxl.com;

⌨ www.auctions.yahoo.com.

With Internet shopping the world is literally your oyster and savings can be made on a wide range of goods, including books, CDs, clothes, sports equipment, electronic gadgets, jewellery, wine and computer software, and services such as insurance, pensions and mortgages. Savings can also be made on holidays and travel. Small, high-price, high-tech items (e.g. cameras, watches and portable and hand-held computers) can usually be purchased cheaper somewhere abroad, particularly in the USA, with delivery by courier worldwide within as little as three days.

When buying goods overseas, you should ensure that you're dealing with a bona fide company and that they will work in your country of residence (e.g. electrical equipment or video games). You should also check the vendor's returns policy. Note that you may not be protected by consumer protection legislation when shopping abroad and should anything go wrong it can take eons to get it resolved. If possible, always pay by credit card when buying by mail-order or over the Internet, as you have more security and the credit card issuer may be jointly liable with the supplier. **When you buy expensive goods abroad, always have them insured for their full value.**

When you purchase a large item abroad, it's advisable to have it shipped by air freight to the nearest international airport. The receiving freight company will notify you when it has arrived and you must usually provide them with details of the contents and cost so that they can clear it through customs. They will deliver the goods to you with the bill for taxes, duty and freight, payable on the spot, unless you make alternative arrangements.

Taxes & Duty: When buying overseas, take into account shipping costs, duty, VAT and other taxes. Carefully calculate the total cost in local currency or the currency in which you're paying – you can do this with the universal currency converter (🖳 www.xe.com/ucc). If you live in an EU country, there's no duty or tax on goods purchased within the EU. Most countries levy no taxes on goods imported from abroad below a certain nominal value (e.g. GB£18 in the UK). Don't buy alcohol or cigarettes abroad, as the duty is usually too high to make it pay (and it may be illegal!). When VAT or duty is payable on a parcel, the payment is usually collected by the post office or courier company on delivery.

SOCIAL CUSTOMS

All countries have their own particular social customs, standards of behaviour and rules, which may be based on class, tradition, race or religion. People are much more formal in some countries than in others – particularly more so than most English-speaking countries – and newcomers should tread carefully to avoid offending anyone. Good manners, politeness and consideration for others are important in all countries. As a foreigner you will probably be excused if you accidentally insult your hosts, but you may not be invited again! Some pointers are listed below:

● When introduced to someone you generally follow the cue of the person performing the introduction, i.e. if someone is introduced as Tom you can usually call him Tom, but if someone is introduced as Lord Montague Downton-Cuddlethorpe, it may not be wise to address him as 'Cuddles' (unless he asks you to!). Most people will usually say 'Please call me Tom', after a short time (unless his name happens to be Montague). Note that in many countries it's customary to use a person's title (e.g. doctor, reverend, professor, general or president) when addressing or writing to them, particularly when the title holder is elderly.

● After you've been introduced to someone, you usually say something (in the local language, if you can) such as 'How do you do?', 'Pleased to meet you', 'My pleasure' or 'Delighted' and shake hands. When saying goodbye, it's customary in some countries to shake hands again. In formal circles, gentlemen may be expected to bow and kiss the back of a lady's hand, while in informal gatherings strangers are more inclined to limply shake hands. In many countries it's traditional for men to kiss ladies on the cheek (or once on either cheek) and women may also follow this custom when greeting other women. Men may also kiss and embrace each other in some countries, although this isn't usual among westerners.

- When talking to a stranger, in many languages (e.g. French, German, Italian, Spanish, etc.) you should use the formal form of address and not use the familiar form or call someone by their Christian name until you're invited to do so. Generally, the older or more important person will invite the other to use the familiar form of address and first names. The familiar form is used with children, animals and God, but almost never with your elders or officials. People in many countries are, however, becoming less formal and younger people often use the familiar form and first names with colleagues, unless they're of the opposite sex, when it may imply a special intimacy! It's customary to use the formal form of address in conversations with shopkeepers, servants, business associates and figures of authority (the local mayor), or those with whom you have a business relationship, e.g. your bank manager, tax officials and policemen.

- Some people are a lot more casual than others and more direct in asking questions and voicing their opinions. For example, don't be surprised if an Australian or American gives you the third degree when you meet for the first time. It's nothing personal – they're just being curious and are genuinely interested in strangers.

- If you're invited to dinner, it's customary in most countries to take a small present of flowers, a plant, chocolates or a bottle of wine. Flowers can be tricky: as to some people, carnations mean bad luck, chrysanthemums are for cemeteries and roses signify love. Maybe you should stick to plastic, silk or dried flowers, or a nice bunch of weeds! Wine can also be a problem, particularly if you're a miser and bring a bottle of cheap plonk and your hosts are wine connoisseurs (they almost certainly won't invite you again!). It's customary in some countries to serve wine brought by guests at the meal, although don't expect your hosts to serve your cheap red (particularly if they're serving fish). If you stay with someone as a guest for a few days, it may also be usual to give your host or hostess a small gift when you leave.

- Many people say 'good appetite' before starting a meal. If you're offered a glass of wine, you should wait until your host has made a toast before taking a drink. If you aren't offered a (another) drink, it's time to go home. You should, however, go easy on the wine and other alcohol, as if you drink to excess you're unlikely to be invited back!

- When planning a party, it's polite to notify your neighbours (and perhaps invite them if they're particularly attractive/interesting!).

- In many countries people dress well and formally, and presentation and impression are all important. They may judge people by their dress, the style and quality being as important as the correctness for the occasion. Bathing costumes, skimpy tops and flip-flops or sandals without socks are considered strictly for the beach or swimming pool in many countries, and not, for example, the streets, restaurants or shops (although foreigners and their 'eccentric' behaviour are usually tolerated). Locals may also carefully choose the occasions when they wear jeans, which aren't usually considered appropriate for a classy restaurant or church (even if they're the latest designer fashion). When going anywhere that may be remotely formal (or particularly informal), it's wise to ask in advance what you're expected to wear. Usually when dress is formal, such as evening dress or dinner jacket, it's stated in the invitation and you'll be unlikely to be admitted if you turn up in the wrong attire. If you're invited to a wedding, enquire about the dress, unless you want to stick out like a sore thumb. In many countries, black or dark dress is usually worn at funerals.

● In most countries, guests are expected to be punctual, with the exception of certain society parties when late arrival is *de rigueur* (unless you arrive after the celebrity guest!) and at weddings (when the bride is often late). Dinner invitations may be phrased as 8pm for 8.30pm, which means arrive at 8pm for drinks and dinner will be served (usually promptly) at 8.30pm. Anyone who arrives extremely late for dinner (unless his house has burnt down) or horror of horrors, doesn't turn up at all (when death is a good excuse), should expect to be excluded from future guest lists. If you're confused by a multitude of knives, forks and spoons (the rule is to start at the outside and work in), don't panic, but just copy what your neighbour is doing. If he is another ignorant foreigner, you will at least have some company in the social wilderness to which you will both be consigned.

● You should introduce yourself before asking to speak to someone on the telephone. In many countries, local people have a siesta in the afternoon and it isn't advisable to telephone during the siesta hours (e.g. 2 to 4pm). If you call between these times it's polite to apologise for disturbing the household if you know people are likely to be having a siesta (particularly very young children and elderly people).

● If you have a business appointment with a foreigner he'll usually expect you to be on time, although he may be five or ten minutes late. However, if *you're* going to be more than five minutes late, it's advisable to telephone and apologise. Note that people in many countries exchange business cards on business and social occasions.

TELEVISION & RADIO

Although most people complain endlessly about the poor quality of television (TV) programmes in their home countries, many find they cannot live without a TV when they're abroad. Fortunately the growth of satellite TV in the last few decades has enabled people to enjoy TV programmes in English and a variety of other languages almost anywhere in the world. Cable TV is also available in many countries, and often includes English-language stations such as BBC World News, CNN and Sky News. The quality of local radio (including expatriate stations in some countries) is generally excellent, and if you have a high quality receiver (or a satellite TV system) it's possible to receive radio stations from around the globe. Note that a TV licence is required in many countries and a separate radio licence may also be necessary.

Television

The standards for TV reception **aren't the same in all countries**. For example, TVs and video cassette recorders (VCRs) operating on the PAL system or the North American NTSC system won't function in France and TVs manufactured for a foreign market won't operate in North America. Most western European countries use the PAL B/G standard, except for the UK, which uses a modified PAL-I system that's incompatible with other European countries. France has its own standard called SECAM-L, which is different from the SECAM standard used elsewhere in the world, e.g. SECAM B/G in the Middle East and North African countries, and SECAM D/K in some eastern European and many African countries.

If you want a TV that will operate in France and other European countries, and a VCR that will play both PAL and SECAM videos, you must buy a multi-standard TV and VCR. These are widely available in some countries and contain automatic circuitry that switches from PAL-I (the UK), to PAL-B/G (rest of Europe) to SECAM-L (France). Some multi-standard TVs also incorporate the North American NTSC standard and have an NTSC-in jack plug connection allowing you to play American videos. If you have a PAL TV it's also possible to buy a SECAM to PAL trans-coder that converts SECAM signals to PAL. Some people opt for two TVs, one to receive local programmes or satellite TV and another to play their favourite videos. A British or US video recorder won't work with a French TV unless it's dual-standard (with SECAM), and, although you can play back a SECAM video on a PAL VCR, the picture will be in black and white. **Generally it's simpler just to buy a new TV and video locally!**

Cable TV: Cable TV is available in many countries, particularly in North America and Western Europe, where some countries (such as Belgium, Holland and Switzerland) have around 90 per cent coverage. There are a number of cable TV companies in most countries, although if you live in an apartment or townhouse with a communal aerial you'll usually be billed automatically for the services of the communal satellite TV service (unless you have no TV). All you need to do to receive cable TV is connect your TV aerial to a special wall socket. Cable TV consists of cable relays of local and foreign TV stations, dedicated cable-only stations and satellite stations. The number of stations available varies and may run from 20 to over 100, according to the package you (or your community/development) choose. In Europe, English-language cable TV stations are widely available and include BBC World News, Bloomberg, CNBC, CNN, Eurosport, ITN News, MTV and Sky News. In addition to unscrambled TV channels, scrambled TV channels are available in many areas. Like some satellite TV stations (see below), you require a decoder (which can be hired from and installed by most TV shops) to receive some stations and must pay a monthly subscription. Cable companies also offer pay-per-view services, where you pay to watch a particular live event, such as a sporting event or concert.

International Satellite TV: Wherever you live in the world it's likely that you will be able to receive satellite TV, although the signal strength and number of stations that can be received will depend on your equipment and your exact location. But note, that in some countries the use of satellite receivers is banned, as the nervous local authorities don't want their citizens to be influenced by 'subversive' foreign TV broadcasts. Europe is best served by satellite TV, where a number of geo-stationary satellites carry hundreds of TV channels broadcasting in a variety of languages.

Europe: Satellite TV has proved popular in Europe in recent years, particularly in countries and regions where there's no cable TV. Although it wasn't the first in Europe (which was Eutelsat), the European satellite revolution took off with the launch of the Astra 1A satellite in 1988 (operated by the Luxembourg-based Société Européenne des Satellites or SES), positioned 36,000km (22,300mi) above the earth. TV addicts are offered a huge choice of English and foreign-language stations, which can be received throughout most of Europe (the dish size required varies). Since 1988 a number of additional Astra satellites have been launched, increasing the number of available channels to 64 (or over 200 with digital TV). An added bonus is the availability of radio stations via satellite, including the major BBC stations (see **Satellite Radio** on page 143).

Among the many English-language stations available on Astra are Sky One, Movimax, Sky Premier, Sky Cinema, Film Four, Sky News, Sky Sports (three channels), UK Gold, Channel 5, Granada Plus, TNT, Eurosport, CNN, CNBC Europe, UK Style, UK Horizons, the Disney Channel and the Discovery Channel. Other stations broadcast in Dutch, German, Japanese, Swedish and various Indian languages. The signal from many stations is scrambled (the decoder is usually built into the receiver) and viewers must pay a monthly subscription fee to receive programmes. You can buy pirate decoders for some channels. The best served by clear (unscrambled) stations are German-speakers (most German stations on Astra are clear).

BSkyB TV: You must buy a receiver with a Videocrypt decoder and pay a monthly subscription to receive BSkyB or Sky stations, except Sky News (which isn't scrambled). Various packages are available costing from around

GB£12 to around GB£35 a month for the premium package offering all movie channels plus Sky Sports. To receive scrambled channels such as Movimax and Sky Sports, you need an address in the UK or Ireland. Subscribers are sent a coded 'smart' card (similar to a credit card), which must be inserted in the decoder to activate it (cards are periodically updated to thwart counterfeiters). Sky won't send smart cards to overseas viewers as they have the copyright only for a British-based audience (expatriates will need to obtain a card through a friend or relative in the UK). Satellite companies (some of which advertise in the expatriate press) can in most countries, however, supply genuine BSkyB cards.

Digital TV: English-language digital satellite TV was launched on 1st October 1998 by BSkyB in the UK. The benefits include a superior picture, better (CD) quality sound, wide-screen cinema format and access to many more stations, including around ten stations showing nothing but movies. To watch digital TV you require a Digibox and a (digital) dish, which can be purchased at a subsidised price by customers in the UK and Ireland. Customers have to sign up for a 12-month subscription and agree to have the connection via a phone line (to allow for future interactive services). In addition to the usual analogue channels (see above), BSkyB digital provides BBC 1, BBC 2, ITV3, Channel 4 and Channel 5, plus many digital channels (a total of 200 with up to 500 possible later). Ondigital launched a rival digital service on 15th November 1998, which although it's cheaper, provides a total of just 30 channels (15 free and 15 subscription), including BBC 1 and 2, ITV3, Channel 4 and Channel 5. The future of Ondigital is, however, in doubt, because of heavy losses. Digital satellite equipment is offered by a number of satellite companies throughout Europe (although getting a Sky Card isn't easy). Further information about BSkyB digital is available on the Internet (🖥 www.digiguide.co.uk).

Eutelsat: Eutelsat was the first company to introduce satellite TV to Europe (in 1983) and it runs a fleet of communications satellites carrying TV stations to over 50 million homes. Until 1995, they broadcast primarily advertising-based, clear-access cable channels, but, following the launch in March 1995 of their Hot Bird 1 satellite, Eutelsat hoped to become a major competitor to Astra, although its channels are mostly non-English. The English-language stations on Eutelsat include Eurosport, BBC World and CNBC. Other stations broadcast in Arabic, French, German, Hungarian, Italian, Polish, Portuguese, Spanish and Turkish.

BBC World-wide Television: The BBC's commercial subsidiary, BBC World-wide Television, broadcasts two 24-hour channels: BBC Prime (general entertainment) and BBC World (24-hour news and information), transmitted via the Eutelsat Hotbird 5 satellite (13 deg. East). BBC World is unencrypted (clear) while BBC Prime is encrypted and requires a D2-MAC decoder and a smart card, available on subscription from BBC Prime, PO Box

5054, London W12 0ZY, UK (☎ 020-8433 2221, ▤ 020-8433 3040, ⊠ bbc prime@bbc.co.uk). For further information and a programming guide, contact BBC World-wide Television, Woodlands, 80 Wood Lane, London W12 0TT, UK (☎ 020-8576 2555). A programme guide is also available on the Internet (▤ www.bbc.co.uk/schedules) and both BBC World and BBC Prime have their own websites (▤ www.bbcworld.com and www.bbc prime.com). When accessing them, you need to enter the name of the country so that schedules are displayed in local time.

Equipment: A satellite receiver should have a built-in Videocrypt decoder (and others such as Eurocrypt, Syster or SECAM if required) and be capable of receiving satellite stereo radio. A system with an 85cm (34in) dish (to receive Astra stations) costs from around GB£200 or US$300, plus installation, which may be included in the price. A digital system is more expensive, for example a BskyB system costs around GB£650 or US$1,000 in most European countries (excluding the UK and Ireland). Shop around as prices vary considerably. With a 1.2m (4ft) or 1.5m (5ft) motorised dish, you can receive hundreds of stations in a multitude of languages from around the world. If you wish to receive satellite TV on two or more TVs, you can buy a satellite system with two or more receptors. To receive stations from two or more satellites simultaneously, you require a motorised dish or a dish with a double feed antenna (dual LNBs). There are satellite sales and installation companies in most countries, some of which advertise in the expatriate press. Shop around and compare prices. Alternatively, you can import your own satellite dish and receiver and install it yourself. **Before buying a system, ensure that it can receive programmes from all existing and planned satellites.**

Location: To receive programmes from any satellite, there mustn't be any obstacles between the satellite and your dish, i.e. no trees, buildings or mountains must obstruct the signal, so it's wise to check this before renting or buying a home. It's also recommended, before buying or erecting a satellite dish, that you check whether you need permission from your landlord, development or local council. Some towns and buildings (such as apartment blocks) have regulations regarding the positioning of antennae, although in some countries owners can mount a dish almost anywhere without receiving any complaints. Dishes can usually be mounted in a variety of unobtrusive positions and can also be painted or patterned to blend in with the background. Note, on the other hand, that in some countries, private dishes in apartment blocks are prohibited and have been replaced by a single communal antenna with a cable connection to individual homes.

Programme Guides: Many satellite stations provide Teletext information and most broadcast in stereo. Sky satellite programme listings are provided in a number of British publications such as *What Satellite*, *Satellite Times* and *Satellite TV Europe* (the best), which are available on subscription and from local newsagents in some countries. Satellite TV programmes are also listed in expatriate newspapers and magazines in many countries. The annual *World Radio TV Handbook* edited by David G. Bobbett (Watson-Guptill Publications) contains over 600 pages of information and the frequencies of all radio and TV stations world-wide.

Radio

Radio flourishes in most countries, where it's often more popular than TV with a much larger audience. Numerous public and private, local, regional, national and foreign radio stations can be received in most countries, with programme standards ranging from excellent to agonisingly amateurish. There's a wealth of excellent FM (VHF stereo) and AM (medium waveband) stations in the major cities and resort areas in most countries, although in remote rural areas (particularly mountainous areas) it may be difficult to receive any of the FM stations clearly. The long wave (LW) band is not used very much in most countries, although LW stations are available in the UK and Ireland. A Short Wave (SW) radio is useful for receiving international stations.

English & Other Expatriate Stations: There are English-language and other foreign-language commercial radio stations in the major cities and resort areas in many countries, where the emphasis is usually on music and chat with some news. Some expatriate stations broadcast in a variety of languages (not simultaneously), including English, Dutch, German and various Scandinavian languages, at different times of the day. Unfortunately (or inevitably), expatriate radio tries to be all things to all men (and women) and, not surprisingly, usually falls short, particularly with regard to music, where it tries to cater for all tastes. On the other hand, it generally provides a good service and is particularly popular among retirees. The main drawback of expatriate radio (and most commercial radio) is its agonising, amateurish ads, which are obtrusive and repetitive, and make listening a chore. English-language radio and other foreign radio programmes are published in the expatriate press in many countries.

BBC & Other Foreign Stations: The BBC World Service is broadcast on short wave on several frequencies (e.g. short wave 12095, 9760, 9410, 7325, 6195, 5975 and 3955 kHz) simultaneously and you can usually receive a good signal on one of them. The signal strength varies according to where you live, the time of day and year, the power and positioning of your receiver, and atmospheric conditions. The BBC World Service plus BBC Radio 1, 2, 3, 4 and 5 are also available via the Astra (Sky) satellite. For a free BBC World Service programme guide and frequency information, write to BBC World Service (BBC World-wide, PO Box 76, Bush House, Strand, London WC2B 4PH, UK (☎ 020-8752 5040). The BBC publish a monthly magazine, *BBC*

On Air, containing comprehensive programme listing for BBC World Service radio, BBC Prime TV and BBC World TV. It's available on subscription from the BBC (On Air Magazine, Room 207 NW, Bush House, Strand, London WC2B 4PH, UK (☎ 020-7240 4899, ✉ on.air.magazine@bbc.co.uk) and from newsstands in some countries.

Many other foreign stations also publish programme listings and frequency charts for expatriates keen for news from home, including Radio Australia, Radio Canada International, Denmark Radio, Radio Nederland, Radio Sweden International and the Voice of America. Don't forget to check for websites, where you can often download and hear broadcast material as well as view schedules.

Cable & Satellite Radio: If you have cable or satellite TV, you can also receive many radio stations via your cable or satellite link. For example, BBC Radio 1, 2, 3, 4 and 5, BBC World Service, Sky Radio, Virgin 1215 and many foreign-language stations are broadcast via the Astra satellites (see page 139). Satellite radio stations are listed in British satellite TV magazines such as *Satellite Times*. If you're interested in receiving radio stations from further afield, you should obtain a copy of the **World Radio TV Handbook** edited by David G. Bobbett (Watson-Guptill Publications).

TIME DIFFERENCE

When living abroad it's important to be aware of the difference between local time and the time in countries where you have friends or family. World time is calculated as the difference (plus or minus) between Greenwich Mean Time (GMT), which is the time at Greenwich in England from where world time is calculated. Many countries change to 'summer' time in the spring (usually on the last Sunday in March), when people put their clocks forward one hour, and back to 'winter' time in autumn (usually on the last Sunday in October), when clocks are put back one hour. Time changes are announced in local newspapers and on radio and TV, and usually officially take place at 2 or 3am.

In many countries, times in timetables are written using the 24-hour clock, when 10am is written as 10h and 10pm as 22h . Midday is 1200 and midnight is 2400, while 7.30am is written as 07.30. Note, on the other hand, that the 24-hour clock is rarely referred to in speech. In some countries, times are given using the 12-hour clock ('am' and 'pm'), in which case they may be printed in timetables in light type to indicate before noon (am) and in **bold** type to indicate after noon (pm).

When making international telephone calls or travelling long distance by air, you should check the local time difference of the country you are calling or visiting (one way to upset most people is to wake them at 3am). Time differences are usually shown in the 'International Dialling' section of telephone books and they can also be found on numerous websites, including

⌨ www.worldtimeserver.com/country.asp, ⌨ www.timeanddate.com/world clock, ⌨ www.worldtime.com and ⌨ www.worldtimezone.com. Note that many countries have a number of time zones, e.g. Australia has three and continental USA four.

The time difference between the UK (when it's noon GMT) and some major international cities is shown below:

LONDON	CAPE TOWN	BOMBAY	TOKYO	LOS ANGELES	NEW YORK
1200	1400	1730	2100	0400	0700

7.

ARRIVAL & SETTLING IN

On arrival abroad, your first task will be to negotiate immigration and customs. Fortunately this presents few problems for most people, particularly those moving between Canada and the USA or from one European Union (EU) country to another. A visa is, however, required to enter many countries, irrespective of the purpose of your visit. Note that you may also be required to enter via a particular airport, port or land border.

In addition to information about immigration and customs, this chapter contains checklists of tasks to be completed before or soon after arrival abroad and when moving house, plus suggestions for finding local help and information.

Immigration

When you arrive abroad, the first thing you must do is pass through immigration. If you have a single-entry visa it will be cancelled by the immigration official – if you require a visa to enter a country and attempt to enter without one you will be refused entry. Some people may wish to get a stamp in their passport as confirmation of their date of entry into a country. Immigration officials may ask you to produce a return ticket, proof of accommodation, health insurance and financial resources, e.g. cash, travellers' cheques and credit cards. The onus is on you to prove that you're a genuine visitor or retiree and that you won't violate the immigration laws. Immigration officials aren't required to prove that you will break the law and can refuse you entry on the grounds of suspicion. In most countries they're usually polite and efficient, although they're occasionally a little over-zealous in their attempts to exclude illegal immigrants, and certain nationalities or racial groups may experience harassment or even persecution.

Customs

Customs regulations vary considerably according to the country, your nationality, and whether your home country has an agreement with the country where you're planning to live or is a member of an organisation such as the EU or the North American Free Trade Association (NAFTA). The shipment of (household) belongings from one EU country to another isn't subject to customs formalities, although an inventory must be provided on request. Note, on the other hand, that those arriving in an EU country (including EU citizens) are still subject to customs checks and limitations on what may be imported duty-free. There are no restrictions on the import or export of local or foreign bank notes or securities within the EU, although if you enter or leave a country with more than a certain amount in cash or negotiable instruments (see **Importing & Exporting Money** on page 91), you must make a declaration.

The rules regarding the importation of furniture and possessions usually vary according to whether you will be a temporary or permanent resident. Before making any plans to ship goods to any country, check the latest regulations with a local embassy or consulate in your home country. You may need a special application form (available from local embassies), plus a detailed inventory of the items to be imported and their estimated value in local currency. All items to be imported should be included on the list, even if some are to be imported at a later date. Customs documents may need to be signed and presented to an embassy or consulate abroad with your passport. EU nationals planning to take up residence in another EU country are permitted to import their household belongings and possessions free of duty or taxes, provided they were purchased tax-paid within the EU or have been owned and used for at least six-months. Non-EU nationals must have owned and used their possessions for at least six months to qualify for duty-free import into an EU country.

It's usually necessary to show proof of having rented or purchased a home, and in some countries you may need to pay a deposit or obtain a bank guarantee equal to the value (or a percentage) of all the possessions to be imported. The deposit is returned after a specified period, e.g. one or two years, or when the goods are exported or you've obtained a residence permit. Belongings imported duty-free mustn't be sold within a certain period, e.g. one or two years of their importation, and, if you leave the country within this period, everything imported duty-free must be exported or duty paid.

If you use a shipping company to transport your belongings, they will usually provide all the necessary forms and complete the paperwork. Always keep a copy of all forms and communications with customs officials, both with those abroad and in your 'home' country. Note that, if the paperwork isn't in order, your belongings may end up incarcerated in a customs storage depot for a number of weeks or months. If you personally import your belongings, you may need to employ a customs agent at the point of entry to clear them. You should have an official record of the export of valuables in case you wish to re-import them later.

Prohibited & Restricted Goods: Certain goods are subject to special regulations in all countries and in some cases their import and export is prohibited or restricted. These usually include the following:

● animal products;

● plants;

● wild fauna and flora and products derived from them;

● live animals;

● medicines and medical products (except for prescribed drugs and medicines);

- firearms and ammunition;
- certain goods and technologies with a dual civil/military purpose;
- works of art and collectors' items.

If you're unsure whether anything you're importing falls into one of the above categories, check with the local customs authorities. If you're planning to import sporting guns, you may require a certificate from an embassy or consulate abroad, which is usually issued on production of a local firearm's licence. Those travelling to western European countries and North America from 'exotic' regions, e.g. Africa, South America, and the Middle and Far East, may find themselves under close scrutiny from customs and security officials looking for illegal drugs.

Car Importation: Car importation is a popular topic among retirees in many countries, where importing a car often entails a long, drawn-out battle with the local authorities. The process has been simplified in recent years for EU citizens moving between EU countries, although it still involves completing a mountain of forms and can take a number of weeks. Many countries allow new residents to import a car that has been owned for a limited period, e.g. six months. In most countries a permanent resident isn't permitted to operate a car on foreign registration plates and must import it and operate it on local plates. Note also that a vehicle must be de-registered in its original country after it has been re-registered abroad. A vehicle that's imported tax and duty-free mustn't usually be sold, rented or transferred within a minimum of one year of its registration. Note that the registration of a right-hand drive vehicle in a country where traffic drives on the right may be prohibited (the same applies to left-hand drive vehicles in countries that drive on the left). In many countries (e.g. the UK) you can buy a tax-free car and operate it for six months before exporting it, which may help reduce your tax liability.

An imported vehicle must comply with certain safety and other requirements (called homologation) before it can be registered, although this isn't necessary when taking a locally-registered car from one EU country to another or between Canada and the USA. When necessary, homologation can be prohibitively expensive in some countries. Local taxes must usually be paid when importing a car, depending on its year of manufacture, where it was manufactured and its current registration. These may include value added tax, sales tax, registration or car tax and import duty. The amount payable is usually based on the vehicle's original price with a reduction for its age. The procedure for the importation of a boat, caravan or motorcycle (with an engine capacity above 49cc) is usually the same as for a car. Mopeds with engines below 49cc can be freely imported into most countries as part of your possessions and require no special paperwork.

Non-residents: Non-residents can operate a foreign-registered vehicle in most countries for up to six months in a calendar year without paying local taxes and may be permitted to keep a foreign-registered vehicle permanently at a holiday home abroad. The vehicle must be road-legal in its home country, meaning that it must be inspected (for roadworthiness) and taxed each year in its country of registration (which may entail taking it home each year to have it tested!), and must be insured for local use. Non-residents can operate a car on tax-free (or 'tourist') plates in some countries. **Note that anyone who illegally operates a vehicle on foreign or tax-free plates can be fined and the vehicle confiscated.**

Residence

Foreigners (legally) residing in a country for longer than 90 or 180 days must usually either obtain an extension as a visitor or apply to become a resident. If you don't have a regular income or adequate financial resources, your application may be refused. Failure to apply for a residence card within the specified time is a serious offence and can result in a heavy fine or even deportation. Residence in a country may depend on your nationality and whether a reciprocal agreement exists between your home country and the country where you're planning to live.

Retirees planning to become residents abroad must check the rules and regulations *before* travelling abroad (see page 135).

Embassy Registration

Nationals of some countries are required to register with their local embassy or consulate after taking up residence abroad. Registration isn't usually mandatory, although most embassies like to keep a record of their country's citizens abroad. Many countries maintain a number of consulates in certain countries, e.g. most major European countries maintain consulates in the major cities in North America and in many areas in European countries where their nationals reside. This also applies to American and Canadian consulates in European countries. Consulates are an important source of local information and can often provide useful contacts.

Finding Help

One of the major problems facing retirees in a foreign country is where to get help with day-to-day problems. How successful you are at finding local help depends on the town or area where you live (e.g. those in cities and resort areas are far better served than those living in rural areas), your nationality, how many other foreigners live in the town or area, your language proficiency and your sex (women are usually better catered for than men through women's clubs). There's often an abundance of information available in the local language(s), but little in English and other foreign languages. An additional problem is that much of the available information isn't intended for foreigners and their particular needs. You may find that your friends, neighbours and colleagues can help as they can often offer advice based on their own experiences and mistakes. **But take care!** Although they mean well, you're likely to receive as much false and conflicting information as accurate (it may not necessarily be wrong, but often won't apply to your particular situation).

If a woman lives in or near a major town she is able to turn to many English-speaking women's clubs and organisations for help. The single foreign male (who, of course, cannot possibly have any problems) must usually fend for himself, although there are men's expatriate clubs in some areas and mixed social clubs in most countries. Among the best sources of information and help for women are the American Women's Clubs (AWC) located in major cities. AWC clubs provide comprehensive information in English about both local matters and topics of more general interest, and many provide data sheets, booklets and orientation programmes for newcomers. Membership in the organisation is sometimes limited to Americans or those with active links to the US, e.g. through study, work or a spouse who works for a US company or the US government, but most publications and orientation programmes are available to non-members for a fee. AWC clubs are part of the Federation of American Women's Clubs Overseas (FAWCO), which can be contacted via their website (⌨ www.fawco.org).

In addition to the above, there are many social clubs and expatriate organisations for foreigners in most countries, whose members can help you find your way around. They may, however, be difficult to locate, as most clubs are run by volunteers and operate out of the president's or secretary's home, and they rarely bother to advertise or take out a phone listing. If you ask around among your neighbours and friends, it's possible to find various Anglo 'friendship' clubs or English-speaking organisations. Finally, don't neglect to check the Internet, where local newspapers, government offices, clubs and organisations often have their own websites. Contacts can also be found through expatriate magazines and newspapers.

Your town hall may be a good source of information, but you usually need to speak the local language to benefit and may still be sent on a wild goose chase from department to department. Nevertheless, town halls in some countries where there are many foreign residents sometimes have a foreigners' department, where staff may speak English and other foreign languages such as Dutch, French, German and Swedish – an advantage of living somewhere where there are lots of other foreigners!

Many businesses (particularly large multinational companies) produce booklets and leaflets containing useful information about clubs or activities in the area. Book shops may have some interesting publications about the local region, and tourist and information offices are also good sources of information. Most embassies and consulates also provide their nationals with local information, which may include the names of lawyers, interpreters/translators, doctors, dentists, schools, and social and expatriate organisations. See also **Appendices A, B** and **C**.

Checklists

Before Arrival

The checklists on the following pages list tasks which you must (or may need to) complete before and after arrival abroad.

- Check that your passports are valid!

- Obtain a visa, if necessary, for all your family members. Obviously this must be done before travelling abroad.

- Arrange health and travel insurance for your family (see pages 82 and 114 respectively). This is essential if you aren't already covered by a private insurance policy and won't be covered by a country's national health service.

- Open a local bank account and transfer funds – you can open an account with many banks from abroad or even via the Internet. It's best to obtain some local currency (if possible) before your arrival, which will save you having to exchange money immediately on arrival. Failing this, take some GB£ or US$, which are readily accepted in most countries.

- Obtain an international driver's licence, if necessary. If you don't already have one, it's advisable to obtain an international credit card, which will prove invaluable during your first few months abroad.

- If you plan to become a permanent resident, you may also need to organise the shipment of all your possessions.

- Obtain as many credit references as possible, e.g. from banks, mortgage companies, credit card companies, credit agencies, companies with which you've had accounts, and references from professionals such as lawyers and accountants. These will help you establish a credit rating abroad.

- If you're planning to become a permanent resident, you should also take your official documents with you. These may include birth certificates, driving licences, marriage certificate, divorce papers or death certificate (if a widow or widower), medical and dental records, bank account and credit card details, insurance policies (plus records of no-claims' allowances), and receipts for any valuables. You also need the documents necessary to obtain a residence permit plus certified copies, official translations and a number of passport-size photographs.

After Arrival

The following checklist contains a summary of the tasks to be completed after arrival abroad (if not done before arrival):

- On arrival at an airport, port or land border post, have your visa cancelled and your passport stamped, as applicable.
- If you aren't taking a car with you, you may wish to rent (see page 33) or buy one locally. Note that it's difficult to get around in many countries without a car, if you don't live in a major city, and it's practically impossible in rural areas.
- Open a bank account (see page 93) at a local bank and give the details to any companies that you plan to pay by direct debit or standing order.
- Arrange whatever insurance is necessary such as health, car and home.
- Contact offices and organisations to obtain local information.
- It's advisable to make courtesy calls on your neighbours and the local mayor within a few weeks of your arrival. This is particularly important in villages and rural areas if you want to be accepted and integrate into the local community.
- If you plan to become a resident abroad, you may need to do the following within the following few weeks (if not done before your arrival):
  - Apply for a residence permit.
  - Register for membership of the state national health service.
  - Register with a local doctor and dentist.
  - Apply for a local driving licence (see page 35).

Moving House

When moving abroad permanently there are many things to be considered and a 'million' people to be informed. Even if you plan to spend only a few months a year abroad, it may still be necessary to inform a number of people and companies in your home country. The checklist below is designed to make the task easier and help prevent an ulcer or a nervous breakdown –

provided of course you don't leave everything to the last minute! (See also **Moving House** on page 60 and **Moving In** on page 63).

- If you live in rented accommodation you must give your landlord notice (check your contract).

- If you own your home, if applicable, you will need to arrange to sell or let it (see page 66), well in advance of your move abroad.

- Inform the following:
  - Your local town hall or municipality. You may be entitled to a refund of your local property or other taxes.
  - If it was necessary to register with the police in your home country, you should inform them that you're moving abroad.
  - Your electricity, gas, water and telephone companies. Contact companies well in advance, particularly if you need to get a deposit refunded.
  - Your insurance companies (e.g. health, car, home contents and private pension), banks, post office (if you have a post office account), stockbroker and other financial institutions, credit card, charge card and hire purchase companies, lawyer and accountant, and local businesses where you have accounts.
  - Your local tax and social security offices.
  - Your family doctor, dentist and other health practitioners. Health records should be transferred to your new doctor and dentist abroad.
  - Your family's schools. Try to give a term's notice and obtain copies of any relevant reports or records from current schools.
  - All regular correspondents, subscriptions, social and sports clubs, professional and trade journals, and friends and relatives. Give them your new address and telephone number abroad and arrange to have your mail redirected by the post office or a friend (or a property management company).

- Return any library books or anything borrowed.

- Arrange shipment of your furniture and belongings by booking a shipping company well in advance (see page 61). International shipping companies usually provide a wealth of information and can advise on a wide range of matters regarding a move abroad. Find out the procedure for shipping your belongings to your new home from a local embassy or consulate.

- Arrange to sell anything you aren't taking with you (e.g. house, car and furniture). If you're selling a home, you should obtain expert legal advice, as you may be able to save tax by establishing a trust or other legal vehicle. Note that if you own more than one property, you may need to pay capital gains tax on the profits from the sale of second and subsequent homes.

- If you have a car that you're exporting, you must complete the relevant paperwork in your home country and re-register it abroad after your arrival. You may also need to return the registration plates. Contact a local embassy or consulate for information.

- Arrange inoculations, documentation and shipment for any pets that you're taking with you (see page 129).

- You may qualify for a rebate on your tax and social security contributions. Contact your local tax and social security offices for information.

- It's advisable to arrange health, dental and optical checkups before leaving your home country (see page 73), and have any necessary or recommended inoculations. Obtain a copy of health records and a statement from your private health insurance company stating your present level of cover.

- Terminate any outstanding loan, lease or hire purchase contracts and pay bills (allow plenty of time as some companies may be slow to respond).

- Check whether you're entitled to a rebate on your road tax, car and other insurance. Obtain a letter from your motor insurance company stating your no-claims' discount.

- Check whether you need an international driving licence or a translation of your foreign driving licence(s) for your new country. Note that some foreign residents are required to take a driving test to drive in some countries (see page 35).

- Give friends and business associates an address and telephone number where you can be contacted abroad.

- If you will be living abroad for an extended period (but not permanently), you may wish to give someone 'power of attorney' over your financial affairs in your home country so that they can act for you in your absence. This can be for a fixed period or open-ended and can be for a specific purpose only. **Note, on the other hand, that you should take expert legal advice before doing this!**

- Allow plenty of time to get to the airport, register your luggage, and clear security and immigration.

Have a good journey!

8.

COUNTRY PROFILES

This chapter contains profiles of the most popular countries for those planning to retire abroad. Property prices are shown in local currency and are intended as a rough guide only. Exchange rates and interest rates shown are official rates (March 2002) and mortgage rates are usually one or two percentage points higher. Note that for all the euro-zone countries, the interest rate is the same and is set by the European Central Bank.

AUSTRALIA

Background Information

Capital: Canberra
Population: 19 million
Foreign Community: Australia is largely a nation of immigrants and has assimilated some 4 million people since the Second World War. It's an extremely cosmopolitan country and although the bulk of post-war immigrants have come (and still come) from the UK and other European countries, many now arrive from Asia.
Area: 7,682,300km^2 (2,966,368mi^2)
Geography: Australia is the world's largest island, with an area equal to the continental USA and a coastline of 36,755km (22,827mi). It's around 25 times the size of the British Isles and almost twice the combined area of India and Pakistan. The average elevation in Australia is less than 300m (984ft), compared with a world-wide average of around 700m (2,297ft). The highest point is Mount Kosciusko 2,228m (7,310ft) in the Australian Alps in the south-east of the country. Australia is one of the oldest and driest land masses in the world, with vast uninhabitable arid and semi-desert areas. It's a land, nonetheless, of great contrasts with rain forests and vast plains in the north, desert in the centre, fertile croplands in the east, south and south-west; and snowfields in the south-east. On the west coast is the Indian Ocean and on the east the Coral and Tasman seas of the South Pacific Ocean.
Climate: Australia's climate ranges from tropical in the northern 40 per cent of the country (above the Tropic of Capricorn) to temperate in the rest of the country. It's less subject to climatic extremes than other regions of comparable size because it's surrounded by oceans and has no high mountain ranges. Clear skies and low rainfall are characteristic of the weather in most of the continent. Coastal regions generally enjoy an excellent year-round climate, with no state capital averaging less than 5.5 hours of sunshine per day. Australia's seasons are the opposite of the northern hemisphere, e.g. summer is from December to February and winter from June to August. In mid-summer (January) average temperatures range from 29°C (84°F) in the north to 17°C (63°F) in the south, and in mid-winter (July) from 25°C (77°F) in the north to 8°C (46°F) in the south. Average annual rainfall is 46.5cm

(18in), although rainfall varies, considerably depending on the region, from less than 15cm (6in) in the centre to over 2m (79in) in parts of the tropics and western Tasmania. The wettest cities are Darwin, Sydney, Brisbane and Perth. Adelaide, Canberra, Hobart and Melbourne receive around half the rainfall of Sydney. The northern (tropical) region experiences heavy rainfall and oppressive temperatures between November and March.

Language: English is the national language, although there are some regional variations in pronunciation and phraseology.

Political Stability: Australia's system of government is based on the British parliamentary model and is very stable. It consists of three tiers: commonwealth, state and local governments, and is a member of the British Commonwealth, although 45 per cent of Australians voted for a republic in a referendum in 1999. and Australia is expected to become a republic within the next decade.

Finance

Currency: Australian dollar (A$)
Exchange Rate: £1 = A$2.70, US$1 = A$1.92
Exchange Controls: None.
Interest Rate: 4.25 per cent
Cost/Standard of Living: Living costs vary from state to state and even within states, and much depends on the actual area where you live and your lifestyle. Overall it's similar to most northern European countries. Prices are relatively low for essentials such as food, drink and clothes, however, manufactured goods are generally expensive as many are imported. Car prices are around 25 per cent higher than in most western European countries and up to twice those in the USA (imported cars are particularly expensive). Australians enjoy a high standard of living.
GDP Per Head (US$): 20,640
Banks: There are four national banks, as well as numerous regional, state and local banks. You should make sure that a bank is a member of the Australian Bankers' Association (ABA), which implements a Code of Banking Practice, although there's no deposit protection scheme. Electronic banking accounts for most banking transactions and telephone and Internet banking are becoming more popular. To open a bank account you need a tax file number, obtainable from your local Australian Tax Office (ATO).

Taxation

Income Tax: Australia has a PAYG (pay as you go) scheme with the basic rate starting at 17 per cent on annual income over A$6,000 to A$20,000 and rising to 47 per cent on incomes above A$60,000.

Concessions/Tax Breaks For Retirees: There's a tax rebate for pensioners, although pensions are subject to income tax. In some states, pensioners receive a concession on property taxes.

Social Security: Social security in Australia is non-contributory and is financed by general taxation. The system is one of the most comprehensive in the world and provides benefits such as retirement and disability pensions, unemployment and sick pay, family and accommodation allowances, and health care. New immigrants, however, must wait two years before they can take advantage of benefits, with the exception of health care.

Capital Gains Tax (CGT): There's no CGT on the sale of a taxpayer's principal residence. CGT is 33 per cent on gains on property by non-residents, although gains are indexed to allow for inflation. Capital gains made by residents are taxed as income in the tax year in which they were realised.

Inheritance & Gift Tax: None.

Value Added Tax (VAT): Australia introduced a Goods and Service Tax (GST) in July 2000, which is levied at a flat rate of 10 per cent on most goods and services. Basic food items and certain medical aids are exempt.

Accommodation

Market: Australia has a flourishing property market and around 80 per cent of Australians possess their own homes, one of the highest rates in the world. A huge choice of homes is available including apartments, townhouses and a wide range of standard and individually-designed, detached homes. Apartments (called 'units' or 'home units') are common in inner cities and coastal areas, and townhouses are common in the suburbs of the major cities. Outside the major cities most people have a home built to a standard (or their own) design on their own plot of land. Package deals including a plot of land and a house are common. Waterfront homes are in short supply and are a good investment. Property magazines are published by local property associations in major cities and states.

Areas: Australia is a highly urbanised society with over 70 per cent of the population living in the main cities situated on the coast, i.e. Adelaide, Brisbane, Darwin, Hobart, Melbourne, Perth and Sydney, all of which have their own character and particular attractions. Only some 15 per cent of Australians live in rural areas.

Cost: Property prices vary considerably throughout the country and in the various suburbs of the major cities. Not surprisingly, the further you are from a town or city the lower the price of land and property. Two-bedroom apartments (of approximately 75m^2) start at around A$80,000 in city suburbs and rise to over double this in a central or popular beach location. A two or three-bedroom, single-storey home in most city suburbs costs between A$60,000 and A$100,000, and four-bedroom, two-storey homes cost from around A$80,000 to A$200,000. Sydney has the most expensive property, where a reasonable two-bedroom apartment in a nice building with water views costs around A$500,000.

Land prices reduce considerably from around 15km (9.5mi) outside a city and are at their lowest over 25km (15.5mi) from cities. The cost of land varies from as little as A$25,000 for an average size suburban plot over 25km (15.5mi) from cities such as Adelaide, Hobart and Perth to over A$200,000 for a plot within 15km (9.5mi) of central Sydney. The cost of building a home depends on the location, quality and the materials used, e.g. brick (most expensive), brick veneer, weatherboard and fibre cement (cheapest). Brick veneer is the most popular and costs from around A$550 to A$650 per metre, depending on the location. For up-to-date prices obtain a copy of the *Cost of Living and Housing Survey Book* published by the Commonwealth Bank of Australia.

Local Mortgages: Mortgages are available from a large number of banks and building societies. They're usually for a maximum of 75 or 80 per cent of the value, although loans of up to 100 per cent are available. The maximum term is 30 years, although the repayment period is usually between 15 and 25 years. Both variable and fixed-rate loans are available.

Property Taxes: Property taxes differ considerably, depending on the municipality, and are based on the 'rateable value' of the property. Rates are levied annually, but are usually paid quarterly, and can be very high in some areas. Pensioners receive concessions in some states.

Purchase Procedure: Most land and property in Australia is owned freehold, the only exception being the Australian Capital Territory (ACT) or Canberra, where *all* land is sold on a 99-year lease. Once you've found a suitable property and agreed a price, the estate agent completes a Contract of Sale, signed by both the buyer and seller. Contracts of Sale are standard, countrywide documents published by the Law Society and the Real Estate Institute, and carry a government statement informing the buyer about the importance of seeking legal advice, cooling-off periods and the payment of deposits. A deposit (usually 10 per cent of the purchase price) is paid by the buyer to the agent and deposited in the agent's escrow (trust) account until completion, which is usually around a month later. Once the Contract of Sale has been signed, both parties are legally obliged to go through with the deal, subject to cooling-off rights in some states where you may have from two to five working days to cancel the contract subject to paying a penalty of 0.25 per cent of the purchase price.

In the period between signing the Contract of Sale and completion, searches and checks are done (usually by a lawyer or conveyancer) on the property to ensure, among other things, that it has the correct title and no restrictive covenants. Once you and your legal representative are satisfied that all is in order you can proceed with the purchase.

Fees: These usually total 4 to 5 per cent of the purchase price. The main fees are stamp duty and legal fees. Stamp duty costs depend on the state and is lowest in New South Wales and highest in the Northern Territory and Victoria. Some states waive or reduce stamp duty for first-time buyers. Legal fees are usually 1 to 2 per cent of the purchase price, but costs may be based on the actual work involved. Land transfer registration is imposed by each state and may be a flat or variable fee.

Precautions: Buying a property in Australia is generally safe, but you should take all the usual precautions regarding deposits and obtaining proper title. Experts recommend you have a termite and pest inspection done on the property, which is compulsory in some states. If you're buying an apartment, it's advisable to have a strata inspection, which will tell you if there are any structural or administrative problems with the building. It's strongly recommended that you contract the services of a legal expert (lawyer or conveyancer) to carry out the searches and checks on the property. You can do this yourself but it's complicated and a potential minefield. When buying property in Australia, always use a licensed estate agent who must have professional indemnity and adhere to a code of ethics.

Restrictions on Foreign Ownership: All proposed acquisitions of urban property by non-resident foreigners must be approved by the Australian authorities. There are no restrictions for residents.

Building Standards: Generally excellent. Construction varies from brick to brick veneer (a timber inner frame lined with plasterboard), weatherboard and fibre cement.

Belongings: Belongings can be imported duty-free, but must have been owned for a minimum of one year. Immigrants can import a car, but duty and sales tax are payable on its value. The duty rate on cars is 15 per cent plus 10 per cent GST, and there's a 25 per cent tax on vehicles valued at over A$55,134.

Rental Accommodation: The rental market isn't particularly strong in Australia and rental accommodation can be scarce in major cities, particularly in Sydney and Melbourne. It's therefore advisable to secure accommodation before you arrive. Costs for a small apartment range from A$120 to A$180 a month and for a three-bedroom house from A$160 to A$350 a month, although accommodation in city centres is considerably more expensive. Accommodation is usually let unfurnished.

Retirement Homes: Purpose-built retirement homes and developments are widely available in Australia, where there are over 2,300 retirement villages. Retirement villages are hugely popular and places are usually in short supply. The price range is very varied, depending on the location and facilities offered, although prices for a small self-contained apartment generally start at around AS$80,000. Weekly or monthly service charges are also levied. Most state governments have a code of practice regulating retirement villages, and information and advice can be obtained from the Council on the Aging (💻 www.cota.org.au).

Utilities: Electricity (240/250V) is provided by individual state companies, some of which have been privatised. Electricity charges differ considerably, depending on the state and local competition, and most electricity companies offer different rates for peak and off-peak times. Mains gas is available in all major cities, although not all homes are connected to the supply. In country areas, bottled gas is available. Water is a precious commodity in Australia, the world's driest continent, which is subject to frequent and prolonged droughts.. Water restrictions are commonplace in many states. In metropolitan areas, water is metered and households are charged according to use, whereas in rural areas there may be a fixed charge.

Services

Post Office: The Australian postal service, run by Australia Post (AP), is one of the best in the world in terms of cost, speed and reliability. There are post offices in most towns and in rural areas businesses such as stores or petrol stations act as post office agents. AP also provide services such as the payment of bills, the sale of stationery products and money orders.

Telephone: Australia has one of the highest standards of telecommunications in the world and almost all homes have a telephone. There are several telecommunications companies, although the original monopoly-holder, Telstra, dominates the market. The cost of international calls has fallen dramatically in recent years, and calls to the UK can cost as little as 21¢ a minute. Mobile phones are popular and charges are reasonable.

Internet: Australia has the highest number of Internet users per capita outside the USA and enjoys one of the lowest Internet access charges, thanks to un-timed local calls. Most cities have a good choice of ISPs with competitive rates and 'broad band' access is available in metropolitan areas.

English TV & Radio: Australian television is among the best in the world, with over half the programmes purchased from the UK and the USA. There are five national TV channels, two government-owned and the rest private enterprises. There are also several regional networks. Pay TV is available, although it isn't as popular in Australia as in Europe and North America. There are hundreds of radio stations, most of which are commercial. Australia has no TV or radio licence.

General Information

Getting There: Given Australia's remoteness, air travel is, for most people, the only option. The country's main entry points of Melbourne, Perth and Sydney are well-served by international flights from many destinations, particularly Asia. Flights are expensive, although you can find less expensive tickets on the most competitive routes, such as the UK to Australia or during low-season.

Getting Around: The sheer size of Australia means flying is the easiest and quickest way of getting round the country. Domestic flights are operated by Qantas and Ansett Australia (which was pulled out of bankruptcy by a group of businessmen in late 2001) and fares are generally competitive, particularly if you book well in advance. Australia has a rail network covering part of the country (the south-east has the best network), although because of the long journey times and the slowness of trains, rail travel is considered more of a tourist attraction rather than a means of travel. Some main cities have a suburban rail network. Public transport within cities and large towns is usually comprehensive and efficient, and Sydney has a good ferry commuter service. Tasmania and the mainland are linked by passenger and car ferries.

Shopping: Australia isn't one of the world's great shopping countries, and although the choice and variety of goods has improved considerably in recent years, it's still limited somewhat compared to Europe and North America. Shopping centres are popular and there's a wide variety of department and chain stores. Note that in remote areas (i.e. most of Australia!) and small towns there may be only one shop.

Crime Rate: Violent crime in Australia is rare, although car and house crime is common in the major cities.

Driving: Australians love their cars, the main means of transport, and the quality of roads is generally excellent, although in the outback roads are often no more than dirt tracks. Traffic congestion and pollution are chronic problems in some cities, particularly Sydney. Traffic drives on the *left* in Australia and driving standards are generally good. Foreign driving licences are valid for one year, after which residents must exchange their driving licence for an Australian licence, a process which includes taking road knowledge and driving tests. Cars are generally expensive in Australia, although prices have remained static for the last few years. Petrol prices are reasonable, although they tend to be higher in outback areas and in Tasmania.

Medical Facilities: Excellent. Australia has a contributory (1.5 per cent of taxable income) national health scheme called Medicare. It pays for 85 per cent of medical costs (the scheduled fee) and provides free hospital treatment. Private health insurance is necessary for non-residents and retirees who aren't covered by Medicare. The cost of health insurance starts at A$500 annually, depending on the cover required. Reciprocal agreements cover visitors from many countries, but not the UK.

Pets: Australia has strict quarantine laws to protect its unique wildlife and livestock. To import a pet (e.g. a cat or dog) you must obtain a permit from the Australian Quarantine and Inspection Service, GPO Box 858, Canberra ACT 2601, Australia (☎ 1800-020504, 🖥 www.aqis.gov.au).

Reciprocal Agreement with the UK: British citizens entitled to a state pension in the UK can continue to receive it in Australia, but the amount is frozen at the rate it was when they left the UK.

Residence Permits: Australia has a permanent programme of immigration with an annual quota, e.g. 85,000 in 2001/2002. Immigration is decided on a selective policy based on a points system, with preference given to those with special skills that are in demand and those wishing to start a business. Retirees must be aged 55 or over and need to transfer at least A$650,000 or A$200,000 with an annual pension or income of at least A$45,000. An initial permit is granted for four years and extensions may be granted. Everyone except New Zealand passport holders requires a visa to enter Australia.

Work Permits: Authorisation is required from an Australian Consulate under the points system mentioned above.

Visas: Nationals of all countries except New Zealand require a visa.

Reference

Further Reading

Living and Working in Australia, David Hampshire (Survival Books, 🖳 www.survivalbooks.net). Everything you need to know about living and working in Australia.

Australia (Australian Government Publishing Service).

Australia's Foreign Investment Policy: A Guide for Investors (Australian Government Publishing Service).

Australian News, 1 Commercial Road, Eastbourne, East Sussex BN21 3XQ, UK (☎ 01323-726040; 🖳 www.outbound-newspapers.com).

Australian Outlook, 3 Buckhurst Road, Bexhill-on-Sea, East Sussex TN40 1QF, UK (☎ 01424-223111; 🖳 www.consylpublishing.co.uk).

The Cost of Living and Housing Survey Book (Commonwealth Bank of Australia).

Useful Addresses

Australian Embassy, 1601 Massachusetts Ave., NW, Washington, DC 20036, USA (☎ 202-797 3000).

Australian High Commission, Australia House, Strand, London WC2B 4LA, UK (☎ 020-7379 4334, 🖳 www.australia.org.uk).

Australian Tourist Commission, 1st Floor, Gemini House, 10-18 Putney Hill, London SW15 6AA, UK (☎ 020-8780 2227, 🖳 www.australia.com).

Foreign Investment Review Board, Department of the Treasury, Parkes Place, Parkes, ACT 2600, Australia (☎ 02-6263 3795, 💻 www.firb.gov.au). Provides information about buying property in Australia for non-residents and retirees.

Useful Websites

💻 www.immi.gov.au – Department of Immigration and Multicultural Affairs (DIMA). Useful information for visitors and immigrants.

💻 www.ato.gov.au – Australian Tax Office (ATO).

BELIZE

Background Information

Capital: Belize City
Population: 240,000
Foreign Community: Several thousand expatriates from North America and Europe live in Belize, although the exact number isn't known since many expatriates aren't official residents.
Area: 22,923km² (8,866mi²)
Geography: Belize is a small country situated in the Western Caribbean and Central America, and lies in the Yucatan peninsula. The country has borders with Guatemala to the west, Mexico to the north and the Caribbean to the east. Belize has spectacular rainforest and jungle in the south of the country, with an abundance of rare wildlife and the world's second-largest barrier reef situated to the east of the mainland. Off the mainland are several islands, known as 'cayes', including the large Ambergris Caye, Belize's most popular tourist resort.
Climate: Belize has a subtropical climate with high humidity year round, although this is tempered in coastal areas and cayes by sea breezes. Daily temperatures during most of the year are around 30°C (85°F) in the day and around 18°C (65°F) at night, although in mountainous areas night time temperatures are lower. Annual rainfall is high in the south and lower in the north, and tropical storms are common from September to November. Belize is in the hurricane belt, although the western Caribbean doesn't experience as many hurricanes as the east and north. Hurricanes can on the other hand hit Belize as did Hurricane Keith in 2000, causing four deaths and extensive property damage.
Language: English
Political Stability: Very good. The country has a healthy democracy modelled on the British system since its independence in 1971. Belize is a member of the British Commonwealth.

Finance

Currency: Belize dollar (BZ$) and the US dollar (US$). The Belize dollar is worth US$0.50 and most shops and businesses accept both currencies. Note, however, that it's sometimes difficult to exchange Belize dollars for other currencies and it's wise to keep a minimum amount of money in Belize dollars.

Exchange Rate: £1 = BZ$3

Exchange Controls: None, although any companies wishing to invest in Belize must register their investment with the Central Bank of Belize.

Interest Rate: 12 per cent

Banks: Recent legislation has brought great improvements to the Belize banking system, which is now efficient, secure and on a par with western standards. Belize is an offshore financial centre and many international banks are present there. Banking services are good and non-residents can open bank accounts.

Cost/Standard of Living: The cost of living in Belize is generally low compared to Western Europe and North America, although luxury and imported items are expensive.

GDP Per Head (US$): 3,100

Taxation

Belize is one of the world's tax havens, particularly if you retire to the country under the Retiree Incentive Program.

Income Tax: All foreign income is exempt from income tax if you have a Retirement Visa. Income tax on income generated within Belize is levied at progressive rates from 15 to 45 per cent, although there's an annual exemption of BZ$10,400.

Concessions/Tax Breaks For Retirees: If you retire to Belize under the Retiree Incentive Program (see **Residence Permits** on page 26) you're exempt from paying Belize taxes on income originating from outside Belize.

Social Security: Employees in Belize must make compulsory social security contributions, which range from BZ$0.55 to BZ$320 a week depending on your income. Benefits include retirement pensions and injury allowances.

Capital Gains Tax (CGT): None.

Wealth Tax: None.

Inheritance & Gift Tax: None.

Value Added Tax (VAT): The unpopular VAT at 15 per cent was abolished in 1999 and a Sales Tax introduced, which is levied at 8 per cent on most goods and services. Basic food items and some medical items are exempt.

Accommodation

Market: In international terms, the property market in Belize is healthy and prices are generally low, although there are now few bargains. The year 2001was particularly strong for property sales, and this trend is expected to continue over at least the next five years. Some parts of the country are currently experiencing a massive property boom and house construction is especially popular at present. Apartments and condominiums are plentiful on the coast, but there's a shortage of houses and villas, although many are currently under construction. In more remote areas you can buy large areas of land, and some of Belize's islands can be purchased.

Areas: The most popular place to buy property is the island of Ambergris Caye, Belize's top tourist destination just south of the Yucatan peninsula in Mexico. The island has a high expatriate population and good amenities, and most transportation on the island is by golf cart. In keeping with its popularity, Ambergris Caye has the most expensive real estate in Belize, although you can still find the occasional bargain. There are several large developments currently under construction mainly targeted at the foreign market. The northern part of the island is, as yet, mostly undeveloped.

The Placencia peninsula in southern Belize, with its excellent beaches and good amenities, is popular with expatriates, although the real estate market is rather limited and many people prefer to build their own homes. Further south on the coast is the town of Hopkins, which is quieter than Plasencia and popular with expatriates. Punta Gorda is a quiet resort situated in the far south surrounded by fruit farms. Amenities are limited, but there's a daily shuttle flight to and from Belize City. Punta Gorda is expected to become a major development area in the near future.

Cost: Real estate is generally good value in Belize, although the recent influx of buyers from North America means there are fewer bargains to be found. Prices on Ambergris Caye range from US$75,000 to US$300,000 for a condominium and up to US$500,000 for a house. In rural areas, on the other hand, and outside the main tourist areas, you can buy a large modern house for US$50,000 to US$100,000. Plots of land are available throughout the country and a small front-line beach plot costs from US$50,000 in Ambergris Caye and Placencia, although a larger plot in the less popular Corozal costs from US$15,000 to US$20,000. Building costs range from US$125 to US$250 per m² depending on the type and quality of construction. Small private islands start at US$100,000.

Local Mortgages: Belize banks offer mortgages to foreigners, typically for up to 90 per cent of the value over ten years. Note, however, that interest rates are high (around 12 to 16 per cent) and many expatriates prefer to obtain an overseas mortgage, although permission from the Central Bank of Belize is required in order to secure a loan from outside Belize in foreign currency. This is usually a formality for *bona fide* enterprises.

Property Taxes: Property taxes are generally low in Belize and you can expect to pay between 1 and 1.5 per cent of the value a year, but rates are slightly higher in cities.

Purchase Procedure: Property purchase in Belize is based on the British system (see page 290) and is generally safe, although you're strongly advised to employ a reputable lawyer. A lawyer's duties include taking care of the paperwork and registration of the property, as well as making sure that the title deeds to the property are correct and have no debts.

Fees: Purchase fees include 3 per cent transfer tax and 5 per cent stamp duty if the buyer isn't a Belize citizen. The transfer tax and stamp duty fees may be shared between the buyer and seller. Lawyers' fees are around 1 to 1.5 per cent of the purchase price. Estate agents charge a commission of between 7 and 10 per cent of the purchase price, which is usually paid by the buyer.

Precautions: Before purchasing a property you should make sure that the title deeds are correct, that the property has no debts attached to it and all payments, such as annual property tax, are up to date. It's also important to check that the property has no deed restrictions on it. These checks should be carried out by a lawyer.

Holiday Letting: Generally none.

Restrictions on Foreign Ownership: Generally none, although if a plot is larger than ten acres outside a metropolitan area or larger than 1.5 acres within a metropolitan area, government approval is required.

Building Standards: Variable, but generally good for new properties.

Belongings: If you retire to Belize under the Retiree Incentive Program (see **Residence Permits** on page 26) you can import belongings and household goods up to the value of US$15,000 duty-free. You're also permitted to import a car (which cannot be more than three years old), a boat and a light aircraft duty-free. Importation of all goods must be completed within one year of moving to Belize.

Rental Accommodation: Outside the main tourist areas rental accommodation is easy to find and is generally inexpensive. Typical monthly rentals are US$150 for a small house and US$300 to US$700 for a larger North American-type house. Popular tourist areas such as Ambergris Caye and Placencia have a shortage of rental accommodation and rents are expensive. Expect to pay up to US$1,500 a month for a small apartment and up to US$2,500 for a detached house.

Retirement Homes: There are currently no purpose-built retirement homes and developments in Belize, although given the growing retiree population it will probably be only a matter of time before they're introduced.

Utilities: Within towns and main residential areas, the electricity supply (110V) is generally good, although the cost of electricity in Belize is one of the highest in the world. Outside residential areas, the electricity supply can be erratic or non-existent and many residents rely on generators. Bottled gas is widely available and is popular for cooking and for running some appliances, such as refrigerators, as it's cheaper than electricity. Tap water is safe to drink only in Belize City and many areas outside towns don't have mains water.

Services

Post Office: Belize has a generally efficient postal service, certainly much more so than other countries in the region, and delivery is usually quick.

Telephone: Within towns and residential areas, telecommunications are generally modern and good, although call charges can be high, particularly international calls. Outside these areas, telephone communications can be poor or non-existent. Belize Telecomm has a monopoly.

Internet: The Internet has been slow to take off in Belize, although gradually more companies are going online. At present Belize Telecomm is the only ISP and charges are relatively high.

English TV & Radio: Belize has three TV stations (all English-language) and satellite TV is also available, although reception can be poor in remote areas. The Broadcasting Corporation of Belize transmits two radio stations in English. There's no TV or radio licence.

General Information

Getting There: Belize is easily reached by air from many countries, particularly the US airports of Houston and Miami, from where the flight times are just two hours. The country can also be reached by road from Mexico, although the journey is long, taking around four days to travel from Texas to Belize.

Getting Around: Several airlines operate within Belize and the country has a good and frequent air service connecting the main towns with the capital. Public transport varies and is reasonable within the capital. There are several bus services from the capital to the major provincial towns.

Shopping: Belize City has good shopping facilities, including modern supermarkets. Outside the capital shopping amenities vary hugely, although in the main tourist areas facilities are good. Most towns and villages have a weekly food market.

Crime Rate: Statistically, Belize has a high crime rate and violent crime is a particular problem in some areas of the capital. Criminal activities are highly publicised, but most expatriates are unaffected by it, although it's wise to take precautions against theft and avoid certain areas of the capital.

Driving: Road standards are generally poor in Belize with many roads unpaved, although the government has been investing in the road infrastructure recently, and the situation is slowly improving. The country's four main highways are generally good. Traffic drives on the right and driving standards leave a lot to be desired. Petrol is expensive and there's a shortage of petrol stations outside urban areas.

Medical Facilities: Medical facilities have improved greatly in Belize in recent years and local medical care is generally good and inexpensive. Most Belize medical staff receive their training in the USA or Mexico, and many towns have doctor and dental surgeries. Some expatriates, however, prefer to travel to the USA for specialist treatment. Although medical costs are low (a visit to the doctor typically costs from US$15 to US$20), private medical insurance is recommended and can be obtained at competitive rates from local companies.

Pets: To import a pet into Belize you must present the correct importation forms, available from the Belize immigration authorities, and current health and vaccination certificates.

Reciprocal Agreement with the UK: None.

Residence Permits: In theory all foreign residents in Belize require a residence permit, although in practice many foreign residents stay in Belize as tourists and renew their entrance permit every month for up to six months when they must leave the country for 48 hours. Belize introduced a Retired Persons Incentive Act in 2000 in a bid to attract more retirees. The programme is open to Canadian, UK and USA citizens over 45 years of age who must deposit in a Belize bank account a minimum of US$1,000 a month if the funds come from a pension or a minimum of US$2,000 a month if the funds come from investment sources. Applications cost around US$700 and you're also required to submit medical and good conduct certificates. Under this programme you cannot work in Belize.

Work Permits: Work permits for foreigners are difficult to obtain and are usually issued only if there are no Belize nationals available for a job.

Visas: Foreign nationals require an entrance permit which is valid for 30 days and renewable for up to six months, after which period you must leave the country for at least 48 hours or obtain a residence permit. Entrance permits are issued on arrival.

Reference

Further Reading

Belize: A Guide to Business, Investment and Retirement (Offshore Consultants of Southwest)

Belize First, a magazine about living in Belize (🖳 www.belizefirst.com).

Belize Retirement Guide, Bill & Claire Gray (Preview Pub, 🖳 www.belize retire.com).

Belize: The Owners' Manual (International Living, 🖳 www.international living.com)

How to Invest or Retire in Belize, Emory King (International Living, 🖳 www.internationalliving.com)

Useful Addresses

Belize Tourist Board (for Retiree Program Applications), PO Box 325, Belize City, Belize (☎ 501-231913, 🖳 www.belizeretirement.org).

Belize Embassy, 2535 Massachusetts Ave., NW, Washington DC 20008 (☎ 0202-332 9636).

Belize Embassy, 22 Harcourt House, 19 Cavendish Square, London W1M 9AD (☎ 020-7149 99728).

Useful Websites

🖳 www.belizenet.com – A directory of services and companies in Belize.

🖳 www.ambergiscaye.com – A comprehensive website with a wealth of information about life and leisure activities on Ambergris Caye.

CANADA

Background Information

Capital: Ottawa
Population: 30 million
Foreign Community: Canada is a cosmopolitan country due to the large number of immigrants (Toronto and Vancouver are among the most multi-racial cities in the world). Over 40 per cent of the population is of British origin and 30 per cent of French origin, and the country also has large German, Dutch and Ukrainian communities. There has been a large influx of Asian immigrants in the last decade, particularly from Hong Kong. Most new immigrants come from Asia, Africa and Latin America.
Area: 9,976,185km^2 (3,852,106mi^2)
Geography: Canada is the largest country in the world with an area equal to that of Europe (40 times that of the UK and 18 times the size of France) and a coastline of 250,000km (155,000mi). Sparsely populated, Canada has huge areas of wilderness, including forests (one third of the country), mountains, prairies, tundra and polar desert in the north and west. Almost 8 per cent of

the country consists of inland fresh water, including four of the world's largest lakes (Huron, Superior, Great Bear and Great Slave). In the east are the maritime provinces of Newfoundland, Nova Scotia, New Brunswick and Prince Edward Island, and the predominantly French-speaking province of Québec.

The central province of Ontario borders the Great Lakes, extending north across the shield to Hudson Bay. Further to the west are the prairie provinces of Manitoba, Saskatchewan and Alberta, with fertile farmlands to the south and lake-strewn forest on the sub-arctic wastelands in the north. South-western Alberta contains a substantial part of the Rocky Mountains with peaks rising to over 4,000m (13,120ft). The western-most province of British Columbia is mountainous with forests, lakes and sheltered valleys with rich farmland. The vast, largely unpopulated, northern areas include the Yukon Territory bordering Alaska and the extensive Northwest Territories.

Climate: The Canadian climate is noted for its extremes of hot and cold weather, which are more pronounced inland than on the coast. Regional climates vary enormously. The Pacific coast (e.g. Vancouver) is warm and fairly dry in summer and mild, cloudy and wet in winter. Inland conditions are more extreme, depending on the altitude. The region from the Great Lakes to the Rocky Mountains experiences cold winters and warm summers with low rainfall. The southern areas of central Canada are humid with hot summers and cold winters and rain throughout the year, while the Atlantic regions have a humid but temperate climate.

The northern regions, comprising some 40 per cent of the country, experience arctic conditions with temperatures below freezing for most of the year and falling as low as -40°C (around 10°F) in winter. Average daily temperatures are around 21°C (69°F) in summer (July) in Montreal and Toronto, falling to between -7°C and -10°C (27°F to 23°F) in winter (January). In Vancouver, average temperatures are around 17°C (63°F) in July and 2.5°C (36°F) in January.

Language: Canada has two official languages, English and French (spoken mostly in Québec), which enjoy equal status. English is spoken by some 65 per cent of the population and French by 25 per cent, although only around 15 per cent are fluent in both languages. Chinese is Canada's third most widely-spoken language due to the large number of Asian immigrants in recent years.

Political Stability: Canada is one of the most politically stable countries in the world, although tensions have been running high for some years between Québec and the rest of Canada, because of the agitation of the separatist *Parti Québécois* for independence, an issue still unresolved. Canada has two tiers of government, federal and provincial, with the provinces having considerable autonomy. Canada is a member of the North American Free Trade Association (NAFTA), with the USA and Mexico, NATO and the British Commonwealth.

Finance

Currency: Canadian dollar (C$)
Exchange Rate: £1 = C$2.27, US$1 = C$1.59
Exchange Controls: None.
Interest Rate: 3.5 per cent
Banks: The Canadian banking system is regulated by the Bank of Canada, the federal government institution responsible for monetary policy. Over 90 per cent of banking assets are controlled by the six main banks, although there are smaller domestic banks and over 40 foreign banks represented. In order to open a bank account in Canada you need a Social Insurance Number (SIN) or proof that you've applied for one.
Cost/Standard of Living: Canada enjoys one of the highest standards of living in the world. It has a relatively low cost of living (lower than most western European countries) with low inflation and high salaries. The economy was hard hit by the recession in the early '90s when unemployment soared, although it has since fallen back. The quality of life in Canada is frequently rated the highest in the world by the United Nations.
GDP Per Head (US$): 19,170

Taxation

Income Tax: For tax purposes you require a Social Insurance Number (SIN), which should be applied for as soon as possible after your arrival in Canada. Residents in Canada must pay both federal and provincial income tax. Federal income tax rates range from 17 per cent on earnings up to C$30,004 and to 29 per cent on earnings above C$60,009. Provincial income tax rates depend on the province and are calculated as percentages of taxable income ranging from around 42 to 51 per cent. All taxpayers must file an annual tax return, in which federal and provincial taxes are calculated together with the exception of Québec, where taxpayers must file two returns, one for federal income tax and the other for provincial tax.
Concessions/Tax Breaks For Retirees: Retirees may be entitled to discounts on transport.
Social Security: Social security (social insurance) contributions are compulsory for most Canadian residents and are deducted from gross monthly salary payments. Employees pay 2.4 per cent of their gross salary on earnings over C$3,500 a year towards social security for benefits that include health care, retirement and disability pensions, and income supplements.
Capital Gains Tax (CGT): CGT is levied on the sale or purchase of any asset excluding your principal home. The taxable portion of capital gains and the deductible portion of capital losses are each 75 per cent. Non-resident property owners must also pay CGT on the sale of property in Canada.

Inheritance & Gift Tax: None, although beneficiaries may be required to pay income tax on a bequest.

Value Added Tax (VAT): An 8 per cent Goods and Services Tax (GST) is levied by the federal government on most goods and services. Most provinces also levy a direct Provincial Sales Tax on retail sales, which ranges, depending on the province, from 6 to 12 per cent. Note that in all provinces except Alberta, sales tax isn't shown in sales prices, but is added at the checkout.

Accommodation

Market: Canada has a flourishing housing market. In common with most of Europe, prices peaked in the late '80s and have since fallen some 10 to 30 per cent in most areas. The more expensive properties (C$150,000 plus) have fallen the furthest. There's a huge variety of property for sale from apartments (condominiums) to large detached properties with a substantial plot of land. Condominiums (apartments) usually have communal garages and sports facilities.

Areas: Apart from buying a home in major cities such as Montreal, Toronto and Vancouver, many foreign buyers seek a holiday home for winter skiing or summer 'wilderness' holidays (or both). The most popular ski resorts include Banff, Jasper, Lake Louise, Okanagan Valley, Whistler, Kananaskis, Blue Mountain Resort and various resorts in Québec.

Cost: Prices vary considerably with the province, e.g. from under C$100,000 in Saskatchewan to around C$300,000 in Vancouver (British Columbia) for a three-bedroom detached property, the average price for a three-bedroom detached home in a major city being around C$175,000, although cheaper properties are available in many suburbs and rural areas. Co-operative apartments and condominiums are common in cities and start at around C$110,000 for a small one-bedroom apartment. Small studio apartments in major ski resorts start from around C$75,500. Building plots in remote areas cost from as little as C$7,500 for those who wish to get 'back to nature'.

Local Mortgages: Mortgages of up to the legal maximum of 75 per cent of the purchase price are available from local banks and other financial institutions. The term is traditionally for 25 to 30 years, although shorter terms are available. New residents in Canada may find getting a mortgage difficult, as you must provide proof of a perfect credit record (preferably in Canada) to obtain one. Note that mortgage interest isn't tax deductible in Canada.

Property Taxes: Property taxes are levied by local municipalities and vary considerably. Those living in apartments also pay monthly community fees.

Purchase Procedure: Buying a home in Canada is generally very safe and there are few traps for the unwary, but it's advisable to engage a buyer's broker who acts solely for you and has your best interests in mind.

Fees: The fees associated with buying a home in Canada total just 2 to 3 per cent of the purchase price and include an appraisal, survey, legal costs, land transfer tax, title registration and a compliance certificate. Legal fees are usually 0.75 to 1 per cent and land transfer tax is from 0.5 to 2 per cent of the purchase price. New houses are subject to GST and in some provinces Provincial Sales Tax is also levied.

Precautions: It's important to have a structural survey completed before buying a resale home, which should include a termite inspection, particularly when homes are located near water.

Holiday Letting: No restrictions.

Restrictions on Foreign Ownership: None.

Building Standards: Excellent. Buildings have a high degree of insulation due to the extremely cold winters in most regions.

Belongings: Can be imported duty-free, but must have been owned and used prior to entry and must be retained for a minimum of one year. A detailed list of all items to be imported must be provided.

Rental Accommodation: Rental accommodation is generally easy to find in Canada, although in city centres there's considerably less choice. Accommodation is usually let unfurnished and costs depend on the location. A two-bedroom apartment costs from C$500 to C$700 a month and a three-bedroom house from C$850 to C$1,600. Leases are usually for one year, although some accommodation can be rented by the month.

Retirement Homes: There are numerous purpose-built retirement home developments in Canada, which are usually situated in rural areas, but within easy reach of nearby towns and cities. They typically comprise apartments and small detached houses, and have from 500 to 1,000 residents. Retirement villages (known as 'adult communities') are popular and places are in short supply. Prices for accommodation differ greatly depending on the location and amenities provided. A small bungalow typically costs from C$120,000 plus weekly service charges.

Utilities: The electricity supply (110/120V) is reliable and provided by private companies, local municipalities or the provincial government. Rates depend on the season, with daily peak and off-peak times. All but the remotest areas of Canada are connected to the gas supply, although most modern properties are all electric. Bottled gas is available outside cities and in remote areas. Water rates are either included in local property taxes or, if a property has a water meter, billed separately. Some provinces occasionally have water shortages with restrictions in the summer months.

Services

Post Office: Canada Post operates the postal service and there are post offices or post office outlets throughout the country. Mail delivery is reasonable, although it can be slow and isn't always reliable. No banking services apart from money orders are available at Canadian post offices.

Telephone: Canadians are avid telephone users and practically every household has a fixed line phone. The service is one of the most modern and cheapest in the world, and is provided by several companies depending on the province. Local calls are free. Mobile phones are popular.

Internet: The Internet is increasingly popular in Canada where over one third of all households are online. There are many service providers offering competitive services and rates, and online time (local calls) is free.

English TV & Radio: Canada has four nationwide TV stations as well as many regional and commercial networks, all of which broadcast in English except for some stations in Québec. The standard of programmes varies enormously, but news broadcasting is generally excellent. Cable television is popular and satellite television has recently been legalised and regulated, and is popular in remote areas. There's no TV licence in Canada.

General Information

Getting There: Canada's main airports have excellent links to and from most international destinations, with flights from the UK and USA competitively priced.

Getting Around: The sheer size of the country and the inaccessibility of some remote areas means that standards of roads and public transport differ enormously, and in remote areas private transport is essential. Air travel is popular with Canadians who have some of the most comprehensive and cheapest airline services in the world. As a consequence, air travel has largely replaced the train and car as a means of crossing the country. Canada has an extensive rail network, although cross-country trains are slow and not a popular travel option nowadays. Major cities have excellent urban and suburban transit rail systems, which are efficient, fast and economical. There are regular car and passenger ferries connecting the maritime provinces to the islands, and toll-free ferries operate on some rivers in major population centres.

Shopping: Shopping is a popular 'leisure' activity in Canada, where there's an abundance of large shopping centres (malls) with a wide choice of shops and department stores. Small towns usually have a good choice of general stores, although remote areas may have no shopping facilities at all.

Crime Rate: The crime rate in Canada is one of the lowest in the world. Canada has strict gun control laws and a low murder rate, which is similar to most western European countries.

Driving: Canada has a massive road network and one of the highest car densities in the world. Road standards are generally very good, although in remote areas road quality varies and progress can be slow. Bear in mind the size of Canada and that distances are huge, meaning journeys cross-country are long. Cars are cheaper than in most European countries and all vehicles must comply with strict safety and emission regulations. Traffic drives on the right and you can drive with an international licence for a short time, after which you need to take a Canadian driving test to remain licensed to drive.

Medical Facilities: Excellent. Canada has one of the best emergency services in the world, although treatment can be very expensive. There's a government-sponsored health scheme (Medicare) for qualifying residents which provides basic health care 'free' of charge. To qualify for free medical treatment you must be in possession of a health insurance card, which can usually be obtained as soon as you arrive from provincial health offices, although in a few states you have to wait three months before you can apply. Private health insurance is vital for anyone who isn't covered by the government scheme and most Canadians have private medical insurance to cover the shortcomings of Medicare.

Pets: All animals are subject to a veterinary inspection at the port of entry. Some (e.g. birds) are required to undergo a period of quarantine. Domestic animals such as cats and dogs can be imported from rabies-free countries (e.g. the UK) without a rabies vaccination or a quarantine period. Pets from countries with rabies must have a rabies vaccination at least one month prior to their importation.

Reciprocal Agreement with the UK: British citizens entitled to a state pension in the UK can continue to receive it in Canada, but the amount is frozen at the rate it was when they left the UK.

Residence Permits: Resident permits are difficult to obtain unless you qualify for a work permit or start a business in Canada (see below). It's quite difficult for retirees to emigrate to Canada, although if you own property there or are sponsored by a 'very close' relative, e.g. by a son or daughter, your chances are improved considerably.

Work Permits: Canada has a permanent programme of immigration with an annual quota of around 180,000 immigrants, one of the highest quotas in the world. It operates a selective policy based on a points system, with preference given to those with special skills that are in demand, those wishing to start a business, and those with family ties and refugees. Being bi-lingual (English/French) is an advantage for employees. Note that you cannot enter Canada as a visitor or tourist and change your status.

Visas: All persons wishing to live or work in Canada require an immigration visa in order to enter the country. Visitors to Canada from many countries such as the EU states, Australia, New Zealand and the USA don't require a visa to enter as a tourist. Visitors must be able to produce a valid passport and a return or onward travel ticket.

Reference

Further Reading

Living and Working in Canada, David Hampshire (Survival Books, 💻 www.survivalbooks.net). Everything you need to know about living and working in Canada.

Canada News, 1 Commercial Road, Eastbourne, East Sussex BN21 3XQ, UK (☎ 01323-726040, 💻 www.outbound-newspapers.com).

Immigrating to Canada, Gary L. Segal.

Living in Canada (Canadian Ministry of Employment and Immigration).

Useful Addresses

Canadian High Commission, 501 Pennsylvania Ave., NW, Washington, DC 20001, USA (☎ 0202-682 1740).

Canadian High Commission, Macdonald House, 1 Grosvenor Street, London W1X 0AB, UK (☎ 020-7258 6600, 💻 www.canada.org.uk).

Canadian Real Estate Association, 334 Slater St., Suite 1600, Canada Building, Ottawa, ON K1R 743, Canada (☎ 0613-237 7111, 💻 http://crea.ca).

Canada Customs & Revenue Agency, International Taxation Office, 2204 Walkley Road, Ottawa, ON K1A 1A8, Canada (☎ 0613-952 3741).

The Visit Canada Centre, PO Box 5396, Northampton, NN1 2FA, UK (☎ 0870 161 5151, ✉ visitcanada@dial.pipex.com).

Useful Websites

💻 www.cic.gc.ca – Citizenship and Immigration Canada. In addition to giving information on immigration policy, this website also has a range of very useful fact sheets and information about living and working in Canada.

💻 www.travelcanada.ca – A good tourist information site.

💻 www.over50.ca – A website with information and links specifically for retirees in Canada.

THE CARIBBEAN

Background Information

Countries: The Caribbean Sea region contains two major chains of islands: the Greater Antilles (which comprise almost 90 per cent of the region's total land area) and the Lesser Antilles (made up of the Leeward Islands in the north and the Windward Islands in the south). The Caribbean islands extend almost 4,000km (2,500mi) in a wide arc from the Bahamas 100km (62 mi) off the east coast of Florida to Trinidad 24km (15mi) off the coast of Venezuela. Most of the major islands are independent countries, although retaining close ties with their former colonial rulers, and some remain colonies or dependent territories of the UK, France, the Netherlands or the USA. The countries which attract most foreign property buyers include those listed below.

Population: The populations of the Caribbean countries most favoured by foreign home buyers are:

- Antigua & Barbuda (77,000);
- Bahamas (285,000);
- Barbados (260,000;
- Bermuda (60,000);
- Cayman Islands (33,000);
- Dominica (75,000);
- Guadeloupe (350,000);
- Jamaica (2.4 million);
- Martinique (345,000);
- Montserrat (13,000);
- Puerto Rico (3.6 million);
- St Christopher (St Kitts) & Nevis (45,000);
- St Lucia (150,000);
- St Vincent & The Grenadines (115,000);
- Trinidad & Tobago (1.25 million);
- Turks & Caicos Islands (10,000);
- British Virgin Islands (13,000);
- US Virgin Islands (117,000).

The majority of inhabitants are of African descent, their ancestors having been shipped to the Caribbean as slaves and indentured servants. Some islands also have a large Indian population whose forebears were brought to the Caribbean as indentured labourers by the British. The population of many islands swells considerably in the winter, when many visitors stay for the whole season.

Foreign Community: There's a significant foreign community in most of the Caribbean islands, mainly consisting of British and American retirees, and expatriate workers engaged in the financial services and tourist industries. Many visitors spend up to half the year in the Caribbean.

Area: The overall surface areas of the most popular countries among foreign home buyers are:

- Antigua & Barbuda 442km² (179mi²);
- Bahamas 13,938km² (5,382mi²);
- Barbados 430km² (166mi²);
- Bermuda 53km² (20mi²);
- Cayman Islands 259km² (100mi²);
- Dominica 748km² (289mi²);
- Guadeloupe 1,710km² (666mi²);
- Jamaica 10,990km² (4,243mi²);
- Martinique 1,100km² (425mi²);
- Montserrat 102km² (39mi²);
- Puerto Rico 8,897km² (3,435mi²);
- St Christopher (St Kitts) & Nevis 360m² (139mi²);
- St Lucia 622km² (240mi²);
- St Vincent & The Grenadines 388km² (150mi²);
- Trinidad & Tobago 5,130km² (1,981mi²);
- Turks & Caicos Islands 430km² (166mi²);
- British Virgin Islands 153mi² (59mi²);
- US Virgin Islands 340km² (130mi²).

Geography: The Caribbean islands comprise a total land area of 234,000km² (90,350mi²) and with the exception of the Bahamas lie between latitude 10deg north and the Tropic of Cancer (23deg 27min north). There are literally thousands of tropical islands and cays (*cayes*), (the Bahamas alone comprises some 700), the vast majority of which are tiny and uninhabited. The islands are noted for their dazzling, white sandy beaches (some of the finest in the world) and fine coral reefs, warm clear seas, lush vegetation and exotic flora and fauna (rainforests, tropical plants and flowers), mountains, rivers and waterfalls, and cloudless blue skies. Some islands have live volcanoes, including Guadeloupe, Martinique, St Vincent and Montserrat, which was devastated in 1997 when its Soufriere Hills volcano erupted, spewing ash and lava over half the island and burying the capital Plymouth.

Climate: The Caribbean islands enjoy a tropical or sub-tropical (in the northern Bahamas) climate, which is one of the healthiest in the world, with 3,000 hours (some 300 days) of sunshine a year. The climate does, however, differ considerably between the islands as a result of their different topography. In most islands, daytime temperatures rarely drop below 16°C (61°F) or rise above 32°C (90°F) and the average annual temperature is around 25°C (77°F). In winter the weather is usually pleasant with temperatures between around 18 to 25°C (64 to 77°F). The difference between the highest and lowest temperature varies throughout the year by just 3°C (5.5°F) in the southern Antilles to 6°C (11°F) in the Bahamas.

Average sea temperatures range from around 28°C (82°F) in the warmest months to 25°C (77°F) in the coolest (in the sub-tropical Bahamas the temperature is a few degrees lower). Many islands experience high humidity, particularly during the summer months, although the heat is tempered by cooling trade winds. Annual rainfall varies considerably, but in most islands is between 1m and 1.5m (39 to 59in), with the wettest months between May and November and the driest from December to April, although on some islands rainfall is more or less constant throughout the year. The region is susceptible to violent storms and hurricanes between June and November, and most islands experience severe tropical storms around every ten years (hurricanes less frequently). During the northern hemisphere's winter, the Caribbean is the world's cruise centre.

Language: The official language is English, French, Dutch or Spanish, depending on an island's former (or current) colonial allegiance. On the majority of islands the official language is English, while many also have their own colloquial languages such as Creole and Papiamento, the *patois* spoken in the former British possessions.

Political Stability: Political stability varies according to the island, but is generally good to excellent. Many islands are colonies or dependent territories (by choice) and are therefore very stable. Most ex-British colonies have a system of government based on the British parliamentary model. Some governments have been involved in corruption scandals in recent years, although this is the exception.

Finance

Currency: Various, many of which are tied to the US$ at a fixed exchange rate. Some islands share a currency, such as the Eastern Caribbean dollar (EC$). US$ bank notes and travellers' cheques are widely accepted (the US$ is the *de facto* currency in the Caribbean) and the US$ is the official currency on some islands. Many islands are popular tax havens, particularly the Bahamas and the Cayman Islands.

Exchange Controls: None on most islands, although some have limited restrictions. On some islands, the export of local currency is subject to severe restrictions and sometimes totally prohibited. Some islands require foreign currency to be declared on entry and exit, and only imported currency can be exported.

Banks: Banking is generally secure in the Caribbean, one of the world's leading off-shore banking centres, although on some islands, e.g. Jamaica, the banking system is being restructured. Numerous local commercial banks and several foreign banks, mainly North American, trade on the islands. Note, on the other hand, that in recent months, many Caribbean offshore banks and their clients have been under international scrutiny and it's now difficult to have a 'secret' bank account. Banking services and transactions are generally fast and efficient.

Cost/Standard of Living: The cost of food and essential services is reasonably low on most islands, although imported goods (which include most consumer durables) are expensive. Cars, clothing and consumer appliances are comparatively expensive, while items such as jewellery, perfumes and alcohol are generally inexpensive. The cost of living is similar to most western European countries, but higher than the USA and Canada.

GDP Per Head (US$): 16,554 (Bahamas), 39,063 (Bermuda)

Taxation

Income Tax: There's no income tax on many Caribbean islands and where there is, it's relatively low.

Concessions/Tax Breaks For Retirees: On some islands, retired foreign nationals may be exempt from paying income tax on income earned abroad.

Social Security: Contributions to social security and benefits vary from island to island. For example, in Barbados employees contribute around 8 per cent of their gross monthly salary. In Bermuda employees must pay around 4.75 per cent, while in the Bahamas it's 3.4 per cent up to an annual maximum of B$20,800.

Capital Gains Tax (CGT): Most Caribbean countries have no capital gains tax.
Wealth Tax: None.
Inheritance & Gift Tax: Most Caribbean countries have no inheritance tax, although some islands such as Bermuda impose an estate tax of between 0 and 15 per cent.
Value Added Tax (VAT): A few islands have a value added or sales tax, e.g. 15 per cent in Trinidad and Tobago. The main source of income for most governments is import duties, which are levied on most imported goods. Some islands have special taxes, such as a tax on hotel bills.

Accommodation

Market: There's a buoyant market in luxury homes on most islands, although prices are high. Beach front properties are in particularly high demand. New homes are built mostly of wood and older wooden cottages are also available on many islands. Detached homes usually have their own swimming pools. New developments normally provide a wide range of amenities which may include restaurants, bars, shops, tennis courts, swimming pools, water sports facilities, private beaches, boat moorings and on-site management offices. Most developers provide a management and letting service.
Cost: Homes on most islands are expensive on account of the high cost of land and because most building materials and fixtures and fittings must be imported. On the most popular islands, apartments start at around US$300,000 and detached villas at US$500,000, although cheaper property is available on some islands. Property is cheaper on the smaller, less developed islands, but these are generally for those seeking almost complete solitude. Prices have risen considerably in the last decade, and beachfront properties are prohibitively expensive on many islands. Most new developments comprise luxury condominiums (apartments) or luxury detached homes. Prices are usually quoted in US$.
Local Mortgages: Mortgages are available from local banks on most islands. Maximum loans are usually 50 to 60 per cent on second homes with repayment over a maximum of 15 years. A small duty may be imposed on mortgages. Loans are available in the local currency or US$, which usually offers a lower interest rate. Lenders generally insist that properties are insured for their full value and borrowers may also require life insurance.
Property Taxes: Property taxes are levied on most islands and are based on the market or rental value. Taxes are usually low, e.g. in the Bahamas they're 1 per cent of the market value up to B$500,000 and 2 per cent of the market value above B$500,000 for non-residents (taxes are slightly lower for permanent residents). There may be an annual fee for refuse collection.

Purchase Procedure: It's usual to retain a local lawyer to complete the formalities. Foreign buyers may require police clearance from their country of residence and must usually produce evidence of their funds. The purchase procedure on most islands is modelled on the British system (see page 290). Most islands have an efficient and safe legal system and problems are rare.

Fees: Most countries levy duty and/or transfer tax on property purchases at between 5 and 10 per cent, e.g. up to 8 per cent on properties costing over B$100,000 in the Bahamas and 10 per cent in Antigua/Barbuda and Barbados. Estate agents' fees are usually between 5 and 10 per cent for developed property. Legal (conveyance) fees are usually 2.5 to 3 per cent of the sale price.

Precautions: Before buying building land, you must ensure that you have planning permission (or that it will be approved) for the size and type of property you plan to build, and that services will be provided. In view of the occasional severe storms (and erupting volcanoes!) it's important that a home is insured for the full cost of rebuilding.

Holiday Letting: Generally no restrictions, although on some islands, e.g. Bermuda, if you hold a residence certificate you cannot let property for long periods of time and require permission for short periods.

Restrictions on Foreign Ownership: Official government permission is usually required for foreigners to purchase land or property, although this is a formality and may be required only for properties above a certain land area, e.g. 2 hectares (5 acres) in the Bahamas. The amount of land that can be purchased for residential purposes without a permit is usually limited to between 1 and 5 acres.

Building Standards: Generally excellent for new properties. The quality of older properties is variable. Homes are usually built in the local style employing local materials (e.g. wood) whenever possible.

Belongings: These can be freely imported without any restrictions, although duty is payable on some large items (such as motor vehicles) and these can be high. In some cases, items of high value such as photographic equipment, portable computers, electronic apparatus and sports equipment must be declared.

Rental Accommodation: Short-term rentals are widely available in most Caribbean countries, although long-term rentals are less easy to find and can be very expensive.

Retirement Homes: There are currently no purpose-built retirement developments in the Caribbean islands.

Utilities: The electricity supply (generally 100V) is reasonably reliable, although power cuts are commonplace in bad weather. Tap water is generally safe to drink but the taste can be quite saline and most people prefer to drink bottled water. Bottled gas is available on some islands.

Services

Post Office: The efficiency of the postal service varies from island to island, although delivery is usually fast and secure.

Telephone: Telecommunications are generally modern and efficient, and usually operated by a monopoly on each island, although the market is gradually being privatised. Call charges (particularly international) are high.

Internet: The Internet is steadily gaining in popularity, although some islands are still a long way behind others. There are numerous subscription ISPs.

English TV & Radio: State television on English-speaking islands broadcasts in English and satellite TV (usually consisting of American cable stations) is available on all but the smallest islands.

General Information

Getting There: The Caribbean is well connected by flights from most countries, particularly the UK and USA, although some islands are served only by connecting flights from Puerto Rico. Ferries serve the islands from Miami and the Caribbean is one of the world's top cruise ship destinations.

Getting Around: The Bahamas have probably the best domestic flight service and there are also inter-island flights, although services and frequencies vary greatly. Ferries connect the islands with each other, but, again, services can be erratic and dependent on the weather. Most islands have a bus service or 'collective' (shared) taxis. Private transport is often the best way to see an island and there are numerous car rental companies.

Shopping: Most towns on the islands have good shopping facilities, although the choice of goods may be limited. On smaller and more remote islands shopping facilities are limited or even non-existent.

Crime Rate: Low on most islands, although crime has risen considerably on many islands in recent years and you should always keep an eye on your belongings. Violent and serious crime is relatively low, but increasing, particularly in Jamaica. Some areas on some islands are to be avoided, particularly at night. Organised crimes, such as drug trafficking and money laundering, are a problem on some islands.

Driving: Road standards vary greatly, although they're generally good on main roads. Driving standards also vary, but tend to be poor. Cars and petrol are expensive. Traffic drives on the right. An international driving licence is generally necessary, although you can only usually drive for a period before you must exchange your licence for one issued by the country you're living in. In Bermuda no foreign licences are valid and you must take the Bermudan driving test if you wish to drive.

Medical Facilities: Good on most islands, although some facilities aren't available on the smaller islands. In the less developed islands you must be

flown to a hospital if you fall seriously ill and it may be necessary to be evacuated to the USA or a neighbouring country to be treated for a serious health problem (which must be covered by your insurance). Private international health insurance is highly recommended, as the best hospitals are often private. **On some islands, e.g. Barbados, dengue fever is endemic.**
Pets: There's no quarantine for pets on most islands, but it's advisable to check with the local authorities before importing a pet. All animals require a current vaccination certificate including rabies.
Reciprocal Agreement with the UK: Barbados, Bermuda and Jamaica are the only Caribbean states with reciprocal agreements with the UK. British citizens entitled to a UK state pension can continue to receive it and the amount will be increased annually at the same rate as in the UK.
Residence Permits: Usually a formality, provided you have adequate means of financial support and own a property (or have made an investment) above a certain minimum amount, e.g. B$250,000 in the Bahamas. In most cases a temporary (e.g. annual) or permanent residence certificate must be obtained, for which there are high fees, e.g. up to B$10,000 in the Bahamas. On some islands the fee for a residence certificate is based on the value of your property, e.g. 5 per cent of a property's value in Antigua and Barbuda. Note that some islands also levy high fees for those wishing to become tax residents. Citizenship based on investment is also available on some islands.
Work Permits: Difficult to obtain unless you plan to start a business and create employment, when there are minimum levels of investment. Employers must usually show that there isn't a similarly qualified local resident available to fill a position.
Visas: Nationals from the European Union (EU), Canada and the USA generally don't require a visa for stays of up to three months, although US citizens can stay for up to eight months in the Bahamas and British nationals for up to six months on the British Virgin Islands. Australians and New Zealanders generally don't require a visa, although on some islands such as Martinique they require a French visa (from a French consulate or embassy). All foreigners require a visa for employment.

Reference

Further Reading

Baedeker Caribbean (AA/Baedeker).

Useful Addresses

The High Commission of the Commonwealth of the Bahamas, Bahamas House, 10 Chesterfield Street, London W1X 8AH, UK (☎ 020-7408 4488).

High Commission for Antigua and Barbuda, Antigua House, 15 Thayer Street, London W1M 5LD, UK (☎ 020-7486 7073/5, 🖥 www.antigua-barbuda.com).

The High Commission for Barbados, 1 Great Russell Street, London WC1B 3JY, UK (☎ 020-7631 4975).

Office of the High Commission of the Commonwealth of Dominica, 1 Collingham Gardens, London SW5 0HW, UK (☎ 020-7370 5194/5, 🖥 www.dominica.co.uk).

High Commission of the Republic of Trinidad and Tobago, 42 Belgrave Square, London SW1X 8NT, UK (☎ 020-7245 9351).

Embassy of Antigua & Barbuda, 3216 New Mexico Ave, NW, Washington, DC 20016, USA (☎ 0202-362 5122).

Embassy of The Commonwealth of The Bahamas, 2220 Massachusetts Ave, NW Washington, DC 20008, USA (☎ 0202-319 2660).

Embassy of Barbados, 2144 Wyoming Ave, NW, Washington, DC 20008, USA (☎ 0202-939 9200/2).

Embassy of The Commonwealth of Dominica, 3216 New Mexico Ave, NW, Washington, DC 20016, USA (☎ 0202-3643 6781/2).

Embassy of Grenada, 1701 New Hampshire Ave, NW, Washington, DC 20009, USA (☎ 0202-265 2561).

Embassy of Jamaica, 1520 New Hampshire Ave, NW, Washington, DC 20036, USA (☎ 0202-452 0660, 🖥 www.emjam-usa.org).

Embassy of St. Kitts and Nevis, 3216 New Mexico Ave, NW, Washington, DC 20016, USA (☎ 0202-686 2636, 🖥 www.stkittsnevis.org).

Embassy of St. Lucia, 3216 New Mexico Ave, NW, Washington, DC 20016, USA (☎ 0202-364 6792/93).

Embassy of St. Vincent and the Grenadines, 3216 New Mexico Ave, NW, Washington, DC 20016, USA (☎ 0202-364 6730).

Embassy of the Republic of Trinidad and Tobago, 1708 Massachusetts Ave, NW, Washington, DC 20036, USA (☎ 0202-467 6490).

Useful Websites

🖥 www.caricom.org – The official website of the Caribbean community.

🖥 www.caribbean.com – A useful website with links and information about each island.

CYPRUS

Background

Capital: Nicosia (Lefkosia)
Population: 665,000
Foreign Community: The population of Cyprus is 78 per cent Greek, 18 per cent Turkish and 4 per cent other nationalities. There's a sizeable foreign community, including some 5,000 British residents concentrated primarily in resort areas.
Area: 9,250km^2 (3,572mi^2)
Geography: Cyprus is situated at the eastern end of the Mediterranean 64km (40mi) from Turkey and 122km (76mi) from Syria. It's 240km (149mi) long and 96km (60mi) wide, with a coastline of 782km (486mi). The northern coast is backed by the long limestone range of Kyrenia. The central plain between Morphou and Famagusta is fertile and well irrigated, and produces fruit, flowers and early vegetables.
Climate: Cyprus is the sunniest island in the Mediterranean with over 300 days of sunshine a year and long, hot, dry summers and mild winters. Most rainfall is between November and March. August is the hottest month, when temperatures are between 21 and 40°C (70 and 104°F), and January the coldest with temperatures between 6 and 13°C (43 and 55°F). Sea temperatures range from 16°C (61°F) in January to 32°C (90°F) in August. In winter it's possible to ski on Mount Olympus in the Troodos mountains. Cyprus suffered an earthquake in 1995 measuring 5.2 on the Richter scale, which damaged around 700 homes in 50 villages. Modern homes, on the other hand, are generally built to withstand the occasional earth tremors.

Language: National languages are Greek and Turkish, although most Turkish Cypriots now live in the self-declared Turkish Republic of Northern Cyprus. English is spoken by some 90 per cent of Greek Cypriots.

Political Stability: Cyprus has had a turbulent history since the '50s and was partitioned in 1974 when Turkish forces invaded the north. The northern part of Cyprus (40 per cent of the island) remains under the jurisdiction of the Turkish Cypriots backed by the Turkish army, with the capital Nicosia partitioned. The Turkish Cypriots have declared a Turkish Republic of Northern Cyprus, a pariah 'state' recognised only by Turkey. There's little communication between the Greek and Turkish Cypriot communities. Today, at least as far as most foreigners are concerned, Cyprus effectively consists of the southern region governed by the Greek Cypriots, and the information in this section refers exclusively to this area. It should be noted that partition is of little or no concern to foreigners living in the southern part of Cyprus. Cyprus is a member of the British Commonwealth and is expected to join the EU in 2004.

Finance

Currency: Cyprus pound (C£)
Exchange Rate: £1 = C£0.95, US$1 = C£0.66
Exchange Controls: Yes. Funds imported to buy a property should be officially documented so that when it's sold the proceeds can be repatriated.
Interest Rate: 6 per cent
Banks: The Cypriot banking system closely follows the British model and Cypriot banks are modern, efficient and equipped with the latest technology. There are nine commercial banks and some 30 foreign banks represented on the island. Residents and non-residents can open bank accounts.
Cost/Standard of Living: The cost of living is low by European standards, but has increased considerably in recent years, although Cyprus remains one of the cheapest countries in Europe. Some imported items are expensive, although car prices are as much as 50 per cent lower than in some northern European countries.. Residents can import a new car, tax and duty-free. Prices are expected to rise when Cyprus joins the EU, probably in 2004.
GDP Per Head (US$): 16,000

Taxation

Income Tax: Income tax is levied on income remitted to Cyprus. The rate is just 5 per cent on pensions and investment income remitted to Cyprus by residents (the first C£4,000 is exempt for a single person or C£8,000 for a couple). After deducting their allowances, a retired couple would pay only around C£600 tax on C£15,000 remitted to Cyprus. There's a PAYE system for resident employees with progressive tax rates from 20 to 40 per cent (on earnings above C£5,000).

Concessions/Tax Breaks For Retirees: There are significant tax breaks for pensioners (see **Income Tax** above).

Social Security: All employees must contribute 6.3 per cent of their gross monthly salary (up to a maximum of C£1,495) to the Cypriot social security system. The self-employed contribute 11.6 per cent of their monthly income. Benefits include free or low-cost health care, retirement and disability pensions, and sickness and unemployment benefits.

Capital Gains Tax (CGT): Gains from the sale of property in Cyprus are taxed at 20 per cent, although there's a lifetime exemption (i.e. once only) of between C£10,000 and C£50,000 depending on the type of property. You can export the initial purchase price plus C£50,000 profit, but any balance can be exported only at the rate of C£50,000 a year (plus interest), commencing the year following the sale.

Wealth Tax: None.

Inheritance & Gift Tax: Inheritance tax ranges from 10 to 30 per cent and is payable on estates in excess of C£20,000, although there are generous allowances for spouses and children. Inheritance tax must be paid on the worldwide assets of someone who was domiciled in Cyprus. If, on the other hand, he purchased a property there after 1st January 1976 while resident abroad and with imported funds, the estate isn't taxable. Inheritance tax is payable by non-residents on property owned in Cyprus. There's no gift tax.

Value Added Tax (VAT): VAT is levied at a standard rate of 10 per cent and a reduced rate of 5 per cent applies to hotel and restaurant bills and alcohol. Certain essential goods and services are zero-rated or exempt, including most food, medicines and financial transactions.

Accommodation

Market: Cyprus has a flourishing property market and it's traditionally a popular location for both holiday and retirement homes. A wide range of properties is available, both new and old, including restored and un-restored old village houses. New developments abound, although many are uninspiring and few have swimming pools or sports facilities such as tennis courts; there's just one golf course on the island (in Paphos). Over-development and mass-market tourism has ruined many coastal areas with the notable exception of Paphos, where there are strict building regulations. Most inland villages are unspoilt and full of character.

Areas: The most popular locations for foreign buyers are in and around the coastal towns of Ayia Napa, Limassol, Larnaka and Paphos. The Troodos mountains and the capital Nicosia are also popular.

Cost: A wide choice of properties is available, including apartments, townhouses and villas. The prices vary according to the location, size and quality of the property. One-bedroom apartments cost from around C£25,000, two-bedroom apartments from C£35,000, two-bedroom townhouses from C£45,000, and two-bedroom detached bungalows and villas from around C£60,000. Beachfront properties attract a premium of around 20 per cent. Resale properties are often sold furnished. The cost of building land depends considerably on the area, price start from around C£50 to C£300 per m².

Local Mortgages: Mortgages of 70 or 75 per cent are available from local banks for a period of five to ten years. There's a mortgage registration fee of at least 1 per cent of the amount borrowed. Some new properties are sold on 'hire purchase' terms by developers, e.g. a 25 per cent deposit with the balance payable in monthly instalments over two to five years. Other schemes require a third of the whole amount on signing, a third during construction and the remaining third to be paid in monthly instalments over two or three years.

Property Taxes: A local authority tax of between C£30 and C£100 a year is payable for services such as refuse collection and street lighting. There's also an annual tax based on a property's value: 2 per cent on properties valued between C£101,000 to C£250,000, 3 per cent between C£250,001 and C£500,000, and 3.5 per cent above C£500,000.

Purchase Procedure: Foreign currency must be imported to pay for property and an Import of Foreign Currency certificate is required by the Land Registry office. The purchase procedure is based on the British legal system. Both parties sign a preliminary contract which binds them to the transaction on mutually agreed terms. Contracts are subject to good title and any necessary government permits. A deposit is lodged with a lawyer or notary, and searches are carried out to ensure that the vendor has good title to a property. An application to purchase a property must be made to the Council of Ministers, although it's only a formality. When the searches have been completed and the permits approved, a final contract is drawn up and lodged with the Land Registry office.

Offshore Companies: Offshore companies may be used to purchase property in Cyprus, in which case exchange controls don't affect the sale of a property and full repatriation of funds is possible. In addition, no land registry fees are payable, which can result in a large saving.

Fees: Fees generally total around 10 per cent of the purchase price. Lawyer's fees are between C£200 and C£500 or 1 per cent of the purchase price up to C£75,000. Stamp duty is C£1.50 per C£1,000 of value up to C£100,000 and C£2 per C£1,000 above this amount. The application to the Council of Ministers costs around C£200. A land registry fee or transfer tax is levied at between 3 and 8 per cent, depending on the value of the property. When a couple are buying a property together as co-owners, they can split the transfer tax between them.

Precautions: Buyers should engage a local lawyer, although it isn't required by law. Always ensure that the deeds are produced (as required in the contract) and make this a condition of a purchase. Note that the signing of a contract and payment of a deposit can lead to a buyer being irrevocably committed, even if the title is defective or there are flaws in the contract.

Holiday Letting: Holiday letting isn't permitted by foreign property owners in Cyprus, although it isn't strictly enforced and many foreigners let their properties.

Restrictions on Foreign Ownership: Foreigners are permitted to own only one property or building plot at a time and the maximum plot size is usually two 'donums', i.e. $2,675m^2$ ($28,800ft^2$) or approximately two-thirds of an acre. In certain cases, foreigners can own up to three donums (1 acre).

Building Standards: The design of new properties and developments has improved greatly in recent years, although it still lacks inspiration, and the construction quality of new properties is generally high. The quality of older resale properties is variable and a survey is recommended on older detached properties.

Belongings: Belongings can be imported duty-free, including vehicles (retirees are permitted to import two duty-free cars). Non-residents are allowed to import a car and use it for three months. Household effects must have been owned and used for 12 months, and must be imported within 12 months of taking up residence. A government levy, known as the Temporary Refugee Levy (TRL), applies to all imported goods, whether new or used. The rate is 1.7 per cent of the declared value and you can expect to pay between C£75 and C£150 for a typical shipment.

Rental Accommodation: Rental properties are readily available in Cyprus, particularly in coastal and resort areas, although in high season prices are considerably higher and properties more difficult to find. Rental properties are usually let furnished and a two-bedroom apartment costs between C£200 and C£400 a month.

Retirement Homes: There are no purpose-built retirement developments in Cyprus, although given the growing retiree population it will probably only be a matter of time before they're introduced.

Utilities: Electricity (220-240V) is provided by the Electricity Authority of Cyprus (EAC). Charges are reasonable and billed bi-monthly. Mains gas isn't available in Cyprus but bottled gas is widely used and costs around C£3 for a 10kg bottle. Water is a precious commodity in Cyprus and droughts and water shortages are commonplace, particularly in the long summer months. Tap water is safe to drink.

Services

Post Office: The Cypriot mail service is generally efficient and there are post offices in most towns and villages. In addition to postal services, post offices provide limited financial transactions, such as transfers and currency exchange.

Telephone: Telecommunications in Cyprus are operated by the Cyprus Telecommunications Authority (CTA) as a monopoly. Massive investment in the latest technology means telecommunications are excellent and reliable. Call charges are reasonable.

Internet: Cyprus is well-served with Internet facilities, including ISDN lines, mainly on account of huge investment by CTA. Most Cypriot companies have websites and e-mail, and there's a number of ISPs.

English TV & Radio: Cyprus Broadcasting (CyBC) broadcasts news bulletins in English and films are usually shown in English with Greek subtitles. Satellite reception is good throughout the island. CyBC radio also broadcasts frequently in English and the British forces' stations broadcast in English 24 hours a day.

General Information

Getting There: Cyprus has two international airports and is well-served by flights from most major countries; prices are competitive, particularly in high season. You can also travel to Cyprus by ferry from Greece and the Middle East, although services are infrequent in the winter months.

Getting Around: The only form of public transport in Cyprus are buses and although the main centres have good and frequent services, other areas are poorly served. 'Service taxis', similar to mini-buses and shared by several passengers, are a popular, economical means of getting around.

Shopping: Shopping facilities are generally good in Cyprus and there's a reasonable selection of shops in the main towns, where most goods are available.

Crime Rate: Cyprus has one of the world's lowest crime rates, and both serious crime and crime against property are relatively low.

Driving: Private transport is the best way of getting around Cyprus, where road conditions are generally good with excellent dual carriageways linking the main towns, although in rural areas some roads are barely more than tracks. Note that Cypriot driving leaves much to be desired and the accident rate is relatively high. Cars are inexpensive in Cyprus (around half the price in most Western countries) and are mainly Asian makes. Traffic drives on the *left*. If you drive a Cyprus-registered car you will need to exchange your driving licence for a Cypriot one. Petrol is cheap.

Medical Facilities: Very good. Many doctors are trained in the UK or USA and inexpensive health services are provided at government hospitals. Private health insurance is necessary for retirees.

Pets: Pets must be vaccinated against echinoochus and have an import licence issued by the Department of Veterinary Services. A dog or cat must be quarantined for six months, although this may be at your own home. Dogs aren't permitted to roam freely and must be kept in an enclosed area (e.g. with a fence) or on a lead.

Reciprocal Agreement with the UK: British citizens entitled to a state pension in the UK can continue to receive it in Cyprus and the amount will be increased annually at the same rate as in the UK.

Residence Permits: Property owners with an adequate income can obtain a residence permit and foreign retirees are encouraged to take up residence. The annual income requirements in 2001 were C£7,000 for a single person and C£10,000 for a couple without children.

Work Permits: Work permits are difficult to obtain and a government permit is required under the Alien Immigration Law.

Visas: Visas aren't required by visitors from Australia, Canada, EU states, New Zealand and the USA for stays of less than three months. If you're visiting Cyprus to live, seek employment or study, or are a national of a country not listed above, you must obtain a visa. EU nationals can apply for a visa in Cyprus but non-EU nationals must apply for one before their arrival.

Reference

Further Reading

Buying a Home in Greece & Cyprus, Joanna Styles (Survival Books, ⌨ www.survivalbooks.net). Everything you need to know about buying a home in Cyprus.

Cyprus Magazine, PO Box 45Y, London W1 45Y, UK. Bi-monthly magazine.

Cyprus Daily/Weekly, PO Box 21144, 1502 Nicosia, Cyprus.

Useful Addresses

Centre for Overseas Retirement Studies, PO Box 3293, P Lordos Centre, 1st Floor, Block B, Byron Street, Limassol, Cyprus (☎ 05-354371).

Cyprus Embassy, 2210 R St, NW, Washington, DC 20008, USA (☎ 0202-462 5772).

Cyprus High Commission, 93 Park Street, London W1Y 4ET, UK (☎ 020-7499 8272).

Cyprus Real Estate Agents Association, PO Box 1455, Nicosia, Cyprus (☎ 02-449 500).

Cyprus Tourism Organisation, PO Box 24535, 1390 Nicosia (☎ 02-337715, 💻 www.cyprustourism.org).

Ministry of the Interior, Migration Officer, Department of Aliens and Immigration, D. Severis Ave, Nicosia, Cyprus (☎ 02-804533).

Useful Websites

💻 www.cyprusweekly.com.cy –The Cyprus English-language newspaper online.

💻 www.windowoncyprus.com – Plenty of tourist and practical information about visiting or living in Cyprus.

FRANCE

Background

Capital: Paris
Population: 58.8 million
Foreign Community: France has a large foreign community in its major cities and in some rural areas (e.g. Dordogne, where there are many British residents).
Area: 543,965km² (210,025mi²)
Geography: France is one of the largest countries in Europe, stretching 1,050km (650mi) from north to south and almost the same distance from West to East (from the tip of Brittany to Strasbourg). Its land and sea border extends

for 4,800km (3,000mi) and includes 2,700km (2,175mi) of coastline. France also incorporates the Mediterranean island of Corsica (*Corse*) situated 160km (99mi) from France and 80km (50mi) from Italy, covering 8,721km² (3,367mi²) and with a coastline of 1,000km (620mi). France is bordered by Andorra, Belgium, Germany, Italy, Luxembourg, Spain and Switzerland, and the opening of the Channel Tunnel in 1994 connected it with the UK (by rail only).

Climate: France is the only country in Europe that experiences three distinct climates: continental, maritime and Mediterranean. It isn't easy to generalise about French weather, as many regions are influenced by mountains, forests and other geographical features, and have their own micro-climates. Generally, the Loire river is considered to be the point where the cooler northern European climate begins to change to the warmer southern climate. Spring and autumn are usually fine throughout France, although the length of the seasons varies according to the region and altitude.

In Paris, it's rare for the temperature to fall below -5°C (30°F) in winter or to rise above 30°C (86°F) in summer. The capital, on the other hand, receives its fair share of rain. The west and north-west (e.g. Brittany and Normandy) have a maritime climate tempered by the Atlantic and the Gulf Stream, with mild winters and warm summers, and most rainfall in spring and autumn. Many people consider the western Atlantic coast has the best summer climate in France, with the heat tempered by cool sea breezes. The Massif Central (which acts as a weather barrier between north and south) and eastern France have a moderate continental climate with cold winters and hot and stormy summers; but the centre and eastern upland areas have an extreme continental climate, with freezing winters and sweltering summers.

The Midi, stretching from the Pyrenees to the Alps, is hot and dry except for early spring, when there's usually heavy rainfall. The Cévennes region is the wettest in France, with some 200cm (500in) of rain per year. Languedoc has hot dry summers and much colder winters than the Côte d'Azur, with snow often remaining until May in mountainous inland areas. The South of France enjoys a Mediterranean climate of mild winters (daytime temperatures rarely drop below 10°C (50°F) and humid, hot summers, with the temperature often above 30°C (86°F). The average sunshine on the Côte d'Azur is five hours in January and 12 hours in July.

Language: French. France also has a number of regional languages including Alsatian (spoken in the Alsace), Basque (Pyrenees), Breton (Brittany), Catalan (Roussillon), Corsican (Corsica) and Occitan (Languedoc). Local dialects (*patois*) are also common in many areas.

Political Stability: Extremely stable, although periodically shaken by national strikes and riots. After many years of Socialist rule, a conservative coalition of the *Rassemblement pour la République* (RPR) and the Union for a Democratic France (*Union pour la Démocratie Française* (UDF) won the general election in 1993 but lost to a Socialist/Communist coalition in 1997. President Jacques Chirac was re-elected in 2002. France is a founder member of the EU.

Finance

Currency: Euro (€)
Exchange Rate: £1 = €1.60, US$1 = €1.15
Exchange Controls: None.
Interest Rate: 3.25 per cent
Banks: Banks in France are either commercial or co-operative and most have branches in all towns and cities. Many foreign banks, particularly British, are present in France, although branches tend to be concentrated in Paris. Both residents and non-residents may open a bank account, although current accounts receive no interest. Note that it's illegal to go overdrawn even by one euro and transgressors are heavily penalised.
Cost/Standard of Living: Salaries are generally high in France and the French enjoy a high standard of living. With the exception of Paris, where the higher cost of living is offset by higher salaries, the cost of living in France is lower than the EU average, particularly in rural areas.
GDP Per Head (US$): 24,210

Taxation

Income Tax: Income tax for most people in France is below the average for EU countries, particularly for large families. On the other hand, when the high social security contributions (regarded as a form of taxation in France) and other taxes are added, French taxes are among the highest in the EU. Tax rates range from 0 per cent on annual earnings under €4,000 to 54 per cent on annual earnings over €44,980.
Concessions/Tax Breaks For Retirees: There are imminent plans to exempt retirees over 60 from residential tax (*taxe d'habitation*). Over 60s qualify for discounts on transport, including up to 50 per cent on SNCF, and the over 70s may qualify for a free TV licence.
Social Security: Social security contributions are high, although corresponding benefits such as sick pay, child benefit and pensions are generous. An employee contributes between 15 to 18 per cent of his monthly salary to the state social security fund.
Capital Gains Tax (CGT): Gains on profits made on the sale of a second home in France that has been owned for less than two years are taxed at 33.3 per cent. On properties owned for over two years, the difference between the purchase and selling price is reduced by 5 per cent for the third and

subsequent years up to 22 years, multiplied by an index-linked multiplier of the sale price. CGT isn't payable on a profit made on the sale of a principal residence in France, provided it has been occupied since its purchase or for a minimum of five years. CGT at 7 per cent is payable on articles such as antiques, art and jewellery, and at 19.4 per cent on securities.

Wealth Tax: A tax of between 0.55 and 1.8 per cent is levied on French residents with worldwide assets valued at over €716,463.

Inheritance & Gift Tax: Inheritance tax in France is paid by individual beneficiaries, irrespective of where they're domiciled, and not by the estate. The rate of tax and allowances vary according to the relationship between the beneficiary and the deceased. There are allowances for close relatives, after which inheritance tax is levied on a sliding scale at 5 to 40 per cent.

Value Added Tax (VAT): The standard rate of VAT in France is 19.6 per cent, which is included in the purchase price of properties less than five years old when sold for the first time. There are reduced rates of 2.1 per cent on medicines, subject to reimbursement by social security, and daily newspapers, 4 per cent on magazines, and 5.5 per cent on food, agricultural products, medicines, books, public transport, gas, electricity, canteen food, cinema, theatre and concert tickets, hotel accommodation and travel agency fees.

Accommodation

Market: The property market has generally been buoyant since 1997, when the French franc fell in value by around 20 per cent against sterling (and against other currencies). Rural property remains excellent value, particularly if you're after a sizeable plot of land, and some excellent bargains are available. However, coastal and city properties are at a premium and cost up to double the price of similar rural properties. Property on the French Riviera remains among the most expensive in the world and Paris is one of Europe's most expensive cities, although property in the capital remains a good long-term investment. New properties are widely available and include coastal and city apartments, ski and golf developments, and a wide range of individually designed houses and chalets. Many new properties are part of purpose-built developments, often located along the coast or in mountain areas, encompassing a golf course, swimming pool, tennis and squash courts, a gym or fitness club, and a restaurant.

Areas: The most popular areas for foreign buyers include Paris, the Loire Valley (famous for its *châteaux*), the South of France (particularly the French Riviera or Côte d'Azur and Provence), south-west France (e.g. Charente, Dordogne and Gascony), and Brittany and Normandy, which are particularly popular with the British. Winter holiday homes in alpine ski resorts are also popular, especially in fashionable resorts such as Chamonix, Courchevel,

Mégève, Méribel, Val d'Isère and Val Thorens. Properties in French ski resorts are usually an excellent investment and also make fine summer holiday homes, above all if you're a keen hiker.

Cost: Apart from obvious points such as size, quality and land area, the most important factor influencing the price of a house is its location. A restored or modernised two-bedroom house costs between €50,000 and €80,000 in the north-west (e.g. Normandy) but sells for double or treble that price in the south-east (e.g. Provence). Similarly, the closer you are to the coast or Paris the more expensive property is, although properties on the French Riviera are the most expensive (and among the most expensive in Europe). A Charente farmhouse with a barn and a sizeable plot of land costs around the same as a tiny studio apartment in Paris or on the Côte d'Azur.

In most rural areas it's still possible to buy an old property for as little as €20,000 to €35,000, although you usually need to carry out major renovation or restoration which will double or treble the price. Modern one-bedroom apartments in main cities or in resorts cost from around €100,000 and two-bedroom apartments from €150,000. A rural two-bedroom renovated cottage costs from around €30,000 and a modern two-bedroom bungalow from €80,000. Villas situated near the south coast with a swimming pool cost from €300,000. Property in ski resorts varies considerably in price according to the resort and the location of the property. A tiny studio in a purpose-built resort costs from around €37,500, while a one-bedroom apartment close to the ski lifts in a resort such as Courchevel, Méribel or Tignes costs from €55,000, rising to around €75,000 in Chamonix or Val d'Isère. Small chalets start at €100,000, although you need to spend around €125,000 or more to buy a family-size chalet in a top resort.

Local Mortgages: Mortgages are available from all major French banks (both for residents and non-residents) and many foreign banks. Crédit Agricole is the largest French lender with a 25 per cent share of the market. Mortgages can be obtained for any period from 2 to 20 years, although the usual term is 15 years. French mortgages are usually limited to 70 or 80 per cent of a property's value.

Property Taxes: There are two property-based taxes in France. Property tax (*taxe foncière*) is similar to the property tax (or rates) levied in most countries and is paid by property owners based on the average (notional) rental value of the property in the previous year, adjusted for inflation (as calculated by the land registry). Rates vary considerably according to the region and even within a region, from as little as €300 to €1,500 or more per year. Residential tax (*taxe d'habitation*) is payable by whoever is residing in a property on 1st January, whether as an owner, tenant or rent free, and is calculated according to income, number of children, etc. It's normally around half as much as property tax.

Purchase Procedure: The purchase of property in France is strictly controlled and regulated. Property sales are conducted by a notary (*notaire*), who's a government official representing neither the vendor nor buyer (although you can engage another notary to act solely for you). It's wise, nevertheless, to hire a local lawyer to protect your interests and carry out the usual checks concerning title, outstanding debts, etc. A good estate agent is invaluable when buying in France, but he shouldn't be relied upon with regard to legal matters. There are various types of purchase contract, the most common being a bilateral agreement (*compromis de vente*), which is binding on both parties.

When the preliminary contract is signed a deposit is payable, which is usually 5 per cent for a new property and 10 per cent for a resale property. An agent must be bonded to hold money on behalf of clients and must display the sum of his financial guarantee (*pièce de garantie*). Note that the deposit isn't returnable unless you're unable to obtain a mortgage or there are serious legal problems involved in the purchase. The balance of the purchase price and all fees are due on completion of the sale, which is a fixed time after the signing of the purchase contract (normally six weeks), when the deed of sale (*acte de vente*) is signed.

Offshore Companies: Offshore companies can be used to purchase property in France, but for most people there's little or no advantage.

Fees: The total fees payable when buying a house in France are between 10 and 15 per cent of the price for a small to medium-size property over five years old. Fees for new properties less than five years old are 3 or 4 per cent, but VAT at 19.6 per cent is included in the purchase price. The fees comprise the notary's fee (2 to 5 per cent), stamp or transfer duty (0.6 per cent on new homes, 7.5 per cent on old homes), registration fees (6 to 7 per cent) and agent's fees. Note that prices may be quoted inclusive or exclusive of agent's fees, so you should check whether these are included in the price quoted and who's to pay them.

Precautions: The legal procedure in France regarding the purchase of real property is very safe. Any particular conditions regarding a purchase *must*, however, be included as conditional clauses in the preliminary contract. It's wise to have a survey on an older habitable dwelling or at the very least have it checked by a building expert, as a property is purchased 'as seen' and the vendor isn't liable for any defects unless he knowingly withheld information at the time of sale. Buyers should take particular care when buying an old property requiring extensive restoration, as the cost can escalate wildly. Before going ahead with a purchase you should obtain written detailed quotations (*devis*) from *at least* two local builders. You should *always* expect the final cost of restoration to be higher than the highest estimate you receive! If a property has already been renovated, you should check who did it, how it was done (i.e. professionally or by cutting corners) and whether there's a guarantee for the work.

Holiday Letting: There are no restrictions, although tax is payable by non-residents on letting income.

Restrictions on Foreign Ownership: None.

Building Standards: Excellent. The standard of new buildings in France is strictly regulated and most homes are built to official quality standards that are higher than in many other countries. The quality of renovation and restoration varies considerably according to the builder.

Belongings: Goods purchased within the EU can be imported duty-free and don't need to be retained for a minimum period. An inventory must be provided. If you're a non-EU resident planning to take up permanent or temporary residence in France, you're permitted to import your furniture and belongings free of duty. These include vehicles, mobile homes, pleasure boats and aircraft. However, to qualify for duty-free import, articles must have been owned and used for at least six months and cannot be sold for one year after import. All items should be imported within one year of the date of your change of residence, in one or a number of consignments.

Rental Accommodation: In Paris and other major cities, rental accommodation is in high demand and short supply, and rents are among the highest in Europe. Monthly rent for a small apartment costs from €750 to €1,500, although rents in a fashionable area can be much higher. Detached houses are almost impossible to rent in Paris and are prohibitively expensive. Outside Paris and in cities such as Cannes, Lyon and Nice, a small apartment rents for around €600 a month and a three-bedroom house from €950 a month.

Retirement Homes: There are several purpose-built retirement developments in France, although they're in short supply. Unlike most other countries where you usually buy a property within a retirement development or village, in France you generally rent a home. Monthly rents for self-contained apartments range from €600 to €1,250 and monthly rents in retirement villages range from €1,000 to €1,500, depending on the amenities and services provided.

Utilities: Electricity is provided by EDF throughout the country and consumers must choose the maximum power supply they require for domestic use. In rural areas, the power supply may be frequently interrupted. Mains gas is available in most large towns and cities, and the consumer can choose between four tariffs to suit his requirements. In rural areas and smaller towns, bottled gas or a tank are the only available options. Water is metered in France and the cost varies from region to region, with the most expensive tariffs in towns. Water is a scarce commodity in some regions of the country, particularly in the south-east where droughts are common, and in rural areas there may be shortages.

Services

Post Office: Most towns and villages have a post office, which provides a wide range of services, including money transfers and the payment of utility bills. The French mail service is reputably among the slowest in Europe, although services have improved in recent years.

Telephone: Three companies operate the telephone service in France, which has one of the most modern and efficient telephone systems in the world. Tariffs are reasonable by European standards.

Internet: France was slow off the mark with the Internet mainly because of Minitel (now superseded by the Internet) competition and the relatively low computer ownership, yet massive government investment has meant that by 2002 some 20 per cent of households were online. There are numerous ISPs and, with increased competition, prices are competitive.

English TV & Radio: Most television stations broadcast all programmes in French, although some films and news programmes are in English with French subtitles. There's a mandatory TV licence of around €115 a year for a colour TV. Satellite television reception is good throughout France and cable TV is available in the major towns and cities. Some French radio stations broadcast news bulletins in English and in the South of France there are several English-language stations.

General Information

Getting There: There are several international airports in France, including two in Paris, and direct flights are available from most countries. France is easily accessible by road from the rest of Europe and there are frequent ferry services across the Channel to the UK and Ireland, as well as the Eurotunnel car train service.

Getting Around: Communications are excellent in France and one of the country's investment priorities. Public transport in the cities is excellent and Paris has one of the most efficient and cheapest public transport systems in the world. France has Europe's most extensive railway network and the world's fastest passenger trains (TGV), which serve the main routes and a number of European destinations. Fares are reasonable.

Shopping: France has excellent shopping facilities and Paris is one the world's top shopping destinations, particularly for luxury goods. Vast hypermarkets and shopping centres are found throughout the country.

Crime: France has a similar crime rate to most other major European countries and, in common with them, crime increased considerably in the '90s as unemployment increased. Inner-city violence is a particular problem, and house-breaking and burglary are rampant in some areas, where holiday or second homes are a popular target. Car theft and theft from cars is also rife in Paris and other cities. The crime rate is low in rural areas, on the other hand, and it's common for people in many villages and small towns not to lock their homes and cars.

Driving: France has an excellent road network with toll motorways connecting most major cities, although toll charges are high. The heavily congested roads around Paris and in the city itself are one of Europe's motoring nightmares. Driving standards are general poor and the accident rate is high. Traffic drives on the right. EU nationals can drive in France with an EU driving licence. Nationals from other countries need to take the French driving test.

Medical Facilities: Excellent. French doctors are highly trained and general hospitals are superbly equipped, although they're few and far between in some rural areas. There are foreign-run hospitals in major cities, e.g. American and British hospitals in Paris. France has an excellent national health scheme for those contributing to social security, and retirees. If you aren't covered by the national health scheme, private health insurance is essential and often obligatory for residents.

Pets: You can take up to three animals into France at a time, one of which may be a puppy (three to six months old), although no dogs or cats under three months of age can be imported. There's generally no quarantine period. If you're importing a dog into France, it must be vaccinated against rabies or have a health certificate signed by an approved veterinary surgeon and issued no more than five days before your arrival. For visitors with pets, a rabies vaccination is compulsory only for animals entering Corsica, being taken to campsites or holiday parks, or participating in shows in a rabies-affected area. Resident dogs must be vaccinated against distemper and hard-pad and need an annual rabies booster. Cats aren't required to have rabies vaccinations, although if you let your cat roam free outside your home it's wise to have it vaccinated annually. Cats must, just the same, be vaccinated against feline gastro-enteritis and typhus.

Reciprocal Agreement with the UK: EU nationals are entitled to social security and health benefits in all EU member states, although the French rules of eligibility for entitlements (including pensions) apply. British citizens entitled to a state pension in the UK can continue to receive it in France and the sum will be increased annually at the same rate as pensions in the UK.

Residence Permits: A formality for EU nationals, although non-working residents must have sufficient income or financial resources to live in France without working. Visitors can stay in France for a maximum of 90 days at a time, although many nationalities require a visa. Non-EU nationals require a long-stay visa (*visa de long séjour*) to live in France for more than three months.

Work Permits: Work permits are unnecessary for EU nationals, but are difficult for non-EU nationals to obtain.

Visas: Most nationalities (other than EU citizens) require a visa for stays in France longer than three months, irrespective of the purpose of their stay. The appropriate long-stay visa must be obtained *before* arrival, from a French embassy or consulate in your home country. Visa requirements change frequently, so it's advisable to check with the French authorities well before your planned travel date.

Reference

Further Reading

Buying a Home in France, David Hampshire (Survival Books, 💻 www. survival books.net). Everything you need to know about buying a home in France.

Living and Working in France, David Hampshire (Survival Books, 💻 www.survivalbooks.net). Everything you need to know about living and working in France.

The Alien's Guide to France, Jim Watson (Survival Books, 💻 www. survivalbooks.net). A humorous look at France and the French people.

English-French Dictionary of Building and Property, J. Kater Pollock (Flowerpoll).

Focus on France, Outbound Publishing, 1 Commercial Road, Eastbourne, East Sussex BN21 3XQ, UK (☎ 01323-726040). Quarterly property magazine.

France Magazine, Dormer House, Stow-on-the-Wold, Glos. GL54 1BN, UK. Monthly lifestyle magazine (💻 www.francemag.com).

French Property News, 6 Burgess Mews, Wimbledon, London SW19 1UF, UK (☎ 020-8543 3113, 💻 www.french-property-news.com). Monthly property newspaper.

Living France, The Picture House, 79 High Street, Olney MK46 4EF, UK (☎ 01234-713203, 💻 www.livingfrance.com). Monthly lifestyle magazine

The News, Brussac SARL, BP 23, Chancelade, France. Monthly English-language newspaper.

The Riviera Reporter, 56 Chemin de Provence, 06250 Mougins, France (☎ 0493-457719, ✉ info@riviera-reporter.com). Monthly magazine.

Traditional Houses of Rural France, Bill Laws (Collins & Brown).

Useful Addresses

French Embassy, 4101 Reservoir Rd., NW, Washington, DC 20007, USA (☎ 0202-944 6000).

French Embassy, 58 Knightsbridge, London SW1X 7JT, UK (☎ 020-7201 1000).

French Government Tourist Office, 178 Piccadilly, London W1V 0AL, UK (☎ 090-6824 4123, 💻 www.franceguide.com).

Club Français des Retraités et Préretraités (CFRP), 56 Rue de Monceau, Paris (☎ 0145-611154). A retirement association who provide a wealth of information for retirees in France. An annual subscription is payable.

Useful Websites

💻 www.paris-anglo.com – Expatriate website.

💻 www.parlerparis.com – A website aimed at foreigners in Paris. Includes a free online weekly newsletter.

💻 www.franceguide.com – The official French tourist site.

💻 www.French-news.com – An English-language newspaper.

GREECE

Background Information

Capital: Athens
Population: 10.7 million
Foreign Community: Although becoming more popular with northern Europeans, particularly retirees, Greece doesn't have a large foreign community. A significant number of Britons and other EU nationals are, however, resident in Corfu, Crete and other islands.

Area: 131,990km^2 (50,965mi^2)

Geography: Mainland Greece consists of a mountainous peninsula extending some 500km (310mi) into the Mediterranean from the south-west corner of the Balkans, with the Aegean Sea to the east, the Ionian Sea to the west and the Mediterranean Sea to the south. Greece also has 3,000 islands, around 150 of which are inhabited, comprising around 20 per cent of Greek territory. The mainland and islands have a combined coastline of 13,350km (8,300mi).

The principal feature of Greece is the Pindos Mountains extending south-eastwards from the Albanian border and covering most of the peninsula. Some 80 per cent of the mainland is mountainous with 20 mountains over 2,000m (6,560ft) – the highest peak is Mount Olympus at 2,900m (9,500ft) – and permanently covered in snow. Greece has little flat or cultivated land, and woodland covers around half the country (almost 90 million hectares). Greece has borders with Albania, Bulgaria, Turkey and the former Yugoslavian state of Macedonia (now independent).

Climate: Greece has a Mediterranean climate with long, hot, dry summers and mild sunny winters in the south, although winters can be cold in northern areas. It has some 3,000 hours of sunshine a year and average temperatures above 25°C °(77F) in summer, when the oppressive heat is often tempered by a cooling breeze. Spring and autumn are the most pleasant seasons, sunny, but not too hot. Annual rainfall varies from around 1.5m (59in) in the north to under 50cm (20in) in the south and is rare anywhere in summer. Athens has the worst air pollution in western Europe and is often choked with smog, particularly in summer.

Language: Greek. English and other foreign languages such as German are widely spoken in tourist areas.

Political Stability: The least stable country in the EU (only Italy provides any competition), although it has been reasonably stable in recent years. Greek politics are traditionally volatile and are characterised by shaky coalition governments and political and financial scandals. The country was ruled by a military dictatorship from 1967 to 1974. Membership of the EU (since 1981) has brought much needed political and economic stability, although economic performance remains the lowest in the EU. Greece is an enthusiastic member of the EU, although it's unpopular and frequently out of step with its EU partners. It has historically poor relations with its neighbour Turkey, which are exacerbated by Turkey's continuing military occupation of northern Cyprus, although diplomats from both countries have recently been making efforts to resolve the situation, as Cyprus bids to join the EU.

Finance

Currency: Euro (€)

Exchange Rate: £1 = €1.60, US$1 = €1.15

Exchange Controls: None, but funds imported to buy a property should be officially documented so that the proceeds can be re-exported when it's sold.

Interest Rate: 3.25 per cent

Banks: Greece has generally good banking facilities, which are safe and reasonably efficient, although foreigners used to northern European banking practices will find the service somewhat 'leisurely'. There are some 50 domestic banks as well as around 20 foreign-owned banks (based almost exclusively in Athens) operating in Greece and no restrictions on the opening of bank accounts.

Cost/Standard of Living: Greece has a lower living standard and cost of living than most other EU countries, although cars and luxury items are expensive, and a relatively high rate of inflation. Athens is much more expensive than the rest of the country and is expected to be even more so in the period leading up to the 2004 Olympic Games.

GDP Per Head (US$): 11,740

Taxation

Income Tax: Greece has a PAYE system of income tax with rates ranging from 5 to 45 per cent. Annual income below €5,869 is exempt from income tax. Income tax evasion is rife and tax can be increased by the authorities if they decide that your lifestyle is incompatible with your declared income! Tax returns must be filed if you earn over €1,174 a year or, surprisingly, if you own a car. There are numerous allowances and deductions, particularly for families.

Concessions/Tax Breaks For Retirees: The annual non-taxable tax threshold is increased for pensioners.

Social Security: Working residents must contribute to the Greek social security fund, usually the state-run IKA, although some collectives have their own insurance funds. Employees contribute around 16 per cent of their gross salary, and benefits include health care, sickness and disability allowances, pensions and unemployment pay.

Capital Gains Tax (CGT): Gains made by individuals in Greece on the sale of personal assets and property generally aren't subject to CGT. Companies are, however, liable for CGT at 30 per cent on gains from the transfer of any right connected with a company (e.g. a sublease), and there's a 20 per cent tax on gains from the transfer of an entire company or of shares in a limited liability company.

Wealth Tax: Greece has an annual property tax of between 0.3 and 0.8 per cent on property valued above €205,040, although there are generous personal allowances.

Inheritance & Gift Tax: Inheritance and gift tax are based on the value of the bequest and the relationship between the donor and recipient. Rates are between 25 per cent for relatives of the first degree (spouses and children) and 60 per cent for unrelated beneficiaries.

Value Added Tax (VAT): The standard rate of VAT is 18 per cent. There are reduced rates of 8 per cent (food, medicines, water, transport services) and 4 per cent (books, magazines, newspapers and theatre tickets). Note that on certain island groups such as the Dodecanese, north-eastern Aegean and the Sporades, the standard and reduced rates are 12.6 and 5.6 per cent respectively.

Accommodation

Market: Greece has a fairly lively property market, as the country has become more popular with foreign homebuyers in recent years. It is largely undeveloped, with most areas as unspoilt as Portugal and Spain were 20 or 30 years ago. It has a largely untapped holiday-home market and many areas have good investment potential. There are strict controls over development and renovation to ensure that the local character is preserved, particularly in coastal and country areas. Old village houses are reasonably priced and in plentiful supply in most areas, although they usually require extensive renovation. Note that buying and renovating a property in a remote area is unlikely to be a good investment, however low the initial cost. Many foreigners buy a plot of land and build a new house. You can expect to pay a premium for a coastal or island property. Prices are stable in most areas and largely unaffected by world recessions.

Areas: A large number of areas and islands attract foreign property buyers in Greece. The most popular islands include Crete, the Cyclades (e.g. Ios, Mykonos, Naxos, Paros), the Dodecanese (e.g. Rhodes, Kos, Kalymnos), the Ionian Islands (e.g. Corfu, Paxos, Zakynthos), the Sporades (e.g. Skiathos, Skopelos, Alonissos and Skyros), the Saronic Gulf Islands and the Peloponnese Islands. Crete is the most favourable location if you're seeking winter sunshine. The most popular mainland area among foreigners is the Peloponnese.

Cost: Costs vary considerably according to the location and whether you buy a new or old property. Athens is expensive (although not popular with foreign buyers). New apartments on the islands cost from around €60,000 for one bedroom, €75,000 for two bedrooms and €100,000 for three bedrooms. A new two-bedroom townhouse or villa costs from around €100,000, although prices rise to €150,000 or more in a good location on a small island. A three-bedroom, two-bathroom villa costs from €150,000 (plus €15,000 to €25,000 for a pool). Inland properties are much cheaper than coastal properties.

Old stone houses are common in many areas (e.g. Crete) and can be purchased from around €14,000. But renovation costs are around two to three times the purchase price. Note that most old village houses tend to be small, e.g. 50 to 75m², with only a few rooms. Like houses, building plots vary considerably in price, although the average cost of a 4,000m² (around an acre) plot in the country is around €60,000. Houses can be built on small plots, e.g. 250m², which can cost as little as €15,000 in a coastal location. Minimum plot sizes, on the other hand, vary with the location (e.g. whether the plot is in a village or in the country), as does the size of building that can be built. A 200m² building usually requires a one-acre site. For smaller plots, the permitted floor area is usually a maximum of 60 to 70 per cent of the plot size.

Local Mortgages: Interest rates in Greece are in line with the Central European Bank's rates, but local mortgages are only obtainable by Greek residents (Greek banks don't like lending on property). Foreigners therefore usually have to obtain a mortgage or loan abroad. It's possible, nonetheless, to obtain repayment mortgages using a Greek property as security and you can usually borrow up to 80 or 90 per cent of a property's value and repay it over 5 to 30 years.

Property Taxes: In 1997 a property tax was introduced, which is levied at between 0.3 and 0.8 per cent on property valued at over €205,040, although there are generous personal allowances.

Purchase Procedure: All property in Greece is owned freehold. A deposit of 10 to 30 per cent (normally 10 per cent) is usually paid after a preliminary agreement is signed, detailing the price and date of completion (usually within 30 days). The balance of the purchase price (less the deposit) is payable on signing the purchase deed before a public notary in Greece (or a Greek Consulate General abroad). A property must have full and unencumbered title, or the notary won't proceed with the sale. Your lawyer will pay the transfer and local community tax and register the property deeds with the Land Registry. Note that the origin of funds used to buy property in Greece must be declared to the Bank of Greece using an official import document.

Offshore Companies: Offshore companies can be used to purchase property in Greece and have various financial advantages (as well as making a property easier to sell). Expert legal advice is, however, essential.

Fees: The fees associated with buying a home in Greece are high and usually total around 15 per cent of the purchase price. Transfer (or purchase) tax is 10 per cent and an extra 2 per cent is charged on properties in areas covered by the public fire protection service. The tax is assessed on a property's 'objective value' by the local tax office, based on tables issued by the Greek Ministry of Finance. The assessed value is usually around two-thirds of the purchase price. Land registry fees are 0.3 per cent of the assessed value plus a small sum for stamp duties and certificates. A community tax equal to 3 per cent of the property transfer tax is paid to the local municipality for general public services such as road maintenance. Lawyer's fees are normally 1 to 1.5 per cent and notary's fees around 1 to 2 per cent of a property's value. Estate agent's fees are usually paid by the vendor.

Precautions: It's essential that all contracts are checked by a Greek lawyer before you sign any documents or pay any money. You must ensure that the vendor has full title and that a property is free of debts. There are Greek lawyers based in many countries outside Greece (ask your local Greek embassy for a list).

Holiday Letting: No restrictions, although tax is payable on rental income.

Restrictions on Foreign Ownership: There are a few restrictions on foreign property ownership for security reasons, e.g. in some border areas and islands close to Turkey. EU citizens have the same rights as Greeks in most of Greece.

Building Standards: New homes are generally well built and designed. The quality of old properties and restored buildings is variable.

Beongings: No duty is payable on imported belongings, although a five-year residence permit must have been issued by the authorities and an import certificate is required from a Greek embassy or consulate listing all items to be imported. A car can be imported duty-free, but must have been owned and used for at least six months abroad.

Rental Accommodation: Rentals in resort areas and Athens, particularly long-term rentals, are in high demand and short supply. A small two-bedroom apartment costs between €450 to €750 per month in an average Athens suburb. In a resort area, rentals can be much more expensive in high season, although relatively inexpensive outside the main tourist season.

Retirement Homes: There are no purpose-built retirement developments in Greece, although given their popularity in other countries it will probably be only a matter of time before they're introduced in areas popular with foreign property buyers.

Utilities: Electricity (220-240V) is provided by the DEH and is subject to frequent cuts in some areas, where it may be necessary to install a generator. In remote rural areas there's often no mains electricity and the installation of a generator is mandatory. Mains gas is available only in Athens, although bottled gas is available throughout Greece. Water is an expensive and precious commodity in Greece, where drought is often a serious problem. In drought-affected areas, water supplies may be restricted or cut for lengthy periods. Tap water is safe to drink in all urban areas, although, due to its poor quality, many people prefer to drink bottled water. Water in rural areas isn't always safe to drink.

Services

Post Office: The Greek postal service is one of the slowest in Europe, although services have improved in recent years. Post to islands without an airport can be particularly slow. Post offices are provided in most towns and villages, and offer a wide range of services, including cash transfers and currency exchange.

Telephone: The Greek telephone service is run by OTE (currently a monopoly), which has invested heavily in the modernisation of services which are now on a par with the rest of western Europe. Calls are expensive, although charges are expected to fall once much needed competition is introduced. Note that the installation of a telephone line in remote and rural areas can take a long time, particularly if telephone poles need to be installed as telephone-pole workers service certain areas only once or twice a year!

Internet: The Internet has been slow to take off in Greece, mainly due to the shortage of lines from providers. Improvements are being made, nevertheless, almost daily and most large Greek companies now have websites, although the number of households online is considerably lower than in the rest of Western Europe.

English TV & Radio: The majority of Greek channels broadcast English-language programmes and films in the original language with Greek subtitles. Satellite television reception is good throughout most of the country.

General Information

Getting There: Greece is well served by international flights, mainly to Athens, although in high season there are charter flights to the main islands. You can also reach several parts of Greece by ferry from neighbouring countries, although many services only operate in high season or have a much-reduced timetable in winter.

Getting Around: Communications are reasonable in Greece, although the quality and quantity vary considerably from region to region. Athens has a good public transport system, which is under extensive improvement and expansion in preparation for the 2004 Olympics, and some resorts have a good network. Outside the main towns and cities, public transport can be scarce and most people find private transport necessary. There's a comprehensive domestic air service to some 30 airports but fares are high. Rail services are limited to mainland Greece and services are slow in rural areas, although fares are low. There's an extensive ferry service, both from mainland Greece to the islands and between islands, although services are reduced out of season and bad weather often leads to cancellations. There have been a number of ferry disasters in recent years, which has led to a review of safety.

Shopping: Greece has a surprisingly large number of shops, most of which are family enterprises and main towns and cities have good shopping facilities. Some shopping centres have been built in recent years but they aren't nearly as popular as in the rest of Europe. Bear in mind that, in some resort areas and on smaller islands, shops may close during the winter.

Crime Rate: Greece is generally safe and serious crime is rare, although 'petty' crime such as burglary is common.

Driving: Road conditions vary greatly and although the limited network of motorways (mainly toll) is good, great care must be exercised when using other roads. Greece has some of the worst traffic problems in Europe (e.g. jams and pollution, particularly in Athens) and the second highest accident rate in the EU after Portugal. Petrol is among the cheapest in the EU but cars are expensive and the importation of vehicles is complicated. Some islands, such as Hydra, are car-free. Traffic drives on the right. EU issued driving licences are valid in Greece. Non-EU nationals may drive in Greece for up to six months with an international driving licence, although residents must apply for a Greek driving licence.

Medical Facilities: Greece has a national health service for those paying social security, although there are long waiting lists for non-essential treatment. Private health insurance is recommended, even for those covered by social security. Greece has reciprocal health agreements with many countries, and retirees from EU countries enjoy free medical treatment. Note that local medical facilities vary considerably according to the area, and you should check the location of the nearest general hospital with emergency facilities, which, if you live on an island, may be on the mainland or another island.

Pets: All animals must have a health certificate issued within ten days of importation stating that they're in good health and free from contagious diseases. Dogs (except those under three months old) must be vaccinated against rabies not less than 20 days or more than 11 months before importation.

Reciprocal Agreement with the UK: EU nationals are entitled to social security and health benefits in all EU member states, although Greek rules of eligibility for entitlements (including pensions) apply. British citizens entitled to a state pension in the UK can continue to receive it in Greece and the sum will be increased annually at the same rate as pensions in the UK.

Residence Permits: A formality for EU nationals, although non-working residents must have sufficient income to maintain themselves in Greece. Visitors can stay for three months without formalities, but a residence permit is required for longer stays. A temporary residence permit valid for six months is usually issued followed by a five-year permit.

Work Permits: Work permits are unnecessary for EU nationals, but are difficult for other nationals to obtain.

Visas: For visits of over 90 days, all nationalities from non-EU countries require a long-stay visa. If you're a non-EU national, you cannot enter Greece as a tourist and then change your status. Visa requirements are subject to continual change and the latest regulations should be checked with a Greek embassy or consulate in your home country. Note that Greece refuses entry to foreigners whose passports indicate that they've visited Northern Cyprus since November 1993.

Reference

Further Reading

Buying a Home in Greece & Cyprus, Joanna Styles (Survival Books, 💻 www.survivalbooks.net). Everything you need to know about buying a home in Greece.

Useful Addresses

Greek Embassy, 2221 Massachusetts Ave., NW, Washington, DC 20008, USA (☎ 0202-939 5800, 💻 www.greekembassy.org).

Greek Embassy, 1A Holland Park, London W11 3TP, UK (☎ 020-7229 3850, 💻 www.greekembassy.org.uk).

National Tourist Office of Greece, 4 Conduit Regent Street, London W1R 0DJ, UK (☎ 020-7734 5997).

National Tourist Office of Greece, 645 Fifth Avenue, Olympic Tower, New York, NY 10022, USA (☎ 0212-421 5777).

Useful Websites

💻 www.geocities.com/Athens/7243 – Expatriate information.

💻 www.vacation.forthnet.gr – The Greek National Tourist Organisation.

💻 www.travelinfo.fr – A good travel information website.

IRELAND

Background Information

Capital: Dublin
Population: 3.7 million
Foreign Community: Britons make up the largest expatriate community in Ireland and there's also a sizeable American community in Dublin.
Area: 70,280km² (27,137mi²)
Geography: Ireland is the large island situated to the west of Britain in the North Atlantic and is part of the British Isles. However, the Republic of Ireland, with which this section deals, comprises only some 80 per cent of the island of Ireland (or 26 of the 32 counties of Ireland) and excludes the six counties in Northern Ireland that remained part of the United Kingdom when the Republic of Ireland was formed in 1921. Ireland is separated from Britain by the Irish Sea. The Irish landscape consists of rich farmland interspersed with rolling hills, bleak moors and lakes, surrounded by a rocky coastline. The country is largely unspoilt and has little industry and no large cities apart from Dublin.
Climate: Ireland is wet at most times of the year, particularly in the west, hence its green countryside and popular name, the 'Emerald Isle'. It has cold winters and warm summers, when July and August are the hottest months. The climate is similar to that of the UK (see page 287), i.e. cool, damp and changeable for most of the year.
Language: Ireland has two official languages: Irish (or Gaelic) and English. It's mandatory for many government employees to speak Irish, although relatively few people speak it fluently. The everyday language is English, which is spoken by virtually everybody.
Political Stability: Ireland is very stable and the 'troubles' in Northern Ireland have rarely caused much political unrest in the Republic. Ireland has a conservative coalition government, which is no longer slow to effect change. Ireland is a member of the EU, which it joined with the UK and Denmark in 1973. EU subsidies created the highest growth rate in Europe between 1994 and 2000, but this has now slowed and zero growth is predicted for 2002. Relations with the UK government have improved in recent years and both countries have co-operated to achieve peace in Northern Ireland.

Finance

Currency: Euro (€)
Exchange Rate: £1 = €1.60, US$1 = €1.15
Exchange Controls: None.
Interest Rate: 3.25 per cent

Banks: There are eight national banks in Ireland, plus branches of several foreign banks in Dublin. Banking is secure and efficient with a wide range of banking services available. Both residents and non-residents can open a bank account; you're required to show two forms of identification, including your passport, when you open an account.

Cost/Standard of Living: The cost of living is high in Ireland, particularly in relation to salaries, which are relatively low in rural areas. Cars, petrol and luxuries are particularly expensive, although the country also has a rapidly rising standard of living. An increasing number of Britons retire to Ireland, often to take advantage of the high level of benefits paid to pensioners which include free public transport and TV licences, free phone rental plus a number of free calls, free healthcare, and allowances for clothing, electricity and gas.

GDP Per Head (US$): 18,710

Taxation

Income Tax: Ireland has a PAYE system of income tax with rates from 20 to 44 per cent (above €215,190). The first €5,950 is exempt. There's a special dispensation for artists, writers and sports stars, who don't pay tax on their royalties. Non-residents are taxed only on their income from Irish sources. There are large tax allowances for those with a mortgage and dependants.

Concessions/Tax Breaks For Retirees: There are higher tax exemption limits and age credits for resident retirees over 65 in Ireland. Retirees over 70 can receive free electricity or gas allowances, a free TV licence and free phone rental. Those aged between 66 and 70 may also be entitled to these, although eligibility is means tested. All retirees over 66 are entitled to certain free travel services.

Social Security: All employees must contribute to the Pay Related Social Insurance (PRSI) scheme, which provides a wide range of benefits. Employees pay 4.5 per cent on earnings up to a maximum of €35,789. The self-employed pay 3 per cent.

Capital Gains Tax (CGT): CGT is levied at 20 per cent (except on development land, which attracts CGT at 40 per cent). Gains made on the sale of your principal residence are exempt.

Wealth Tax: None.

Inheritance & Gift Tax: Inheritance tax is called Capital Acquisition Tax (CAT) and is levied at 20 per cent above certain thresholds. The wife and children of a donor are granted exemptions of up to €379,747 each. CAT is payable by the recipient and not the estate. The tax on lifetime gifts is 75 per cent of the inheritance tax rates, with the first €633 exempt.

Value Added Tax (VAT): The standard rate of VAT is 20 per cent. There are reduced rates of 12.5 and 10 per cent on certain goods and services including adults' clothing, footwear and theatre tickets. Most food, children's clothing, medicines and books are zero-rated, and services such as insurance, health, education and finance are exempt.

Accommodation

Market: Ireland has a flourishing property market, with home ownership around 80 per cent and the highest in Europe. It has always been popular with the British for holiday homes and an increasing number of Britons retire there. It's particularly popular with outdoor sports enthusiasts (e.g. the hunting, fishing and shooting fraternity) and is becoming a popular destination for continental Europeans seeking holiday homes (e.g. Dutch and Germans). For those with deep pockets, there are period 'stately' homes and large estates in all areas. For those of more modest means, there's a multitude of picturesque cottages and farmhouses. Less attractive, modern bungalows are also popular in all parts of the country. Irish property has been a good investment, with annual price rises of up to 40 per cent, although prices have now stabilised in most areas. (Note that Northern Ireland also has a strong property market and is a popular location for holiday homes – see the **United Kingdom** on page 287).

Areas: Those who don't need to live close to Dublin or another town can choose from a wealth of unspoilt rural settings throughout the country. Among the most popular areas are almost anywhere on the southern and western coasts, most of which are only a short journey from a regional or international airport. The southern counties are especially popular with foreign buyers, particularly Cork, Kerry and Waterford.

Cost: Property is expensive in Dublin, where the average price is around €112,500 and suburban family homes sell for up to €450,000. As the cost of houses rises, apartments are becoming more popular, particularly in Dublin where a one-bedroom apartment costs from €160,000 and two bedrooms from €250,000. Property in rural areas, on the other hand, is good value and a modern semi-detached three-bedroom house costs from around €90,000, a detached three-bedroom house from €105,000 and a four-bedroom bungalow around €130,000. Smaller rural properties in need of modernisation can be purchased from around €50,000, and renovated cottages from around €80,000. Many old rural properties have a large plot of land. Note, however, that in fashionable regions, such as the south-west, prices have risen considerably in recent years as a result of high demand from foreign buyers and you may pay a premium of up to 100 per cent. There are also many large country houses and estates at prices upwards of €1 million, some of which have been converted into expensive apartments with golf and country club facilities.

Local Mortgages: Mortgages are available from Irish banks. The maximum loan is usually 90 per cent, payable over a period of 15 years. There's a small stamp duty (0.1 per cent) on mortgages above €25,316.

Property Taxes: There's no property tax in Ireland. The only charge normally made to householders is for refuse collection, which ranges from nothing to €650 a year or more, depending on the location of a property.

Purchase Procedure: The purchase procedure is similar to the UK (see page 290), completion taking place six to eight weeks after signing a preliminary contract.

Fees: The fees associated with buying a property in Ireland amount to between 2 and 12 per cent of the price. Legal fees are 1 to 1.5 per cent of the purchase price plus VAT (20 per cent) and there are small fees for land registration (between €125 and €650) and a surveyor (if necessary). VAT is included in the price of new properties. The main fee is stamp duty, which ranges from 0 per cent on properties costing up to €126,582 to 9 per cent on properties costing over €632,911 and all properties purchased for investment. Stamp duty is waived for first-time buyers and isn't payable on new properties.

Holiday Letting: No restrictions.

Restrictions on Foreign Ownership: None.

Building Standards: Generally very good.

Belongings: Belongings (including a motor vehicle) can be imported duty-free provided they've been owned and used for six months. Importation must take place within six months of your arrival or 12 months after the date of the transfer of your normal residence. VAT is payable on vehicles imported into Ireland from outside the EU.

Rental Accommodation: A one-bedroom apartment in the capital costs upwards of €650 per month and as much as €950 in areas such as Ballsbridge, whereas a similar apartment can be rented in a small town for as little as €350 per month. Two-bedroom apartments in Dublin start at €900 per month and houses at €1,500.

Retirement Homes: Purpose-built retirement developments have increased in popularity in Ireland and there are now several private retirement villages.

Utilities: Electricity (230V) is provided by the Irish Electricity Supply Board (ESB) and the service is reliable and relatively inexpensive. Mains gas (supplied by *Bord Gáis*) is available in most parts of the country and bottled gas is also available. Domestic water is free and safe to drink, although many people prefer bottled water.

Services

Post Office: The Irish postal service is operated by the state-controlled *An Post*, although the impending liberalisation of the postal market means that around a quarter of postal services will be privatised by the year 2003. *An Post*'s service is as efficient, reliable and inexpensive as any in Europe. Most towns and villages have a post office, where you can use banking services, pay bills and licences, as well as the usual postal services.

Telephone: Irish telephone services began to be deregulated in 1994, but the semi-state company *Eircom* still provides all domestic services. The telephone system is generally excellent and Ireland is at the forefront of telecommunications technology. The number of mobile phones recently outstripped the number of fixed phones in use.

Internet: The Internet has been slow to take off in Ireland and there are relatively few ISPs to choose from. This is gradually changing, however, and an increasing number of companies and households are now online. Online shopping is also becoming more popular.

English TV & Radio: Irish television broadcasts in English on three channels and British TV stations can also be received, as well as numerous satellite and cable channels. An annual TV licence of around €90 is payable. Irish national radio transmits in English on four channels, as do many local radio stations.

General Information

Getting There: Ireland is well connected by international flights and prices are competitive, particularly from the UK. There's also a regular year-round ferry service from the UK and France.

Getting Around: Ireland has a good domestic air service with frequent shuttle flights between Dublin and other major cities, although tickets can be expensive. Public transport varies considerably from good, within Dublin and other major centres, to limited, in rural areas where private transport is essential. A comprehensive bus service and limited rail network connect the provinces with the capital.

Shopping: The Irish are keen shoppers and shopping facilities are generally good in towns and cities. Most small towns and villages have at least one well-stocked general store.

Crime Rate: The crime rate is low in Ireland, particularly serious crime, although burglary and car theft are a problem in some areas, particularly parts of Dublin. The capital also has a significant amount of drug-related crime.

Driving: Road conditions range from good on main roads, which have been subject to major investment in recent years, to poor on minor roads. Driving standards are generally good and traffic drives on the *left*. Car purchase and hire are expensive. EU driving licences are valid and licences from other countries are valid for up to one year, after which a foreign licence must be exchanged for an Irish driving licence.

Medical Facilities: Medical facilities are generally excellent in Ireland, which has a national health scheme for residents paying social security and retirees. .On the other hand, there's a limited number of public hospitals and practitioners, and it's wise to have private health insurance.

Pets: There are no restrictions on cats and dogs imported from the UK and the Channel Islands, and no documentation is required. Pets imported from most other countries must spend six months in quarantine, although regulations are in process of change, so pet owners should check with a local embassy or consulate before making arrangements.

Reciprocal Agreement with the UK: EU nationals are entitled to social security and health benefits in all EU member states, although the Irish rules of eligibility for entitlements (including pensions) apply. British citizens entitled to a state pension in the UK can continue to receive it in Ireland and the sum will be increased annually at the same rate as pensions in the UK.

Residence Permits: Residence permits are a formality for EU nationals, although non-working residents must have sufficient income to maintain themselves. Visitors can stay for three months without formalities, after which a residence permit must be obtained from the Department of Justice.

Work Permits: Unnecessary for EU nationals, but difficult for other foreigners to obtain.

Visas: Visa requirements for non-EU nationals wishing to live or work in Ireland are extremely complicated and immigration regulations are subject to change. Non-EU nationals should consult an Irish embassy or consulate in their home country before making any plans to live or work in Ireland.

Reference

Further Reading

Buying a Home in Ireland, Joe Laredo (Survival Books, 🖳 www.survival books.net). Everything you need to know about buying a home in Ireland.

Living and Working in Ireland, Joe Laredo (Survival Books, 🖳 www. survivalbooks.net). Everything you need to know about living and working in Ireland.

Choose Ireland for Retirement, Patti Cleary (Globe Pequot)

Live Well in Ireland, Steenie Harvey (Avalon Travel)

Useful Addresses

Department of Justice, 72/76 St. Stephen's Green, Dublin 2, Ireland (☎ 01-602 8415).

The Incorporated Law Society of Ireland, Blackhall Place, Dublin 7, Ireland (☎ 01-672 4800, 🖳 www.lawsociety.ie).

The Irish Auctioneers' and Valuers' Institute, 129 Lower Baggot St, Dublin 2, Ireland (☎ 01-678 5685, 🖳 www.ipav.ie).

Irish Embassy, 2234 Massachusetts Ave, NW, Washington, DC 20008, USA (☎ 0202-462 3939, 🖳 www.irelandemb.org).

Irish Embassy, 17 Grosvenor Place, London SW1X 7HR, UK (☎ 020-7235 2171, ✉ ir.embassy@lineone.net).

Irish Tourist Board, 150 New Bond Street, London W1Y 0AQ, UK (☎ 020-7493 3201).

Useful Websites

🖳 www.ireland.com – Website of the *Irish Times*.

🖳 www.ireland.travel.com – Comprehensive travel and tourist information.

🖳 www.shamrock.org – The Irish Tourist Board website.

ITALY

Background

Capital: Rome
Population: 56.8 million
Foreign Community: There are many foreigners in the major Italian cities and also foreign communities in many resorts and rural areas, particularly in central and northern Italy, including some 40,000 Britons.
Area: 301,302km² (116,342mi²)
Geography: Italy has a wide variety of landscape and vegetation, characterised by its two mountain ranges, the Alps and the Apennines (almost 80 per cent of the country is covered by hills and mountains). The Alps, where there are a number of peaks over 4,000m (13,000ft), extend across northern

Italy and include the Dolomite range in the east. The Apennines, where the Corno Grande 2,912m (9,554ft) is the highest peak, form the backbone of the Italian peninsula. The Alpine foothills are characterised by the vast Po Valley and the lakes of Como, Garda and Maggiore. The Po is Italy's longest river, flowing from east to west across the plain of Lombardy in the north into the Adriatic. Northern Italy has large areas of wood and farmland, while the south is mostly scrubland. Italy's principal islands are Sicily (with the active volcano of Mount Etna at 3,342m (10,965ft) and Sardinia, plus Elba, Capri and Ischia. Italy, which is shaped like a boot, has a vast coastline of some 7,500km (4,660mi) and borders with Austria, France, Slovenia and Switzerland.

Climate: Italy has a temperate climate influenced by the Mediterranean and Adriatic Seas. Summers are generally very hot everywhere, with average temperature in July and August around 24°C (75°F). Winters are cold and dry in the Alps, damp in the Po Valley and mild on the Italian Riviera and in Sicily. Rainfall is moderate to low in most regions and is rare anywhere in summer; fog is common in the north in autumn.

Language: Italian. Minorities speak German (Alto Adige), French (Valle d'Aosta), Slovene and Ladino, and there are also numerous regional dialects. French is widely understood and English is spoken in the major cities and tourist centres.

Political Stability: Italy is one of the most politically unstable countries in the EU, although this appears to have little effect on the country's economy. There have been numerous changes of government since the Second World War, largely because Italy's system of proportional representation almost guarantees fragmented and shaky coalition governments (an electoral reform in recent years appears to have had little effect). In April 2001, the country held its 59th general election since 1945, which was won by a right-wing coalition led by Silvio Berlusconi, who has several trials pending for corruption and misuse of public funds! Italy is a founder member of the EU.

Finance

Currency: Euro (€)
Exchange Rate: £1 = €1.60, US$1 = €1.15
Exchange Controls: None. Sums above €10,000 must be declared and their source registered.
Interest Rate: 3.25 per cent
Banks: There are over 900 banks in Italy, including some 50 branches of foreign banks (mostly found in Rome and Milan), although the number of banks is decreasing as banks merge or are taken over. Despite modernisation in recent years, Italian banking services aren't as efficient or varied as other

western European banks and bank charges are high, although banking is secure. Residents can open accounts but usually must have a residence permit. Non-residents can only open non-resident accounts into which you can only pay foreign currency and imported euros.

Cost/Standard of Living: There's a huge disparity between the cost and standard of living in the prosperous north and central regions of Italy, and the relatively poor south. The cost of living in the major cities is much the same as in cities in France, Germany and the UK, although, overall, Italy has a slightly lower cost of living than northern European countries. Luxury and quality products are expensive, as are cars, but wine and spirits are inexpensive.

GDP Per Head (US$): 20,090

Taxation

Income Tax: Income tax (IRPEF) is high in Italy and ranges from 19 (up to €7,745) to 46 per cent (over €82,350). Tax evasion is widespread. Residents require a fiscal number (*codice fiscale*) which must be used in all communications with the tax authorities. Non-residents must file a tax return stating the details of their Italian property, as property is considered to provide an income whether it's let or used as a private residence. The 'assumed' income is based on the cadastral value (*rendita catastale*).

Concessions/Tax Breaks For Retirees: None, although pensioners are eligible for deductions on their taxable income.

Social Security: All employees must make monthly contributions to the state security fund of around 10 per cent of their gross salary. Benefits include sickness, accident, unemployment, pensions and family allowances. Health care is also included, although you must pay a small percentage of the cost and for prescriptions.

Capital Gains Tax (CGT): CGT isn't levied on property but gains made on stocks and shares are levied at two rates: 12.5 and 27 per cent, depending on the gain.

Wealth Tax: None.

Inheritance & Gift Tax: Inheritance tax varies between 3 and 33 per cent according to the relationship of beneficiaries to the deceased. Estates valued below €152,500 left to a spouse, children or parents and estates valued below €61,000 left to direct relatives are exempt.

Value Added Tax (VAT): The standard rate of VAT is 20 per cent and there are reduced rates of 10 and 4 per cent. Some services, such as postal and medical, are exempt. VAT is payable on new properties at 4 per cent for non-luxury property and 20 per cent for luxury property.

Accommodation

Market: There's a lively property market in Italy where there's a high and steady demand for second homes from both Italians and foreigners, although few developments are built solely for foreigners, particularly holiday-home developments such as are common in some other European countries. In many areas the countryside and coastline have been damaged by uncontrolled development (only around 10 per cent of Italy's 7,500km (4,630mi) coastline remains undeveloped, while others (such as Tuscany) have hardly changed in centuries. New development in Tuscany and some other areas is prohibited and renovation is strictly regulated, e.g. existing buildings must be replaced with properties built in the same style and/or the same size.

Many inland towns and villages are almost totally unspoilt. In cities, people generally live in apartments, houses being rare and prohibitively expensive. The best buys are old rural or village period houses requiring renovation or restoration. Properties are advertised in local property newspapers such as *Panorama Casa* in Tuscany and national property magazines such as the weekly *Casa per Casa* or the monthly *Ville & Casali* (mainly for up-market properties). Despite high prices in many areas, Italian property is generally an excellent investment, particularly in cities and popular resort areas.

Areas: There are numerous alluring areas for foreign property buyers in Italy. The most popular areas are those north of Rome including Tuscany, Liguria, Umbria, Lombardy, Le Marche, Veneto and Piedmont. So many Britons have purchased homes in Tuscany that the Chianti region has been dubbed 'Chiantishire'. Much of Tuscany, however, is *extremely* expensive and poor value, although it can still be a good investment. Reasonably priced homes can be found in northern Tuscany (e.g. in Lunigiana north of Lucca), which offers much better value than most of southern Tuscany. Rising prices in Tuscany have led British and other foreign buyers to cast their nets wider and many have turned to Umbria, le Marche and Liguria.

The northern Adriatic coast, the Italian Lakes, the Italian Riviera (e.g. Portofino, San Remo), and the Amalfi coast (e.g. Positano, Sorrento) are also popular for holiday homes, as are Sardinia and Sicily. Property on the Italian Riviera is expensive, but is better value than the French Riviera. Italy also has a wide choice of resorts for those seeking a winter holiday home, including Bormio, Cervinia, Cortina, Courmayeur and Sestriere.

Cost: Property prices in Italy vary considerably and are generally high in cities and towns and relatively low in rural areas (except where high demand from foreign buyers has driven them up). Prices were flat or slumped in Italy's major cities during the recession in the early 1990s, in stark contrast to the most popular areas for second homes where they remained stable or even rose. Although you can spend hundreds of thousands of euros on a luxurious *palazzo* or a large country estate, it's also possible to buy a small one or two-bedroom renovated apartment or village house from around €50,000. In many areas, old village houses in need of complete restoration can be purchased from as little as €30,000. You should, on the other hand, expect to pay two or three times the purchase price in restoration costs (which are around €700 to €800 per m² plus architect's and surveyor's fees). In many rural areas, around €100,000 will buy a restored two-bedroom farmhouse and a bit of land. You can, however, pay over €400,000 for a small farmhouse in a fashionable area of Tuscany.

Prices have remained stable in recent years on the Italian Riviera and are between €6,000 and €7,000 per m² for a quality apartment with a view, in a top resort such as Portofino. In the Cinque Terre villages of Liguria, apartments can be purchased for around €2,500 per m². In some Riviera towns, small one-bedroom apartments cost from around €120,000 and two-bedroom apartments from €140,000. The Italian lakes are another popular area, which is reflected in the above average prices, e.g. €100,000 for a new or restored one-bedroom apartment on Lake Como or Maggiore and €150,000 for a two-bedroom apartment. If you dream of living in Venice, a studio on the Grand Canal will set you back over €500,000! On the other hand, holiday apartments in Sicily start at around €65,000. Winter holiday homes in ski resorts are a good investment and have good letting potential, although they're relatively expensive. In a top resort such as Cortina, you will pay around €95,000 to €130,000 for a studio, €130,000 to €160,000 for a one-bedroom apartment, and up to €240,000 for a two-bedroom apartment. **Always barter over the price of property in Italy, as owners invariably ask for more than they expect to get (but don't show too much enthusiasm or the price is likely to increase suddenly!).**

Local Mortgages: Mortgages are available from Italian banks, although they usually take a long time to be approved and you can generally obtain better terms and a larger loan from a foreign lender. Maximum loans from Italian banks are generally 50 or 60 per cent for second homes and 75 per cent for principal homes. The usual term is 5 to 15 years. If you import funds to buy a property in Italy, it should be officially registered by your Italian bank.

Property Taxes: A local community tax (*imposta comunale sugli immobili* (ICI)) is paid by all owners of property or land in Italy, whether they're resident or non-resident. It's levied at between 0.4 to 0.7 per cent of a property's cadastral value (*valore catastale*), the actual rate being decided by the local municipality depending on a property's size, location, class and category. ICI is paid in two instalments in June and December.

Purchase Procedure: When buying a property in Italy, you must sign a preliminary contract (*contratto preliminare di vendita*, *promessa di vendita* or *compromesso di vendita*), which may be drawn up by the vendor, the estate agent or a lawyer. The preliminary contract, which can be hand-written or a standard printed document, may be preceded by a binding 'buying proposal', where the buyer is legally bound to buy, but the vendor and agent are free to consider other offers. On signing the preliminary contract, both parties are bound to the transaction. A deposit (*capara penitenziale*) of around 10 per cent (but possibly up to 30 per cent) is paid to a notary (*notaio*), which is forfeited if the buyer doesn't go through with the purchase (if the vendor reneges, he must pay the buyer double the deposit). Note that the deposit should be described as *caparra penitenziale* and not as *caparra confirmatoria*, as the latter allows the vendor to take legal action to force a buyer to go through with a purchase.

The preliminary contract contains the essential terms of the sale, including the purchase price, the financing plan, the closing date, and any conditions that must be fulfilled prior to completion. A sale must be completed within the period stipulated in the *compromesso*, usually six to eight weeks (although it can be from two weeks to three or four months). The sale is completed before a notary when the final deed or 'conveyance of transfer' (*atto di compravendita* or *scrittura privata*) is signed. The notary issues a certified copy of the deed of sale and registers the original document with the Land Registry office (*Registro Immobiliare*). Registration is of paramount importance, as until a property is registered you aren't the legal owner. Note that there are two kinds of deed in Italy: a private deed and a public instrument, which provides more protection but is more expensive. When a property is purchased by private deed and is subsequently found to have a charge against it, such as a mortgage, the notary isn't responsible. When buying by public instrument, you can happily sue the notary for professional misconduct. All properties in Italy are owned freehold.

Offshore Companies: It's possible to buy a property in Italy through an offshore or overseas company.

Fees: Total fees when buying a property in Italy are usually between 8 and 15 per cent of the purchase price. Registration tax or stamp duty ranges from 4 to 19 per cent of the declared price plus a fixed fee.

Notary fees depend on the price of a property and are higher (as a percentage of the price) on cheaper properties. They're generally between 2 and 4 per cent of the declared price and legal fees around 2 per cent. A surveyor's fee is usually from around €300, but can be €800 or more for a large property with an extensive plot. The estate agent's fee (and who pays it) varies considerably, although it's usually shared between the vendor and buyer, e.g. around 3 per cent each. VAT is payable on new homes at 4 per cent (on non-luxury buildings) or 20 per cent (for luxury homes with a rating of A1 in the property register) and is included in the price. Registration tax on new homes is levied at a flat rate of €77.

Precautions: It's important to deal only with a qualified and licensed agent, and to engage a local lawyer (*avvocato*), before signing anything or paying a deposit. A local surveyor (*geometra*) may also be necessary, particularly if you're buying an old property or a property with a large plot of land. Your lawyer or surveyor will carry out the necessary searches regarding such matters as rights of way. Enquiries must be made to ensure that the vendor has a registered title and that there are no debts against a property (e.g. mortgages or taxes). It's also important to ensure that a property has the relevant building licences, conforms to local planning conditions and that any changes have been notified to the local town hall. If a property is owned by several members of a family, which is common in rural areas, *all* owners must give their consent before it can be sold. With regard to a rural property, it's important to ensure that there's a reliable water supply.

Holiday Letting: No restrictions.

Restrictions on Foreign Ownership: None.

Building Standards: Vary from excellent to poor. New buildings are generally well made. The quality of renovations varies, but is usually good.

Belongings: Belongings (including a motor vehicle) can be imported duty-free provided they've been owned and used for at least six months. A certificate of residence or proof of having purchased a home is required, and belongings must be imported within six months of taking up residence. It's necessary to make an inventory of all items being imported and to have it stamped by an Italian consulate.

Rental Accommodation: Italy has a strong rental market and virtually every type of accommodation is available, although rental property is in short supply in Rome and Milan. Bear in mind that property is usually let unfurnished, which in Italy means empty of everything, including kitchen appliances! A two-bedroom apartment costs around €600 to €1,500 a month and a three-bedroom apartment from around €900 to €1,850 a month. Note that prices in central Rome and in major northern cities can be up to three times higher.

Retirement Homes: There are no purpose-built retirement developments in Italy.

Utilities: The electricity supply (220V) is generally reliable, although power cuts are commonplace in some rural areas and charges are higher than the EU average. Mains gas is only available in the north of the country, although bottled gas is widely available elsewhere. Water charges are among the most expensive in Europe and water shortages and cuts are common in central and southern parts of the country.

Services

Post Office: The Italian postal service is probably the worst in Western Europe in terms of speed and efficiency, although modernisation and investment are slowly improving services. There are post offices in most areas, which also provide banking services

Telephone: Several companies provide telephone services in Italy, of which Telecom Italia is the main provider with a monopoly on local calls and the installation of phone lines. Competition between the various companies means call charges are continually being reduced.

Internet: The Internet was slow to take off in Italy but it's now catching up fast with the rest of the EU and most companies and many households are now online. There are numerous ISPs in Italy, both free and subscription.

English TV & Radio: There are various state and privately-owned TV and radio stations in Italy, but apart from the occasional news broadcast and some expatriate radio stations, there's little in English. There's no cable TV, but satellite reception is good in most regions. An annual TV and radio licence is payable.

General Information

Getting There: Italy is well served by international flights to around 15 airports, although to get to some parts of the south, e.g. Sardinia, you may have to take a connecting flight. Fares are generally reasonable but vary greatly from one airline to another. Italy is easily accessible from France and Switzerland by rail or by road via toll tunnels or mountain passes, which may be closed in winter. Ferries from several European countries including France, Greece and Spain also travel to Italy, although some services only operate during high season when fares are at their highest.

Getting Around: Northern Italy has the best communications network, where public transport services in the cities are excellent. The south is less well-served and in rural areas private transport is essential. There's a good domestic air service with frequent shuttle flights between the major cities. Most of Italy is covered by the rail network, which includes high-speed Eurostar trains between the main cities in the north. Fares have risen in recent years but are still lower than the EU average. City buses usually provide an excellent and inexpensive service. Regular ferry services connect Italy's islands with the mainland and several lakes also have ferry and hydrofoil services.

Shopping: Italy is a shopper's paradise, particularly with regard to luxury designer items, and Rome and Milan rank among the world's top shopping destinations. Food shopping is excellent in Italy, where small local shops and markets are preferred by the locals to supermarkets. Bear in mind that prices for most food products are high, even Italian produce, and imported foreign foods are difficult to find.

Crime Rate: The crime rate in Italy varies considerably from region to region. Violent crime is rare, although muggings do occur in resort areas and there are armed (and dangerous) bandits in some parts of southern Italy. Burglary is a problem in most areas and car crime is widespread. Vespa (motor scooter) thieves are common in some cities. Although organised crime and gang warfare is rife in some areas, it has no discernible impact on the lives of most foreigners in Italy (particularly in rural areas).

Driving: Northern Italy has excellent roads and the main north-south routes are also good. Most motorways are expensive toll roads. In the south and in rural areas the quality of roads varies considerably. Italian driving leaves an awful lot to be desired and anarchy and chaos are widespread, particularly in the major cities where traffic congestion is a major problem. Traffic drives (mostly) on the right. Cars are expensive to buy in Italy and importation is a much cheaper option. Car rental is also expensive. EU nationals don't need to exchange their EU driving licence in Italy, but non-EU nationals (depending on their nationality) may need to have their licence transcribed or take a driving test.

Medical Facilities: Medical facilities in Italy vary from poor to excellent. Italy has a public health service, although it's over-stretched and under-funded, and the quality of service varies considerably according to the region. Private health insurance is highly recommended.

Pets: There's no quarantine period for pets in Italy, but they need a certificate of health from an approved veterinary surgeon. Cats and dogs over 12 weeks old need a rabies vaccination not less than 20 days or more than 11 months prior to the date of issue of the health certificate. A veterinary officer may examine animals at the Italian port of entry.

Reciprocal Agreement with the UK: EU nationals are entitled to social security and health benefits in all EU member states, although the Italian rules of eligibility for entitlements (including pensions) apply. British citizens entitled to a state pension in the UK can continue to receive it in Italy and the sum will be increased annually at the same rate as pensions in the UK.

Residence Permits: Prospective residents must obtain a residence permit within eight days of arrival, which is valid for one year and renewable annually. Visitors may remain for three months and extensions can be obtained.

Work Permits: Unnecessary for EU nationals, but difficult for others to obtain.

Visas: Non-EU nationals require a visa if they plan to stay longer than 90 days or intend to work or study there. Visas should be applied for well in advance from an Italian consulate or embassy in your home country.

Reference

Further Reading

Buying a Home in Italy, David Hampshire (Survival Books, 🖥 www. survivalbooks.net). All you need to know about buying a home in Italy.

Living and Working in Italy, Nick Daws (Survival Books, 🖥 www.survival books.net). Everything you need to know about living and working in Italy.

Belle Cose, c/o Brian French & Associates, The Nook, Sowerby St, Sowerby Bridge, West Yorkshire HX6 3AJ, UK (☎ 0870-730 1910, 🖥 www.brian french.com). Quarterly property magazine.

Casa e Country, Via Burigozzo 5, 20122 Milan, Italy (☎ 02-58219). Glossy home decoration and country homes magazine with some property listings.

Casa per Casa, Via Valtellina 21, 20092 Cinisello Balsamo (MI), Italy (☎ 02-660 6161). Weekly free property magazine published in regional editions.

The Informer, BuroService Snc, Via dei Tigli 2, 20020 Arese (MI), Italy (☎ 02-935 81477, 🖥 www.informer.it). Monthly Internet magazine for people living in Italy.

La Mia Italia (Italian State Tourist Board). Free booklet.

A Small Place in Italy, Eric Newby (Picador).

Urban Land and Property Markets in Italy, Gastone Ave (UCLP).

Ville e Casali, Via Anton Giulio Bragaglia, 33, 00123 Rome, Italy (☎ 06-3088 4122, ✉ direzione@eli.it). Glossy monthly property and home style magazine.

Useful Addresses

Italian Embassy, 1601 Fuller St, NW, Washington, DC 20009, USA (☎ 0202-328 5500).

Italian Embassy, 14 Three Kings Yard, Davies St, London W1Y 2EH, UK (☎ 020-7312 2200, 🖥 www.embitaly.org.uk).

Italian Government Travel Office, 630 Fifth Avenue, Suite 1565, New York, NY 10111, USA (☎ 0212-245 4822).

Italian State Tourist Board, 1 Princes St, London W1R 8AY, UK (☎ 020-7408 1254, 🖥 www.enit.it/uk).

Useful Websites

🖥 www.goitaly.about.com – A useful travel website with plenty of links.

🖥 www.informer.it – Subscription website providing useful practical information about living and working in Italy.

🖥 www.italiantourism.com – Comprehensive travel and tourism information.

MALTA

Background

Capital: Valletta
Population: 375,000
Foreign Community: There are around 5,000 British residents in Malta and many more holiday homeowners, but relatively few residents from other countries.
Area: 316km² (122mi²)
Geography: Malta is situated in the middle of the Mediterranean 93km (58mi) south of Sicily and 290km (180mi) from North Africa (Libya), and consists of three main islands, Malta, Gozo, Comino, and the small uninhabited islands of Cominotto and Filfla. The island of Malta, by far the largest, is 27km (17mi) long and 14.5km (9mi) wide at its maximum and has a coastline of 137km (85mi), indented with natural harbours, sandy beaches and rocky coves. Most of Malta consists of an undulating limestone plateau with no mountains, woodland, rivers or lakes. All available land is under cultivation.
Climate: Malta has hot, dry summers and mild, damp winters. The temperature ranges from 10 to 21°C (50 to 70°F) in January and 25 to 33°C (77 to 91°F) in July. Malta enjoys an average of eight hours sunshine a day. Most rain falls in winter and spring, with around 7.5cm (3in) between October and March and just 1cm (0.4in) in the remaining six months.
Language: Maltese. Most Maltese speak English, which is also an official language. Italian is widely understood.
Political Stability: The political stability of Malta has been excellent in recent years and the government encourages (through tax breaks) foreign retirees to live in Malta. Malta is a member of the British Commonwealth and has applied for membership of the European Union. It has had a high growth rate and low inflation in recent years, and is an offshore financial centre.

Finance

Currency: Maltese lira (Lm)
Exchange Rate: £1 = Lm0.60, US$1 = Lm0.46
Exchange Controls: Yes. Funds imported to buy a property should be officially documented so that on its sale the proceeds can be re-exported.
Interest Rate: 4.5 per cent
Banks: Banking activity in Malta is modern and secure, and is controlled by the Central Bank of Malta. The island is also an offshore banking centre.

Many foreign banks are present. Both residents and non-residents may open bank accounts.

Cost/Standard of Living: Malta's cost of living is around 10 to 20 per cent lower than northern European countries. Although food and essential services are reasonably priced, on the other hand, imported 'luxury' goods are expensive.

GDP Per Head (US$): 10,100

Taxation

Income Tax: Malta has a PAYE income tax system for employees at rates of 15 to 35 per cent. There are a number of tax concessions for retirees and temporary residents. Foreign residents must have an income of at least Lm10,000 a year or assets of Lm150,000 and must remit to Malta at least Lm6,000 (for a single person) a year plus Lm1,000 a year for each dependant. Tax is assessed on these remittances at 15 per cent, less personal allowances, with a minimum income tax bill of Lm1,000 per year. Income that isn't remitted to Malta isn't taxed there. Visitors can spend six months a year in Malta without paying income tax; those whose stay exceeds six months per year are taxed at between 10 and 35 per cent on remittances to Malta.

Concessions/Tax Breaks For Retirees: There are a number of concessions (see **Income Tax** above).

Social Security: Social security contributions are compulsory for all employees in Malta who contribute 1/12 of their gross annual salary. Benefits include health care, retirement and disability pensions, and unemployment and maternity benefit.

Capital Gains Tax (CGT): CGT at 7 per cent is levied on gains made since January 1993 on income and property, although property is exempt from CGT after three years' ownership.

Wealth Tax: None.

Inheritance & Gift Tax: Malta levies a transmission (transfer) tax of 5 per cent on property inherited in Malta. If the recipient is the spouse, transfer tax is levied on half the property's value.

Value Added Tax (VAT): The standard rate of VAT is 15 per cent, with a reduced rate of 10 per cent for hotel and holiday accommodation and restaurant food.

Accommodation

Market: A wide range of properties are available, both old and new. Old character village homes and farmhouses that have been restored and modernised are popular with foreigners. Old properties are usually full of charm, although garages are rare and much sought-after. Modern properties are generally larger than the average in many other countries, although modern apartment buildings are often uniform in style and externally unattractive. A number of new developments are targeted at the foreign retirement market. All property is sold freehold.

Areas: There are numerous attractive areas to live in Malta, including both inland villages and coastal areas. Among the most popular towns are Bugibba, Mellieha, Marsaxlokk, Qawra, St Pauls Bay and Xemxija. Other popular areas include Mdina, Mosta, Rabat and Sliema (particularly St Julians). The island of Malta has a high population density, particularly in the area surrounding Valletta, where 2/3 of the population lives. Gozo is quieter than Malta with a slower pace of life, although its population has increased considerably in recent years.

Cost: Property prices are lower than in northern Europe, although strong local demand has pushed them up in recent years. The minimum price of a property purchased by a non-resident foreigner must be Lm15,000 and to qualify as a permanent resident the minimum cost is Lm30,000 in the case of an apartment and Lm50,000 for a house. Typical prices are two or three-bedroom apartments from Lm30,000, converted two-bedroom village houses from Lm70,000, two or three-bedroom townhouses from Lm80,000, and three-bedroom detached bungalows and houses from Lm180,000 (although a detached house in a fashionable area can cost around Lm350,000). Prices on Gozo are lower and include two-bedroom apartments from Lm20,000, three-bedroom bungalows from Lm75,000 and three-bedroom detached villas from Lm120,000.

Local Mortgages: Mortgages are available from Maltese banks, although facilities are limited and you can usually obtain better terms from a foreign lender. Local mortgages are usually for a maximum of 25 per cent of a property's value and terms are limited to 10 years.

Property Taxes: None.

Purchase Procedure: Permission is required from the Ministry of Finance to buy a property, although this is only a formality. Documentary evidence is required confirming that the funds used to purchase a property originated abroad. A preliminary or 'promise of sale' agreement is signed, binding both vendor and purchaser to the sale, subject to good title and the issue of any appropriate permits. A deposit of 10 per cent is paid and deposited in a trustee (escrow) account. The preliminary agreement is usually valid for three months (or longer if both parties agree), during which time a public notary undertakes searches to prove good title and submits applications for government permits. The final purchase contract is signed once the permits are issued, when the balance is paid plus all fees. Contracts may be written in English.

Fees: Total fees are around 6.5 per cent of the purchase price. They include 5 per cent stamp duty, 1 per cent notary's fee, a Ministry of Finance fee of

Lm100, and search and registration fees. Estate agents' fees are usually paid by the vendor.

Precautions: No particular precautions are necessary when buying property in Malta, although you should deal with a reputable local agent and engage a local lawyer to carry out the necessary checks.

Holiday Letting: Foreigners can let a home only if it's a villa, bungalow or farmhouse with a privately owned swimming pool, although apartments in some new developments in designated areas (e.g. such as Portomaso and Cottonera Waterfront) may also be let. Applications to let must be made through an estate agent and the annual licence fee is around Lm350.

Restrictions on Foreign Ownership: Foreigners are permitted to buy only one property per family. Permits to build new properties are almost impossible to obtain.

Building Standards: Good, although the design of new buildings, particularly apartment blocks, often leaves much to be desired.

Belongings: There's no import duty on belonging (including one car) for anyone who spends at least 200 days a year in Malta. Goods must have been owned and used for at least six months and must be imported within six months of your arrival. A motor vehicle imported duty-free must not be sold in Malta for three years. Holiday homeowners must obtain an import licence and pay customs duty on imported goods.

Rental Accommodation: Rental accommodation is readily available, although in high season rents are higher and property is in short supply. Rental properties are usually let furnished and cost around Lm70 a week for a two-bedroom apartment and Lm200 a week for a small house. Rental contracts are usually for one year and renewable.

Retirement Homes: There are currently no purpose-built retirement developments in Malta, although given the growing retiree population it will probably be only a matter of time before they're introduced.

Utilities: The electricity supply (240V) is reliable and charges are reasonable. Mains gas isn't available in Malta, but bottled gas is widely available. Tap water is generally safe to drink in the main population centres, but may not be in rural areas. Many people prefer the taste of bottled water.

Services

Post Office: The Maltese postal service is good and reliable, with fast delivery within the island and to mainland Europe.

Telephone: The telephone service is reliable and modern, but call charges can be high.

Internet: The Internet is gradually gaining in popularity, especially with Maltese businesses. There are several ISPs offering Internet connections and a few cyber cafés in the capital.

English TV & Radio: Maltese television and radio broadcast regularly in English, and cable and satellite TV are also available.

General Information

Getting There: Malta's international airport at Valletta is well connected by flights from mainland Europe and the Middle East. You can also reach the island in summer by ferry from Sicily and Genoa.

Getting Around: Public transport is generally good and there's a comprehensive bus service complemented by taxis. Frequent ferries operate between Malta and Gozo, as well as between Comino and other islands.

Shopping: Malta isn't known for its great shopping and many residents prefer to take a shopping trip to Sicily.. Prices in Malta can also be high, especially for clothing. Most towns have a small supermarket but in some resort areas shops may be closed out of season.

Crime Rate: The crime rate in Malta is exceptionally low, although precautions must be taken against burglary.

Driving: Road conditions vary in Malta, although main roads are generally good but signposting is poor. Maltese driving standards are dreadful and extreme care should be exercised when driving, particularly on secondary roads. Traffic drives on the *left*. Car hire is inexpensive. It's cheaper to import a car (duty-free if you spend at least 200 days a year in Malta) than buying one on the island. You can drive with a foreign driving licence for up to three months, after which time you must endorse your licence with the Maltese authorities.

Medical Facilities: Medical facilities are generally good and there's a major general hospital on the island, with mostly British-trained medical staff, and a number of 24-hour health centres. Free health care is provided for permanent residents and reduced hospital charges for holders of temporary residence permits. Residents and visitors who aren't covered by reciprocal agreements need private health insurance.

Pets: There's a quarantine period of three weeks for dogs and cats imported from Australia, New Zealand and the UK; for pets imported from other rabies-free countries the quarantine period is six months. Pets cannot be imported from countries which aren't free of rabies.

Reciprocal Agreement with the UK: British citizens entitled to a state pension in the UK can continue to receive it in Malta and the amount will be increased annually at the same rate as pensions in the UK.

Residence Permits: Permanent residents need to purchase a property of a minimum value and have a minimum income level (see page 99 under **Income Tax** and **Cost**). Visitors may remain for three months and can obtain a three-month extension. A special category of 'temporary residence' allows foreigners to remain in Malta 'permanently' without becoming residents.

They must provide evidence, however, that they have sufficient income to support themselves.

Work Permits: Very difficult to obtain.

Visas: Nationals from many countries, including Australia, Canada, New Zealand and EU member states, don't require a visa for visits of under three months. For longer visits and for employment purposes, a visa may be required.

Reference

Further Reading

Guide to Buying Property in Malta, Frank Salt, 2 Paceville Avenue, Paceville, Malta (🖳 www.franksalt.com.mt). Free bi-monthly property magazine.

Malta: The Owners' Manual (International Living, 🖳 www.international living.com)

Malta Property News, Frank Salt (see above).

Useful Addresses

Acquisition of Immovable Property Section, Ministry of Finance, St Calcedonius Square, Floriana CMR 02, Malta (☎ 236-306).

Association of Estate Agents in Malta, PO Box 18, Sliema, Malta (☎ 343-370, 🖳 www.maltaestateagents.com).

Department for Citizenship and Expatriate Affairs, 3 Castille Place, Valletta CMR 02, Malta (☎ 250-569).

Maltese Consulate, 2017 Connecticut Ave, NW, Washington, DC 20008, USA (☎ 0202-462 3611).

Maltese High Commission, Malta House, 36–38 Piccadilly, London W1V 0PP, UK (☎ 020-7292 4800).

Malta National Tourist Office, Suite 300, Mappin House, 4 Winsley Street, London W1N 7AR, UK (☎ 020-7292 4900).

Useful Websites

🖳 www.visitmalta.com – The official Maltese tourism website.

🖳 www.tourism.org.mt – Useful tourist and general information.

MEXICO

Background Information

Capital: Mexico City, known by Mexicans as Mexico DF (*Distrito Federal*).
Population: 81 million
Foreign Community: There's a large foreign community in Mexico comprised mainly of North Americans, particularly in the coastal areas of Guadalajara and Cancun in the Yucatan peninsula. It's estimated that some 400,000 North Americans have retired to Mexico.
Area: 1,970,000km² (760,676mi²)
Geography: Mexico lies in both North and South America, occupying most of Central America and bordering with the USA in the north (the border is over 3,200km (2,000mi) in length), the Pacific Ocean in the west, Belize and Guatemala in the south, and the Gulf of Mexico in the east. Mexico is a mountainous country and much of it is arid or semi-arid. In the north are the vast empty plains of the Mesa Central, while the mountains of central Mexico are an earthquake zone and home to a large part of the population; mountains are also the main feature in the south of the country. In the south-east is the low-lying Yucatan peninsula, popular with tourists and as a retirement destination.
Climate: The climate in Mexico depends very much on the altitude and can range from tropical in the lowlands to continental in the mountains, many of which are snow-capped for much of the year. There's very little rainfall in the north, while the central area (including the capital) has a rainy season from June to September and is dry for the rest of the year. Winters are cold and night-time temperatures are low all year round.
Language: The official language is Spanish and there are also over 50 indigenous languages. English is widely spoken.
Political Stability: This is good but fragile. In late 2000, Eduardo Fox, leader of the right of centre Alliance for Change party, became president of Mexico and was the first Mexican leader in 70 years not to come from the PRI party who governed the country under a corrupt pseudo-democratic regime. Mexico has huge problems of debt, poverty, corruption and internal armed conflict, mainly in the Chiapas region which is currently occupied by the army in an attempt to suppress a guerrilla uprising. Mexico has recently begun a new political era of hope among the majority of the population, for a better standard of living and a better understanding with its mighty neighbour, the USA.

Finance

Currency: Mexican peso. Prices are often quoted, however, in US$.
Exchange Rate: £1 = 12.5 pesos, US$1 = 9.08 pesos
Exchange Controls: None.
Interest Rate: In late 2001 the interest rate was an all-time low of 7 per cent, down from 17.6 per cent in 2000. Note, however, that interest rates in Mexico remain volatile.
Banks: There are many commercial banks in Mexico led by Banamex, BBVA, Bancomer and Bital, plus a number of foreign banks. Mexican banks offer a wide range of banking services, although transactions can be slow and time consuming. Loan interest rates are high. To open an account, foreigners need a residence or work permit (see **Permits** sections on page 26) and a credit reference. Note that it's illegal to go overdrawn (even by one peso) and you're liable for high penalties and bank charges.
Cost/Standard of Living: The standard of living in Mexico is low and wealth is unevenly distributed. Local goods and produce are cheap, but imported goods are expensive and prices rose significantly during 2001.
GDP Per Head (US$): 3,840

Taxation

Income Tax: Income tax is deducted at source (PAYE) and employers usually file tax returns on behalf of employees. If, on the other hand, you're resident and employed by a non-resident company, you must file a monthly income tax return yourself. There are some deductions and an annual tax credit. Income tax rates are adjusted for inflation quarterly and range from 3 to 40 per cent.
Concessions/Tax Breaks For Retirees: Retirement benefits and pensions provided by public institutions are exempt from income tax and private pensions are partially exempt.
Social Security: Employees are required to contribute 4.395 per cent of their gross monthly salary up to an annual maximum of around P11,000. Benefits include medical treatment and retirement and disability pensions.
Capital Gains Tax (CGT): CGT is levied at the same rates as income tax and for real estate purposes is levied on the difference between the purchase and selling prices after adjustment for inflation. If real estate has been used as a principal residence for at least two years, it's exempt from CGT, when you must provide your residence permit (see **Residence Permits** on page 26) plus water and electricity bills as proof that you've been using the property as a principal residence.
Wealth Tax: None.
Inheritance & Gift Tax: No inheritance tax is levied. Gifts from people other than direct family members are included in your annual taxable income.

Value Added Tax (VAT): VAT is levied at a flat rate of 15 per cent. It was revised in early 2002 when nearly all exemptions and zero rates were eliminated.

Accommodation

Market: Despite the erratic Mexican economy, real estate in popular tourist areas is generally a good investment and in recent years demand and prices have risen. The market is particularly strong in areas favoured by North Americans, seven million of whom travel to Mexico every year and some 400,000 have retired there. There's a huge demand for large quality villas and condominiums, which has fuelled a construction boom in popular areas.

Areas: The most popular parts of Mexico with retirees are mainly concentrated in two areas. The main area is in the province of Guadalajara on the Pacific coast in central Mexico, where the resorts of Lake Chapala (where the world's largest North American expatriate community is situated), Puerto Vallarta and Los Cabos are particularly popular. This area has a year-round warm climate and there are good facilities and leisure opportunities in the resorts. The second area is the Yucatan peninsula, situated on the Gulf of Mexico coast to the north of Belize and Guatemala, where tourism has been a massive growth industry in recent years. The Yucatan is famous for its natural beauty and is less developed and has fewer facilities than the Guadalajara resorts. It's expected, however, to experience substantial growth over the next decade and is already one of Mexico's top tourist resorts. Other popular areas with foreigners are the beautiful mountain town of Oaxaca and the world-famous resort of Acapulco.

Cost: Real estate in Mexico is generally considered to be a good investment, although prices in popular resort areas have risen by between 5 and 10 per cent in recent years. Prices are highest around Lake Chapala and Puerto Vallarta, where a two-bedroom apartment costs around $130,000 and a three-bedroom house from $240,000. Large villas with five or more bedrooms are in short supply and cost at least $900,000. Property in the Yucatan peninsula and Quintana Roo is cheaper and real bargains can be found in towns and villages in areas outside resorts. Property prices in the Yucatan peninsula are expected to increase substantially in the next five to ten years. Construction costs are around $150 per m^2, although building your own property in Mexico can be complicated (see **Precautions** below).

Local Mortgages: Property in Mexico was, until recently, always paid for in cash and mortgages are a relatively new concept. Until the mortgage market is more firmly established, it's advisable to obtain a foreign mortgage. In 2001, several American mortgage lenders entered the Mexican mortgage market offering up to 70 per cent of the purchase price over a period of up to 15 years.

Property Taxes: 1 per cent of the assessed value.

Purchase Procedure: Before committing yourself to a property purchase in Mexico you should obtain legal advice (see **Precautions** below). When your offer is accepted for a property you must pay a deposit (usually 10 per cent of the purchase price), which is generally paid into an escrow (trust) account. Your lawyer then makes the necessary checks on the property, including a title search. If necessary, your lawyer applies for a trust deed on your behalf. When your lawyer is satisfied that the property is free of debts and liens you go to a notary where the title deeds are signed. On the day of signing, a non-lien certificate (*certificado de no adeulo*) is obtained. The time from paying the deposit to completion is usually one to two months.

Fees: Fees total around 6 per cent of the purchase price and include 2 per cent sales tax and 4 per cent for legal fees and registration.

Precautions: Expert legal advice in Mexico is essential as title deeds are a potential minefield of problems. You should make sure that your lawyer is licensed to practise law in Mexico, which you can check by asking to see his licence (*cédula profesional*). To date there are no regulations governing real estate transactions or real estate agents and you should beware of unscrupulous estate agents. Some foreign consulates may be able to provide you with a list of reputable agents.

Building your own home in Mexico isn't recommended for foreigners and you should take expert legal advice before embarking on any construction as the paperwork and bureaucracy involved is extremely complex. Among the many Mexican peculiarities, a property owner becomes the employer of anyone working on the construction of a house and is responsible for all contracts, social security payments and taxes etc.!

Holiday Letting: No restrictions, but rental income generated in Mexico by non-residents is subject to withholding tax at 21 per cent.

Restrictions on Foreign Ownership: None unless you wish to buy on the coast or near a border, in which case you must obtain a trust deed (*fideicomiso*) and a permit from the Ministry of Foreign Affairs. The trust deed is held by a bank and is valid for 50 years, after which it can be renewed for a further 50 years. It costs around US$360 and can usually be obtained in a few days.

Building Standards: Variable, although good in modern properties.

Belongings: Personal and household effects can generally be imported duty-free if you import them personally or on your work permit, but regulations are subject to change and it's advisable to obtain current information from a Mexican consulate or embassy.

Rental Accommodation: Rental accommodation is generally easy to find, although properties in popular resort areas in high season can be in short supply. Rents are at a premium from November to April and during July and August. Small apartments generally cost from US$300 to US$600 per month and houses between US$350 and US$1,200 per month, depending on the location. Ensure that your rental contract states the rental amount in pesos, as contracts with the rent in a foreign currency aren't legally binding in Mexico. **Retirement Homes:** There are a number of purpose-built retirement developments in Mexico, where the influx of foreign (mainly American) retirees has boosted demand. There are several well-established communities, which are mainly situated in the province of Guadalajara around the resorts of Lake Chapala and Puerto Vallarta. These are well-equipped with sports and leisure activities, although prices are high.

Utilities: The electricity supply (100-127V) is erratic and unreliable, so a generator may be necessary, particularly in more remote areas. Tap water isn't generally safe to drink, although bottled water is widely available. Propane gas is available in the main cities, where most properties have tanks filled by the local gas company. Otherwise bottled gas is available.

Services

Post Office: The postal system is organised on a federal basis and is generally slow and unreliable, and many people prefer to use courier services for mail delivery.

Telephone: The telephone service is reasonable and operated by several companies, of which Teléfonos de Mexico SA is the main carrier. Inter-provincial and international call charges are high.

Internet: Mexico has one of the world's fastest growing rates of Internet use, although it's limited outside the main population areas. There are many service providers, some of which provide free Internet access.

English TV & Radio: If you're close to the US border you can pick up US TV. Otherwise, one cable TV and two satellite providers are available. Cable TV is more reliable, but satellite TV offers more choice.

General Information

Getting There: Direct flights to Mexico are available from most countries, mainly terminating at Mexico DF or Cancun, from where there's an excellent domestic flight service linking other destinations. Several highways, including the Pan American, link Mexico with the USA and the rest of Central America.

Getting Around: The best way to travel around Mexico is by air and the domestic flight service is excellent with frequent flights and reasonable fares. There's a good countrywide bus service, both for long and short distances, as well as an extensive rail network, although they can be rather slow. Mexico DF has a metro system, although its use isn't recommended because of the high crime rate and many people use the efficient private taxi service.

Shopping: Shopping facilities in resort areas have improved considerably in recent years and there's now a good variety of shops and goods catering for the foreign population. Outside resort areas, facilities vary greatly, but most small towns and villages have some sort of general store and a weekly food market.

Crime Rate: Outside the capital the crime rate is average, although petty street crime is common and car-jacking is a nationwide problem. In the capital, crime is a huge problem (there are between 2,000 and 3,000 crimes committed daily) and foreigners should take special precautions and avoid travelling at night, on public transport and in street taxis.

Driving: Road conditions in Mexico are generally reasonable and major investment is currently underway. Driving standards are poor, however. Traffic drives on the right. Cars and petrol are inexpensive. Foreign driving licences aren't valid in Mexico and if you drive a locally registered car you must obtain a Mexican driving licence, which involves taking a written test. Note that all cars driven in Mexico must have local insurance.

Medical Facilities: Medical facilities are reasonable in most cities, although standards are lower than in North America and Western Europe, and in some rural and more remote areas facilities are limited. Private medical treatment is generally of a high standard, but is expensive so that comprehensive medical insurance is essential. **Health warning:** vaccination against cholera, dengue fever, hepatitis A and B, malaria (particularly in the south-east and rural areas), polio, tetanus and typhoid is highly recommended. Much of Mexico is situated at high altitudes (causing fatigue) and pollution in the capital is a major problem.

Pets: Pets require a current vaccination certificate (including rabies, hepatitis and leptospirosis) as well as a health certificate signed by a registered veterinary surgeon no more than 72 hours before importation into Mexico.

Reciprocal Agreement with the UK: None.

Residence Permits: All foreign residents wishing to live in Mexico must apply for a residence permit (FM2) from the Ministry of the Interior. Permits are initially granted for one year and then extended annually for five years, when you can become a permanent resident. Residence permits are granted to those with work permits, with family ties and those wishing to retire to Mexico with sufficient financial means.

Work Permits: All foreigners require a work permit (FM3), which are difficult to obtain because preference is given to Mexican nationals and permits are restricted to jobs where there's a lack of local expertise. Foreign nationals may be self-employed in Mexico and no minimum investment is required, but you must be able to show sufficient financial resources and business experience.

Visas: Nationals from the EU, Australia, Canada, New Zealand and the USA don't require a visa to visit Mexico for stays of under three months. For longer stays, visas may be necessary. Consult the Mexican authorities before travelling for current information. Note that if you don't have the correct visa you may face a heavy fine and risk deportation.

Reference

Further Reading

Choose Mexico for Retirement, John Howells & Don Merwin (Globe Pequot)

How to Buy Real Estate in Mexico, John Peyton Dennis (Law Mexico Pub.)

Live Better South of the Border in Mexico, Mike Nelson (Fulcrum)

Live Well in Mexico: How to Relocate, Retire and Increase Your Standard of Living, Ken Luboff (John Muir)

Living Easy in Mexico, Hayes C. Schlundt & Philip H. Hersey (Woodbridge)

Living Overseas: Mexico, Robert Lawrence Jonston & Robert Johnson (Lawrence International)

Your Guide to Retiring to Mexico, Costa Rica and Beyond, Shelley & Shelly Emling (Avery)

Useful Addresses

British Embassy, Lerma 71, Colonia Cuauhtemoc, Mexico DF 06500 (☎ 207-2089).

US Embassy, 305 Reforma, Colonia Cuauhtemoc, Mexico DF 06500 (☎ 211-0042).

Mexican Embassy, 42 Hertford Street, Mayfair, London W1Y 7TF, UK (☎ 020-7499 8586).

Mexican Embassy, 1911 Pennsylvania Avenue, NW, Washington DC 20006, USA (☎ 202-728 1600; 🖳 www.embassyofmexico.org)

Useful Websites

🖳 www.solutionsabroad.com – A comprehensive expatriate website that includes a useful question and answer service.

🖳 www.mexconnect.com – A comprehensive website for foreigners living in Mexico.

🖳 www.mexpatriate.net – An interesting expatriate website with good links.

🖳 http://go2mexico.com – A good tourist website with lots of useful information.

NEW ZEALAND

Background

Capital: Wellington
Population: 3.7 million
Foreign Community: New Zealand is largely a nation of immigrants (around 75 per cent of the population is of European descent) and a cosmopolitan country, although less so than Australia. The bulk of immigrants still come from the UK (and a few other European countries), although in recent years there has been an increasing number of Asian and South African immigrants. The indigenous Maori race makes up around 10 per cent of the population (some 350,000) and Polynesians (mostly from Fiji, Samoa and Tonga) 4 per cent. Auckland has the largest concentration of Polynesians in the world. Chinese and Indians each comprise around 1 per cent of the population.
Area: 268,680km² (103,737mi²)
Geography: New Zealand is situated in the South Pacific, some 2,200km (1,370mi) east of Australia. It comprises two main islands, named simply North Island and South Island, which differ considerably in geography, vegetation and character. The country is almost 1,600km (994mi) long and 420km (260mi) wide at its widest point. New Zealand also comprises a number of outlying islands, including Stewart and Chatham Islands and territories in the Pacific such as the Kermadec Islands and Kiribati. It's a mountainous country with some 75 per cent of land above 200m (650ft) and over half forested. The highest peak is Mount Cook in the Southern Alps 3,764m (12,349ft) on the South Island, which divides the wet rain forests on the west coast from the dry pasture lands on the east coast. New Zealand is one of the world's most beautiful and unspoilt countries, with some 30 per cent of the land consisting of protected conservation sites. The country is noted for its wealth of volcanoes, geysers, glaciers, fjords (lakes), rivers and

lush vegetation. The South Island in particular has an abundance of unspoilt mountain scenery and a thriving skiing industry in winter.

Climate: Most of New Zealand has a temperate oceanic climate (the exception being the far north, which is subtropical) and four distinct seasons that are the opposite of those in the northern hemisphere. Summers are hot throughout the country and there are sometimes heat waves in December or January. Winters are cold and temperatures sometimes fall below freezing during the day on the east coast, and snow isn't uncommon in Christchurch (South Island). The northern part of the South Island usually has the mildest weather and the most sunshine (an average of around 6.5 hours a day). Average rainfall in the North Island is 135cm (53in) per year, while in the South Island it varies considerably between the east and west coasts. Rainfall is extremely high (usually torrential) on the west coast, where many areas receive over 5m (195in) of rain per year! The eastern coasts of both islands are much drier, e.g. in Auckland it rains on around 12 days a month in winter and six days a month in summer, while Christchurch has rain on around six days a month all year round. New Zealand's major cities also suffer from strong winds, Wellington being the windiest capital city in the world, well deserving its nickname of 'The Windy City'. Temperatures are moderate outside the mountainous areas, averaging 23°C (73°F) in summer and 14°C (57°F) in winter in Auckland, 22°C (72°F) and 11°C (52°F) in Christchurch, 19°C (66°F) and 11°C (52°F) in Dunedin, and 20°C (68°F) and 14°C (57°F) in Wellington.

Language: English and Maori are both official languages, and most official signs and forms are bi-lingual.

Political Stability: Excellent. New Zealand is a parliamentary democracy modelled on the British system. Politics have traditionally been dominated by the Labour (left) and National (conservative) parties, although a system of proportional representation introduced in recent years has made it more difficult for one party to obtain an overall majority. New Zealand is a member of the British Commonwealth and Queen Elizabeth II is head of state.

Finance

Currency: New Zealand dollar (NZ$)
Exchange Rate: £1 = NZ$3.35, US$1 = NZ$2.35
Exchange Controls: None.
Interest Rate: 5.57 per cent
Banks: There are several banks in New Zealand led by the 'big three', ANZ, BNZ and Westpac Trust, and several foreign banks have branches mainly in Wellington. Banking is secure and efficient, although bank charges are high. Telephone and Internet banking are growing in popularity. Residents and non-

residents can open a bank account; a minimum opening balance of at least NZ$200 is usually required.

Cost/Standard of Living: New Zealand enjoys a high standard of living, ranked as the tenth highest in the world according to a recent survey and exceeding that of Australia. The cost of living is reasonable, with food and essential goods and services relatively inexpensive. Imported goods such as motor vehicles and electrical goods are expensive, although prices have fallen in real terms in recent years. Many New Zealanders own second homes (known as a *bach* or a *crib*) in the country or on the coast.

GDP Per Head (US$): 14,600

Pensions: If you come to New Zealand from a country with a reciprocal agreement (including Australia, Canada, Ireland and the UK) you can claim a pension (known as superannuation in New Zealand) without a minimum period of residence, provided you would have been entitled to a state pension in your home country, although your overseas pension will probably be deducted from New Zealand Superannuation.

Taxation

Income Tax: New Zealand has a PAYE system where income tax is deducted from gross salaries at source. Income tax rates are 19.5 per cent (on income up to NZ$38,000), 33 per cent (NZ$38,000 to NZ$60,000), and 39 per cent (over NZ$60,001).

Concessions/Tax Breaks For Retirees: None.

Social Security: New Zealand has a unique social security scheme, known as the Accident Compensation Corporation, which provides accident cover for everyone in New Zealand, including visitors. Contribution to the ACC is compulsory for all employees who contribute NZ$1.10 for each NZ$100 of 'liable' income up to a maximum amount of liable earnings of NZ$85,795 (2002 figures). Benefits are comprehensive but most immigrants to New Zealand aren't eligible for benefits until a minimum resident period has passed (usually 24 months) unless they're nationals of a country with a reciprocal agreement.

Capital Gains Tax (CGT): None.

Wealth Tax: None.

Inheritance & Gift Tax: There's no inheritance tax in New Zealand. Gifts above NZ$27,000 in any year are taxed on a graduated scale up to 25 per cent (on gifts exceeding NZ$72,000).

Value Added Tax (VAT): New Zealand has a goods and services tax (equivalent to VAT) of 12.5 per cent. It's usually included in the advertised price rather than added when you pay (as in the USA). There are various exemptions, including residential property, financial services and rented accommodation.

Accommodation

Market: New Zealand has a thriving property market with some 75 per cent of families owning their own homes. The most common home is a single-storey detached house built on a plot known as a section, traditionally a quarter of an acre and dubbed 'the quarter acre paradise' (although plots are now often smaller, as many sections have been subdivided by developers). Apartments (usually called units) and townhouses are common in cities, but are rare elsewhere. Most homes are constructed of wood and brick, and the variety of architecture is limited. Wooden Victorian villas are popular. (Most older houses are made of Kauri wood.). The year 2001 was a boom time for property sales in New Zealand, when prices increased on average by some 9 per cent, although rises were much higher in the main cities. This trend looks set to continue for the next few years.

Areas: The most popular areas are the major cities, i.e. Auckland, Christchurch and Wellington. Popular regions for second homes are the Coromandel Peninsula and the Bay of Islands in the extreme north of the North Island, and the Southern Alps, the Glaciers, Mount Cook and Milford Sound on the South Island. The most popular areas for retirement homes on the North Island include the Coromandel Peninsula, the Bay of Islands, the Bay of Plenty and the Kapati Coast (north of Wellington). In the South Island, the northern Marlborough region (e.g. Blenheim, Nelson and Picton) is popular, as is Banks Peninsula south of Christchurch.

Cost: The average price of a three-bedroom detached house ranges from around NZ$110,500 in Otago to NZ$258,000 in Auckland, the average being around NZ$180,000. Apartments are often more expensive than houses and townhouses, as they're invariably located in inner cities (inner city living has become fashionable in recent years), whereas most houses are located in suburbs or in the country. Advertised prices are usually up to 10 per cent above a property's actual market value.

Local Mortgages: Mortgages of up to 90 per cent are available from major banks, building societies and increasingly, mortgage brokers. The maximum repayment term is 25 years, although the current trend is for 20 or even 15 years.

Property Taxes: Property taxes (residential rates), which usually include water charges, are levied by local authorities according to the size of a property. The annual bill for an average family house is between NZ$1,000 and NZ$2,000 (the average in Auckland is NZ$1,200). In some areas there are additional fees for certain services, e.g. refuse collection and water.

Purchase Procedure: A deposit of 10 per cent is payable when a contract is signed. This is usually non-refundable, but most contracts include a clause requiring its return if the title to the property isn't clear or land is subject to government requisition (compulsory purchase).

Fees: Lawyer's fees are usually between NZ$1,000 and NZ$2,000, and there's a land transfer registration fee of NZ$148. Banks levy a mortgage processing fee of 1 per cent of the mortgage amount and require a deposit (usually a minimum of NZ$500) on application, but you may be able to negotiate.

Precautions: It isn't wise to sign a contract before taking legal advice and confirming that the title is clear, as this commits you to the purchase. Many estate agents try to get buyers to sign as soon as a sale is agreed. If you feel obliged to sign a contract before the conveyance checks are complete, you should ask your lawyer to insert a clause in the contract to the effect that the contract is null and void if any problems arise.

Holiday Letting: No restrictions.

Restrictions on Foreign Ownership: Foreigners can buy property of less than one acre without any restrictions. For property exceeding one acre, permission is required from the District Land Registrar or the Land Value Tribunal. Permission isn't required if permanent residence has been granted.

Building Standards: Generally excellent, although corrugated iron roofs and weatherboard (wooden) exterior walls are used on cheaper houses, which don't always stand up well to the inclement weather.

Personal Effects: Permanent residents can import goods owned for 12 months (including a car) without payment of duty, subject to restrictions.

Rental Accommodation: Rental accommodation is generally easy to find in New Zealand with the exception of Auckland, which accounts for almost half the rental market and where properties are in short supply. A two-bedroom apartment costs from NZ$250 per month in Auckland and Wellington and a three-bedroom apartment from NZ$325. Outside these cities, monthly rental costs are much lower and you can expect to pay around NZ$150 for a two-bedroom apartment and NZ$200 for a three-bedroom apartment.

Retirement Homes: There are numerous purpose-built retirement developments in New Zealand, including many retirement villages. Prices start at NZ$90,000 plus weekly service rates (from NZ$50) which vary according to the facilities provided.

Utilities: The electricity supply (230V) in New Zealand is reliable and has been completely privatised in recent years. Most areas have at least two suppliers, which offer competitive prices, so it's worthwhile shopping around. Prices are generally reasonable. Mains gas is available throughout most of North Island, but only in Christchurch and Dunedin on South Island. Bottled gas is available throughout the country. Tap water is safe to drink and usually of good quality, and New Zealand rarely suffers from droughts.

Services

Post Office: The New Zealand postal service is generally reliable and delivery is secure and quick. There are numerous post offices (known as post shops) throughout the country offering a wide variety of services including (from 2002) banking services.

Telephone: The telecommunications market in New Zealand has been deregulated, but is still dominated by Telecom New Zealand, the previous monopoly holder. Telephone services are modern and efficient, and call charges are generally reasonable, particularly for local calls.

Internet: New Zealand has taken to the Internet with gusto and the government has made a huge investment in getting the country's companies and organisations online. As a consequence, New Zealand is one of the world's Internet leaders. There are numerous ISPs offering a variety of free or subscription access.

English TV & Radio: There are four national TV stations in New Zealand, as well as regional stations in some areas. Programme standards aren't particularly good and most are imported from Australia, the UK and the USA, although the government-funded organisation, NZ On Air, is attempting to boost home-made programmes. Satellite TV and, to a lesser extent, cable TV are popular and show many major sporting events. There are numerous national and local radio stations. New Zealand no longer has a TV licence.

General Information

Getting There: New Zealand is well connected by international flights, the majority of which terminate in Auckland or Wellington. Outside the high season, tickets are more competitive, particularly from the UK.

Getting Around: New Zealand has excellent communications, including a frequent ferry link between the two islands. Public transport is efficient and well co-ordinated, and includes a comprehensive long-distance bus service, which is reasonably priced and provides a good alternative to air travel. Domestic air services are good and there are frequent flights linking most parts of the country, but fares can be high. NZ Rail operates a limited network but the service is neither frequent or fast, and is mainly used by tourists. Auckland and Wellington both have fast and reliable suburban rail services.

Shopping: Although New Zealand isn't one of the world's great shopping countries, the choice and number of shops have grown significantly in recent years, boosted mainly by the proliferation of shopping centres on the outskirts of the main cities and towns. There are numerous supermarkets and general stores (known as dairies) throughout the country.

Crime Rate: Low. New Zealand is a safe country with a low rate of violent and serious crime. On the other hand, in common with most other western countries, crime has risen in the last decade. Auckland has a substantially higher crime rate than rural areas.

Driving: New Zealand's roads are generally good and not congested, except in Auckland where jams are frequent and pollution an increasing problem.

The country has one of the world's highest accident rates, but this has been reduced in recently by increased speeding controls and fines. New cars are expensive, although there's a competitive used car market and it's usually cheaper to buy a car in New Zealand rather than import one. If you have a driving licence written in English you may drive in New Zealand for up to a year before you need to exchange it for a New Zealand one. Depending on your nationality, you may have to take both the theoretical and practical tests. Traffic drives on the *left*.

Medical Facilities: Very Good. New Zealand has a national health system for residents, although there are long waiting lists for non-urgent hospital treatment. The state scheme doesn't pay for doctors' visits, prescriptions (although they're subsidised), optometrists (opticians) or dental treatment. Over 30 per cent of New Zealanders have supplementary private health insurance, which is highly recommended as it pays the cost of treatment that isn't covered by the state system and includes private hospital care. Reciprocal agreements cover visitors from many countries, including the UK, and treatment for injuries sustained in an accident is provided free for all visitors.

Pets: The regulations for importing animals into New Zealand are rigorous and include vaccinations and veterinary checks. An import permit is required and most pets are subject to a quarantine period. The exceptions are animals from Australia, Norway, Sweden, the UK and Hawaii, which aren't subject to quarantine but must undergo veterinary checks.

Reciprocal Agreement with the UK: British citizens entitled to a state pension in the UK can continue to receive it in New Zealand, but the amount is frozen at the rate it was when they left the UK.

Residence Permits: New Zealand has a permanent programme of immigration with an annual quota, e.g. 45,000 in 2002. As in Australia, immigration is decided on a selective policy based on points, with priority given to those with skills that are in demand and those wishing to start a business.

Work Permits: Authorisation is required from a New Zealand Consulate under the points system mentioned above.

Visas: Nationals of all countries, except Australia, require a visa to enter New Zealand, whatever their status. Visas are available from a New Zealand embassy or consulate in your home country.

Reference

Further Reading

Living and Working in New Zealand, Mark Hempshell (Survival Books, 🖥 www.survivalbooks.net). Everything you need to know about living and working in New Zealand.

Destination New Zealand, 1 Commercial Road, Eastbourne, East Sussex BN21 3XQ, UK (☎ 01323-726040, 🖳 www.outbound-newspapers.com).

New Zealand Outlook, 3 Buckhurst Road, Bexhill-on-Sea, East Sussex TN40 1QF, UK (☎ 01424-223111, 🖳 www.consylpublishing.co.uk).

New Zealand News UK, PO Box 10, Berwick-upon-Tweed, Northumberland TD15 1BW, UK (☎ 01289-306677).

Useful Addresses

Harcourts Group, 28 Grey Street, PO Box 151, Wellington, New Zealand (☎ 0800-804805, 🖳 www.harcourts.co.nz). New Zealand's largest estate agency group. Publishes 'Blue Book' guides to the property market in the major areas.

The New Zealand High Commission, New Zealand House, Haymarket, London SW1Y 4TQ, UK (☎ 020-7930 8422, 🖳 www.nzembassy.com).

New Zealand Embassy, 37 Observatory Circle, NW, Washington, DC 20008, USA (☎ 202-328 4800, 🖳 www.nzemb.org).

New Zealand Tourism Board, New Zealand House, Haymarket, London SW1Y 4TQ, UK (☎ 020-7973 0360).

New Zealand Immigration Service, PO Box 27 149, Wellington (☎ 04-384 7929, 🖳 www.immigration.govt.nz). As well as information on immigration, this website also offers a useful insight into living and working in New Zealand.

Useful Websites

- 🖳 www.purenz.com – New Zealand Tourism. An excellent website about all aspects of visiting New Zealand.

- 🖳 www.retirementvillages.org.nz – Retirement Villages Association. Contains information about retirement villages in New Zealand, including a nation-wide directory.

- 🖳 www.stats.govt.nz – Statistics New Zealand. A government organisation providing a wealth of useful information and links about New Zealand.

PANAMA

Background Information

Capital: Panama City
Population: 2.8 million

Foreign Community: Panama has become in recent years a popular tourist and retirement destination, particularly among North Americans, and there are large foreign communities situated mainly around the resort areas and in the capital.

Area: 75,990km² (30,134mi²)

Geography: Panama is a long, narrow country situated in the middle of Central American joining the continents of South and North America. Panama borders with Costa Rica to the west, the Caribbean Sea to the north, Colombia to the east and the Pacific to the south. Much of the country is mountainous of volcanic origin and covered in fertile agricultural land. It's divided into two by the Panama Canal, sometimes referred to as the 'Eighth Wonder of the World', one of the world's busiest shipping lanes. Panama has over 1,600km (1,000mi) of coastline and around 1,600 islands.

Climate: Panama has a subtropical climate with mild temperatures year round. Average temperatures are around 24°C (75°F) during the day and 16°C (60°F) at night. The wet season runs from April to December when thunder storms and heavy rains are common.

Language: The official language is Spanish, although English is widely spoken.

Political Stability: Good. After the overthrow of General Noriega in 1989, Panama has progressed to become a stable and health democracy.

Finance

Currency: Balboa (B/.), although the US dollar (US$) is also legal currency and the two currencies are worth the same.

Exchange Rate: £1 = B/.1.41

Exchange Controls: None.

Interest Rate: Panama has no central bank and interest rates depend on individual banks. In 2001 the lowest rate was around 8 per cent.

Banks: Over 150 commercial banks operate in Panama, which in recent years has become an important international banking centre, second only to Switzerland, with the most modern banking system in Latin America. Note, however, that there's no central bank. There are strict privacy laws regarding banking and offshore banking is popular. Both residents and non-residents can open bank accounts.

Cost/Standard of Living: Panama has a low cost of living compared to North America and Western Europe, and utilities and locally-produced food are particularly cheap. There are also generous discounts for expatriate retirees with a 'Retired Tourist Visa' (see below). Imported items can be expensive, however.

GDP Per Head (US$): 6,000

Taxation

Income Tax: Income tax is deducted at source (PAYE) and is levied at rates ranging from 0 per cent on annual income below B/. 3,000 to 30 per cent on annual income in excess of B/.200,000. Taxable income earned in Panama by non-residents is generally subject to the same rates as residents, plus an education tax levied at 2.75 per cent. Foreign professionals working in Panama under specific contracts for less than 180 days a year are taxed at 15 per cent. Deductions and allowances are available. Tax returns must be filed by everyone with more than one salary or with other taxable income by 15th March following the calendar year. Panama has no double taxation treaties.

Concessions/Tax Breaks For Retirees: If you have a retirement visa you're entitled to many discounts ranging from 15 to 50 per cent on goods and services, such as transport, medical services and utilities.

Social Security: Employees are required to contribute 7.25 per cent for social security tax and 1.25 per cent for educational tax from their gross monthly salary. Benefits include sickness and retirement benefits, and injury compensation.

Capital Gains Tax (CGT): CGT is levied at the same rate as income tax on all capital gains. To calculate CGT on real estate the following items are deducted from the sale price: the original cost of the property, the cost of any improvements, sale expenses and 10 per cent of the original price of the property for each year it has been owned. The resulting figure is then divided by the number of complete years the property was owned and this is then added to your other taxable income to determine the tax rate. Note that you can choose to pay a 5 per cent annual income tax on the value of the property, in which case you aren't liable for CGT when you sell.

Wealth Tax: None.

Inheritance & Gift Tax: None.

Value Added Tax (VAT): Panama levies a sales tax of 5 per cent on most goods and services.

Accommodation

Market: There's a buoyant property market in Panama owing to increased interest from foreign buyers (particularly North Americans) and the Panamanian government is keen to promote foreign investment in real estate by offering a variety of tax and residence incentives. There's a wide variety of property available, including typical stilt-houses on water, waterfront plots and newly-built apartments, and real estate represents good value. Construction is currently undergoing a boom.

Areas: The most popular area with foreign retirees is the province of Chiriqui, situated in the west of Panama bordering Costa Rica. This scenic mountainous area includes the towns of Boquete and Volcan, and the popular Bocas del Toro archipelago in the Bay of Chiriqui. The archipelago, whose centre is the small town of Bocas, has several islands, including Isla Solarte, a new 'eco-friendly' development where no cars are allowed. Other popular areas include the Pacific Coast near and around the capital.

Cost: Real estate in Panama is generally considered to be a good investment and, although they have risen in recent years, prices are still low compared to other popular retirement countries. Houses are available from US$50,000 and outside resort areas real bargains can be found. Plots are available from US$20,000 and construction costs around US$150 per m²; new homes are exempt from real estate taxes for 20 years.

Local Mortgages: There are five main mortgage banks in Panama who receive generous tax incentives from the Panamanian government if they provide loans to foreign buyers. Rates are competitive and loans are usually for 15 years, although some banks offer a longer repayment period.

Property Taxes: Property tax is payable annually on the official value of a property and cannot be higher than 2.1 per cent of its value. Homes with an official value of less than US$20,000 are exempt. If your home in Panama is your only residence, you're also exempt from property taxes.

Purchase Procedure: All property purchases in Panama are overseen by a notary public in the district where the property is located. The two parties first dictate the terms of the sale to the notary who prepares the title deeds (*escrituras*) where all details of the property such as size, description and location are included. After all taxes have been paid, the notary checks the deeds, which are then signed by both parties. The deeds are taken to the national Land Registry who register the property in the buyer's name after checking that there are no encumbrances or debts. Despite the fact that the deeds are checked by a notary, it's advisable to use the services of a lawyer.

Fees: Panama has low fees for property purchase, which include legal fees and transfer tax levied at 2 per cent, although this is usually paid by the seller.

Precautions: You're advised to proceed with a property purchase only after taking expert legal advice.

Holiday Letting: No restrictions. Note that if you let your property for a monthly rent of between US$250 and US$500, you cannot increase the rent without prior permission from the Ministry of Housing.

Restrictions on Foreign Ownership: None, except for property situated within 10km (6mi) of the country's borders.

Building Standards: Variable and good for most new properties.

Belongings: Permanent residents and holders of the Retired Tourist Visa may bring in possessions and household goods duty-free to Panama. Retired Tourist Visa holders may also import a new car every two years.

Rental Accommodation: Rental properties are fairly easy to find in Panama, although they can be in short supply in popular areas in high season.

Retirement Homes: There are no purpose-built retirement developments in Panama, although given the influx of foreign (mainly American) retirees, this is expected to change in the near future.

Utilities: The electricity supply in Panama is generally reliable and charges are reasonable. Most areas are connected to the mains supply, although in some remote areas a generator may be necessary. Mains gas isn't available in Panama, although bottled gas is widely available. Mains water in the main urban areas is safe to drink, but it may not be in more remote areas.

Services

Post Office: The Panama postal system is reasonably efficient, although courier services are preferred for urgent or valuable mail.

Telephone: Telecommunications in Panama are the best in Central America with an excellent and modern infrastructure. The sector is partially privatised, although INTEL, the original monopoly holder, still controls much of the market. Call charges, particularly international, can be high.

Internet: Panama has a good Internet infrastructure and there are several ISPs offering a range of services.

English TV & Radio: Panama television broadcasts on five channels almost exclusively in Spanish. Satellite and cable TV are available providing over 40 channels, the majority of which are in English. Local radio is in Spanish, but English-language radio is available by satellite or cable.

General Information

Getting There: Panama's strategic location between the two Americas means the country is easy to reach by air, with frequent flights from South America, Europe and, in particular, the USA. Airports such as Miami and Dallas are just two to three hours away from Panama City. You can also enter the country via the Pan-American Highway from Costa Rica by car or bus (in which case you must walk between the two borders) and from Costa Rica or Columbia via the Atlantic coast. Note that unless you're a permanent resident, you must pay US$5 for a tourist visa when you enter Panama and present the second half of the visa when you leave.

Getting Around: The quality of public transport varies hugely in Panama, although the capital has a good network of buses and taxis are relatively cheap. Most of the country can be reached by a comprehensive bus network. In the islands there are water taxis and ferries serving the main destinations. Retired Tourist Visa holders are entitled to generous discounts on public transport, including a 25 per cent reduction on domestic airfares.

Shopping: Contrary to popular belief, Panama has plenty of shops and restaurants, many of which are American-owned such as Sears, and the capital has an excellent selection of stores where you can buy just about anything. In rural areas, on the other hand, shops may be no more than a tiny counter selling basic items, although fresh-food markets are common.

Crime Rate: Panama has an average crime rate, which is considerably higher in the main cities and low in rural areas.

Driving: The modern and well-maintained Pan-American highway runs the length of Panama and is the main route. Other road conditions vary, but the government is currently investing heavily in road infrastructure. Traffic drives on the right. You may drive for up to 90 days with a foreign driving licence, after which you must obtain a Panamanian licence, which is valid for the same period as your identity card.

Medical Facilities: Medical facilities are generally good in Panama and medical staff are highly trained. The Hospital Nacional in Panama City is one of the best in Central America and provides treatment under several international insurance policies. Many expatriates, however, prefer to fly to the USA for specialist medical treatment. Medical treatment costs are low in Panama, although medical insurance is recommended. Retired Tourist Visa holders with no medical insurance are entitled to discounts on hospital treatment, visits to the doctor and medicine.

Pets: Pets must have current health and vaccination (including rabies) certificates to enter Panama.

Reciprocal Agreement with the UK: None.

Residence Permits: The main residence option for retirees is the Retirement Visa, for which you require certificates of good character and health, and proof that you have a minimum income of US$500 per month plus US$100 per month for each dependent. You can apply for a retirement visa when you're in Panama, which costs around US$500.

Work Permits: Work permits are difficult to obtain in Panama and are usually granted only if there are no Panamanians available for the job. There are also strict quotas for foreign workers in companies (usually no more than 10 per cent of the workforce).

Visas: Most foreign nationals must obtain special tourist cards or tourist visas to visit Panama, except for nationals of the following countries: Austria, Chile, Costa Rica, Finland, Germany, the Netherlands, Spain, Switzerland, the UK, Uruguay and the USA. Tourist visas are initially valid for 30 days and other temporary visitor visas are usually valid for up to one year.

Reference

Further Reading

Panama: The Owners' Manual (International Living, 💻 www.international living. com)

Useful Addresses

Panama Consulate, 1212 Avenue of the Americas, 6th Floor, New York, NY 10036, USA (☎ 212-840 2450, 🖥 www.nyconsul.com).

Panama Consulate, Panama House, 40 Hereford St, London W1J 7SH, UK (☎ 020-7409 2255, 🖥 www.panaconsul.com).

The Retiree Association of Panama, Apartado 4078, Boquete, Chiriqui, Republic of Panama (✉ retirepanama@yahoo.com). Produces a Panama Information Package and offers membership.

Useful Websites

🖥 www.explorepanama.com – Comprehensive information about life in Panama.

🖥 www.panamainfo.com – Official information about Panama.

🖥 www.panamatravel.com – Extensive travel information.

PORTUGAL

Background Information

Capital: Lisbon
Population: 10.3 million
Foreign Community: Portugal has large expatriate communities from the UK, Germany and various Scandinavian countries, mostly on the Algarve and in Lisbon, plus a considerable number of Brazilians.
Area: 92,000km² (32,225mi²)
Geography: Portugal is situated in the extreme south-west corner of Europe, occupying around one sixth of the Iberian peninsula, with an Atlantic

coastline of over 800km (500mi). It has a huge variety of landscapes including sandy beaches, rugged mountains, rolling hills, vast forests (over a quarter of the country is forested) and flat grasslands. Portugal also owns Madeira (and its neighbouring island of Porto Santo) and the Azores in the Atlantic. Madeira, which is situated off the West African coast north of the Canary Islands and around 1,000km (620mi) south-west of Lisbon, is 56km (34mi) in length and 21km (13mi) wide and has a population of 300,000. Like the Azores it has volcanic origins and is green and mountainous with few beaches. The Azores, north-west of Madeira and approximately 1,500km (932mi) west of Lisbon, comprise nine islands covering an area of 2,350sq km (907sq mi), with a population of around 250,000.

Climate: Mainland Portugal is noted for its generally moderate climate with mild winters and warm summers, with the notable exception of the north-east, which has long, cold winters and hot summers. The Algarve has one of the best year-round climates in Europe, with hot summers tempered by cooling breezes from the Atlantic and warm winters. Most rain falls in winter, with the heaviest rain in the north-west. Average temperatures in the Algarve are 12°C (°54F) in January and 24°C (75°F) in July/August, although temperatures may fall to 5°C (41°F) in winter and can be over 30°C (86°F) in summer. Lisbon and Oporto are only a few degrees cooler than the Algarve for most of the year. Madeira is subtropical with wet winters and hot summers. The average temperature is around 16°C (61°F) in winter (January) and 22°C (72°F) in summer (July/August).

Language: Portuguese. English is widely spoken in resort areas.

Political Stability: Since the bloodless revolution in 1974, which overthrew 50 years of dictatorship, Portugal has had a stable democracy. Its stability was enhanced in 1986 when it joined the EU (at the same time as Spain), a move which has brought huge economic benefits, although Portugal remains one of the EU's poorest members.

Finance

Currency: Euro (€)
Exchange Rate: £1 = €1.60, US$1 = €1.15
Exchange Controls: None.
Interest Rate: 3.25 per cent
Banks: There are many banks in Portugal and banking is efficient (if slow) and secure. Several foreign banks have branches, mainly in Lisbon, and supermarket banking is popular. To open a bank account in Portugal you require a fiscal number from the local tax office.
Cost/Standard of Living: Portugal has a relatively low cost of living, although it has increased considerably since the country joined the EU and it's

no longer an inexpensive country in which to live. Food and wine are relatively inexpensive, but imported goods are expensive.
GDP Per Head (US$): 10,670

Taxation

Income Tax: Foreign property owners require a tax card and a fiscal number (*número de contribuinte*). Portugal has a PAYE system of income tax with rates from 12 to 40 per cent. There are numerous tax credits. Non-residents must pay tax on income received in Portugal, e.g. letting income, at a flat rate of 15 per cent. When a property is owned by an offshore company tax on letting income is paid at a flat rate of 25 per cent, although the offshore company must fulfil certain requirements.
Concessions/Tax Breaks For Retirees: There are special low tax rates for pensioners who are residents in Portugal.
Social Security: All employees must make compulsory monthly contributions to the Portuguese social security system of around 11 per cent of their gross monthly salary. Benefits include almost free health care, retirement and disability pensions, and unemployment benefit.
Capital Gains Tax (CGT): In general, CGT is levied at the same rates as personal income tax rates up to a maximum of 40 per cent, although tax on gains from real estate apply only to 50 per cent of the gain. Property acquired before 1st January 1989 is exempt as are gains from a principal home if the proceeds are reinvested in another principal home in Portugal within two years. Gains from property are indexed to allow for inflation according to an official government coefficient.
Wealth Tax: None.
Inheritance & Gift Tax: Inheritance tax is levied at between 3 and 50 per cent, depending on the relationship between the donor and the beneficiary. It's payable by the beneficiary and not the estate.
Value Added Tax (VAT): The standard rate of VAT is 17 per cent, which is levied on most products including new homes. There's a reduced rate of 12 per cent for some foodstuffs, restaurants, farming equipment and miscellaneous items, and a rate of 5 per cent on books. In Madeira and the Azores there are VAT rates of 12, 8 and 4 per cent.

Accommodation

Market: The Portuguese property market is fairly lively in most areas and there's a strong market in properties on luxury developments (offering a wide range of leisure and sports facilities) and retirement homes. At the start of the new millennium, the property market was strong, particularly in the Algarve, and this looks set to continue (there's currently a shortage of top quality resale properties). In the past, overdevelopment has spoilt some areas of the Algarve and there are now much stricter planning controls. A planning law (*Plano Regional de Ordenamento do Território Algarve*/PROTAL) was introduced in 1993 to curb development, which has stabilised and increased prices. Most new developments are tasteful and in harmony with their surroundings. Older properties requiring renovation are available in rural areas.

Areas: The most popular area for foreign buyers is the Algarve in the south, which extends from the Spanish coast to Cape St Vincent in the west, although the main tourist area is between Faro and Lagos. Apart from a few towns (e.g. Albufeira, Quarteira and Vilamoura), few Algarve towns have been spoilt by overdevelopment and there are still many unspoilt fishing villages, particularly east of Faro, an area largely ignored by tourists. Other coastal areas popular with foreign buyers include Cascais and Estoril west of Lisbon, the Obidos lagoon area (silver coast) north of Lisbon, and the Costa Verde north of Oporto. Those seeking a peaceful life in completely unspoilt surroundings may wish to investigate developments in central Portugal (e.g. Beita Litoral), which has been discovered by developers from Belgium and the Netherlands. There's a relatively small property market in Madeira and few foreign agents.

Cost: Property prices in Portugal vary considerably and are generally higher than Spain because of the higher cost of land and the often superior quality of developments. The boom in property sales in recent years has also increased prices and there are no longer many bargains available except in remote rural areas. Some estimates claim that prices have doubled in the last five years, although it's now expected that prices will stabilise. Resale apartments on the Algarve cost from around €65,000 for one bedroom, from €124,700 for two bedrooms and from €140,000 for three bedrooms. Two-bedroom detached villas cost from around €140,000 and three-bedroom villas from €175,000. Note that it can be cheaper to build a new villa than to buy a resale property, with building costs from around €400 per m². In inland areas, old cottages and houses on large plots in need of total restoration can be purchased from around €40,000. You should, however, expect to spend two or three times the purchase price on renovation costs.

In the last decade the Algarve has seen many luxury developments (mostly built by foreign, often British, developers) with a wide range of leisure and sports facilities, including golf courses. Prices can be high, e.g. €150,000 for a tiny studio or one-bedroom apartment, €200,000 for a two-bedroom apartment, from €250,000 for a three-bedroom apartment or townhouse and from €450,000 for a three-bedroom villa with pool. The price usually includes free golf membership plus the use of country club facilities. Luxury developments generally have high annual maintenance fees, e.g. from around €1,000 for a studio apartment to over €3,000 for a three-bedroom villa. Prices in other areas (apart from major cities and a few fashionable areas such as Cascais and Estoril) are generally lower than on the Algarve, although prices vary considerably with a property's age, location, size and quality.

Local Mortgages: Local mortgages on second homes are difficult for foreigners to obtain, as Portuguese banks are reluctant to lend to non-Portuguese nationals. In any case, you can usually get better terms and a larger loan from a foreign lender.

Property Taxes: Property or municipal tax (*contribuiçao predial*) is based on a property's value, location and the standard of local services. It ranges from 0.7 to 2 per cent of a property's fiscal value (*valor matrical*) per year and is paid in two instalments in April and November. Principal homes in urban areas costing less than €50,000 are exempt for ten years. It's likely that municipal taxes will be raised in the near future to 20 per cent for property owned by offshore companies.

Purchase Procedure: Foreign property buyers must obtain a fiscal number (*número de contribuinte*). It's no longer necessary to declare the funds imported to buy a property in Portugal, but it's still recommended. When buying a property in Portugal, the buyer signs a preliminary or promissory contract (*contrato de promessa de compra e venda*) containing the property details, price, completion date and date of possession. When buying off plan, a small holding deposit, e.g. €750, is necessary to reserve a property until a promissory contract is signed (usually around four weeks later). The deposit is agreed between the parties and is usually between 10 and 30 per cent of the purchase price, depending on the price and the date of completion. It's forfeited if the buyer fails to go through with the purchase; if the vendor withdraws, he must pay the buyer double the deposit. A buyer should engage a lawyer (*advogado*) to check for outstanding debts such as a mortgage, charges or restrictive covenants.

Completion is performed by a notary when the deeds (*escritura de compra e venda*) are signed by both parties and the balance of the purchase price is paid. The original deeds are stored in the notary's office and a stamped certified copy is given to the buyer. Ownership is registered at the local land registry office (*Conservatória de Registo Predial*) by the buyer or his legal representative. Note that it can take several months to complete the registration. Most properties in Portugal are owned freehold.

Offshore Companies: There are many advantages to buying a home in Portugal through an offshore company. These include no conveyance costs (the shares of the company are simply transferred to the new owner), no property transfer tax (SISA), no capital gains tax and no inheritance tax. The cost of buying a property through an offshore company is around €750 plus annual fees of around the same amount. Owning a property through an offshore company is a big advantage when you're selling and may increase its value.

Fees: The fees when buying a property in Portugal are usually between 10 and 15 per cent of the purchase price. Notary and registration fees are between 3 and 3.5 per cent and legal fees usually between 1 and 2 per cent of the price. VAT (at 17 per cent) is included in the price of new properties. The main fee is stamp duty or transfer tax (SISA), which ranges from 8 to 10 per cent of the purchase price.

Precautions: When buying property in Portugal, you should deal only with a government-registered estate agent (*mediador autorizado*) and employ an English-speaking lawyer to protect your interests and carry out the necessary searches. It's necessary to ensure that a property is free of debts and liens via a certificate (*certidao de registro*) from the local land registry. The deeds (*escritura*) must be registered as soon as possible after completion.

Holiday Letting: No restrictions.

Restrictions on Foreign Ownership: None.

Building Standards: Generally excellent, particularly for luxury developments. The quality of renovations is variable.

Belongings: Household goods and cars can be imported duty-free provided they've been owned for at least six months, although you must produce a property deed (*escritura*) or a residence permit (*residência*). VAT and duty is payable on vehicles imported from outside the EU.

Rental Accommodation: Rental accommodation is generally easy to find, although long-term rentals may be difficult to find in resort areas. Rental prices in the capital and popular resort areas are from €600 a month for an apartment and from €1,200 a month for a small house, although in high season rents are far higher.

Retirement Homes: There are a few purpose-built retirement developments in Portugal, although the market is still in its infancy and is expected to grow rapidly in the next decade. There are a few residential apartment blocks on the Algarve, where prices for a small apartment start at €150,000 with weekly service charges of around €100.

Utilities: Electricity is provided by *Electricidade de Portugal*, who have a monopoly and levy among the highest prices in the EU. The electricity supply (220V) is generally reliable, although power cuts are frequent during bad weather. Mains gas is only available in Lisbon but bottled gas is in widespread use elsewhere. Water is expensive and shortages are common in the south during the summer months.

Services

Post Office: The postal service is generally slow and unreliable, although there have been improvements in recent years. It's advisable, however, to send valuable or urgent mail by courier. No banking services are provided by the post office.

Telephone: A huge investment in telecommunications in recent years has led to great improvements in telephone services, which are generally good in Portugal, particularly in the capital and on the Algarve. Call charges are, however, relatively high compared to other EU countries.

Internet: The Internet has been slow to take off in Portugal, although demand has grown significantly in recent years and most companies are now online. Personal usage isn't widespread but is growing. There are several ISPs, mainly in Lisbon and on the Algarve, offering a range of services.

English TV & Radio: Satellite TV is popular in Portugal, particularly in the capital and expatriate areas. There are several English-language radio stations, mainly on the Algarve.

General Information

Getting There: Portugal has good international connections from its three main airports in Lisbon, Porto and Faro (which has frequent charter flights during the tourist season). The country can also be reached by train, road and ferry via Spain. The southern connection from Spain (Seville) was much improved in late 2001 when the motorway was finished.

Getting Around: Portugal has a good, but expensive domestic air service and other public transport ranges from good in Lisbon (where trams, metro, buses and funiculars operate) and Porto, to poor in rural areas. The rail network is somewhat limited, although there's an excellent countrywide express coach service. A high-speed rail link from Faro to Lisbon will be completed by 2004.

Shopping: Shopping is generally good in Lisbon and facilities have improved greatly on the Algarve in recent years with the opening of several large shopping centres. Most towns and villages have a general store and a weekly food market.

Crime Rate: Portugal has a relatively low crime rate, particularly regarding serious and violent crime, although as in most European countries, crime has risen dramatically in the last decade. It's important to protect your property against burglary, particularly if it's a holiday home.

Driving: Road conditions vary considerably in Portugal from excellent on motorways to poor in remote areas. Road infrastructure has been given a much-needed boost by the European Football Championships in 2004 when the IP1 motorway linking Lisbon to the Algarve will be complete as will the East-West Via do Infante extension to Lagos. Driving standards are poor and Portugal has the highest accident rate in the EU. Parking and traffic congestion are major problems in most towns and cities. Traffic drives on the right. Cars and petrol are expensive.

Medical Facilities: Health care in Portugal has greatly improved in the last decade or so and is generally of a high standard. There are many English-speaking and foreign doctors in resort areas and major cities, although hospital facilities are limited in some rural areas. Residents who aren't covered by social security need private health insurance.

Pets: Pets must be vaccinated and have an import permit and a health certificate issued by an authorised veterinary surgeon not less than 14 days prior to import. Dogs over the age of four months must be vaccinated against rabies and be kept isolated in your home for a period after importation (as indicated on the import permit or determined by the Portuguese Animal Health Services).

Reciprocal Agreement with the UK: EU nationals are entitled to social security and health benefits in all EU member states, although the Portuguese rules of eligibility for entitlements (including pensions) apply. British citizens entitled to a UK state pension can continue to receive it in Portugal and the sum will be increased annually at the same rate as pensions in the UK.

Residence: Residence permits are a formality for EU nationals, although non-working residents must have sufficient income to maintain themselves. A residence card is required (valid for five years) and a fiscal number. Visitors can remain for three months, after which a residence permit is necessary.

Work Permits: Unnecessary for EU nationals; difficult for others to obtain.

Visas: Non-EU nationals require a visa if they plan to stay longer than 90 days or intend to work or study there. Visas should be applied for well in advance from a Portuguese consulate or embassy in your home country.

Reference

Further Reading

Buying a Home in Portugal, David Hampshire (Survival Books, 🖳 www. survivalbooks.net). Everything you need to know about buying a home in Portugal.

Algarve Resident Magazine (weekly), Rua 16 de Janeiro, Nº 6, 8400 Lagos, Portugal (☎ 282-342936).

Anglo-Portuguese News (APN), Avda Sao Pedro 14-D, 2765 Monte Estoril, Portugal.

Essential Algarve Magazine (bi-monthly), HDP, Apt 59, 8400 Lagoa, Portugal.

Madeira Island Bulletin, Apt 621, 9008 Funchal, Madeira, Portugal (🖳 www.madeiraonline.com).

Useful Addresses

The Anglo-Portuguese Society, Canning House, 2 Belgrave Square, London SW1X 8PJ, UK (☎ 020-7245 9738).

The Association for Residents and Home Owners in Portugal, Apartado 23, Alvor, 8500 Portimao (Algarve), Portugal.

Portuguese Embassy, 2125 Kalorama Rd, NW, Washington, DC 20008, USA (☎ 202-462-3726).

Portuguese Embassy, 11 Belgrave Square, London SW1X 8PP, UK (☎ 020-7235 5331, 💻 www.portembassy.gla.ac.uk).

Portuguese National Tourist Office, 2nd Floor, 22–25a Sackville Street, London W1X 1DE, UK (☎ 020-7494 1441, 💻 www.portugal.org).

Useful Websites

💻 www.portugal.org – Official government website.

💻 www.portugalinsite.pt – Portugal's official tourism website.

💻 www.portugaltravelguide.com –Extensive travel and general information.

SOUTH AFRICA

Background Information

Capital: Pretoria
Population: 41.5 million
Foreign Community: South Africa has some 6 million residents of European origin, including over 500,000 Britons. After the second world war, South Africa was one of the most popular countries for immigrants from Europe, particularly from France, Germany, Holland and the UK. It's an extremely cosmopolitan country, and although the bulk of post-war immigrants came from Europe, many African-Americans have migrated to South Africa since the end of apartheid. In recent years, on the other hand, there has been a net outflow of qualified workers, those leaving (including a high number of professionals) outnumbering new arrivals by around two to one.
Area: 1,221,040km^2 (471,444mi^2)
Geography: South Africa is the second-largest country in southern Africa (five times the size of the UK), occupying the southernmost region of the African continent. It's an ancient land comprising two natural zones: the interior and the coastal fringe, which is separated from the interior by the Fringing Escarpment, a major communications barrier. The coastline covers almost 2,900km (1,800mi) and borders the Atlantic Ocean in the south-west and the Indian Ocean (which is much warmer than the Atlantic) in the south and east. South Africa is one of the world's most beautiful countries and contains a wealth of breathtaking natural beauty. It contains a wide variety of landscapes, including majestic mountains extending to over 2,500m (8,000ft),

tranquil lakes and raging rivers, vast plains, huge tracts of dense forest and jungle, and many magnificent game parks and reservations.
Climate: South Africa has a temperate and subtropical (on the Kwazulu-Natal coast) climate, with the southern coast around Cape Town enjoying an almost Mediterranean climate, recognised as one of the best in the world. Being in the southern hemisphere, the seasons in South Africa are the opposite of those in the northern hemisphere, which makes the country a popular choice for a winter holiday home for Europeans and North Americans. Coastal regions enjoy a hotter climate than inland regions, although the extreme summer heat is tempered by balmy sea breezes. The coolest months are June to September (winter), which is also the rainy season.
Language: The main languages are English and Afrikaans, although South Africa has 11 official languages. The major African languages are Xhosa and Zulu. Over 60 per cent of the population speaks English.
Political Stability: Currently good but with an uncertain future. Apartheid officially ended in 1991 and a government of National Unity was established after the general election in 1994, with Nelson Mandela (African National Congress) as president. Mandela retired in 1999 leaving his successor, Thabo Mbeki, with many social and economic problems, particularly high unemployment and widespread AIDS. While South Africa's democracy seems to be stable, there are sporadic outbreaks of violence and civil unrest in the country. The South African government, however, encourages foreign investment.

Finance

Currency: Rand (R)
Exchange Rate: £1 = R16.67, US$1 = 10.93
Exchange Controls: None for import, although there are controls on the export of foreign currency.
Interest Rate: 11 per cent
Banks: Over 70 foreign banks operate in South Africa, where the banking sector is generally secure and stable, and a wide range of modern banking services are available. Bank charges tend to be high and you may be required to maintain a minimum balance. Non-residents and residents can open bank accounts.
Cost/Standard of Living: The cost of living in South Africa is lower than most western European countries, but higher than in North America. Food and alcohol are inexpensive, but imported goods are expensive, including motor vehicles (although there are concessions for immigrants). Homes are a bargain by international standards.
GDP Per Head (US$): 3,310

Taxation

Note that as from 1st March 2001 South African residents are taxed on their worldwide income.

Income Tax: South Africa has a PAYE system of income tax, with rates from 18 per cent (on annual income up to R38,000) to 42 per cent (on income above R215,000). There are rebates for individuals. Income tax is payable on all income earned in South Africa, even by non-residents.

Concessions/Tax Breaks For Retirees: There are several tax concessions for retirees over 65 including exemption from withholding tax on up to R4,000 interest, deductions for retirement pension funds, deductible medical expenses for physical disabilities and a higher tax threshold of R39,154.

Social Security: The social security system in South Africa is undeveloped and provides few benefits. Low to middle range earners pay contributions to the unemployment insurance fund, but higher earners neither contribute to or benefit from this fund.

Capital Gains Tax (CGT): CGT was introduced on 1st October 2001 and is applied on gains made on or after this date at the rate of 25 per cent. Primary residences are exempt from CGT unless the gain is higher than R1 million.

Wealth Tax: None.

Inheritance & Gift Tax: A donations (gift) tax of 25 per cent is levied on gifts, and an estate (inheritance) tax, also of 20 per cent, on estates valued at over R1 million.

Value Added Tax (VAT): VAT at 14 per cent is levied on goods and services, with the exception of basic foodstuffs. Duty at 57.5 per cent is payable on motor vehicles, although this is waived for tourists, business people and first time immigrants (provided the vehicle has been owned for one year). VAT is, however, still payable after an addition of 10 per cent to the vehicle's value. Visitors may apply for a refund of VAT on goods taken out of the country when their value exceeds R250.

Accommodation

Market: In the last decade there has been a booming market for second and permanent homes in South Africa, prompted by the relatively stable political climate and low prices, although property prices have risen somewhat as a result. The market has been fuelled by a strong demand from overseas buyers, particularly Britons and Germans. There are many superb examples of colonial architecture, including beautiful Dutch gable houses, thatched cottages and 19th century homesteads. New marina and golf apartment and townhouse developments are also attracting foreign buyers. Larger homes contain a wealth of luxury features such as swimming pools, Jacuzzis, saunas, tennis courts, large landscaped gardens, barbecue patios and extensive security features. Many older homes (including most detached properties) contain self-contained apartments, which were originally designed as servants' quarters. Most property is sold freehold, although it can also be leasehold, sectional title (condominiums) or share block.

Areas: The most popular provinces with foreign buyers are the Western and Eastern Capes, followed by Kwazulu-Natal. The coastal areas around Cape Town on the Western Cape, Port Elizabeth, Port Alfred and East London on the Eastern Cape, and Durban in Kwazulu-Natal are the most popular areas among foreign buyers. Cape Town is one of the world's most attractive cities and is noted for its beautiful countryside and magnificent coastline. There are numerous prestigious residential areas including the suburbs of Claremont, Constantia and Kenilworth, and the nearby towns of Somerset West and Stellenbosch. Hout Bay on the Atlantic coast is also popular, as are Fish Hoek and Simon's Town on the Indian Ocean, which, although not as attractive, are cheaper than the Central and Western Cape areas. Knysna on the Western Cape (between Cape Town and Port Elizabeth) has become a prime retirement area and Port Alfred is also becoming increasingly popular. The Northern Cape, which runs north of Cape Town to the Botswana and Namibia borders, mainly appeals to those looking for tranquillity.

Cost: Property in South Africa is excellent value (because of the low value of the rand and the emigration of many white residents in recent years), and is among the least expensive in the world. Prices have, however, been increasing in recent years and have risen by 25 per cent or more in many areas, particularly in Cape Town where the property market is booming. In many coastal areas you can buy new apartments and townhouses from R135,000 and resale three-bedroom detached houses with servants' quarters from around R300,000. New marina apartments are available in Cape Town for around R250,000 and a four-bedroom detached house on a large plot in a good area costs as little as R400,000. Large colonial-style homes are in high demand and a five or six-bedroom property with a swimming pool and a few acres of land can be purchased from around R800,000 rising to over R1,200,000 in exclusive areas such as Constantia Valley.

Local Mortgages: Mortgages (called bonds in South Africa) of up to 90 or even 100 per cent over 10 to 20 years are available to residents from local banks and building societies, although interest rates are high. Mortgages up to 50 per cent of the purchase price are available to non-residents. Stamp duty of 0.2 per cent is payable on a mortgage. Most buyers find it's cheaper to obtain a mortgage abroad.

Property Taxes: Property taxes are levied by local communities and vary with the size of a property and other factors. There are plans to unify the criteria in the near future.

Purchase Procedure: Buying property in South Africa is usually trouble-free and the country has a highly efficient system of land registration. Agents must be qualified and register with the Estate Agents Board. Offers must be made in writing and when an offer is accepted, a deposit of 10 per cent is paid to the seller's agent, which is held in a trust (escrow) account. Contracts contain the obligations of both vendor and buyer, and the buyer has the right to nominate a lawyer to carry out the necessary checks and register the new ownership at the Registrar of Deeds office. Deeds are held by the buyer's bank when there's a mortgage. Completion usually takes two to three months.

Offshore Companies: It's possible to buy property in South Africa through an offshore company, which provides certain advantages regarding inheritance.

Fees: The tariffs for legal fees, conveyance costs and transfer duty are set by the government. Transfer duty is levied at 1 per cent on the first R60,000, 5 per cent on the amount between R60,001 and R250,000, and 8 per cent on the balance. Where the purchaser is a legal entity, transfer duty is a flat 10 per cent. Transfer duty isn't payable on new properties when VAT (at 14 per cent) is included in the purchase price. Conveyance costs (payable to the seller's lawyer) are variable and are usually between 1 and 2 per cent of the purchase price. Legal and other fees total around 1 per cent.

Precautions: It's usual to have a survey (inspection), which should include checks for damp and termites. It's also necessary to engage a lawyer to oversee a sale and carry out the necessary checks.

Holiday Letting: No restrictions.

Restrictions on Foreign Ownership: None.

Building Standards: Variable but generally good.

Belongings: Can be freely imported without any restrictions, but you must pay a deposit equivalent to the duty payable on the goods. This deposit is refunded when you leave the country permanently or become a resident. Immigrants may import a motor vehicle (that has been owned for at least a year) up to an insured value of R100,000 duty-free.

Rental Accommodation: Rental accommodation is generally easy to find except in the capital, where it's in short supply. Rental contracts are usually for a minimum of six months and accommodation is generally let unfurnished. Monthly rents start at R600 for a small apartment.

Retirement Homes: Purpose-built retirement developments are becoming increasingly popular, where they're mainly situated in the southern provinces. Retirement villages are springing up around Cape Town and prices start at around R200,000 for a one-bedroom unit with an alarm and on-site medical attention. There's also a monthly charge of from R1,200 for services.

Utilities: The electricity supply (usually 200V, but 240V in Pretoria and 250V in Port Elizabeth) is reliable and charges are among the lowest in the world.

Many remote areas, however, aren't connected to the mains supply. Mains gas is available in most major cities and bottled gas is widely available. Tap water is generally safe to drink in the major cities, but may not be so in rural or remote areas. Bottled water is popular and widely available.

Services

Post Office: Postal services are erratic and unreliable, and courier services are recommended.
Telephone: The main telephone operator in South Africa, Telkom, has recently been partially privatised and as a result, services have improved. Call charges are reasonable.
Internet: The Internet has taken off in South Africa in recent years, during which demand has risen sharply. Many companies are now online, although personal use remains low. There are many ISPs offering a wide range of services and competitive rates.
English TV & Radio: The South African Broadcasting Corporation (SABC) broadcasts mainly in English, but the standard of programming isn't high. There are private TV channels and cable and satellite TV are also available.

General Information

Getting There: South Africa is well connected by international flights, although fares are expensive during the high season and you must book months in advance.
Getting Around: Two domestic airlines provide a comprehensive route network, although fares are high. Main towns and cities are well connected by modern express trains and luxury intercity buses, and fares are reasonable. The public transport network within the main cities is generally good.
Shopping: South Africa has good shopping facilities in its large towns and cities, where there's a wide variety and choice of goods. In smaller towns and remote areas shops may be few and far between.
Crime Rate: The crime rate is *extremely* high in some cities and urban areas, particularly crimes against property and robberies (including muggings). South Africa's murder rate is the highest in the world, but is distorted by the high level of inter-tribal fighting (over 5,000 have died in the last decade), and most 'white' areas where foreigners buy property, for example in the Eastern and Western Capes, are relatively crime-free. It's necessary, nevertheless, to take precautions to protect your property and avoid high crime areas. In many areas, private properties and estates have extensive security systems (including barbed wire and high walls) and many employ private security guards. The hijacking of cars is rife in some cities (such as Johannesburg), where it can be dangerous to stop a car at night, even at a red light. Police

corruption is widespread and up to 25 per cent of police officers have a criminal record (many officers are linked to robbery, rape and murder).

Driving: Road conditions vary greatly, although main highways are generally good and well-maintained. Driving standards are poor. Traffic drives on the *left*. You can drive on an international driving licence for up to one year, after which you must exchange it for a South African licence. Car prices have traditionally been on a par with European prices, but were set to rise by as much as 20 per cent in 2002 owing to a weak rand. Petrol is cheap.

Medical Facilities: Good to excellent, depending on the town or city. South Africa has no national health scheme, although one is planned, and private health insurance is essential.

Pets: To import pets into South Africa you need a permit from the State Veterinarian (the forms are available from immigration offices or embassies) and the application for the permit must be made at least six weeks before your pet's scheduled arrival. Pets need current health certificates, but there's no system of quarantine in South Africa.

Reciprocal Agreement with the UK: None.

Residence Permits: Note that *all* applications for immigration to South Africa have a *non-refundable* fee of R1,112. Among those who qualify for immigration are:

● financially independent people (who must transfer around R1.5 million, of which R700,000 must be invested in South Africa for a period of three years);

● close relatives (under the family reunion scheme);

● retirees, who must provide evidence that they have sufficient income (at least R8,000 a month for a couple) to support themselves and that they can transfer funds to South Africa immediately;

● business investors, who require a minimum investment of around R250,000 (the precise figure is decided by the Immigrants Selection Board). If you plan to employ South Africans, your application will be looked upon more favourably.

Work Permits: South Africa doesn't have a points system and those wishing to work (aged 18 to 51) require an offer of employment; employers must produce evidence as to why a position cannot be filled by a South African. Immigrants must pay a deposit (R400 in early 2001), which is refunded when they leave South Africa.

Visas: Nationals of Australia, Canada, New Zealand, the EU, Norway and Switzerland don't require visas for holiday and business visits. For any other purposes a visa is required. Other nationals usually require a visa, but you should check current regulations with the South African authorities.

Reference

Further Reading

Live and Work in South Africa, Avril Harper (Grant Dawson).

South Africa News, Outbound Newspapers, 1 Commercial Road, Eastbourne, East Sussex BN21 3XQ, UK (☎ 01323-726040, 💻 www.outbound-newspapers.com). Monthly newspaper for those planning to live or work in South Africa.

Useful Addresses

Institute of Realtors of South Africa, Suite 15, Howard Centre, Forest Drive, Pinelands, 7405, South Africa (☎ 021-531 3180).

South African Embassy: 3051 Massachusetts Ave, NW, Washington, DC 20008, USA (☎ 202-232 4400, 💻 www.southafrica.net).

South African High Commission, South Africa House, Trafalgar Square, London WC2N 5DP, UK (☎ 020-7451 7299, 💻 www.southafricahouse.com).

Useful Websites

💻 www.gov.sa – South African government online.

💻 www.southafrica.com – Travel and general information.

💻 www.southafrica.net – The official South African tourism site.

SPAIN

Background Information

Capital: Madrid
Population: 40 million
Foreign Community: Spain has a large expatriate community in its major cities and resort areas, including many Americans, British, Germans, Scandinavians and other Europeans.
Area: 510,000km² (197,000mi²)
Geography: The Spanish mainland measures 805km (500mi) from north to south and 885km (550mi) from east to west, making Spain the second largest country in western Europe after France. The Balearic Islands off the eastern coast comprise the islands of Mallorca (Majorca), Ibiza, Menorca (Minorca) and Formentera, and cover an area of 5,014km² (1,936mi²), while the Canary Islands, situated 97km (60mi) off the west coast of Africa, cover 7,272km² (2,808mi²). Spain also has two North African enclaves, Ceuta and Melilla, administered by the provinces of Cadiz and Malaga respectively. The Pyrenees in the north form a natural barrier between Spain and France, while to the west is Portugal. To the north-west is the Bay of Biscay and the province of Galicia with an Atlantic coast. In the east and south is the Mediterranean. The southern tip of Spain is just 16km (10mi) from Africa across the Strait of Gibraltar, a British territory claimed by Spain and a constant source of friction between the UK and Spain. Spain's mainland coastline totals 2,119km (1,317mi).

The country consists of a vast plain (the *meseta*) surrounded by mountains and is the highest country in Europe after Switzerland, with an average altitude of 650m (2,132ft) above sea level. The *meseta* covers an area of over 200,000km² (77,000mi²) at altitudes of between 600 and 1,000m (2,000 and 3,300ft). Mountains fringe the coast on three sides with the Cantabrian chain in the north (including the Picos de Europa), the Pénibetic chain in the south (including the Sierra Nevada, which has the highest peaks in Spain) and a string of lower mountains throughout the regions of Catalonia and Valencia in the east. The highest peak on the mainland is the Pico de Mulhacén in the Sierra Nevada range, 3,482m (11,423ft), which is topped by Mount Teide 3,718m (12,198ft) on the Canary island of Tenerife.
Climate: Spain is the sunniest country in Europe and the climate (on the Costa Blanca) has been described by the World Health Organisation as among the healthiest in the world. Spain's Mediterranean coast, from the Costa Blanca to the Costa del Sol, enjoys an average 320 days of sunshine per year. Continental Spain experiences three climatic zones: Atlantic, continental and Mediterranean, whereas some areas, particularly the Balearic and Canary

Islands, have distinct micro-climates. Coastal can have huge differences in the weather between the seafront and mountains a few kilometres inland. Mallorca's rainfall varies from 30 to 40cm (12 to 16in) in the south to over 1.2m (47in) in the north, and Menorca experiences strong winds in winter.

Language: Spanish, or more correctly Castilian (*castellano*), is the main language, although Basque, Catalan and Galician are also official languages in their respective regions. There are also a number of dialects including *Mallorquin* (Mallorca), *Menorquin* (Menorca) and *Ibiçenco* (Ibiza). English is widely spoken in resort areas and the major cities.

Political Stability: Very good. Since the death of General Franco on 20th November 1975, which heralded the end of 36 years of dictatorship, Spain has become a parliamentary democracy, with arguably the most liberal constitution in western Europe (since 1978). Spain has been a member of the EU since 1986.

Finance

Currency: Euro (€)
Exchange Rate: £1 = €1.60, US$1 = €1.15
Exchange Controls: None.
Interest Rate: 3.25 per cent
Banks: There are two types of banks in Spain: clearing banks and savings banks, which are controlled by the central Bank of Spain. Banking services are generally efficient and most banks offer a wide range of services, including Internet banking, an increasingly popular option. Foreign banks are well represented, mostly in Madrid and Barcelona, although British and other foreign banks also operate in resort areas. Residents and non-residents can open a bank account.

Cost/Standard of Living: In the last decade or so, inflation has brought the price of many goods and services in Spain in line with most other European countries, although many things remain relatively inexpensive, including property and rents, food, alcohol, dining out and general entertainment. With the exception of the major cities, where the higher cost of living is generally offset by higher salaries, the overall cost of living in Spain is lower than in many other European countries, particularly in rural and coastal areas.

GDP Per Head (US$): 14,100

Taxation

Income Tax: Income tax is levied on a sliding scale from 18 (on annual income up to €3,606) to 48 per cent (on annual income over €66,111). Non-resident property owners in Spain are liable for income tax at a flat rate of 25 per cent on income arising in Spain, including income from letting a property.

All property owners in Spain (both residents and non-residents) must have a fiscal number (*número de identificación de entranjero* (NIE)).

Concessions/Tax Breaks For Retirees: None.

Social Security: All employees make compulsory monthly contributions to the social security system of around 7 per cent of their gross monthly salary (the employer pays a high 33 per cent). Benefits include health care, sickness and maternity leave, unemployment and housing benefits, and pensions.

Capital Gains Tax (CGT): Capital gains tax (*impuesto sobre incremento de patrimonio*) is payable on the profit from the sale of certain assets in Spain, including property. After the first two years there's an annual deduction (for inflation) of 11.11 per cent for property, which means that after 10 years' ownership there's no capital gains tax liability. CGT isn't payable when you're a resident of Spain and sell your principal home, provided the proceeds are used to buy a new home in Spain within two years. The CGT rate is a flat 35 per cent for non-residents and a maximum of 18 per cent for residents. Individuals over 65 are exempt from CGT on property provided they've owned the property for more than three years.

Wealth Tax: Spain has a wealth tax (*impuesto extraordinario sobre el patrimonio*), known simply as *patrimonio*. A resident is exempt from paying tax on assets worth up to €108,182 and pays no tax on a primary residence. If a property is registered in the names of both spouses (or a number of unrelated people), each is entitled to claim the €108,182 exemption. Non-residents must pay tax on the total value of their assets in Spain. The rate ranges from 0.2 per cent on assets of up to €167,130, to a maximum of 2.5 per cent on assets above €10,696,000.

Inheritance & Gift Tax: Inheritance tax (*impuesto sobre sucesiones y donaciones*) in Spain is paid by the beneficiaries and not by the deceased's estate. The amount payable depends upon the relationship between the donor and the recipient, the amount inherited, and the wealth of the recipient, and varies from 0.2 to 34 per cent. There are allowances for close relatives, e.g. direct descendants, direct ascendants and relatives to a third degree.

Value Added Tax (VAT): The standard rate of VAT (called IVA in Spain) is 16 per cent. There are reduced rates of 7 per cent (e.g. drinks other than alcohol and fizzy drinks, fuel, water, communications, drugs and medicines, transport, hotel accommodation, restaurant meals, and theatre and cinema tickets) and 4 per cent (e.g. food and books). Certain goods and services are exempt, including health care (e.g. doctors' and dentists' services), educational services, insurance and banking.

Accommodation

Market: The Spanish property market is lively and the last few years have seen an unprecedented boom in construction in resort areas. Prices have risen sharply in mainland coastal and resort areas, although in early 2002 prices startcd to stabilise. Prices in the major cities have remained fairly stable, being less dependent on foreign buyers and the vagaries of the world economic climate, although Madrid and Barcelona have some of Europe's most expensive property. Resort property remains good value, particularly for those paying in currencies that made large gains against the peseta in recent years (e.g. sterling). Spain suffered in the '80s from a reputation for 'crooked' agents and developers and, although it's now a safer place to buy, it's still plagued by red tape and a plethora of property-related taxes.

Areas: The most popular locations are the Costa Blanca, Costa Del Sol, the Balearics (Ibiza, Mallorca and Menorca) and the Canaries (Gran Canaria, Tenerife and Lanzarote), followed at some distance by the other *costas* (e.g. Costa Brava, Costa Dorada, Costa Almería, Costa Cálida and the Costa de la Luz). The major cities, particularly Barcelona and Madrid, are popular with foreigners, who are also to be found in many inland villages along the *costas*. There is much more to Spain than the Mediterranean coastal resorts and the islands, and less popular regions such as the northern Cantabrian coast and inland cities such as Seville and Granada also have their enthusiasts. The Costa del Sol is Europe's sunniest region during the winter, although if you want really hot weather and wish to swim in the sea during winter without freezing, the only choice is the Canaries.

Cost: Prices in Spain vary considerably with the region and town, and with the size and quality of a property. On the Costa del Sol, resale studios and one-bedroom apartments start at around €60,000, two-bedroom apartments at around €90,000 and three-bedroom apartments at €120,000. Two-bedroom townhouses cost from around €120,000 and three-bedroom townhouses from €180,000. Small two-bedroom detached villas can be purchased from around €180,000 and three-bedroom villas from around €270,000. For those with deep pockets the sky's the limit and there's a huge choice of luxury villas and estates costing from around €500,000 upwards. Prices are generally lower on the eastern Costa del Sol than at the western end (i.e. west of Malaga). Prices on the Costa del Sol are generally around 10 to 20 per cent higher than on the Costa Blanca and property in the Balearics and the Canaries is usually around 20 per cent more expensive than on the *costas*.

There's little difference between the price of new and resale properties, although new properties may be slightly cheaper. Resale properties are often good value in Spain, particularly in resort areas, where the majority of low to medium-priced apartments and townhouses are sold fully furnished. You usually pay a premium for a beachside property or a property with a sea view. Property is less expensive in rural areas, where a farmhouse (*finca*) with outbuildings and a fair amount of land can cost the same as a studio apartment in a fashionable resort. In inland areas, old cottages and houses in need of total restoration can be purchased for around €50,000 or less, although you will need to spend two or three times the purchase price on modernisation and renovation costs. When buying a community property, always check the community fees, which can run into thousands of euros per year.

Local Mortgages: Mortgages are freely available from Spanish banks for both principal and second homes, up to a maximum of 80 per cent of the purchase price (50 to 60 per cent for non-residents). Spanish mortgages are usually payable over 10 to 15 years, although loans can be repaid over 5 to 25 years. You should shop around, as you may be able to obtain better terms from a foreign or offshore bank.

Property Taxes: Property tax (*impuesto sobre bienes inmuebles* (IBI)) in Spain is based on the fiscal value (*valor catastral*) of a property, which may be higher than a property's market value. It's important to check the fiscal value of a property, as a number of taxes are linked to it, including income tax, wealth tax, transfer tax on property sales and inheritance tax. In general, property tax rates in Spain are 0.5 per cent for urban (*urbana*) properties and 0.3 per cent for those on agricultural land (*rústicas*), although in some municipalities they're as high as 1.7 per cent. There's also an imputed 'letting' tax (*rendimientos del capital inmobiliario*) at 0.5 per cent of the fiscal value, the purchase price or the value assessed by the authorities with regard to other taxes whichever is the highest. Many municipalities also charge an annual fee for refuse collection.

Purchase Procedure: When buying an unfinished property off plan, take care when signing a reservation or option contract that it isn't a binding purchase contract. A reservation deposit, e.g. €3,000, usually secures a property for up to 30 days. If you pay a reservation fee, this is usually lost if you back out of the purchase, although some developers will return it. If a property is still to be built or completed, payment is made in stages. **When buying an unfinished property, it's important to ensure that the developer is financially secure and that any money paid is protected if he goes bust.**

When you sign the contract (*contrato privado de compraventa*) for a new or resale property (or a plot), you must pay a deposit. If you're buying a property privately, you must usually pay a deposit of 10 per cent when signing the initial contract, although the actual deposit is negotiable, particularly on expensive properties. Once you've paid the deposit there's a legally binding agreement between you and the vendor. If there's any doubt about whether you can complete a sale in the time specified in the contract, you should sign a contract with an option to purchase (*contrato de opción de compra*). In this case the deposit is paid in the form of an *arras* or *señal* and the contract can be cancelled by either party: if the buyer cancels, he forfeits his deposit; if the vendor cancels, he must pay the buyer double the deposit. A deposit should always be held in a separate bonded (escrow) account. **Always ensure that you know precisely the terms under which a deposit will be repaid or forfeited** *before paying it!*

The final act of the sale is the signing of the deed of sale (*escritura de compraventa*) and the payment of the balance due, usually paid by banker's draft unless otherwise arranged. Non-resident purchasers must obtain a certificate from a Spanish bank stating that the amount to be paid has been exchanged or converted from a foreign currency, and a copy of the certificate is attached to the title deed. It's normal for both parties to be present when the deed of sale is read, signed by both buyer and vendor, and witnessed by the *notario*. In practice, a copy of the *escritura* will usually be available for scrutiny before the official signing and, if you don't understand it, you should obtain an official translation. You can give a representative in Spain general power of attorney (*poder general*) so that he can sign a contract on your behalf.

Since 1993, a notary has been required to check the property register (not more than 48 hours before making the title deed) for any debts against a property or other restrictions which would 'inhibit' a sale. When the contract is signed, the notary will give you a certified copy (*primera copia*) of the deeds. A notarised copy is lodged at the property registry office (*registro de la propiedad*) and the new owner's name is entered on the registry deed. You should ensure that the *escritura* is registered *immediately* after signing it, if necessary by registering it yourself. Registering your ownership is the most important act of buying property in Spain, as until it's registered – even after you've signed the contract before a notary – charges can be levied against it. Only when the *escritura* is registered in your name do you become the legal owner of a property. Following registration, the original deeds are returned to you, usually after a few months.

Offshore Companies: It's possible to buy a property through an offshore company, but the advantages have been largely negated by a law requiring the name of the owner to be declared to the Spanish tax authorities, or a punitive annual tax (*impuesto especial*) equal to 5 per cent of the property's value is imposed. When selling a property owned by an offshore company, you can save fees such as transfer tax, notary and land registry fees, but it's no longer possible to avoid capital gains and inheritance tax. You should therefore buy a property through an offshore company in certain exceptional cases only, e.g. when there's a complicated family or inheritance situation.

Fees: The fees payable when buying a property in Spain amount to around 10 per cent of the purchase price and include the notary's fees, VAT (IVA) or transfer tax, legal fees and a property registration fee. A land tax (*plus valía*) is also payable when a property is sold and should be paid by the vendor (but you should confirm this). Most fees are based on the 'declared' value of the property, which is usually around 80 to 90 per cent of the purchase price or 'market' value. Local authorities maintain tables to calculate the current fiscal value (*valor catastral*) of properties, which should be used when declaring the value of a property.

Property buyers purchasing resale property must pay a transfer tax (*impuesto de transmisiones patrimoniales* (ITP)) of 6 per cent (4.5 per cent in the Canaries). There's no transfer tax on new properties, but VAT at 7 per cent is payable. Legal fees are usually around 1 to 2 per cent of the purchase price for an average property. The notary who officiates at a sale is paid a fixed fee based on a sliding scale depending on the amount of land, the size of the building(s) and the price. The fee for an average property is around €600. The registration fee is usually between €250 and €300, depending on the declared value.

Precautions: Buying property in Spain has been the subject of much adverse publicity, with some commentators even going so far as to advise people *not* to buy at all! It should be noted that most purchasers who had problems weren't the victims of fraud, but suffered from the insolvency of developers. Developers are now required to have financial guarantees and the legal situation has been tightened to prevent fraud, although the possibility must never be ignored. Nevertheless, **it cannot be emphasised too strongly that anyone planning to buy (or sell) property in Spain** *must* **take expert, independent legal advice.** Never sign anything or pay any money until you've sought legal advice in a language in which you're fluent from an experienced, Spanish-registered lawyer. If you aren't prepared to do this, you shouldn't even think about buying property in Spain!

Among the myriad problems experienced by buyers in Spain have been properties purchased without legal title, properties built without planning permission, properties sold that were subject to mortgages or embargoes, properties with missing infrastructure, properties sold to more than one buyer, and even properties sold that didn't exist! Checks must be carried out *both* before signing a 'preliminary' contract *and* before signing the deed of sale (*escritura*). Note that, if you get into a dispute over a property deal, it can take many years for it to be resolved in the Spanish courts, and even then there's no guarantee that you will receive satisfaction.

One of the Spanish laws that property buyers should be aware of is the law of subrogation, whereby property debts, including mortgages, local taxes and community charges, remain with a property and are inherited by the buyer. This is an open invitation for dishonest sellers to 'cut and run'. It is, of course, possible to check whether there are any outstanding debts on a property and this should be done by your legal advisor. It's virtually impossible, however, to prevent a seller fraudulently taking out a loan on a property after you've made a check. The procedure has been tightened in recent years, but still isn't guaranteed. This also applies in some other countries.

Many problems can arise when buying an unfinished property (i.e. buying off plan) or a property on an unfinished development (*urbanisation*). Because of the problems associated with buying off plan, such as the difficulty in ensuring that you actually receive what is stated in the contract and that the developer doesn't go broke, many experts advise buyers against buying an unfinished property. A 'finished' property is a property where the building is complete in every detail (as confirmed by your own architect or legal advisor), all communal services have been completed, and all infrastructure is in place, such as roads, parking areas, lighting, landscaping, water, sewerage, swimming pools, tennis courts, electricity and telephone services.

Holiday Letting: No restrictions. An imputed letting tax is payable by all property owners in Spain, both resident and non-resident, irrespective of whether you let a property. Tax is also payable on letting income at a flat rate of 25 per cent. Note also, that Spanish tenancy law is particularly generous towards the tenant and it can be difficult to evict a long-term tenant legally if there are problems. All contracts should be drawn up and checked by an expert.

Restrictions on Foreign Ownership: None.

Building Standards: Building standards differ enormously from excellent to poor. Care must be taken when buying a property, whether new or old, and unless you're confident that a property is sound you should have a survey carried out. The quality of properties in Spain varies considerably with regard to materials, fixtures and fittings, and workmanship, probably as much or more so than in any other European country.

Belongings: EU nationals planning to take up permanent or temporary residence in Spain are permitted to import their furniture and possessions free of duty or taxes, provided that they were purchased tax-paid within the EU or have been owned for at least six months. Non-EU nationals must have owned and used all goods for at least six months to qualify for duty-free import. A vehicle owned and used for six months in another EU country can be imported into Spain tax and duty-free. VAT (16 per cent) and duty (10 per cent) are payable on vehicles imported from outside the EU, the rates being based on a vehicle's value. A registration tax (*impuesto municipal sobre circulación de vehículos*) of 13 per cent is payable on all vehicles imported into Spain, including those from EU countries, and is calculated on the vehicle's current market value.

Rental Accommodation: Rental accommodation is in short supply in the main cities, but is relatively easy to find in resort areas, although long-term rentals can be difficult to obtain. Tenants are well protected by Spanish law and contracts are usually worded in generous terms, including the first option to buy a property should the owner wish to sell it. For a two-bedroom apartment, rents range from around €300 a month in a resort area and from €500 or more in a major city. A three-bedroom house costs from around €600 per month in a resort area and €1,500 in a major city. **Note, however, that in areas where properties to let are in short supply they can easily be double these levels.**

Retirement Homes: There are few purpose-built retirement developments in Spain, although there are a number of new developments under construction or planned, particularly in resort areas. Prices for a small apartment start at around €90,000 with weekly service charges from around €120.

Utilities: Electricity (220V) is provided in Spain by different companies, depending on the region. Costs have risen considerably in recent years and are now among the highest in the EU. The supply is generally reasonable, although power cuts are commonplace in bad weather. Spain needs to urgently increase its supply to cope with demand in built-up areas if it's to avoid long and frequent power cuts, such as those suffered in the winter of 2001 in Madrid, Barcelona and Valencia. Mains gas is only available in the major cities, but bottled gas is used extensively throughout the country. Water is relatively inexpensive but scarce in most parts of Spain (except the northern third), where drought is commonplace and often a constant problem, particularly in the south and east of the country. In some rural areas, water is provided by wells and may not be safe to drink.

Services

Post Office: The Spanish postal service has historically been one of the least efficient and slowest in Western Europe and, although it's slowly improving, the service remains erratic. It's expected (and hoped!) that the situation will be improved dramatically when the planned and much-needed privatisation takes place. There are post offices in most towns offering the usual postal services plus a limited number of other services such as money transfers and orders. Courier services should be used for valuable or urgent mail.

Telephone: Telecommuncations in Spain are modern and efficient with considerable investment in optic lines. The market is dominated by Telefónica, the previous monopoly holder, although there are around ten other telephone companies. The cost of international calls has fallen dramatically in recent years and there's a continual, on-going price war between the different companies. Mobile phones are extremely popular in Spain where there are more mobile phones than fixed lines.

Internet: Although personal Internet use in Spain is below the EU average, it's increasing rapidly mainly due to the intense competition between the many ISPs. Prices for flat rates are reasonable and ADSL lines are popular.

English TV & Radio: Apart from the occasional film in English with Spanish sub-titles, Spanish television carries no broadcasts in English. Cable TV is available in most cities and satellite TV reception is excellent in most regions. In resort areas, there are a number of expatriate radio stations broadcasting in English (and other languages) for the foreign population.

General Information

Getting There: Spain has several international airports and is served by direct flights from most countries; fares are competitive, particularly to resort areas from Germany and the UK. Road connections from France are good and you can also travel to Spain by ferry from the UK, Morocco and Italy (during the summer only).

Getting Around: Infrastructure has improved dramatically over the last decade and most parts of the country except for remote rural areas can easily be reached by public transport. There's a comprehensive domestic air service provided by several companies who are engaged in a continual price war, meaning fares are competitively priced. The rail network isn't extensive and some regions have no rail connections at all, although the high-speed rail network (AVE) is currently undergoing expansion to Barcelona, Valencia and Malaga. Fares are inexpensive and trains are usually punctual. Madrid, Barcelona and other major cities have excellent public transport systems. The country has a good coach service linking most towns and cities.

Shopping: Shopping facilities in Spain are generally good and in recent years there has been a proliferation of shopping centres, now a popular 'leisure' option among the Spanish. Most towns have at least one supermarket and a weekly food market. Bear in mind that shops in some resort areas may close during low season and that villages in remote areas may have no shopping facilities at all.

Crime Rate: Spain's crime rate is among the lowest in Europe, although in common with most other European countries it has increased considerably in the last decade. Violent crime is rare, although muggings have increased in resort areas. However, 'petty' crime such as handbag snatching, pick-pocketing and theft from vehicles are widespread throughout Spain. You should *never* leave anything on display in your car, including your stereo system, which should be removed when parking in cities and resorts. Burglary is also a big problem throughout Spain, particularly for holiday homeowners. It's necessary to take comprehensive measures to protect your property in Spain to ensure that it's as thief-proof as possible and not to leave valuables or money lying around (a home safe is recommended).

Driving: The road network is generally good in Spain and recent years have seen big investment in motorways, many of which are expensive toll roads. Standards on minor roads vary and can be exceedingly poor. Driving standards leave a lot to be desired and Spain has one of the highest accident rates in the EU. Traffic congestion and pollution are major problems in most towns and cities. Traffic drives on the right. Cars are more expensive in Spain than many other EU countries, although cheaper than the UK. Petrol is relatively inexpensive for Europe.

Medical Facilities: Medical facilities in Spain vary and are generally good in resort areas and major cities but limited in rural areas. There are English-speaking Spanish and foreign doctors and dentists in resort areas and major cities. If you aren't covered by the public health service, private health insurance is essential; it's recommended in any case if you want the widest possible choice of practitioners and the best treatment without waiting.

Pets: A maximum of two pets may accompany travellers to Spain. A rabies vaccination is usually compulsory, although this *doesn't* apply to accompanied pets (including cats and dogs) entering Spain directly from the UK or for animals under three months old. A rabies vaccination is necessary if pets are transported by road from the UK to Spain via France. If a rabies vaccination is given, it must be administered not less than one month or more than 12 months prior to export. Pets over three months old from countries other than the UK must have been vaccinated against rabies. If a pet has no rabies certificate, it can be quarantined.

Reciprocal Agreement with the UK: EU nationals are entitled to social security and health benefits in all EU member states, although the Spanish rules of eligibility for entitlements (including pensions) apply. British citizens entitled to a state pension in the UK can continue to receive it in Spain and the sum will be increased annually at the same rate as pensions in the UK.

Residence: A residence permit is a formality for EU nationals, although non-working residents must have sufficient income to maintain themselves in Spain. There's no fixed income required to obtain a visa to retire to Spain, but proof of income or receipt of a pension is required. An investment of around €90,000 is usually necessary for a non-EU national to start a business in Spain and 30 per cent of this sum must be readily available. Visitors may remain in Spain for up to six months in a calendar year without a residence permit.

Work Permits: Unnecessary for EU nationals, but difficult for other foreigners to obtain.

Visas: All non-EU nationals require a visa to visit and stay in Spain for more than 90 days, which must be obtained from a Spanish consulate or embassy *before* arrival. For visits of less than 90 days, nationals from some countries, including the USA, Canada and New Zealand don't require a visa. Note that visa regulations are subject to continual change and you should obtain the latest information from the authorities.

Reference

Further Reading

Buying a Home in Spain, David Hampshire (Survival Books, 🖥 www. survivalbooks.net). All you need to know about buying a home in Spain.

Living and Working in Spain, David Hampshire (Survival Books, 💻 www. survivalbooks.net). Everything you need to know about living and working in Spain.

Costa Blanca News (✉ cbnews@ctv.es). Weekly English-language newspaper.

Island Connections (✉ info@ic-web.com). Fortnightly English-language newspaper issued in the Canary Islands.

Lookout, Lookout Publications SA, Urb. Molino de Viento, C./Rio Darro, Portal 1, 29650 Mijas Costa (Málaga), Spain (✉ lookout@jet.es). Quarterly lifestyle magazine.

Property World, Edif. Buendía, 1°A, C/España 1, 29640 Fuengirola, Spain (☎ 0952-888 234, 💻 www.propertyworldmagazine.com). A Cost del Sol property magazine with extensive listings.

The Reporter, C./Los Naranjos, 5, Pueblo Lopez, 29640 Fuengirola (Málaga), Spain (✉ thereporter@alsur.es). Free monthly news magazine.

Sur in English, Diario Sur, Avda. Doctor Marañón, 48, 29009 Málaga, Spain (💻 www.surinenglish.com). Free weekly newspaper.

Useful Addresses

Institute of Foreign Property Owners, Apartado de Correos, 418, 03590 Altea (Alicante), Spain (☎ 096-584 2312, 💻 www.fipe.org).

Spanish Embassy, 2375 Pennsylvania Ave, NW, Washington, DC 20037, USA (☎ 0202-452 0100, 💻 www.spainemb.org).

Spanish Embassy, 39 Chesham Place, London SW1X 8SB, UK (☎ 020-7235 5555, 💻 www.cec-spain.org.uk).

Spanish National Tourist Office, Metro House, 57-58 St James's Street, London SW1A 1LD, UK (☎ 020-7499 0901).

Useful Websites

💻 www.okspain.org – Good travel information.

💻 www.spainexpat.com – A website with resources for foreigners living in Spain.

💻 www.spanish-living.com – Comprehensive information about living in Spain.

💻 www.tourspain.es – The official Spanish tourism website.

UNITED KINGDOM

Background Information

Capital: London
Population: 58 million
Foreign Community: Around 5 per cent of the British population is made up of immigrants from British Commonwealth countries and their descendants. There's also a large foreign population from throughout the world, particularly in London, the world's most ethnically diverse city.
Area: 242,432km² (93,600mi²)
Climate: The UK has a generally mild and temperate climate, although it's extremely changeable and usually damp most of the year. Due to the prevailing south-westerly winds, the weather is variable and is affected mainly by depressions moving eastwards across the Atlantic Ocean. This maritime influence means that the west of the country tends to have wetter, but also milder weather than the east. The amount of rainfall also increases with altitude and the high areas of the north and west have more rain (160cm (63in) annually) than the lowlands of the south and east, where the average is 80cm (31in). Rain is fairly evenly distributed throughout the year in all areas, but the driest months are usually March to June and the wettest September to January.

In winter (December to February), it's often cold, wet and windy, although temperatures are higher in the south and west than in the east. Winters are often harsh in Scotland and on high ground in Wales and northern England, where snow is usual. Although winter temperatures drop below freezing at night, it's rarely below freezing during the day and the average temperature is 4°C (39°F). For many, spring is the most pleasant time of year, although early spring is often wet, particularly in Scotland.
Language: English
Political Stability: Excellent. One of the most politically stable countries in the world.

Finance

Currency: Pound sterling (£)
Exchange Rate: US$1 = £0.70
Exchange Controls: None.
Interest Rate: 4 per cent
Banks: There are a number of major banks in the UK and most towns have branches of one or more of them, although branch networks have been reduced in recent years due to mergers and rationalisation. Telephone and Internet banking are provided by most banks and building societies (similar to savings banks). In recent years, there has been a flood of new-style 'banks' (often run by supermarkets or stores) offering innovative accounts and services. Bank accounts can be opened by residents and non-residents.
Cost/Standard of Living: The UK has a high cost of living, particularly food and consumer goods, making it one of the most expensive places to live in the world, although there's a huge disparity between the wealthy, expensive south and the relatively 'poor' (and less expensive) north of England, Scotland, Wales and Northern Ireland. Duty and taxes on cars, petrol, alcohol and tobacco are high. London is one of the world's most expensive cities, although this is largely due to the high cost of property.
GDP Per Head (US$): 21,410

Taxation

Income Tax: The UK has three income tax rates: a lower rate of 10 per cent on the first £1,500, a basic rate of 23 per cent on income from £1,501 to £28,000, and a higher rate tax of 40 per cent on taxable income above £28,000 a year.
Concessions/Tax Breaks For Retirees: For people aged 65 or over, the basic personal tax allowance is increased from £4,385 to £5,790 (2001/02) if annual income doesn't exceed £17,000. For annual income up to £19,810 the amount is reduced by £1 for every £2 above £17,000. For those aged 75 or over, the basic personal tax allowance is £6,050 if annual income doesn't exceed £17,000. For annual income up to £20,190, the amount is reduced as above.
Social Security: Social security (national insurance) payments are compulsory for most employees in the UK and contributions are calculated as a percentage of your salary and depend on which of the five classes you come under. Rates range from 8.4 per cent on a weekly wage of £67, below which you're exempt from contributions, and there are reductions depending on your status. Social security provides a range of benefits, including health care, family allowances, sick and unemployment pay, and pensions.

Capital Gains Tax (CGT): Anything you sell (from a second home to shares or antiques) which reap profits above £7,100 a year (2001/02) is liable to CGT. Net gains over £7,100 are taxed at 20 per cent where the aggregate of income and gains is less than the basic rate limit, and at 40 per cent where they exceed that limit. There's no CGT on a profit made on your primary residence.
Wealth Tax: None.
Inheritance & Gift Tax: Inheritance tax of 40 per cent is payable on any bequests over £231,000, if left to anyone other than your spouse or a registered charity. You're permitted to give away up to £3,000 a year, which can be carried over for one year without paying gift tax. Note that inheritance and gift tax is complicated and professional advice should be sought.
Value Added Tax (VAT): 17.5 per cent (8 per cent on domestic fuels). Most food, new buildings, young children's clothes and footwear, books and newspapers are exempt.

Accommodation

Market: Home ownership in the UK is around 65 per cent and among the highest in the European Union. During the recession in the early '90s, there was an unprecedented collapse in the value of property, although the market has now fully recovered and prices are at an all-time high. There's a flourishing market for homes in central London, where property prices are among the highest in the world, and many areas in the south of England are enjoying a mini-boom. If you want a property for an investment, then the best buy is usually a character, period property.
Areas: The areas most favoured by second home owners include the Lake District (in the north-west of England), the West Country (e.g. Cornwall and Devon), Wales, East Anglia (on the coast or the Norfolk Broads) and the Chilterns. Most foreign residents tend to live in the cities or the south-east of England, where property is the most expensive. Property in central London is among the most expensive in the world, although it remains popular with foreign buyers and is a good long-term investment (particularly properties at the top end of the market). The most popular areas among overseas buyers in central London include Belgravia, Kensington, Knightsbridge, Mayfair and St Johns Wood.
Cost: House prices vary considerably according to the region and whether a property is located in a town or the country. A three-bedroom semi-detached house costing £70,000 in the north of England or Scotland, will usually cost at least 50 per cent more in the south-east of England. The average price of a house in the UK in 2001 was around £100,000, with the cheapest homes in the north of England and Scotland and the most expensive in London, which has the world's most expensive real estate. Older, cheaper houses are

available in some areas, but most have been snapped up and modernised years ago, and those that are left are no longer bargains. Most semi-detached and detached houses have single or double garages included in the price, although they're rare in cities.

Local Mortgages: Mortgage repayments are relatively low in the UK due to the long repayment period, typically 25 to 30 years. Mortgages of up to 95 per cent are widely available and discounts are provided for first-time buyers and those switching lenders, with interest rates up to two percentage points lower than the standard rate for a number of years. The availability and terms of mortgages mean that it's usually cheaper to buy a home than rent one.

Property Taxes: There's no property tax in the UK but instead residents pay 'council tax', which is calculated according to the value of the property, the number of people living there and the area where the property is situated. Annual rates range from £400 in a rural area to over £1,000 in a major city. Payment can be made in instalments.

Purchase Procedure: Most property in the UK is sold freehold, although there's also a system of leasehold for apartments (flats) where buyers buy a lease, e.g. from 99 to 999 years (when the lease expires the property reverts to the original owner, i.e. the freeholder). When buying property in England, Wales or Northern Ireland, prospective buyers make an offer subject to survey and contract. Either side can amend or withdraw from a sale at any time before the exchange of contracts (when a sale is legally binding). In Scotland neither side can pull out once an offer has been made and accepted.

Fees: Fees total around 3 to 5 per cent of the purchase price and include legal fees, land registry fees and stamp duty. Stamp duty is 1 to 4 per cent depending on the purchase price (properties below £60,000 are exempt). There are various fees associated with obtaining a mortgage, including a valuation fee, indemnity insurance and an arrangement or acceptance fee. Survey fees are optional, but are common on older resale properties. The fees for buying a property in the UK are among the lowest in the world.

Precautions: There are a few special precautions that need to be taken when buying property in the UK apart from using an experienced solicitor (lawyer) or conveyancer. It is, however, inadvisable to use the legal adviser or conveyancer who's acting for the seller, in order to avoid potential conflicts of interest. When a property is owned jointly you must ensure that the sales contract is signed by all the co-owners. In some areas (and with some properties) there are problems such as woodworm, subsidence, landslip, overhead electricity cables or sub-stations, radiation (in areas with a high concentration of radon) and flooding. All these problems (if they exist) should be exposed by a survey, which is highly recommended on older properties. Buyers should be wary of buying an apartment in an 'old' apartment block, however much of a bargain it may appear, as many have serious problems (in some cases they cost owners more to rectify than the value of their property).

Holiday Letting: No restrictions.
Restrictions on Foreign Ownership: None.
Building Standards: Generally excellent.
Personal Effects: Household goods purchased within the European Union can be imported duty-free and don't need to be retained for a minimum period. Goods (including vehicles) purchased outside the EU, however, must have been owned for at least six months and cannot be sold for 12 months after importation.
Rental Accommodation: The UK has one of the most unregulated letting markets in Western Europe and the consumer has little protection against voracious landlords. There isn't a strong rental market and there's a chronic shortage of rental properties throughout the country, particularly in London and the Southeast area.. Average rental costs for the Southeast (excluding London) are £350 to £500 a month for a one-bedroom apartment and £600 to £1,250 for a three-bedroom detached house. London rents are around 50 per cent higher and the north of England and Scotland (with the exception of Edinburgh) are considerably lower.
Retirement Homes: Some 30 companies offer purpose-built retirement homes and developments (often termed sheltered accommodation) in the UK, which are popular and tend to be in short supply. Apartments and houses are usually sold on long leases, and prices range from £40,000 to £500,000 according to the size, location and the amenities provided. A weekly service charge of £35 to £50 is usually payable.
Utilities: Electricity (240V) is provided by many companies in the UK, most of which provide a countrywide service. The supply is generally good in most parts of the country and relatively inexpensive. Mains gas is available in all but the remotest areas and is supplied by some 25 companies. Gas is a relatively inexpensive form of energy in the UK, particularly for central heating and hot water. Tap water is safe to drink throughout the country and charges are usually based on the rateable value of a property and included in the council tax (few homes in the UK have water meters). In spite of the wet climate, water charges can be high and there are often water shortages in many areas, particularly the south-east.

Services

Post Office: The British postal service is one of the most efficient and modern in the world. Most towns and villages have a post office, at which you can use banking services, pay bills and licences, in addition to the usual postal services.
Telephone: The phone market in the UK is dominated by British Telecom (BT), although some 100 other telephone companies also have a licence to operate, making the UK one of the most competitive and relatively

inexpensive markets in the world. The telephone system is generally excellent and the UK is at the forefront of telecommunications technology and a world leader in mobile phones.

Internet: The UK is very much 'online' with a large number of companies and homes using the Internet. There are numerous service providers, many of which offer free access and/or flat rate deals.

English TV & Radio: British TV is generally regarded as the best (or least worst) in the world and British TV companies, particularly the BBC, produce many excellent programmes. There are five national free-to-air channels, as well as dozens of cable and satellite stations, an increasingly popular option in the UK. An annual TV licence of around £100 is payable (which finances the BBC). British radio is split between the BBC and commercial stations, which provide a range of music, discussion, sport and entertainment.

General Information

Getting There: There are around 140 airports in the UK serving a comprehensive network of domestic and international destinations. London's Heathrow and Gatwick are among the world's busiest airports. Airfares to and from the UK are the most competitive in Europe and there's fierce competition between airlines offering discount fares. Regular (expensive) car and passenger ferry services operate all year round to continental ports and the Eurotunnel train service links Paris and London.

Getting Around: The transport system in the UK is one of the most congested in Europe and the quality of public transport ranges from excellent to poor, depending on the region or city. The railway network, once famed for its efficiency, has been plagued with problems since privatisation and is in desperate need of massive investment and modernisation. A variety of discounts are available for senior citizens (usually 60 or over) on train, bus, coach and air travel.

Shopping: The UK is 'a nation of shopkeepers' and a shopper's Mecca, with a huge variety of excellent stores throughout the country. Even small villages usually have a well-stocked general store and out-of-town shopping centres abound, where shopping is a popular 'leisure' option.

Crime Rate: The crime rate in the UK is low in most areas, although it has increased considerably in recent years, particularly in inner cities and London where violent crime has risen sharply (although it isn't a high crime country). Much crime is drug-related, particularly violent crime, which is an increasing problem; car crime, burglary and house-breaking are widespread.

Driving: British roads are congested and among the most crowded in Europe. Traffic jams are eternal and roadworks are commonplace in towns and cities, while roads in the south are close to saturation point. In spite of the volume of traffic, the UK has a relatively low accident rate and driving standards are high. Cars are more expensive in the UK than the rest of Europe and it's advisable to buy a new car on the continent. Petrol is also the most expensive in Europe. Traffic drives on the *left*. Driving licences issued within the EU are valid, but other licences must be exchanged for a British licence.

Medical Facilities: Good. Employees and retirees from many countries are covered by the National Health System (NHS), which pioneered state health care in the '40s, although in recent years lack of investment has created staffing and other problems and long waiting lists for non-emergency treatment. All visitors are given free emergency treatment and many countries have reciprocal agreements with the UK. If you aren't covered by the NHS, private health insurance is necessary and may be mandatory for foreign residents.

Pets: Animals imported into the UK from Western Europe and North America must be micro-chipped and have a veterinary certificate of vaccination, including rabies, and a pet 'passport' certifying that it's free from rabies. Animals without the necessary documents or imported from other countries are subject to the toughest quarantine regulations in the world and must spend six months in quarantine on arrival in the UK.

Residence Permits: Residence permits are a formality for EU nationals, although non-working residents must have sufficient income to maintain themselves. Visitors may remain for up to six months. Nationals of most non-EU countries require a visa to work or reside permanently in the UK. Non-EU retirees and persons of independent means must have a minimum of £200,000 in disposable capital or an annual income of at least £25,000, and must be able to prove that they're able to support and accommodate themselves and their dependants indefinitely without working and recourse to public funds. Applicants must also show that they have a 'close connection' with the UK through family or employment.

Work Permits: No restrictions for EU nationals, but difficult for other foreigners to obtain.

Visas: Visa requirements for non-EU nationals wishing to live in the UK are extremely complicated and immigration regulations are subject to change. You should consult a British embassy or consulate in your home country before making any plans to live in the UK.

Reference

Further Reading

Buying a Home in Britain, David Hampshire (Survival Books, 🖥 www. survivalbooks.net). All you need to know about buying a home in Britain.

Living and Working in Britain, David Hampshire (Survival Books, 🖳 www.survivalbooks.net). Everything you need to know about living and working in Britain.

Living and Working in London, Claire O'Brien (Survival Books, 🖳 www. survivalbooks.net). Everything you need to know about living and working in London.

Good non-Retirement Guide, Rosemary Brown (Enterprise Dynamics).

Top Towns (Guinness Publishing).

Useful Addresses

The Association of Relocation Agents, PO Box 189, Diss, IP22 1PE, UK (☎ 08700-737475, 🖳 www.relocationagents.com).

The British Association of Removers (BAR), 3 Churchill Court, 58 Station Road, North Harrow, London HA2 7SA, UK (☎ 020-8861 3331, 🖳 www.bar movers.com).

British Embassy, 3100 Massachusetts Ave, NW, Washington, DC 20008, USA (☎ 0202-588 6500, 🖳 www.britainusa.com).

British Tourist Authority (BTA), Thames Tower, Black's Road, Hammersmith, London W6 9EL, UK (☎ 020-8846 9000, 🖳 www.visit britain.com).

National Association of Estate Agents (NAEA), Arbon House, 21 Jury Street, Warwick CV34 4EH, UK (☎ 01926-496800, 🖳 www.naea.co.uk).

National House Building Council, Chiltern Avenue, Amersham, Bucks HP6 5AP (☎ 01494-434477). Operates the Sheltered Housing Code, which is mandatory for all registered house builders.

Useful Websites

🖳 http://www.ageconcern.org.uk – The premier organization for the elderly in the UK.

🖳 www.atuk.co.uk – UK travel and tourist information.

🖳 www.britain-info.org – Americans in Britain. A website which provides a comprehensive list of fact sheets regarding living and working in Britain.

🖳 www.visitbritain.com – Official government tourist site.

🖳 www.uktravel.com – Travel and tourist information.

USA

Background Information

Capital: Washington DC
Population: 281.4 million
Foreign Community: The USA is extremely cosmopolitan, particularly in the major cities, and a nation of immigrants, although today only some 7.5 per cent of the population is foreign-born. There are large immigrant communities from all major countries.
Area: 9,399,300km² (3,615,125mi²)
Geography: The USA consists of 48 contiguous states on the mainland of North America, plus Alaska and Hawaii, and it's the third-largest country in the world after Canada and China. It measures around 2,500mi (4,023km) from east to west (from the Atlantic to the Pacific coasts) and stretches some 1,200mi (1,931km) north to south, from the Canadian border (mostly along the 49th parallel) to the Gulf of Mexico. Alaska, which joined the Union as the 49th (and largest) state in 1959, is situated north-west of Canada and is separated from Russia by the Bering Strait. Hawaii joined the Union in 1960 as the 50th state and comprises a group of islands in the mid-Pacific Ocean, some 2,500mi (4,023km) to the south-west of continental America.

The USA also administers over 2,000 islands, islets, cays (*cayes*) and atolls in the Pacific and Caribbean, including American Samoa, Guam, Puerto Rico and the US Virgin Islands. The contiguous states consist generally of the highland region of Appalachia in the East, the Rocky Mountains in the West and the Great Plains in the centre. The highest point is Mount McKinley 6,193m (20,320ft) in Alaska and the lowest is Death Valley in California (86m (282ft) below sea level).

Climate: Because of its vast size and varied topography, ranging from subtropical forests to permanent glaciers, from deserts to swamplands, America's climate varies enormously. The range of weather in the contiguous states is similar to what is experienced in Europe (from northern Finland to the south of Spain). In winter it's cold or freezing everywhere, except in the southern states. The coldest areas include the Plains, the Midwest and the Northeast, where temperatures can remain well below freezing for weeks on end. A long hot summer is normal throughout America, with the exception of northern New England, Oregon and Washington state.

Language: English (or American English) is the official language, although it isn't the first language for some 15 per cent of Americans. Spanish is the main foreign language and is spoken by some 17 million people.

Political Stability: The USA is one of the world's most politically stable countries. The Constitution lays down the division of power, which is split between the executive (the President), the legislature (Congress) and the judiciary. Power is also split between federal, state and local governments. Each state has its own semi-autonomous government headed by a governor who's elected for four years. There's no system of proportional representation in America and elections are based on a 'winner takes all' system. This usually results in a very stable government, as coalition governments are unknown and independent politicians rarely get elected. American politics is dominated by just two parties, the Democrats and the Republicans, who fill every seat in Congress and provide most state governors and other posts at state and local government level.

Finance

Currency: US Dollar (US$)
Exchange Rate: US$1 = £0.70
Exchange Controls: None.
Interest Rate: 2.5 per cent
Banks: There are hundreds of independent banks in the USA and the choice can be bewildering for the newcomer. You must choose carefully, however, as the USA has the most volatile banking industry in the western world. It's advisable to choose a large bank covered by the Federal Deposit Insurance Corporation (FDIC). To open a bank account you must provide your social insurance number and your permanent address.
Cost/Standard of Living: The USA enjoys one of the highest standards and lowest costs of living in the world, although it varies considerably with different states and regions, and between cities and rural areas. The cost of 'luxury' imported goods is lower than in almost any other country. Cars are inexpensive and cost up to 50 per cent less than in some European countries.
GDP Per Head (US$): 29,240

Taxation

Income Tax: Federal income tax rates are from 15 to 39.6 per cent, although state and local income taxes are also payable in some counties and states. Non-residents are generally taxed only on income from sources in America. State income tax rates vary considerably from state to state, although guidelines are set by the federal government, and some states have no state income tax, including Alaska, Florida, Nevada, New Hampshire, South Dakota, Tennessee, Texas, Washington and Wyoming. Non-resident homeowners must file an annual tax return. Tax on rental income earned by non-residents is 30 per cent, although mortgage interest and other expenses can be offset against income. **Note that US citizens and residents are subject to tax on their worldwide income, irrespective of its source**, although there are annual exclusions.

Concessions/Tax Breaks For Retirees: None.

Social Security: Social security contributions are paid by both the employer and the employee, who pays around 8 per cent of his gross salary up to a maximum salary of US$62,700. Self-employed persons pay double this amount. Benefits include retirement and disability pensions, supplementary income, welfare payments and two hospital insurance schemes, Medicare and Mediaid. Note that both these schemes are applicable only to residents over 65 years old or those with severe disabilities. Benefits vary from state to state, which independently decide the benefit levels and who's entitled to receive them.

Capital Gains Tax (CGT): Capital gains are included in gross income and must be reported on a non-resident's tax return (form 1040NR). Net gains are taxed at ordinary rates, although the maximum rate for long-term gains is 20 per cent (10 per cent for individuals in the 15 per cent income tax bracket). Once every two years, US taxpayers may exclude up to US$250,000 (US$500,000 for married taxpayers filing jointly) of gains derived from the sale of a principal residence. The residence must have been owned and used for at least two of the five years preceding the sale. Non-residents generally pay CGT at 15 per cent up to US$23,350 and at 28 per cent above this amount. When a non-resident sells a property, the buyer in some states (e.g. Florida) is required to withhold 10 per cent of the purchase price as security against unpaid taxes.

Wealth Tax: None.

Inheritance & Gift Tax: An Estate Tax Return (form 706) must be filed when the gross estate of a US citizen or resident exceeds US$675,000 or the gross US estate of a non-resident exceeds US$600,000 at the time of death. Residents receive a credit against federal estate and gift taxes equivalent to the tax on an estate worth US$600,000. This credit is indexed annually for inflation, up to a maximum estate value of US$1 million in 2006. Non-residents are granted a credit of US$13,000, which effectively exempts the first US$60,000 of an estate from tax. A federal gift tax is imposed on the gratuitous transfer of property and is usually payable by the donor. You can give US$10,000 to any individual during any calendar year without incurring gift tax; a couple can agree to treat gifts to individuals as joint gifts and exclude up to US$20,000 a year. Gift and estate tax rates are from 18 to 55 per cent. In addition to federal estate tax, some 20 states also impose estate tax on estates left to a spouse or child.

Other Taxes: Some states impose a sales tax on letting income and certain counties in some states (e.g. Florida, see page 313) levy other taxes on letting income, such as a tourist development tax, resort tax, tourist impact tax or a convention development tax.

Value Added Tax (VAT): There's no system of VAT in the USA, but sales tax is levied in 45 states at between 3 and 7 per cent. Sales tax must usually be added to advertised or displayed prices.

Accommodation

Market: The USA has a vast and flourishing property market, and there's a huge quantity and variety of homes to choose from. Millions of properties change hands each year and some 1.5 million new homes and apartments are built annually. Although the recession in the early '90s dealt the American property market a severe blow, it has now recovered. The demand for vacation homes by non-residents has increased dramatically in the last decade, particularly in America's 'Sunbelt', stretching from California in the west to Florida in the east.

The choice and variety of property is huge and includes golf and country club developments, marina and waterfront homes with private moorings, and a vast range of inland sites with unique attractions. Developments usually consist of individual plots (e.g. for ranch or villa-style, one-family homes) and/or townhouse and condominium developments with communal swimming pools, Jacuzzis, saunas, heated spas, racquetball and tennis courts, golf courses, health clubs or fitness centres, and picnic and barbecue areas. Homes in ski resorts are also popular, as are residential communities with comprehensive fitness, recreational and social facilities (many free to residents). American homes are generally bigger, more luxurious and better equipped than homes in other western countries, particularly in rural areas. A large number of (usually free) property catalogues, magazines and newspapers are published in all states.

Areas: Every American state has a particular appeal, both for holiday homeowners and permanent residents, and many are ideal locations for both summer and winter holiday homes. Traditionally, the most popular US destinations for foreigners have been California, Florida and New York, although buyers are now spreading their wings, and homes in Georgia, North and South Carolina, Louisiana, Tennessee, Texas, Washington (e.g. Seattle), and Virginia and West Virginia are also in demand. The mountain states of Montana, Idaho, Wyoming, Utah, Colorado, Arizona and New Mexico are becoming increasingly popular with vacation homebuyers, particularly among winter sports enthusiasts.

Although expensive, property in popular cities such as New York and San Francisco is a good investment and there's a constant demand for quality properties. Retirement communities, incorporating a wide variety of sports and leisure facilities, are common in many states. Although many Europeans, particularly the British, still think of Florida as the only American state in which to buy a vacation home, many other states offer excellent year-round weather and aren't as congested as Florida.

Cost: Property prices in America have remained relatively stable and generally offer better value than equivalent homes in Europe (always depending, of course, on prevailing exchange rates), with prices in the Sunbelt states (particularly Florida) kept down by intense competition. Prices differ considerably from region to region and area to area. A typical house of $167m^2$ ($1,800ft^2$) costs around US$400,000 in Washington DC, US$550,000 in Boston and San Francisco, and up to twice as much in New York city. However, in rural areas and small towns (including many areas popular for holiday and retirement homes such as Florida) the same size home can be purchased for as little as US$100,000.

A wide range of quality fixtures and fittings is installed as standard equipment and homes in popular resort areas can be bought 'turn-key furnished' and ready to occupy. Although most foreigners buy new homes, resale homes are often better value. Rural building plots are available from as little as US$6,000 to US$12,000 in many states.

Local Mortgages: Mortgages in America are available from a number of sources, including savings and loan associations (who provide over half of all mortgages), commercial banks, mortgage bankers, insurance companies, builders and developers, and government agencies. Most American lenders won't lend more than 70 or 80 per cent of the value of a property over a period of 10 to 30 years (typically 30 years). Credit and income checks are rigorous, although mortgages of up to 70 per cent are obtainable without proof of income or tax returns. Note that it's difficult and usually more expensive to raise finance for an American property from abroad.

Property Taxes: Property tax is levied annually on property owners in all states to help pay for local services such as primary and secondary education, police and fire services, libraries, public transport, waste disposal, highways and road safety, maintaining trading standards and personal social services. Property taxes on a house of average value range considerably from zero (in some areas houses valued below a certain amount, e.g. US$75,000, are exempt) or around US$500 (e.g. in West Virginia) to some US$6,000 a year in wealthy states (e.g. New Hampshire). Tax rates are fixed by communities and are expressed as an amount per US$100 or US$1,000 (the 'millage' rate) of the assessed market value of a property, e.g. US$15 per US$1,000.

Purchase Procedure: Usually you pay an initial 'good faith' deposit (also known as 'earnest money'), e.g. US$1,000 to US$5,000, to show that you're a serious buyer, and sign a contract that's binding on both parties. The deposit is usually 1 per cent of the purchase price, although it can be as high as 5 per cent. In California and some other states your deposit and all other funds must be placed with a neutral third party, an 'escrow agent', who's usually selected by the buyer's estate agent (but is subject to approval by all parties). He is responsible for compiling and checking documents and ensuring that the transaction can 'close' within the period specified in the purchase contract. Once the deal closes, the escrow agent records the deed and pays the funds to the appropriate parties.

If you withdraw from a purchase, you lose your deposit or can be forced to go through with the deal, so don't sign a contract without taking legal advice. A contract usually contains a number of conditions (riders or contingencies) that must be met before it becomes valid and binding, e.g. house and termite inspections and your ability to obtain a mortgage (if necessary) by a certain date. Conditions may differ from region to region and state to state. Some, such as a termite inspection, may be required by law, while others (e.g. a house inspection or survey) may be insisted upon by your estate agent or lender. The contract must list anything included in the price, such as furniture, fittings and extras, and should specify who pays the fees associated with the purchase. Standard contracts can usually be tailored to individual requirements.

Fees: You should allow around 5 per cent of the purchase price for closing or settlement costs. These may include a lender's appraisal (valuation) fee, legal fees, title search, title insurance, recording fees, survey/home inspection, homeowner's insurance and mortgage tax. Many people use a buyer's broker or agency, which doesn't usually cost any more than buying direct from a developer. Before you engage an agent, make sure that you know exactly who will pay his fees. Usually agents' commissions are split between the buyer and seller, but this isn't always the case.

Precautions: From a legal viewpoint, America is one of the safest countries in the world in which to buy a home. You should, nevertheless, take the usual precautions regarding deposits and obtaining proper title. Owner's title insurance is mandatory in some states and is usually required by lenders. In many states, hiring a lawyer for a property transaction is standard practice, although it isn't always necessary when a state (such as California) has mandatory escrow and title insurance (to protect against a future claim on the title by a third party). Before hiring a lawyer, compare the fees charged by a number of practices and make sure that they're experienced in property transactions. As when buying property in any country, you should never pay any money or sign anything without first taking legal advice.

Most experts believe that you should always have a house inspection (survey) on a resale house, and a termite inspection is almost mandatory on an older home, as America has numerous varieties of wood-boring insects. Make sure that all local taxes and water/sewerage bills have been paid by the previous owner, as these charges usually come with the property (and if unpaid are passed on to subsequent owners). You receive additional protection if you buy from a licensed and registered realtor, rather than an estate agent, as realtors are bound by a strict code of ethics. You must *never* sign anything pertaining to the purchase of property in the USA without going there and checking that the developer and land actually exist (they've been known not to!). As in most countries, there are crooks who prey on 'greenhorn' foreigners.

Holiday Letting: There are restrictions in some communities regarding short-term lets. In some developments, short-term rentals (generally less than 28 or 30 days, but in some cases less than six months) are prohibited, although if this is so you should be notified before buying. For example, Orange and Seminole counties in Florida don't permit lets of less than six months (usually because permanent residents don't wish to live in a community or development where people are coming and going every few weeks or months). Because most foreign property owners are limited to spending a maximum of six months in the USA, most developers (e.g. in Florida) provide management and letting services. Note that agents in America aren't permitted to offer guaranteed rental income, although some do. Rental income earned by non-resident aliens is taxable in America (e.g. 30 per cent in Florida), although if you have a Tax Identification Number and file an annual tax return, the 30 per cent is only levied on profit after deductions for mortgage interest, expenses and depreciation. You must also charge a sales tax on short-term rentals, payable to the state, plus local county taxes in some states (e.g. Florida).

Restrictions on Foreign Ownership: None.

Building Standards: Excellent. Building standards are strictly controlled and high quality fixtures and fittings are usually standard. American property generally provides excellent value with regard to size, construction quality, and fixtures and fittings.

Belongings: When you enter America to take up permanent or temporary residence, you can usually import your belongings duty and tax-free. Any duty or tax payable depends on your country of origin, where you purchased the goods, how long you've owned them, and whether duty or tax has been paid in another country. Possessions owned and used for at least a year prior to import are usually exempt from duty.

Rental Accommodation: In general, rental accommodation isn't difficult to find in the USA with the exception of large cities and their suburbs where there's a strong demand and rents are high. Most property is let unfurnished and even furnished apartments are sparsely equipped. Note that most landlords require a credit report from tenants. Monthly rental costs for similar properties in different parts of the country can vary by as much as 1,000 per cent, although the average monthly rent for a one-bedroom apartment is US$500 to US$800 and US$700 to US$1,200 for a three-bedroom house. The cities of New York and San Francisco have the highest rents.

Retirement Homes: Retirement developments (villages) are very popular in the US, where there's an abundance of different options, including many retirement villages. Villages may be run by co-operatives, religious groups or private companies, with prices varying hugely according to the size of property and the services provided. Before committing yourself to a purchase, you should ensure that the retirement village is registered with the state authorities.

Utilities: Electricity, gas and water are provided by 'utility' companies owned privately or by the local municipality, and are monopolies regulated by state commissions. The electricity supply (110/120V) is reliable and charges are reasonable. Mains gas is available in all but the remotest parts of the USA, although many new homes have only electrical appliances and cannot be connected to the gas supply. In areas without mains gas, bottled gas is readily available. Water costs may be included in local property taxes or charged separately, based on the water meter reading. Water rates are usually relatively low, although Americans tend to use a lot of water. In areas in the west and south of the country, drought and water restrictions are common in the summer.

Services

Post Office: The United States Postal Services (USPS) is generally efficient, although delivery times vary from region to region. There are hundreds of post offices throughout the country operated directly by USPS, handling only mail and selling money orders: no other services are provided.

Telephone: Telecommunications are excellent in America and the Americans are the world's most habitual telephone users. Services are provided by many companies, although AT&T is the leader. Rates are generally lower than most countries, particularly for long-distance calls, where competition between providers is fierce. Local calls are free. There are also many mobile phone companies, although the US was surprisingly slow to introduce them.

Internet: Use of the Internet is almost a way of life in the US, which is the world leader in the number of households and companies online, mainly due to the low price of computers and free local call charges. Broad band access is widely available and popular. There are numerous ISPs providing competitive rates.

English TV & Radio: American TV is the most competitive in the world, with five national networks and numerous local, cable and satellite stations. However, in spite of the choice, the standard of programmes is generally poor. Cable TV is extremely popular and viewers in urban areas can receive up to 50 channels. To receive transmissions from outside the US, you must have a satellite system, although many cities don't allow the installation of private satellite dishes. There's no TV licence in the US. There are thousands of radio stations, mainly local and mostly dedicated to chat, news or music. National Public Radio (NPR) provides the best serious radio.

General Information

Getting There: Most regions of the USA are well served by international flights from most countries, which are competitively priced, particularly from the UK. The USA also has good highway links with neighbouring Canada and Mexico. You can also travel to the USA by sea, although given the length of the journey this is more of a leisure option or cruise.

Getting Around: Communications, particularly by air, are generally good in the USA, although the public transport system is generally slow and inefficient. The USA has the cheapest air travel in the world and there's an enormous choice of destinations and number of flights. Flying is the most popular (and cheaper than using a car) means of travelling between major cities, although the US has the busiest airports in the world and long delays are common. Delays have increased owing to stringent security checks introduced after the terrorist attacks in September 2001. Long-distance coaches are the cheapest form of public transport and urban buses also provide a good service. The best rail services are provided in the north-east and southern California. There are urban and/or underground (subway) railway networks in many major cities, which are efficient, reasonably priced and popular with commuters. Taxis also provide a relatively inexpensive form of transport.

Shopping: America's major cities are a shopper's paradise and there's an infinite variety of shops, including several world-famous department stores. America invented the shopping centre (shopping mall) – although it's also claimed by Canada – and practically all towns have a huge shopping centre on their outskirts.

Crime Rate: One of the major drawbacks of living in the USA is the high crime rate, particularly of violent crime. The crime rate varies considerably with the state, county and city or town, and it's important to check crime statistics and avoid high crime areas. If you come from a country with a relatively low crime rate, e.g. anywhere in western Europe, it's important to bear in mind that **the ground rules aren't the same in America.** Avoid the ghetto areas of inner cities day and night, some of which are even no-go areas for armed policemen. Be extremely wary of where you go at night and always use a taxi rather than walk.

Driving: The car's practically a cult object in the USA, which has the world's highest ratio of vehicles to population as well as the most extensive road network. Cars rule and Americans drive *everywhere* and in many cities there's almost permanent gridlock as well as serious pollution problems. Cars are inexpensive to purchase and to run, although insurance is expensive. Traffic drives on the right and driving standards are generally good. Bear in mind that distances in the USA are huge and journeys take a long time. Driving licence regulations vary from state to state and you should check with the state authorities when you arrive, although as a general rule you will have to exchange your foreign licence for a state one.

Medical Facilities: Health care in the USA is among the best in the world, provided you can afford it! There's no free treatment for visitors to America, and health insurance is essential for both visitors and residents. The health insurance cover required when visiting most other countries is totally inadequate in America, where the recommended minimum annual cover is around US$500,000. Health insurance in America is *extremely* expensive, with a typical policy for a family of four costing thousands of US dollars a year (between US$1,000 and US$2,000 a month is typical). The average American family spends around 15 per cent of its income on health care!

Pets: All animals and birds imported into America must meet health and customs requirements (as do pets that are taken out of America and returned). Pets, particularly cats and dogs, must be examined at the port of entry for signs of disease that can be transmitted to humans. Dogs must be vaccinated against rabies at least 30 days prior to entry. Exceptions include puppies less than three months old and dogs originating from or having been located for at least six months in areas designated by the Public Health Service as being rabies-free. Vaccination against rabies isn't required for cats. Birds must be quarantined upon arrival, at the owner's expense, for at least 30 days in a facility operated by the US Department of Agriculture.

Reciprocal Agreement with the UK: British citizens entitled to a state pension in the UK can continue to receive it in the USA and the sum will be increased annually at the same rate as pensions in the UK.

Residence Permits: Residence permits are difficult to obtain unless you qualify for a green (residence) card, although with official immigration of around 1 million a year, there are many opportunities. The easiest and quickest way for most people to obtain a green card is to buy a business, which qualifies you for an E-2 investor visa. Residence permits aren't issued to retirees (unless they're very rich!). Visitors can stay for 90 days at a time (six months a year), and nationals of most western countries (including the UK) don't need a visa for visits of up to three months.

Work Permits: A work permit (green card) is required to live or work in the USA and is difficult to obtain unless you qualify, for example through birthright, relationship, employment or investment.

Visas: Visitors to the USA, on business or holiday, don't require a visa for stays of under 90 days. For longer stays and to live and work in the USA, you must apply for an immigration or non-immigration visa from the appropriate authorities. Note that if you enter the USA as a visitor, you cannot change your status once in the country.

Reference

Further Reading

Living and Working in America, David Hampshire (Survival Books, 🖳 www.survivalbooks.net). Everything you need to know about living and working in America.

America's 100 Best Places to Retire, Richard L. Fox (Vacation Pubs)

America's Best Low-Tax Retirement Towns, Eve Evans & Richard Fox (Vacation Pubs)

Boomertown: A Baby Boomer's Search for a Retirement Town, Dennis Kitchin (1st Books Library)

Choose the Northwest, John Howells (Globe Pequot)

Choose a College Town for Retirement, Joseph M. Lubow (Globe Pequot)

Choose the South for Retirement, John Howells (Globe Pequot)

Choose the Southwest for Retirement, John Howells (Globe Pequot)

Destination Southwest: A Guide to Retiring and Wintering in Arizona, New Mexico and Nevada, Michael Meyer & Sarah Muir (Oryx)

Going USA, Outbound Newspapers, 1 Commercial Road, Eastbourne, East Sussex BN21 3XQ, UK (☎ 01323-726040, 🖳 www.outbound-newspapers. com). Monthly newspaper for those planning to live, work or holiday in the USA.

Life in America's Small Cities, G. Scott Thomas (Prometheus Books)

Retirement Migration in America, Charles F. Longino Jnr. (Vacation Pubs)

Retirement New Mexico, Jim Burbank (New Mexico Magazine)

Retirement Places Rated, David Savageau (Hungry Minds)

Union Jack, a British newspaper, available free in California and Florida or on subscription elsewhere (▣ www.ujnews.com).

Welcome to New York, Roberta Seret (American Welcome Services Press)

Where to Retire, John Howells (Globe Pequot)

Useful Addresses

American Association of Retired Persons (AARP), 601 East Street, NW, Washington, DC 20049 (☎1800-424 3410, ▣ www.aarp.org).

American Embassy, 24 Grosvenor Square, London W1A 1AE, UK (☎ 020-7499 9000, ▣ www.usembassy.org.uk).

Department of Housing and Urban Development, 451 7th Street, SW, Washington, DC 20410, USA (☎ 0202-708 1112, ▣ www.hud.gov).

United National Real Estate, 4700 Belleview, PO Box 11400, Kansas City, Missouri 64112, USA (☎ toll-free 0800-999 1020, ▣ www.united country.com).

USA Information Resource Centre in London, UK (☎ 020-7894 0925).

Useful Websites

▣ www.britishinamerica.com – Expatriate website.

▣ www.britsonline.com – Expatriate website.

▣ www.ccaonline.com – Continuing Care Accreditation Commission. America's only accrediting body for retirement communities and lists all accredited communities in the USA.

▣ www.retirenet.com – Comprehensive information about retirement in the USA.

▣ www.snowbirds.org – Canada Snowbirds Association. A website for Canadian retirees spending the winter abroad, particularly in the USA.

▣ www.seniorpages.com – A website for retirees with a useful page of links to many American retiree websites.

CALIFORNIA

Background Information

Population: 34 million. California is the USA's most populous state and some 12.5 per cent of the American population live there.

Foreign Community: California is home to millions of immigrants, including a large Hispanic population and a considerable number of Europeans.

Area: 411,013km² (158,693mi²)

Geography: California, the 'Golden State', is the USA's third-largest state. It's situated on the west coast bordering Mexico in the south, Arizona and Nevada in the east, Oregon in the north and the Pacific Ocean in the west. California is a land of contrasts with endless beaches along its nearly 1,300km (800mi) of coastline; high snow-covered mountain ranges along the Sierra Nevada range, which divides the state into two (home to some of America's most popular ski resorts), and hot dry deserts in the south occupying almost a quarter of the state. The state also encompasses the world-famous national parks of Sequoia Canyon and Yosemite. The coastal cities include Los Angeles (LA), one of America's largest cities (pop. 9.9 million), San Francisco and San Diego. California is the USA's most populous state and most of its population is concentrated on the coast.

Climate: Southern California forms part of the so-called 'Sunbelt' and is generally warm and sunny all year round, although Los Angeles suffers from a chronic smog problem during the summer months. Northern California is cooler and fog is often a daily occurrence. Rainfall is usually low but it can rain torrentially for weeks at a time in winter, during this time landslides can be a problem. Snow is common in the mountains from October to June, when many mountain passes are closed. California sits on one of the world's most active earthquake zones, the San Andreas fault, and the area lives in constant threat of the 'Big One'. The last major earthquake was in 1994 at Northridge, although there are significant earth tremors each year. The desert areas are dry and hot all year round – Death Valley is the world's hottest place in summer.

Cost/Standard of Living: The cost of living in California is high and the state has some of America's most expensive real estate. The cost of food, on the other hand, is low compared to other states and the standard of living and quality of life are generally considered to be among the best in the USA (if you can manage to stop thinking about the Big One!).

Taxation

Income Tax: As well as federal income tax you're also liable for state income tax in California. Rates range from 1 per cent on annual income below US$10,528 to 9.3 per cent on annual income above US$69,096.

Value Added Tax (VAT): Sales tax in California is levied on most goods and services at the rate of 7.75 per cent, but food items are exempt.

Accommodation

Market: The housing market in California had a record year for sales in 2000 and, although sales were down nearly 6 per cent in 2001, the market is still considered very healthy, particularly in respect of new construction. California has a buoyant property market and quality resale property is generally in short supply throughout the state. Resale properties spend little time on the market (an average of less than 40 days in San Diego) and there's high demand for large mansion-style homes.

Areas: Popular areas for foreign homebuyers include San Francisco, generally considered to be the state's most beautiful and most European city, where many city buildings are made of wood, Los Angeles, home to Hollywood and a large number of America's millionaires, and San Diego, a popular and quieter city.

Cost: California has some of America's most expensive real estate and some of the largest and most luxurious mansions. Property prices vary according to the location with the most expensive real estate in San Francisco and Los Angeles, where the smallest properties start at around US$300,000. San Diego is cheaper but even here the cheapest properties in the least popular areas start at around US$250,000. In 2001, the average price for a house in California was US$279,000, although the sky's the limit in a state where a mansion can easily cost millions of US dollars. Prices rose by over 12 per cent in 2001 and are expected to continue to rise at around the same rate in the short term. It's calculated that Californian real estate has appreciated by as much as 25 per cent in the last three years.

Property Taxes: Generally property tax is around 1 to 1.2 per cent (1 per cent according to Proposition 13 limiting property taxes plus any voter approved local bonds). Since Proposition 13 didn't provide enough revenue for infrastructure in new areas, a Community Facilities Act was introduced (popularly known as Mello-Roos, after the congressmen who invented it) and many new areas in California have an additional monthly property tax ranging from US$50 to US$200.

Purchase Procedure: The procedure in California is much the same as in the rest of the USA (see **Purchase Procedure** on page 300), except that in California your deposit and all other funds must be placed with a neutral third party, the 'escrow agent', who's usually selected by the buyer's estate agent (but is subject to approval by all parties). He is responsible for compiling and checking documents and ensuring that the transaction can 'close' within the period specified in the purchase contract. Once the deal closes, the escrow agent records the deed and pays the funds to the appropriate parties.

Fees: Fees include Escrow (US$150 plus an additional US$1.50 per US$1,000 of the price), the first year's fire insurance (obligatory in California and costing around US$300) and the Grant Deed (US$40). There are additional fees if you finance a property purchase with a loan.

Precautions: Property purchase in California is generally as secure as in the rest of the USA; if anything, it's safer as the state has mandatory escrow and title insurance (to protect against a future claim on the title by a third party). You should, however, take the usual precautions, including professional legal advice. It's also advisable to make sure that a real estate agent is registered with the Californian authorities and has a state licence number.

Holiday Letting: No restrictions. Rental accommodation in Californian cities is in short supply and the rental market is very strong.

Restrictions on Foreign Ownership: None.

Building Standards: Generally excellent and all new and recently built properties are built with reinforced structures to withstand earth tremors.

Rental Accommodation: California has the highest rents in America and with the exception of the capital Sacramento, rental accommodation is in short supply in all cities. Rents in San Francisco are the highest in the USA (along with New York) and have risen sharply in recent years (by 23 per cent in 2001 alone). Here an apartment costs an average of around US$1,900 a month. San Diego and Los Angeles have lower rental prices at an average of some US$1,000 a month for an apartment, but this is still above the country's average. The monthly rent for an apartment in Sacramento is around US$700.

Retirement Homes: As in all American states, there's an abundance of retirement developments (villages) in California, where they usually have strict age restrictions (over 55s), unlike some other states where younger retirees are accepted. Retirement communities (known as 'adult communities') consist of up to 2,000 homes with a variety of amenities and services. Property prices vary hugely, although in most communities prices start at around US$150,000, with monthly service charges ranging from US$20 to US$250 depending on the amenities and care provided. The California Registry (see **Useful Websites** below) co-ordinates all registered retirement developments in the state, and is a useful starting point for information about the options available.

Utilities: The electricity supply is generally reliable in California, although chaotic privatisation of the electricity companies led to highly-publicised, wide-scale blackouts in Los Angeles in the summer of 2000. Charges are low. Mains gas is available in the major population centres. Water is a precious commodity in southern California where drought and water shortages are common. Tap water is generally safe to drink except in rural and desert areas.

General Information

Getting There: California is easily reached by direct flights from most countries and from the rest of the USA, particularly the international airports at LA and San Francisco. San Francisco is a major port of call on many passenger shipping routes. Good highways connect California with the rest of America.

Getting Around: Public transport is reasonably good in California, although the more remote parts of the state are better reached by private transport. There's a rail route with frequent services running from San Diego in the south to Oakland (San Francisco's nearest station) passing through LA. A second rail route runs through the Central Valley. Bus services link all the main population centres. Public transport in San Francisco is generally good and includes a tram network, in sharp contrast to LA, which was essentially designed for motorists and has relatively poor public transport.

Shopping: LA is one of the world's Meccas for designer shopping where the choice is endless, but prices are high. San Francisco is also noted for its choice of shopping facilities. All main towns and cities have at least one shopping centre, although towns in the north and in the mountains are less well-served.

Crime Rate: LA is notorious for its high crime rate and many areas of the city are 'no-go' areas at night and some even during the day. Many developments have extensive security systems (e.g. security gates), including private security guards. San Francisco and San Diego have lower crime rates, although still high in comparison with most European countries.

Driving: Private transport is essential in LA where the public transport system is poorly-developed and there are practically no pavements for pedestrians! A car's also advisable for California's more remote areas. Car rental is among America's cheapest. If you become a Californian resident or take a job there you must apply for a Californian driving licence within ten days. This involves an eye test and taking both practical and written tests. Likewise, you must register a non-Californian state car within 20 days if you're resident in the state. Visitors don't need to exchange their driving licences.

Reference

Useful Reading

Choose California for Retirement, Joseph M. Lubow (Globe Pequot)

Useful Addresses

Escrow Association of California (☎ 800-337 2769). The Association's help-line gives advice and information regarding the state's escrow system.

Useful Websites

🖥 www.gocalif.ca.gov – The official state tourism site.

💻 www.calregistry.com – California Registry (☎ 800-777 7575), a state-run organisation co-ordinating all registered retirement villages in California.

💻 www.ca.gov – The Californian government online.

FLORIDA

Background Information

Population: 15.69 million. Florida is America's fourth most populous state and some 1,000 people relocate there every day.

Foreign Community: Florida is home to a large foreign community including some two million Cuban exiles in Miami and over 500,000 Britons living mainly around Fort Lauderdale and Miami.

Area: 151,670km² (58,560mi²)

Geography: Florida, the 'Sunshine State', lies on a peninsula in southern USA and borders the states of Georgia and Alabama in the north, the Gulf of Mexico in the west and the Atlantic Ocean in the east. In the north are the Panhandle forests and some excellent beaches. In the south is the Everglades National Park, a wild and undeveloped swampland famous for its population of alligators. At the southernmost point lie the Florida Keys, a string of small islands stretching westwards for some 160km (100mi) into the Gulf of Mexico.

Climate: Not for nothing is Florida known as the 'Sunshine State' and it's warm and sunny practically all-year round. The state has two main climatic zones: the south which has warm, mild winters with low rainfall and hot, extremely humid summers with daily thunder storms; and the north which has colder winters when it can snow, although temperatures on the coast are generally mild, and hot and humid summers. Florida lies in the hurricane zone and during the season (late summer and early autumn) it occasionally suffers from devastating hurricanes.

Language: English is the official language, although the state's large Hispanic population means Spanish is widely spoken and the dominant language in some areas.

Cost/Standard of Living: Florida is one of the USA's cheapest states, particularly as there's no state income tax and property prices are up to two-thirds lower than many other parts of the country.

Taxation

Income Tax: Florida is one of the USA's tax havens and no personal state income tax is payable, although residents are still liable for federal income tax.
Inheritance & Gift Tax: None.
Other Taxes: Florida levies several other taxes mainly on letting income, such as a sales tax, resort tax, tourist tax or a personal property tax.
Value Added or Sales Tax: A sales tax is levied on most goods and services at 6.5 per cent, although basic food and medical items are exempt.

Accommodation

Market: Florida is probably America's cheapest retirement area regarding real estate and most of the state has a very lively property market catering for some 1,000 Americans who relocate there every day, plus many foreign retirees. The south remains popular and central Florida is currently experiencing a boom, particularly the area south of Orlando and north of Tampa. Property in Florida is generally considered to be good investment and the resale market is good.
Areas: The most popular areas in Florida are generally found in the south at resorts such as Fort Lauderdale and West Palm Beach, although in recent years these areas have become overcrowded. Popular western resorts include Clearwater, Sarasota, St Petersburg and Tampa Bay. Orlando and Daytona Beach in the east are also popular locations. The current boom location is central Florida between Orlando and Tampa where the cheapest real estate in Florida is to be found. This rural area has many lakes and fields, and is much quieter than the neighbouring coastal resorts.
Cost: New homes in Florida cost from around US$70,000 for a two-bedroom, two-bathroom detached home with a one-car garage or a two-bedroom, two-bathroom condominium (apartment) with a community pool. A 185m² (2,000ft²) property with Jacuzzi and pool can be purchased for as little as US$120,000. Southern and central Florida have become more expensive in recent years, particularly around Disney World and on the southern Gulf coast (e.g. Naples), and you generally need to look north of Tampa to find the best value. Property in inland central Florida is among the cheapest in the state and new homes can be bought from around US$60,000.
Property Taxes: One of the Florida state authorities' main sources (of income is property tax and annual taxes can be high with millage (see **Property taxes**

in USA section on page 299) rates of 30 (e.g. US$30 per US$1,000 of value) in some areas. Residents may be eligible for a US$25,000 exemption from real estate taxes if their Florida property is their primary residence and they fulfil certain other criteria.

Purchase Procedure: The procedure in Florida is much the same as in the rest of the USA (see page 300).

Precautions: Buying property in Florida is generally safe, although you must take the usual precautions (see page 48). There are numerous construction companies and new construction is currently experiencing a boom, although it's advisable to check a company's credentials before committing yourself to a purchase. You should also check the reputation of an estate agent.

Holiday Letting: Holiday letting in Florida is subject to strict legal and tax requirements and isn't permitted in some parts of the state. You should check your deeds and with the city or county authorities to check whether letting is permitted. In some areas letting may be permitted, but with restrictions: for example, Orange and Seminole counties in Florida don't permit lets of less than six months (usually because permanent residents don't wish to live in a community or development where people are coming and going every few weeks or months). In order to let your property you must obtain a hotel licence, which is valid for one year. Before the licence is issued your property will be inspected and must conform with state regulations on safety requirements such as fire extinguishers and smoke detectors. You must register with the Florida Department of Revenue for Sales Tax, Tangible Personal Property Tax and Tourist Tax (the latter is only levied in some cities and counties). Rental income earned by non-resident foreigners is subject to withholding tax levied at 30 per cent, although if you have a Tax Identification Number and file an annual tax return it's levied only on your profit after making deductions for mortgage interest, expenses and depreciation. Because most foreign property owners are limited to spending a maximum of six months in the USA, most developers provide management and letting services. Note that agents in America aren't permitted to offer guaranteed rental income, although some do.

Restrictions on Foreign Ownership: None.

Building Standards: Generally excellent, particularly in new construction where strict building codes apply.

Rental Accommodation: Rental accommodation is generally easy to find in Florida, although it's in short supply in popular resort areas during the high season and in the Bayshore and Beach areas of Miami all year round. In some counties it's difficult to find a short-term lease (under six months). Monthly rental rates are among America's lowest and range from US$500 a month for a small apartment to US$750 upwards for a house. Note that rentals in high season are considerably more expensive.

Retirement Homes: Florida's popularity with retirees has led to an abundance of retirement developments (villages) in the state. Retirement villages (known as 'adult communities') are generally open to retirees of all ages and some also accept families. Prices are among the lowest in the USA and also compare favourably with those in Europe. Property prices start at US$40,000 for a prefabricated unit or 'mobile home' (known as a 'manufactured home' in the USA) and even the best properties at top communities may cost no more than US$120,000. Amenities and facilities range from very basic to the most luxurious, with many communities having their own golf courses. Monthly service charges vary according to the amenities and care provided.

Utilities: The electricity supply in Florida is supplied by a number of companies and is reliable. Mains gas is available in most main towns and cities, although many new buildings aren't connected. Tap water is generally safe to drink, although many residents prefer to drink bottled water. Note that water is expensive and there are often restrictions in summer.

General Information

Getting There: Miami's international airport (MIA) is the second busiest in the USA and there are some 3,000 flights every week to international and American destinations. Miami is also a popular stop for flights from Europe to South America. Florida can easily be reached by road and rail from the rest of the USA. The Port of Miami is the world's busiest cruise destination and some four million passengers arrive there annually.

Getting Around: Florida's cities, particularly in the south, have a good public transport system, but the state-wide bus and rail system tends to operate only between the main cities and parts of the state that aren't served by public transport. The bus service is good, but fares can be high. The south-east coast has a particularly good public transport system including the excellent Tri-Rail commuter rail link running from West Palm Beach in the north to Miami in the south. Miami-Dade county has the USA's longest elevated rail system, the Metrorail, and a comprehensive Metrobus network. The Florida Key islands are connected to each other and the mainland by a series of causeways.

Shopping: Florida's main population centres have excellent shopping facilities, including several vast new shopping centres such as Sawgrass Mills, with over 270 stores (Florida's second-largest tourist attraction after Disney World), Dadeland in Kendall with over 200 stores and Aventura Mall north of Miami-Dade. Florida is a popular shopping destination for visitors from South America and the Caribbean.

Crime Rate: Like the rest of America, Florida has a high crime rate and in recent years there have been several highly publicised cases of violent crime against tourists. Miami has an infamous reputation as a high-crime city and you should avoid travelling at night on the highways and certain areas of the city at any time. The authorities have, however, been successful in reducing the crime rate in Florida in recent years and most residents experience no problems.

Driving: Communications by road in Florida are good with well-maintained highways and causeways linking the main islands of Miami Beach and Key Biscayne. If you're resident in Florida you must apply for a Florida driving licence. The documents required include proof of Florida registration of your vehicle, a valid driving licence and a social security card. If your driving licence is clean you will have to take an eye test only. If you don't possess a clean licence, you must take a driving test. Imported vehicles must be registered in the state, for which the Vehicle Identification Number (VIN) needs to be verified unless a vehicle is new. Vehicles registered in Florida must be insured with a company registered in Florida.

Reference

Further Reading

Buying a Home in Florida, David Hampshire (Survival Books, 💻 www. survivalbooks.net). All you need to know about buying a home in Florida.

ADL's Comprehensive Guide to Assisted Living Facilities in Central Florida, Georgeann Quealy (ADL)

Choose Florida for Retirement, James F. Gollattscheck & Daniel Murray (Globe Pequot)

The Complete Guide to Life in Florida, Barbara Brumm LaFreniere & Edward N. LaFreniere (Pineapple Press, 💻 www.pineapplepress.com).

Florida Homes and Travel Newsletter, 9438 US Hwy 19, #318, Port Richey, Florida 34668-4623, USA (💻 www.floridahomesandtravel.com). Newsletter for Florida homeowners and frequent visitors published ten times a year.

Florida Trend, 490 First Ave South, St Petersburg, Florida 33701, USA (☎ 0727-821 5800, 💻 www.floridatrend.com). Business magazine.

Florida on My Mind (Globe Pequot/Falcon)

Useful Addresses

Florida Association of Realtors, 7025 Augusta National Drive, PO Box 725025, Orlando, FL 32872-5025, USA (☎ 0407-438 1400, 💻 http://fl. living.net).

Florida Brits Club, Stanhope House, 18 Grange Close, Skelton, York YO3 6YR, UK (☎ 01904-471800, ✉ flabritscl@aol.com).

Florida Department of Revenue (☎ 800-352 3671 within Florida (toll-free) or ☎ 850-488 9750 from outside Florida).

Useful Websites

⌨ www.fl-esi.com/retire – Senior and retirement living in Florida.

⌨ www.florida.com – Extensive travel information.

⌨ www.floridaguide.com/retire – Guide to Florida retirement communities.

⌨ http://floridainfo.com – Information about travel and relocation in Florida.

⌨ www.florida-relocation.com – Relocation and moving guide.

⌨ www.myflorida.com – Comprehensive government website.

APPENDICES

APPENDIX A: USEFUL ADDRESSES

English Language Publications

Miscellaneous

Best Retirement Spots, 17101 E. Baltic Dr., L, Aurora, Colorado, USA (☎ 303-358 0512, 💻 www.bestretirementspots.com).

Condé Nast Traveller, Vogue House, 1 Hanover Square, London W1S 1JU, UK (☎ 020-7499 9080, 💻 www.cntraveller.com) and 4 Times Square, New York, NY 10036, USA (☎ 212-286 2860). Glamorous travel magazine for the well-heeled.

Emigrate, Outbound Newspapers, 1 Commercial Road, Eastbourne, East Sussex BN21 3XQ, UK (☎ 01323-726040, 💻 www.outbound-newspapers.com).

FT Expat Magazine, Castle House, 37–45 Paul Street, London EC2A 4LS, UK (☎ 020-7825 7600, 💻 www.ftexpat.com). Monthly magazine for British expatriates.

Homes Overseas, Blendon Communications, 207 Providence Square, Mill Street, London SE1 2EW, UK (☎ 020-7939 9888, 💻 www.homes overseas.co.uk). Bi-monthly international property magazine.

International Homes, 3 St. Johns Court, Moulsham Street, Chelmsford, Essex CM2 0JD, UK (☎ 01245-358877, 💻 www.international-homes.com). Bi-monthly magazine.

National Geographic, National Geographic Society, 1145 17th St, NW Washington, DC 20036-4688, USA (☎ 202-857 7000, 💻 www.national geographic.com). Also publish National Geographic Traveller.

Nexus Expatriate Magazine, Expat Network Limited, International House, 500 Purley Way, Croydon CR0 4NZ, UK (☎ 020-8760 5100, 💻 www.expat network.co.uk).

Thomas Cook Magazine, 7 St. Martin's Place, London WC2H 4HA, UK (☎ 020-7747 0700).

Transitions Abroad, PO Box 1300, Amherst, MA 01004-1300, USA (☎ 413-256 3414, 💻 www.transitionsabroad.com). Bi-monthly colour magazine about living, working, studying and retiring abroad.

Traveller, Wexas International, 45–49 Brompton Road, Knightsbridge, London SW3 1DE, UK (☎ 020-7581 4130, 💻 www.wexas.com). Long-established, quality travel magazine.

Wanderlust, PO Box 1832, Windsor SL4 1YT, UK (☎ 01753-620426, 🖳 www.wanderlust.co.uk). Monthly magazine for travellers.

Where to Retire (🖳 www.wheretoretire.com). American magazine dedicated to retirement issues in the USA and abroad.

World of Property, Outbound Publishing, 1 Commercial Road, Eastbourne, East Sussex BN21 3XQ, UK (☎ 01323-726040, 🖳 www.outbound-newspapers.com). Bi-monthly international property magazine. Also organise international property shows.

Specific Countries

American Holiday & Life, PO Box 604, Hemel Hempstead, Herts. HP1 3SR, UK.

Australia News, **Canada News**, **Destination New Zealand**, **Focus on France**, **Going USA** and **South Africa News**, all published by Outbound Newspapers, 1 Commercial Road, Eastbourne, East Sussex BN21 3XQ, UK (☎ 01323-726040, 🖳 www.outbound-newspapers.com). Monthly newspapers for immigrants available on subscription.

Australian Outlook, **New Zealand Outlook**, Consyl Publishing, 3 Buckhurst Road, Bexhill-on-Sea, East Sussex TN40 1QF, UK (☎ 01424-223111). Monthly newspapers for immigrants available on subscription.

Britannia Magazine, PO Box 340, Wellington, ON K0K 3L0, Canada (☎ 613-399 2555, 🖳 www.magma.ca/~britanni). Magazine for British expatriates in Canada.

Canada Bound, Canada Bound Newspapers, PO Box 55270, Toronto ON M2J 5B9, Canada.

Canadian Living, PO Box 702, Markham Station, Markham ON L6B 1A3, Canada (☎ 905-946 0275, 🖳 www.canadianliving.com). Monthly women's home and lifestyle magazine.

Caribbean World, 84 Albert Hall Mansions, Prince Consort Road, Knightsbridge, London SW7 2AQ, UK (☎ 020-7581 9009).

Essentially America, Phoenix Publishing and Media, 18–20 Scrutton Street, London EC2A 4TG, UK (☎ 020-7247 0537, 🖳 www.phoenix.wits.co.uk). Bi-monthly magazine for travellers in North America.

France Magazine, Community Media, Dormer House, Stow-on-the-Wold, Glos. GL54 1BN, UK (☎ 01451-833208, www.francemag.com). Monthly lifestyle magazine.

France-USA Contacts, FUSAC, 3 rue La Rochelle, 75014 Paris, France. Free weekly magazine.

Living France, Picture House Publishing, 9 High Street, Olney MK46 4EB, UK (☎ 01234-713203, 💻 www.livingfrance.com). Monthly lifestyle/ property magazine.

New Zealand News UK, Commonwealth Publishing, 3rd Floor, New Zealand House, Haymarket, London SW1Y 4TE, UK (☎ 020-7747 9200).

The South American Explorer, South American Explorers Club, Casilla 3714, Lima 100, Peru (💻 www.samexplo.org).

South East Asia Traveller, Compass Publishing, 336 Smith Street, 04-303 New Bridge Centre, Chinatown, Singapore 0105 (☎ 221-1111).

Southern Cross, **TNT Magazine** and **TNT Magazine New Zealand**, 14–15 Child's Place, Earls Court, London SW5 9RX, UK (☎ 020-7373 3377, 💻 www.tntmag.co.uk). Free weekly magazines for expatriate Australians and New Zealanders.

Other Addresses

American Association of Retired Persons, 601 E St., NW, Washington, DC 20049, USA (☎ 800-424 3410, 💻 www@aarp.org).

American Citizens Abroad (ACA), PO Box 321, CH-1211 Geneva 12, Switzerland (☎ 022-347 6847, 💻 www.aca.ch).

Assist-Card, 745 Fifth Avenue, New York, NY 10022, USA (☎ 212-752 2788 or 1-800-221 4564). Helps members with travel crises such as illness, loss of passport, legal trouble and theft.

The Association of American Residents Overseas (AARO), 34, avenue de New York, Paris 75016, France (☎ 01.47.20.24.15, 💻 www.aaro-intl.org).

The British Association of Removers (BAR) Overseas, 3 Churchill Court, 58 Station Road, North Harrow HA2 7SA, UK (☎ 020-8861 3331).

The British Council, 10 Spring Gardens, London SW1A 2BN, UK (☎ 020-7930 8466, 💻 www.britishcouncil.org).

The Centre for International Briefing, Farnham Castle, Farnham, Surrey GU9 0AG, UK (☎ 01252-721194, 💻 www.cibfarnham.com). Organises briefing courses for people moving overseas.

Corona Worldwide, Commonwealth Institute, Kensington High Street, London W8 6NQ, UK (☎ 020-7610 4407). Provides information for women expatriates.

English Contacts Abroad, PO Box 126, Oxford OX2 6UB, UK.

The Experiment in International Living, Kipling Road, PO Box 676, Brattleboro, Vermont 05302-0676, USA (☎ 802-257-7751, 🖳 www. experiment.org).

Federation of Overseas Property Developers, Agents and Consultants (FOPDAC), PO Box 3524, London NW5 1DQ, UK (☎ 020-7836 9524).

Going Places, 84 Coombe Road, New Malden, Surrey KT3 4QS, UK (☎ 020-8949 8811). Organises tailor-made expatriate briefing courses.

International Living, 5 Catherine Street, Waterford, Ireland (☎ 051-304557, 🖳 www.internationalliving.com).

Medical Advisory Service for Travellers Abroad (MASTA), London School of Hygiene and Tropical Medicine, Keppel Street, London WC1E 7HT, UK (☎ 020-7631 4408, 24-hour Travellers Healthline 0891-224100).

Wexas International, 45–49 Brompton Road, London SW3 1DE, UK (☎ 020-7589 3315, 🖳 www.wexas.com). Provides a comprehensive range of travel insurance.

APPENDIX B: FURTHER READING

The books listed below are just a small selection of the many books written for those planning to live or retire abroad. Some titles may be out of print, but may still be obtainable from book shops and libraries. Books prefixed with an asterisk (*) are recommended by the author. See also the list of books published by Survival Books (page 345 and following) and the books listed under **Further Reading** in **Country Profiles** (Chapter 8).

Retirement

*The Good Retirement Guide, Rosemary Brown (Kogan Page)

Have a Healthy and Happy Retirement, Michael Apple (Help Yourself)

How to Enjoy Your Retirement, Vicky Maud (Sheldon Press)

*Life in the Sun, Nancy Tuft (Age Concern England)

Making the Most of Retirement, Michael Barratt (Kogan Page)

Retirement Abroad, Robert Cooke (Robert Hale)

*The Retirement Handbook, Caroline Hartnell (Age Concern)

Sunset Lives: British Retirement Migration to the Mediterranean, Russell King, Tony Warnes & Allan Williams (NYUP)

*Where to Retire, John Jowells (Globe Pequot)

*The 'Which?' Guide to an Active Retirement, Jane Vass (Which? Books)

*The World's Top Retirement Havens, Margeret J. Goldstein (John Muir)

*Your Retirement: How to make the Most of It, Rosemary Brown (Kogan Page)

Living Abroad

The Adventure of Living Abroad: Hero Tales from the Global Frontier, Joyce Sautters Osland (Jossey-Bass)

*Americans Living Abroad, J. Kepler (Praeger)

**Buying a Home Abroad, David Hampshire (Survival Books)

Guide to Living Abroad, Michael Furnell & Philip Jones (Kogan Page)

Guide to Working Abroad, Godfrey Golzen & Helen Kogan (Kogan Page)

The Insiders' Guide to Relocation, Beverly Roman (Globe Pequot)

Keeping Your Life, Family and Career Intact While Living Abroad, Cathy Tsang-Feign (Hamblan)

Let's Move Overseas, Beverly D. Roman (Anchor Publishing)

Living Overseas, Robert Lawrence Johnston & Robert Johnston (Living Overseas Books)

**Living and Working Abroad, David Hampshire (Survival Books)

*Money Mail: Moves Abroad, Margaret Stone (Kogan Page)

Moving and Living Abroad, Sandra Albright, Alice Chu & Lori Austin (Hippocrene Books).

*Relocation: Escape from America, R. Gallo (Manhattan Loft Publishers)

Survival Kit for Overseas Living: For Americans Planning to Live and Work Abroad, L. Robert Kohis (Nicholas Brealey)

*US Expatriate Handbook, Guide to Living & Working Abroad, John W. Adams

Health & Safety

The ABC of Healthy Travel (British Medical Journal)

*How to Stay Healthy Abroad, Dr. R. Dawood (Oxford University Press)

International Travel and Health 2001 (World Health Organization)

*Merck Manual of Medical Information: Home Edition (Merck)

*Rough Guide to Travel Health, Dr. Nick Jones (Rough Guides)

Travel in Health, Graham Fry & Vincent Kenny (Gill and Macmillan)

*Travel and Health in the Elderly, I. B. McIntosh (Quay)

*Travel Medicine and Migrant Health, Cameron Lockie MBE (Churchill Livingstone)

*Travel Safety, Adler (Hippocrene)

*The Traveller's Handbook (Wexas)

*Travellers' Health, Dr. Richard Dawood (OUP)

Understanding Travel and Holiday Health, Bernadette Carroll (Family Doctor)

*World Wise – Your Passport to Safer Travel, Suzy Lamplugh (Thomas Cook)

APPENDIX C: USEFUL WEBSITES

There are literally dozens of websites of interest to retirees and others living abroad, and as the Internet increases in popularity the number grows daily. Most provide useful information and generally offer free access, although some require a subscription or payment for services. Relocation and other companies specialising in expatriate services often have websites, although these may only provide information that a company is prepared to offer free of charge, which although it can be useful may be rather biased. However, there are plenty of volunteer sites run by expatriates providing practical information and tips. A particularly useful section found on many expatriate websites is the 'message board' or 'forum', where expatriates answer questions based on their experience and knowledge, and offer an insight into what a country or city is *really* like.

Below is a list of some of the best expatriate websites. Note that websites are listed under headings in alphabetical order and the list is by no means definitive. Websites relating to specific countries are listed in **Chapter 8** (Country Profiles) under individual countries.

General Websites

Direct Moving: (🖥 www.directmoving.com) The first world-wide relocation portal with a plethora of expatriate information, tips, advice and good links.

ExpatAccess: (🖥 www.expataccess.com) Unlike other 'expat' sites, ExpatAccess is specifically for those planning to move abroad, with free online moving guides to help you through the relocation process.

ExpatBoards: (🖥 www.expatboards.com) The mega site for expatriates, with popular discussion boards and special areas for Britons, Americans, expatriate taxes, and other important issues.

Escape Artist: (www.escapeartist.com) This is probably the most comprehensive and extensive resource portal for anyone planning to live abroad and it also has a useful section on 'Retirement Abroad'. The site offers free subscription to the Escape Artist e-zine *Escape from America*, which is full of useful articles and advice, often specifically about retiring abroad. Note that Escape Artist is an American based portal and therefore it doesn't include any information about the United States.

ExpatExchange: (🖥 www.expatexchange.com) Reportedly the largest online community for English-speaking expatriates. Provides a series of articles on relocation and also a question and answer facility through its expatriate network.

Expat Forum: (🖥 www.expatforum.com) Provides interesting cost of living comparisons as well as over 20 country-specific forums and chat rooms.

Expat Network: (🖥 www.expatnetwork.com) The leading expatriate website in the UK, which is essentially an employment network for expatriates, although there are also numerous support services plus a monthly online magazine, *Nexus*.

Expat World: (🖥 www.expatworld.net) 'The newsletter of international living.' Contains a wealth of information for American and British expatriates, including a subscription newsletter.

Expatriate Experts: (🖥 www.expatexpert.com) A website run by expatriate expert Robin Pascoe, providing invaluable advice and support.

Global People: (🖥 www.peoplegoingglobal.com) Provides interesting country-specific information with particular emphasis on social and political aspects.

International Living: (🖥 www.internationalliving.com) A useful site based mainly around the subscription magazine *International Living* (see **Appendix A**) and aimed at international retirees. The site offers free subscription to 'weekly postcards' with information from around the world.

Kiplinger's Retirement Report: (🖥 www.kiplinger.com/retreport) Contains interesting information for those planning to retire abroad.

Living Abroad: (🖥 www.livingabroad.com) Provides articles about different countries with information about the practicalities of living there. Contains an extensive and comprehensive list of country profiles, although they're available only on payment. Has a good links page.

Network for Living Abroad: (🖥 www.liveabroad.com) Provides information, resources and links for people living abroad, including a subscription newsletter.

Outpost Information Centre: (🖥 www.outpostexpat.nl) A website containing extensive country-specific information and links operated by the Shell Petroleum Company for its expatriate workers, but available to everyone.

Real Post Reports: (🖥 www.realpostreports.com) Provides relocation services, recommended reading lists and plenty of interesting 'real-life' stories containing anecdotes and impressions written by expatriates in just about every city in the world.

The Retirement Center: (🖥 www.familyhaven.com/retirement) Advice on how to make the most of your finances and what to consider when retiring abroad.

Third Culture Kids: (🖥 www.tckworld.com) A website designed for expatriate children.

Thrifty Traveling: (🖥 www.thriftytraveling.com) Useful information about travel discounts for the over-50s.

Transitions Abroad: (🖥 www.transitionsabroad.com) Useful website with good resources for anyone planning to live or retire abroad. Contains articles about living in popular retirement countries.

Where to Retire: (🖥 www.wheretoretire.com) Comprehensive American website covering all aspects of retirement, both in the USA and abroad.

World Travel Guide: (🖥 www.wtgonline.com) A general website for world travellers and expatriates.

World Wide Seniors: (🖥 www.wwseniors.com) Contains retirement information plus a weekly online newsletter.

There are many websites that provide cost of living comparisons between countries and major cities, including:

Career Perfect: (🖥 www.careerperfect.com/careerperfect/salaryinfo.htm)

ECA: (🖥 www.windhamint.com/html/cd-biz.html)

Economic Research Institute: (🖥 www.salariesreview.com and 🖥 www.erieri.com/sources)

Money Manager: (🖥 www.moneymanager.com.au/personal_finance/calcs/costliving.html)

Runzheimer International: (🖥 www.runzheimer.com)

University of Michigan: (🖥 www.lib.umich.edu/libhome/documents.center/steccpi.html)

North American Websites

50 Plus: (🖥 www.50plus.com) The official website of Canadian retirees with plenty of useful information. Also publish *FiftyPlus* monthly magazine.

Americans Abroad: (🖥 www.aca.ch) This website offers advice, information and services to Americans abroad.

American Association of Retired Persons: (🖥 www.aarp.org) This website includes useful information about retiring around the world, such as economic and social security issues.

Americans in Britain: (🖥 www.britain-info.org) A website providing a comprehensive list of fact sheets regarding living and working in the UK.

American Teachers Abroad: (🖳 www.overseasdigest.com) A comprehensive website with numerous relocation services and advice plus teaching opportunities.

Federation of American Women's Clubs Overseas: (🖳 www.fawco.org) An international network of American women's clubs which support American women living abroad.

US Government Trade: (🖳 www.usatrade.gov) A huge website providing a wealth of information principally for Americans planning to trade and invest abroad, but useful for anyone planning a move abroad.

British Websites

50 Connect: (🖳 www.50connect.co.uk) British website for those aged over 50 containing a wealth of practical information and advice.

Age Concern: (🖳 www.ageconcern.org.uk) The website of this British charity is packed with detailed and up-to-date information and articles about retirement and ageing.

British in America: (🖳 www.britishinamerica.com and www.british-expats.com) Two websites designed for Britons in the USA.

British Expatriates: (🖳 www.britishexpat.com and www.ukworldwide.com) These websites keep British expatriates in touch with events and information about the UK.

FT Expat: (🖳 www.ftexpat.com) Based on the British *FT Expat* magazine, this website offers useful advice for Britons living and investing abroad.

Retirement Counselling Service: (🖳 www.the-retirement-site.co.uk) Provides useful financial advice for those about to retire.

Retirement Matters: (🖳 www.retirement-matters.co.uk) Offers a wealth of information about retirement.

Seniority: (🖳 www.seniority.co.uk) British site providing an interactive community for senior citizens.

Trade Partners: (🖳 www.tradepartners.gov.uk) A government sponsored website whose main aim is to provide trade and investment information on just about every country in the world. Even if you aren't planning to do business abroad, the information is comprehensive and up to date.

Worldwise Directory: (🖳 www.suzylamplugh.org/worldwise) This website, run by the Suzy Lamplugh charity for personal safety, provides a useful directory of countries with practical information and special emphasis on safety, particularly for women.

Australian & New Zealand Websites

Australians Abroad: (⌨ www.australiansabroad.com) Information for Australians concerning relocating plus a forum to exchange information and advice.

Kiwi Club: (⌨ www.kiwiclub.org) Information and support for New Zealanders in Austria, Switzerland, Singapore and North America.

Southern Cross Group: (⌨ www.southern-cross-group.org) A website for Australians and New Zealanders providing information and the exchange of tips.

Travel Information & Warnings

The websites listed below provide daily updated information about the political situation and natural disasters around the world, plus general travel and health advice and embassy addresses.

Australian Department of Foreign Affairs and Trade: (www.dfat.gov.au/consular/advice/advices_mnu.html).

British Foreign and Commonwealth Office: (⌨ www.fco.gov.uk/travel).

Canadian Department of Foreign Affairs: (⌨ http://voyage.dfait-maeci.gc.ca/menu-e.asp). Also publishes a useful series of free booklets for Canadians moving abroad.

Gov Spot: (⌨ www.govspot.com/ask/travel.htm) US government website.

New Zealand Ministry of Foreign Affairs and Trade: (⌨ http://www.mft.govt.nz/travel/report.html).

International Association for Medical Assistance to Travelers: (⌨ www.iamat.org) International non-profit organisation that provides travellers with information about health risks, immunisation requirements and medical care abroad.

SaveWealth Travel: (⌨ www.savewealth.com/travel/warnings).

The Travel Doctor: (⌨ www.tmvc.com.au/info10.html) Contains a country by country vaccination guide.

Travelfinder (⌨ www.travelfinder.com/twarn/travelwarnings.html).

US Department of State: (⌨ http://travel.state.gov/travel_warnings.html and http://travel.state.gov/warnings_list.html) Contains warnings about drugs (⌨ http:// travel.state.gov/drug_warning.html) and a list of useful travel publications (http://travel.state.gov/travel_pubs.html).

World Health Organisation: (⌨ www.who.int).

APPENDIX D: WEIGHTS & MEASURES

New Zealand uses the metric system of measurement. Nationals of a few countries (including the Americans and British) who are more familiar with the imperial system of measurement will find the tables on the following pages useful. Some comparisons shown are only approximate, but are close enough for most everyday uses. In addition to the variety of measurement systems used, clothes sizes often vary considerably with the manufacturer (as we all know only too well). Try all clothes on before buying and don't be afraid to return something if, when you try it on at home, you decide it doesn't fit (most shops will exchange goods or give a refund).

Women's Clothes

Continental	34 36 38 40 42 44 46 48 50 52
UK	8 10 12 14 16 18 20 22 24 26
USA	6 8 10 12 14 16 18 20 22 24

Pullovers	Women's	Men's
Continental	40 42 44 46 48 50	44 46 48 50 52 54
UK	34 36 38 40 42 44	34 36 38 40 42 44
USA	34 36 38 40 42 44	sm medium large xl

Note: sm = small, xl = extra large

Men's Shirts

Continental	36 37 38 39 40 41 42 43 44 46
UK/USA	14 14 15 15 16 16 17 17 18 -

Men's Underwear

Continental	5	6	7	8	9	10
UK	34	36	38	40	42	44
USA	small	medium		large	extra large	

Children's Clothes

Continental	92	104	116	128	140	152
UK	16/18	20/22	24/26	28/30	32/34	36/38
USA	2	4	6	8	10	12

Children's Shoes

Continental	18 19 20 21 22 23 24 25 26 27 28 29 30 31 32
UK/USA	2 3 4 4 5 6 7 7 8 9 10 11 11 12 13

Continental	33 34 35 36 37 38
UK/USA	1 2 2 3 4 5

Shoes (Women's and Men's)

Continental	35 35 36 37 37 38 39 39 40 40 41 42 42 43 44 44
UK	2 3 3 4 4 5 5 6 6 7 7 8 8 9 9 10
USA	4 4 5 5 6 6 7 7 8 8 9 9 10 10 11 11

Weight

Avoirdupois	Metric	Metric	Avoirdupois
1 oz	28.35 g	1 g	0.035 oz
1 pound*	454 g	100 g	3.5 oz
1 cwt	50.8 kg	250 g	9 oz
1 ton	1,016 kg	500 g	18 oz
1 tonne	2,205 pounds	1 kg	2.2 pounds

* A metric 'pound' is 500g, g = gramme, kg = kilogramme

Length

British/US	Metric	Metric	British/US
1 inch	2.54 cm	1 cm	0.39 inch
1 foot	30.48 cm	1 m	3 feet 3.25 inches
1 yard	91.44 cm	1 km	0.62 mile
1 mile	1.6 km	8 km	5 miles

Note: cm = centimetre, m = metre, km = kilometre

Capacity

Imperial	Metric	Metric	Imperial
1 pint (USA)	0.47 litre	1 litre	1.76 UK pints
1 pint (UK)	0.57 litre	1 litre	0.26 US gallons
1 gallon (USA)	3.78 litre	1 litre	0.22 UK gallon
1 gallon (UK)	4.54 litre	1 litre	35.21 fluid oz

Square Measure

British/US	Metric	Metric	British/US
1 square inch	0.45 sq. cm	1 sq. cm	0.15 sq. inches
1 square foot	0.09 sq. m	1 sq. m	10.76 sq. feet
1 square yard	0.84 sq. m	1 sq. m	1.2 sq. yards
1 acre	0.4 hectares	1 hectare	2.47 acres
1 square mile	259 hectares	1 sq. km	0.39 sq. mile

Temperature

° Celsius	° Fahrenheit	
0	32	freezing point of water
5	41	
10	50	
15	59	
20	68	
25	77	
30	86	
35	95	
40	104	

Oven Temperature

Gas	Electric	
	°F	°C
-	225–250	110–120
1	275	140
2	300	150
3	325	160
4	350	180
5	375	190
6	400	200
7	425	220
8	450	230
9	475	240

For a quick conversion, the Celsius temperature is approximately half the Fahrenheit temperature.

Temperature Conversion

Celsius to Fahrenheit: multiply by 9, divide by 5 and add 32.
Fahrenheit to Celsius: subtract 32, multiply by 5 and divide by 9.

Body Temperature

Normal body temperature (if you're alive and well) is 98.4° Fahrenheit, which equals 37° Celsius.

INDEX

W

SUGGESTIONS

Please write to us with any comments or suggestions you have regarding the content of this book (preferably complimentary!). We are particularly interested in proposals for improvements that can be included in future editions. For example, did you find any important subjects were omitted or weren't covered in sufficient detail? What difficulties or obstacles have you encountered which aren't covered here? What other subjects would you like to see included

   If your suggestions are used in the next edition of *Retiring Abroad*, you will receive a free copy of the Survival Book of your choice as a token of our appreciation.

NAME: _____

ADDRESS: _____

_____

_____

Send to: Survival Books, PO Box 146, Wetherby, West Yorks. LS23 6XZ, United Kingdom.

My suggestions are as follows (please use additional pages if necessary):

BUYING A HOME ABROAD

Buying a Home Abroad is essential reading for anyone planning to purchase property abroad and is designed to guide you through the jungle and make it a pleasant and enjoyable experience. Most importantly, it's packed with vital information to help you avoid the sort of disasters that can turn your dream home into a nightmare! Topics covered include:

- Avoiding problems
- Choosing the region
- Finding the right home & location
- Estate agents
- Finance, mortgages & taxes
- Home security
- Utilities, heating & air-conditioning
- Moving house & settling in
- Renting & letting
- Permits & visas
- Travelling & communications
- Health & insurance
- Renting a car & driving
- Retirement & starting a business
- And much, much more!

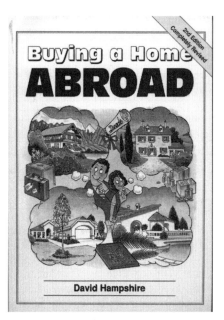

Buying a Home Abroad is the most comprehensive and up-to-date source of information available about buying property abroad. Whether you want a detached house, townhouse or apartment, a holiday or a permanent home, this book will help make your dreams come true.

Buy this book and save yourself time, trouble and money!

Order your copies today by phone, fax, mail or e-mail from: Survival Books, PO Box 146, Wetherby, West Yorks. LS23 6XZ, United Kingdom (☎/📠 +44 (0)1937-843523, ✉ orders@ survivalbooks.net, 💻 www.survivalbooks.net).

ORDER FORM
ALIEN'S GUIDES / BEST PLACES / BUYING A HOME / WINES

Qty.	Title	Price (incl. p&p)*			Total
		UK	Europe	World	
	The Alien's Guide to America	Autumn 2002			
	The Alien's Guide to Britain	£5.95	£6.95	£8.45	
	The Alien's Guide to France	£5.95	£6.95	£8.45	
	The Best Places to Buy a Home in France	Autumn 2002			
	The Best Places to Buy a Home in Spain	Summer 2002			
	Buying a Home Abroad	£13.45	£14.95	£16.95	
	Buying a Home in Britain	£11.45	£12.95	£14.95	
	Buying a Home in Florida	£13.45	£14.95	£16.95	
	Buying a Home in France	£13.45	£14.95	£16.95	
	Buying a Home in Greece & Cyprus	£13.45	£14.95	£16.95	
	Buying a Home in Ireland	£11.45	£12.95	£14.95	
	Buying a Home in Italy	£13.45	£14.95	£16.95	
	Buying a Home in Portugal	£11.45	£12.95	£14.95	
	Buying a Home in South Africa	Summer 2002			
	Buying a Home in Spain	£13.45	£14.95	£16.95	
	How to Avoid Holiday & Travel Disasters	Summer 2002			
	Rioja and its Wines	£11.45	£12.95	£14.95	
	The Wines of Spain	£15.95	£18.45	£21.95	
				Total	

Order your copies today by phone, fax, mail or e-mail from: Survival Books, PO Box 146, Wetherby, West Yorks. LS23 6XZ, UUK (☎/▤ +44 (0)1937-843523, ✉ orders@survivalbooks.net, 🖥 www.survivalbooks.net). If you aren't entirely satisfied, simply return them to us within 14 days for a full and unconditional refund.

Cheque enclosed/please charge my Delta/Mastercard/Switch/Visa* card

Card No. _ _ _ _   _ _ _ _   _ _ _ _   _ _ _ _

Expiry date_____   **Issue number (Switch only)** _____

Signature _____   **Tel. No.** _____

NAME _____

ADDRESS _____

_____

_____

* Delete as applicable (price includes postage – airmail for Europe/world).

LIVING AND WORKING IN AMERICA

Living and Working in America is essential reading for anyone planning to spend some time in America including holiday-home owners, retirees, visitors, business people, migrants, students and even extraterrestrials! It's packed with over 500 pages of important and useful information designed to help you **avoid costly mistakes and save both time and money.** Topics covered include how to:

- Find a job with a good salary & conditions
- Obtain a residence permit
- Avoid and overcome problems
- Find your dream home
- Get the best education for your family
- Make the best use of public transport
- Endure motoring in America
- Obtain the best health treatment
- Stretch your dollars further
- Make the most of your leisure time
- Enjoy the American sporting life
- Find the best shopping bargains
- Insure yourself against most eventualities
- Use post office and telephone services
- Do numerous other things not listed above

Living and Working in America is the most comprehensive and up-to-date source of practical information available about everyday life America. It isn't, however, a boring text book, but an interesting and entertaining guide written in a highly readable style.

Buy this book and discover what it's *really* like to live and work in America.

Order your copies today by phone, fax, mail or e-mail from: Survival Books, PO Box 146, Wetherby, West Yorks. LS23 6XZ, United Kingdom (☎/▤ +44 (0)1937-843523, ✉ orders@ survivalbooks.net, 💻 www.survivalbooks.net).

ORDER FORM

LIVING & WORKING SERIES / RETIRING ABROAD

Qty.	Title	Price (incl. p&p)*			Total
		UK	Europe	World	
	Living & Working Abroad	£14.95	£16.95	£20.45	
	Living & Working in America	£14.95	£16.95	£20.45	
	Living & Working in Australia	£14.95	£16.95	£20.45	
	Living & Working in Britain	£14.95	£16.95	£20.45	
	Living & Working in Canada	£14.95	£16.95	£20.45	
	Living & Working in France	£14.95	£16.95	£20.45	
	Living & Working in Germany	£14.95	£16.95	£20.45	
	Living & Working in the Gulf States & Saudi Arabia	Autumn 2002			
	Living & Working in Holland, Belgium & Luxembourg	£14.95	£16.95	£20.45	
	Living & Working in Ireland	£14.95	£16.95	£20.45	
	Living & Working in Italy	£14.95	£16.95	£20.45	
	Living & Working in London	£11.45	£12.95	£14.95	
	Living & Working in New Zealand	£14.95	£16.95	£20.45	
	Living & Working in Spain	£14.95	£16.95	£20.45	
	Living & Working in Switzerland	£14.95	£16.95	£20.45	
	Retiring Abroad	£14.95	£16.95	£20.45	
				Total	

Order your copies today by phone, fax, mail or e-mail from: Survival Books, PO Box 146, Wetherby, West Yorks. LS23 6XZ, UK (☎/▤ +44 (0)1937-843523, ✉ orders@survivalbooks.net, 💻 www.survivalbooks.net). If you aren't entirely satisfied, simply return them to us within 14 days for a full and unconditional refund.

Cheque enclosed/please charge my Delta/Mastercard/Switch/Visa* card

Card No. __ __ __ __   __ __ __ __   __ __ __ __   __ __ __ __

Expiry date _____   **Issue number (Switch only)** _____

Signature _____   **Tel. No.** _____

NAME _____

ADDRESS _____

_____

_____

* Delete as applicable (price includes postage – airmail for Europe/world).

NOTES

NOTES

NOTES

NOTES